Sustainability in the Entrepreneurial Ecosystem:

Operating Mechanisms and Enterprise Growth

Yang Gao
Dalian University of Technology, China

Sang-Bing Tsai
Regional Green Economy Development Research Center, Wuyi University, China & Research Center for Environment and Sustainable Development of the China Civil Aviation, Civil Aviation University of China, China

Xiaomin Du
Yingkou Institute of Technology, China

Chunlin Xin
Beijing University of Chemical Technology, China

A volume in the Practice, Progress, and Proficiency in Sustainability (PPPS) Book Series

IGI Global
PUBLISHER of TIMELY KNOWLEDGE

Published in the United States of America by
IGI Global
Business Science Reference (an imprint of IGI Global)
701 E. Chocolate Avenue
Hershey PA, USA 17033
Tel: 717-533-8845
Fax: 717-533-8661
E-mail: cust@igi-global.com
Web site: http://www.igi-global.com

Library of Congress Cataloging-in-Publication Data

Names: Gao, Yang, editor. | Tsai, Sang-Bing, 1973- editor. | Du, Xiaomin, 1985- editor. | Xin, Chunlin, 1971- editor.
Title: Sustainability in the entrepreneurial ecosystem : operating mechanisms and enterprise growth / Yang Gao, Sang-Bing Tsai, Xiaomin Du and Chunlin Xin, editors.
Description: Hershey : Business Science Reference, 2020. | Includes bibliographical references and index. | Summary: "This book is a collection of innovative research that systematically explores the operation mechanism of sustainable entrepreneurship ecosystem from macro and micro aspects so as to provide value for promoting economic vitality and regional economic development"-- Provided by publisher.
Identifiers: LCCN 2019054342 (print) | LCCN 2019054343 (ebook) | ISBN 9781799834953 (hardcover) | ISBN 9781799834960 (paperback) | ISBN 9781799834977 (ebook)
Subjects: LCSH: Entrepreneurship--Environmental aspects. | Sustainable development. | Environmental economics. | Regional planning.
Classification: LCC HB615 .S977 2020 (print) | LCC HB615 (ebook) | DDC 338/.04--dc23
LC record available at https://lccn.loc.gov/2019054342
LC ebook record available at https://lccn.loc.gov/2019054343

This book is published in the IGI Global book series Practice, Progress, and Proficiency in Sustainability (PPPS) (ISSN: 2330-3271; eISSN: 2330-328X)

British Cataloguing in Publication Data
A Cataloguing in Publication record for this book is available from the British Library.

All work contributed to this book is new, previously-unpublished material.
The views expressed in this book are those of the authors, but not necessarily of the publisher.

For electronic access to this publication, please contact: eresources@igi-global.com.

Practice, Progress, and Proficiency in Sustainability (PPPS) Book Series

ISSN:2330-3271
EISSN:2330-328X

Editor-in-Chief: Ayman Batisha, International Sustainability Institute, Egypt

MISSION

In a world where traditional business practices are reconsidered and economic activity is performed in a global context, new areas of economic developments are recognized as the key enablers of wealth and income production. This knowledge of information technologies provides infrastructures, systems, and services towards sustainable development.

The **Practices, Progress, and Proficiency in Sustainability (PPPS) Book Series** focuses on the local and global challenges, business opportunities, and societal needs surrounding international collaboration and sustainable development of technology. This series brings together academics, researchers, entrepreneurs, policy makers and government officers aiming to contribute to the progress and proficiency in sustainability.

COVERAGE

- Technological learning
- Knowledge clusters
- Sustainable Development
- Outsourcing
- Global Business
- Global Content and Knowledge Repositories
- E-Development
- Eco-Innovation
- Environmental informatics
- Socio-Economic

IGI Global is currently accepting manuscripts for publication within this series. To submit a proposal for a volume in this series, please contact our Acquisition Editors at Acquisitions@igi-global.com or visit: http://www.igi-global.com/publish/.

The Practice, Progress, and Proficiency in Sustainability (PPPS) Book Series (ISSN 2330-3271) is published by IGI Global, 701 E. Chocolate Avenue, Hershey, PA 17033-1240, USA, www.igi-global.com. This series is composed of titles available for purchase individually; each title is edited to be contextually exclusive from any other title within the series. For pricing and ordering information please visit http://www.igi-global.com/book-series/practice-progress-proficiency-sustainability/73810. Postmaster: Send all address changes to above address.

Titles in this Series

For a list of additional titles in this series, please visit:
https://www.igi-global.com/book-series/practice-progress-proficiency-sustainability/73810

Developing Sustainable Food Systems, Policies, and Securities
Abiodun Elijah Obayelu (Federal University of Agriculture, Abeokuta, Nigeria) and Oluwakemi Adeola Obayelu (Unversity of Ibadan, Nigeria)
Engineering Science Reference • © 2020 • 300pp • H/C (ISBN: 9781799825999) • US $195.00

Building an Entrepreneurial and Sustainable Society
Brizeida R. Hernández-Sánchez (University of Salamanca, Spain) José C. Sánchez-García (University of Salamanca, Spain) and Antonio Carrizo Moreira (University of Aveiro, Portugal)
Business Science Reference • © 2020 • 369pp • H/C (ISBN: 9781799827047) • US $235.00

Toward Sustainability Through Digital Technologies and Practices in the Eurasian Region
Gainiya Tazhina (University of International Business, Kazakhstan) and Judith Parker (Teachers College, Columbia University, USA)
Information Science Reference • © 2020 • 294pp • H/C (ISBN: 9781799825517) • US $195.00

Examining the Environmental Impacts of Materials and Buildings
Blaine Erickson Brownell (University of Minnesota, USA)
Engineering Science Reference • © 2020 • 358pp • H/C (ISBN: 9781799824268) • US $245.00

Cross-Border Cooperation (CBC) Strategies for Sustainable Development
Rui Alexandre Castanho (University of Dąbrowa Górnicza, Portugal)
Engineering Science Reference • © 2020 • 348pp • H/C (ISBN: 9781799825135) • US $225.00

Membrane Technology for Water and Wastewater Treatment in Rural Regions
Rosalam Sarbatly (Universiti Malaysia Sabah, Malaysia)
Engineering Science Reference • © 2020 • 354pp • H/C (ISBN: 9781799826453) • US $205.00

IGI Global
PUBLISHER of TIMELY KNOWLEDGE

701 East Chocolate Avenue, Hershey, PA 17033, USA
Tel: 717-533-8845 x100 • Fax: 717-533-8661
E-Mail: cust@igi-global.com • www.igi-global.com

Table of Contents

Detailed Table of Contents

The incubator of scientific and technological innovation plays an important role in leading scientific and technological innovation, accelerating the transformation of scientific and technological achievements, and promoting industrial upgrading and transformation. The Chinese economy is in the transition stage, so the research on the operating efficiency of the incubator of scientific and technological innovation based on the Chinese context has its unique value. In this study, combined with Chinese context, the business incubator is divided into two main modes: government and private. By using DEA research method, this chapter analyzes a series of problems, such as the overall difference and difference grade of the operating efficiency of incubators among the four major economic zones of China, the comparison of the operating efficiency of different modes between Northeast and Western regions, and the gap between private-led incubators in eastern China and private-led incubators in Northeast and Western China.

Many SMEs lack business competitiveness and sustainability. Their potential for growth and expansion is limited, and they are constrained by institutional challenges (such as high-interest rates and rigid regulatory requirements) which impede their creativity, innovativeness and sustainability. Despite the numerous contributions of the sector to the Ghanaian economy, SME internationalisation in Ghana is at the nascent stage and is bedevilled with a gamut of institutional challenges. Studies of the formal and informal institutional effects on indigenous SME internationalisation in the Ghanaian economy are limited. Furthermore, a stylised framework which serves as a model to aid academics and researchers in investigating the impact of the formal institutions (legal and political) and informal institutions (socio-culture) on Ghanaian-owned businesses is under-canvassed in the Ghanaian entrepreneurial eco-system. Hence, this paper suggests a model for institutions and SME internationalisation to boost their innovativeness and business sustainability.

Dake Jiang, Business School, Dalian University of Technology, China
Hong Zhang, Business School, Dalian University of Technology, China
Lei Wang, Law School, Civil Aviation University of China, China
Jin Liu, Business School, Dalian University of Technology, China
Linlin Chang, Dalian University of Technology, China

In the business ecosystem, the core business niche is not occupied by a structural position; its objectives and strategies are easily dispersed, while the core business can't coordinate the business ecosystem elements. Therefore, the ecological advantages obtained by core enterprises in the process of self-organization evolution are not sustainable. To solve this problem, a possible way is to explore how core enterprises consolidate and form new ecological advantages from the perspective of cross-border business. However, the academic community has not discussed the evolution path of cross-border entrepreneurship in detail. For this reason, based on the perspective of ecological advantages, this chapter discusses the strategic path of cross-border entrepreneurship of core enterprises and constructs an interaction model between ecological advantages and core enterprises' cross-border entrepreneurial paths. The study broadens the understanding of the relationship between corporate strategies and business ecosystems, then provides theoretical value for subsequent research.

Yu Wang, Dalian University of Technology, China
Haoyang Gao, Dalian University of Technology, China
Haomin Du, Dalian University of Technology, China
Kaifeng Wu, Dalian University of Technology, China
Yuqing Chen, Dalian University of Technology, China

This chapter constructs a system of financial ecological environment that is based on the multiple indicators: economic foundation, financial development, and institutional environment of 14 cities in Liaoning Province from 2008 to 2014. In addition, it supplements a measurement of influence of financial quality and uses the factor analysis method and panel threshold model to explore the dynamic evolution characteristics and optimization route of financial ecological environment. The empirical study shows that (1) the whole trend performs as an inversed U shape with the characteristics of rising at first and then declining and its influential mechanisms are disparate in different periods; (2) the financial ecological environment qualities of coastal cities rank in the upper and middle reaches of the overall rankings, while

As business failure is a high probability event that influences the operation efficiency of the entrepreneurial ecosystem, it is necessary to know how to manage business failure experience to promote serial entrepreneurship and improve circulation in the ecosystem. While most scholars agree that it is different between failure and exit, DeTienne suggests that exit could be a way to avoid failure and protect the passion and financial condition of entrepreneurs. Therefore, this chapter analyzes the difference of failure and exit and conducts a model to help entrepreneurs decide whether to exit and how to choose a better way to exit entrepreneurship. In the meantime, this chapter analyzes why entrepreneurial exit can improve the operation efficiency of entrepreneurial ecosystem, and also it would give some ideas about how to bound from failure and benefit from failure to do better next time. After reading this chapter, entrepreneurs have the idea that failure is controllable and exit may be a restart to do business more successfully.

An extraordinary proliferation of entrepreneurship education programs has been underway in recent years. One of key purposes of entrepreneurship education is to foster entrepreneurial intention. So how to predict and interpret the process of entrepreneurial intention becomes a dominant topic in academia. Under related entrepreneurial and psychological theories, reasoning and reviewing related classical entrepreneurial intention models, this chapter analyzes the influencing factors and interacting effects and proposes a path-model of entrepreneurial intentions from combined perspectives of entrepreneurial motivation and cognition in order to reveal the underlying psychological mechanism of entrepreneurial intention. The chapter hopes to have added richness to ongoing further researches among academics and discussions among educators and policymakers regarding the importance of entrepreneurial intention in entrepreneurial education.

Competitive dynamics theory emphasizes that entrepreneurs must be alert to the opportunities, perceiving the tension of competition between firms to implement organizational change strategy. However, empirical studies on the above aspects are very scarce. Based on the literature review, this chapter proposes a research model about opportunity alertness, competitive tension, and organizational change and uses 183 valid questionnaires from the northeast of China to test this model. The empirical results show that opportunity alertness and competitive tension have a significant impact on organizational change strategies respectively, and competitive tension moderates the relationship between opportunity alertness and organizational change strategies. The results show that facing fierce competition, entrepreneurs, who can exert the organizational strategies, should not only improve opportunity alertness, but also strengthen their understanding of the competitive situation among enterprises and the value of competitive tension. Finally, theoretical and practical implications are addressed.

The authors examine the effects of innovation and imitation strategies on new venture competitive advantage during both technological and market turbulence. In turn, they test the moderating effects of dysfunctional competition in these settings. Using data collected from 153 new ventures in China, they find that innovation and imitation strategies have positive effects on new venture competitive advantage. Furthermore, they find that dysfunctional competition increases the positive relationship between imitation strategies and new venture competitive advantage in these settings. However, the negative moderating effects of dysfunctional competition are partly verified. And they find that the consumption attitudes of the younger generation in China may explain why the theory is inconsistent with the empirical results. The theoretical and practical implications of the findings are discussed.

This chapter introduces entrepreneurial self-efficacy, a psychological cognitive factor, into the context of entrepreneurship, trying to sort out the internal mechanism of entrepreneurial self-efficacy, dual entrepreneurial learning, and entrepreneurial performance and construct a theoretical model. The hypothesis is that entrepreneurial self-efficacy has a positive effect on both dual entrepreneurial learning and new venture performance. Dual entrepreneurial learning has a positive impact on the performance of new ventures and acts as a mediator between entrepreneurial self-efficacy and entrepreneurial performance. The empirical results show that entrepreneurial self-efficacy can promote exploratory entrepreneurial learning and the improvement of new venture performance. Exploratory entrepreneurial learning plays a mediating role in the effect of entrepreneurial self-efficacy on the performance of start-ups, while entrepreneurial learning can't play a mediating role in the process of exploitative entrepreneurial learning.

For countries in the process of economic transition, improvement of industrialization is no longer the sole goal of their economic development. While upgrading the level of industrial development, these countries also gradually attach importance to resource utilization efficiency and environmental protection, which is why sustainable entrepreneurship has become increasingly popular in recent years. With the intensification of policy guidance, a new "sea area" named sustainable entrepreneurship ushers in more and more "treasure hunters" exploring "the treasure" therein. Based on this, this chapter constructs the model of "Green Ocean Treasure Hunting" for green entrepreneurial enterprises to analyze the role played by their government's relevant policies and puts forward the research proposition of this chapter based on the relevant literature. On this basis, this chapter chooses

Foreword

The study of entrepreneurial ecosystem in this book is of great academic value and practical enlightenment. At present, the research of entrepreneurial ecosystem has become a hot spot. It is a very meaningful work to understand the operation mechanism of the system, which can not only provide a reference for government policymaking, but also help actors in the system.

After reading each chapter and some main contents in this book, it can be pointed out that the theory used here is very sufficient, the methods are both accurate and effective. From the beginning chapter of this book, research of the entrepreneurial ecosystem is presented on the macro level, including the evaluation of the vitality of entrepreneurial ecosystem, the operation efficiency of innovation incubator, etc. Macro-level research is oriented towards policy making. After that, the book began to focus on micro research, including financial institutions, enterprises, governments and even entrepreneurs in the entrepreneurial ecosystem. Multi-level research coincides with the multi-agent characteristics of the entrepreneur's ecosystem, which has deepened theoretical and practical value. Besides, this kind of research will be thought-provoking which shed light on future research.

It is believed that through reading this book, both scholars and practitioners will get certain enlightenment. First, scholars will broaden their understanding of the theory in this field from both macro and micro levels. Besides, practitioners (government departments and entrepreneurs) could find out a useful way to play their own role in the system.

Finally, I would like to thank Professor Gao Yang for his invitation and the cooperation of Professor Tsai for many years. I believe that this book will benefit more readers.

Chia-Huei Wu
Institute of Service Industries and Management, Minghsin University of Science and Technology, Taiwan
April 8, 2020

Preface

The entrepreneurial ecosystem refers to a dynamic balanced system consisting of new ventures, various interdependent subjects and the entrepreneurial ecological environment. Sustainable entrepreneurial ecosystem. reflects sustainable characteristics in both macro and micro aspects of the entrepreneurial ecosystem. The macro-level includes the sustainable vitality of the entrepreneurial ecosystem, such as the sustainable growth of system performance and regional economic vitality; the micro-level should include the sustainable growth of enterprises, green performance, and the sustainable management of stakeholders. Sustainable Entrepreneurial Ecosystem could not only increase the vitality of entrepreneurship, enhance the level of regional economic development, but also promote the sustainable economic development.

The construction of sustainable entrepreneurial ecosystem is critical for any country in the world. However, at present, the research on entrepreneurial ecosystem in academia is still in the primary stage. Only a few scholars have studied the characteristics and the composition of the ecosystem from macro aspect, it is also rare in the research of the micro-mechanism of individual operation in the ecosystem. Based on this, the purpose of the book is to systematically explore the operation mechanism of sustainable entrepreneurial ecosystem from macro and micro aspects, so as to provide value for promoting economic vitality and regional economic development from sustainable perspective.

The target audiences of this book are professionals, researchers, students, and professors working in fields such as entrepreneurship, entrepreneurial ecosystem, business management, strategic management and the topic is primarily the use of new theories, technologies, methods, and techniques.

Acknowledgements are made to IGI Global for professional assistance in the publication of this book and the authors of all the chapters for their contributions.

This book contains the following 13 chapters.

CHAPTER 1

The Regional Evaluation on the Vitality of Entrepreneurial Ecosystem in China

The research of entrepreneurial ecosystem has become popular and the theory of entrepreneurial ecosystem provides an overall perspective for the research of entrepreneurial activity. However, how to measure the ecosystem vitality still remains an unsolved field. We chose density, diversity and connectivity of each province as the dynamic characteristics to evaluate the vitality of regional entrepreneurship ecosystem. We calculated the vitality scores of entrepreneurial ecosystem of the whole provinces of China, compared them with that of Lianoing province in the northeast China and then suggested some way to improve the vitality of Lianoing province.

CHAPTER 2

Operation Efficiency of Science and Technology Innovation Incubator: A Research Under Different Leading Modes

The incubator of scientific and technological innovation plays a crucial role in leading scientific and technological innovation, accelerating the transformation of scientific and technological achievements, and promoting industrial upgrading and transformation. The transition stage of Chinese economy increases the salience of operating efficiency research on the incubator concerning scientific and technological innovation in China, (i.e., government- and private-led incubators). By employing DEA research method, this paper tackles relevant problems. For example, the current study dives into the differences in the operating efficiency of incubators among the four major economic zones in China, and in the operating efficiency of different modes between Northeast and Western regions, and the technology gap between private-led incubators based in eastern China and in Northeast and Western China. The presentation of these problems revealed the differences in operating efficiency of incubators across four areas in China in terms of scientific and technological innovation, contributing to the emergence of "two-step" routing scheme in the current study.

CHAPTER 3

Innovation and Business Sustainability Among SMEs in Africa: The Role of the Institutions

SMEs have been the key contributor economic development and transformation. Due to the influential role of SMEs various governments have established relevant policies and programmes and implemented structures for an enabling and favourable business atmosphere dedicated to the development, growth and sustainability of the SMEs. Government programmes and policies have been largely focused on establishing SMEs regulatory institutions and government financial institutional support for SMEs. The study shows that the pace of SMEs internationalization is effect by the informal institutional factors. This chapter discusses the various themes connected to SMEs with specific reference to innovative Ghanaian SMEs. Certain crucial factors like social culture, legal, political, and internationalization of SMEs in Ghana are highlight.

CHAPTER 4

Research on Cross-Border Entrepreneurial Path of Core Enterprise Based on Ecological Advantage

With the increasingly industrial environment changes, how to maintain and expand competitive advantage has become a key issue for enterprises. However, traditional theory of competitive advantage is no longer applicable to enterprises at this time. Therefore, domestic scholars have introduced the concept of ecological advantage, with the belief that it is necessary to rethink the source of competitive advantage and strategic choice from an ecological perspective.

In the business ecosystem, the core business niche is not occupied by a structural position, its objectives and strategies are easily dispersed, while the core business can't coordinate the business ecosystem elements. Therefore, the ecological advantages obtained by core enterprises in the process of self-organization evolution are not sustainable. To solve this problem, a possible way is to explore how core enterprises consolidate and form new ecological advantages from the perspective of cross-border business.

However, the academic community has not discussed the evolution path of cross-border entrepreneurship in detail. For this reason, based on the perspective of ecological advantages, this paper discusses the strategic path of cross-border entrepreneurship of core enterprises and constructs an interaction model between ecological advantages and core enterprises' cross-border entrepreneurial paths. The study broadens the understanding of the relationship between corporate strategies and business ecosystems, then provides theoretical value for subsequent research.

CHAPTER 5

The Evaluation of Financial Ecological Environment and Optimization Research in LiaoNing Province: Based on the Empirical Research With Factor Analysis and Panel Threshold 2008-2014

This paper constructs a system of financial ecological environment which is based on the multiple indicators: economic foundation, financial development and institutional environment of 14 cities in Liaoning Province from 2008 to 2014. Besides, it supplements a measurement of influence of financial quality and uses the factor analysis method as well as panel threshold model in order to explore the dynamic evolution characteristics and optimization route of financial ecological environment in Liaoning Province. The empirical study shows that: (1) the whole trend performs as an inversed U shape with the characteristics of rising at first and then declining, and its influential mechanisms are disparate in different periods; (2) the financial ecological environment qualities of coastal cities rank in the upper and middle reaches of the overall rankings, while the financial ecological environment qualities of inland cities comparatively fall behind; (3) the impact of urban financial ecological environment on economic growth in Liaoning Province presents as a non-linear single threshold, and the threshold values of financial ecological environment are 0.48, 0.52, 0.46 and 0.41 respectively, which accordingly reveals the optimization interval of financial ecological environment in Liaoning Province.

CHAPTER 6

Financial Industry Under Entrepreneurial Ecosystem: Internet Finance, Interest Rate Marketization, and Bank Performance

Due to the three functions of cost reduction, disintermediation and information asymmetry, Internet finance continues to impact the traditional banking business in the financial industry, posing a new competitive risk for commercial banks. In developing countries such as China, given the imperfect development of the financial market, the government needs to introduce a series of policies, but new policies will bring the risk of market uncertainty. Due to the double uncertainty of the market and the system in developing countries, commercial banks are caught between competitive and new policy risks. Therefore, exploring the impact of these two risks on the performance of commercial banks is very important to allow commercial banks to discern, resist and respond to risks. This research uses the data of A-share listed banks for the past 10 years. Empirical research shows that Internet finance and interest rate liberalization have a negative impact on bank performance. The liberalization of interest rates further increases the negative impact of Internet finance on bank performance. The results show that commercial banks are currently lacking in both their response to and integration into the market, and national policies currently have short-term failures in the process of the liberalization of the financial industry.

CHAPTER 7

Entrepreneurial Passion, Cognitive Bias, and the Speed of Technology Commercialization of New Ventures: An Empirical Test in China

This paper utilizes cognitive theory to explain how entrepreneurial passion influence the speed of new ventures' technology commercialization, and explore the roles of cognitive bias (illusion of control and risk propensity) played in this process. The results show that both entrepreneurial passion and cognitive bias positively impact on the speed of technology commercialization. We also find that illusion of control and risk propensity play a partial mediating role in the relationship between entrepreneurial passion and the speed of technology commercialization. This conclusion can make up for the gap of existing theoretical research.

CHAPTER 8

Operating Mechanism: Make Use of the Difference of Failure and Exit to Improve the Operation Efficiency of Entrepreneurial Ecosystem

As business failure is a high probability event and influence the operation efficiency of entrepreneurial ecosystem, it is necessary to know how to manage business failure experience to promote serial entrepreneurship and improve circulation in the ecosystem. While most scholars agree that it is different between failure and exit, DeTienne suggests that exit could be a way to avoid failure and protect the passion and financial condition of entrepreneurs. Therefore, this chapter would like to analyze the difference of failure and exit, and conduct a model to help entrepreneurs decide whether to exit and how to choose a better way to exit entrepreneurship. In the meantime, this chapter analyze why entrepreneurial exit can improve the operation efficiency of entrepreneurial ecosystem, and also it would give some ideas about how to bound from failure and benefit from failure to do better next time. We do hope after reading this chapter, entrepreneurs have the idea that failure is controllable and exit maybe a restart to do business more successfully.

CHAPTER 9

Review of Classical Entrepreneurial Intention Models and Research Framework From Combined Perspectives of Entrepreneurial Motivation and Cognition

An extraordinary proliferation of entrepreneurship education programs has been underway in recently years. One of key purposes of entrepreneurship education is to foster entrepreneurial intention. So how to predict and interpret the process of entrepreneurial intention becomes a dominant topic in academia. Under related entrepreneurial and psychological theories, reasoning and reviewing related classical entrepreneurial intention models, this paper analyzes the influencing factors and interacting effects, and proposed a path-model of entrepreneurial intentions from combined perspectives of entrepreneurial motivation and cognition, in order to reveal the underlying psychological mechanism of entrepreneurial intention. The paper hopes to have added richness to ongoing further researches among academics and discusses among educators and policy-makers regarding the importance of entrepreneurial intention in entrepreneurial education.

CHAPTER 10

The Effects of Opportunity Alertness and Competitive Tension on Organizational Change Strategies

Competitive dynamics theory emphasizes the entrepreneurs must be alert to the opportunities, perceiving the tension of competition between firms to implement organizational change strategy. However, empirical studies on the above aspects are very scarce. Based on the literature review, this paper proposes a research model about opportunity alertness, competitive tension and organizational change and uses 183 valid questionnaires from the Northeast of China to test this model. The empirical results show that opportunity alertness and competitive tension have a significant impact on organizational change strategies respectively and competitive tension moderates the relationship between opportunity alertness and organizational change strategies. The results show that facing fierce competition entrepreneurs who can exert the organizational strategies should not only improve opportunity alertness, but also strengthen their understanding of the competitive situation among enterprises and the value of competitive tension. Finally, theoretical and practical implications are addressed. entrepreneurial process as evidence of the propositions we have put forward.

CHAPTER 11

Innovation or Imitation in New Ventures? Contingent Effects of Dysfunctional Competition

We examine the effects of innovation and imitation strategies on new venture competitive advantage during both technological and market turbulence. In turn we then test the moderating effects of dysfunctional competition in these settings. Using data collected from 153 new ventures in China, we find that innovation and imitation strategies have positive effects on new venture competitive advantage. Furthermore, we find that dysfunctional competition increases the positive relationship between imitation strategies and new venture competitive advantage in these settings. However, the negative moderating effects of dysfunctional competition are partly verified. And we find that the consumption attitudes of the younger generation in China may explain why the theory being inconsistent with our empirical results. The theoretical and practical implications of our findings are discussed.

CHAPTER 12

The Role of Entrepreneurs in Entrepreneurial Ecosystem: Self-Efficacy, Dual Learning, and Performance

With the vigorous development of entrepreneurial activities, the role of entrepreneurial psychological factors in the entrepreneurial process has been paid more and more attention. This paper introduces entrepreneurial self-efficacy, a psychological cognitive factor, into the context of entrepreneurship, trying to sort out the internal mechanism of entrepreneurial self-efficacy, dual entrepreneurial learning and entrepreneurial performance, and construct a theoretical model. The hypothesis is that entrepreneurial self-efficacy has a positive effect on both dual entrepreneurial learning and new venture performance, Dual entrepreneurial learning has a positive impact on the performance of new ventures and acts as a mediator between entrepreneurial self-efficacy and entrepreneurial performance. The empirical results show that entrepreneurial self-efficacy can promote exploratory entrepreneurial learning and the improvement of new venture performance, Exploratory entrepreneurial learning plays a mediating role in the effect of entrepreneurial self-efficacy on the performance of start-ups, while entrepreneurial learning can't play a mediating role in the process of exploitative entrepreneurial learning.

CHAPTER 13

Sustainable Entrepreneurship Guided by Policy Support in a Transitional Economy: A Research Based on a Chinese High-Tech Enterprise

For countries in the process of economic transition, improvement of industrialization is no longer the sole goal of their economic development. While upgrading the level of industrial development, these countries also gradually attach importance to resource utilization efficiency and environmental protection, which is why sustainable entrepreneurship has become increasingly popular in recent years. With the intensification of policy guidance, a new "sea area" named sustainable entrepreneurship ushers in more and more "treasure hunters" exploring "the treasure" therein. Based on this, this paper constructs the model of "Green Ocean Treasure Hunting" for green entrepreneurial enterprises to analyze the role played by their government's relevant policies and puts forward the research proposition of this article based on the relevant literature. On this basis, this paper chooses and analyzes a medium-sized, high-tech enterprise in China which follows a certain typical green

Yang Gao
Dalian University of Technology, China

Acknowledgment

We acknowledge IGI Global for their professional assistance in the publication of this book, as well as all the chapter authors for their contributions to this book. These authors were supported by Dalian University of Technology of China; University of Electronic Science and Technology of China Zhongshan Institute; University of KwaZuLu-Natal, Shangdong Normal University; University of Texas at San Antonio; Changwon National University; Jilin University; Yingkou Institute of Technology; Shanghai University; Zhengzhou University; Hebei University of Technology; Tianjin Academy of Social Sciences; Jilin University of Finance and Economics; Beijing Normal University; Civil Aviation University of China; Harbin University of Commerce; Harbin Engineering University; Guangxi University of Finance and Economics; Changchun University of Technology; Guangdong University of Technology; Regional Green Economy Development Research Center, School of Business, WUYI University; Research Center for Environment and Sustainable Development of the China Civil Aviation, Civil Aviation University of China.

Chapter 1
The Regional Evaluation on the Vitality of the Entrepreneurial Ecosystem in China

Sae Woon Park
https://orcid.org/0000-0003-1507-7177
Changwon National University, South Korea

Xingqun Xue
Dalian University of Technology, China

Sunhae Lee
https://orcid.org/0000-0001-8325-1582
Changwon National University, South Korea

Xinya Xu
Dalian University of Technology, China

Yuanyu Zeng
Dalian University of Technology, China

ABSTRACT

With the development of business ecosystems and the depth of entrepreneurship research, the research based on the ecosystem has been popular. The theory of entrepreneurial ecosystem provides an overall perspective for the research of entrepreneurial activity. However, how to measure the system vitality still remains an unsolved problem. This study chooses diversity, density, and connectivity as the dynamic characteristics to construct the assessment index system of a regional entrepreneurship system. The study also takes the old industrial bases in Northeast China, Liaoning Province as an object. It calculates the vitality score and puts forward some targeted suggestions for improving the vitality of entrepreneurial ecosystems in Liaoning Province.

DOI: 10.4018/978-1-7998-3495-3.ch001

INTRODUCTION

With the rapid development of mass entrepreneurship and innovation, entrepreneurs, governments and scholars are gradually realizing the importance of the entrepreneurial ecosystem (EE) (Mack & Mayer, 2016). EE can promote enterprise innovation or the formation of new enterprises by creating a good environment, and achieve regional economic development (Bruton et al., 2010). The vitality of entrepreneurial environment directly affects the development of entrepreneurial activities. The establishment of a systematic and objective evaluation system for entrepreneurial vitality can play a guiding role in regional entrepreneurial activities, thus promoting the overall development of regional economy and improve the living standards of the citizens in the region (Acs & Armington, 2004). However, in the existing researches, there are still some deficiencies in the evaluation of regional entrepreneurial vitality. Although studies on social entrepreneurship activities from the perspective of business ecosystem continue to flourish, few studies can be found on a comprehensive measurement of the vitality of EE in provinces or cities, due to the limitations of research time and research level, which results in lack of pertinence and systematicness in the startup elements.

In order to solve these problems, this paper examines the dynamic evaluation system of business ecosystem. We construct three detailed indicators of the dynamic characteristics of EE: density, diversity and connectivity. Then we choose the appropriate data processing method and use the analytic hierarchy process(AHP) to build a scientific and reasonable evaluation system.

Making use of the established evaluation system, this paper conducts an empirical analysis on the vitality of EE in Liaoning province. The results show that Liaoning province has deficiencies in aspects of entrepreneurship atmosphere, scientific and technological innovation, talent training, entrepreneurship support services and others. Based on the evaluation conclusion, this paper puts forward some targeted suggestions such as strengthening innovation and entrepreneurship education, perfecting government system and improving service system. This paper has important practical value for developing regional economy by promoting entrepreneurial vitality of the old industrial base in the northeastern area, and pioneering theoretical contribution for evaluating the vitality of regional EE.

THEORETICAL REVIEW

Development of Entrepreneurial Ecosystem Theory

Connotation of Entrepreneurial Ecosystem

The study of EE originates from the integration of organizational ecology and entrepreneurship related researches. Moore (1993) put forward the concept of business ecosystem, which is defined as "an economic association based on organizational interaction" (Moore, 1993). Spilling (1996) first proposed the concept of EE to describe entrepreneurial activities within the market (Spilling, 1996).

With the continuous development of the concept of EE, scholars defined EE mainly from the perspective of ecology and network. Starting from the ecological perspective, Vogel (2013) believed that EE is composed of a variety of interdependent entrepreneurial entities (entrepreneurial enterprises, government agencies, etc.) and environmental elements (market, etc.) in a specific region, which coexist and interact to promote the generation of entrepreneurial activities (Vogel, 2013). Scholars from the perspective of network believed that various elements form an EE through network connection. Neck et al. (2004) used taxonomy method to divide EE into two parts: the institutional elements related to incubator in the university, government, professional support services, and intellectual resources; other elements supported by entrepreneurship (Neck, 2004). Cohen (2006) argued that the internet, infrastructure and entrepreneurial culture are the core elements of sustaining an EE. According to Isenberg (2010), EE is a network environment composed of various resources and government policies needed for entrepreneurship. Mason and Brown (2014) argued that EE is a series of interrelated entrepreneurial entities (entrepreneurial enterprises, investment institutions, universities, etc.) and entrepreneurial environment (policies, culture, etc.), which can improve performance through formal and informal connections. Spiegel (2017) believed that EE is a combination of social, political, economic and cultural elements to promote the development of start-ups in a region, which can encourage emerging entrepreneurs or other participants to take risks such as entrepreneurship and financing. Based on the synthesis of several definitions, the EE consists of economic actors and environmental factors existing in a region as influenced by geographical boundaries (Audretsch & Belitski, 2017).

Based on previous studies, this paper defines the regional EE as a dynamic equilibrium system composed of regional entrepreneurial enterprises and regional entrepreneurial environment that influences and co-evolves with each other.

Entrepreneurial Ecosystem Factors

When the theory of EE was put forward, many scholars studied the concept and components of ecosystem. Neck (2004) divided EE into two parts: incubation-related institutions and entrepreneurial support institutions: the former promotes entrepreneurial enterprises, while the latter contains elements like universities, governments, scientific research institutions, capital services, infrastructure and entrepreneurial culture. Cohen (2006) believed that EE is mainly composed of universities, governments, professional service institutions, capital support institutions, human service institutions and other elements. Suresh and Ramraj (2012) argued that EE consists of moral, financial, technological, market, social, networking, policy and environmental support systems. Spigel (2017) believed that EE consists of 11 elements that belong to cultural attribute, social attribute and material attribute, which include entrepreneurial culture support, entrepreneur history, labor quality, investment capital, network, entrepreneurship mentor and model, government policy, university education, support services, basic material facilities and open market. The interaction between the elements promotes the development of EE.

Isenberg (2011) believed that EE needs six major elements, namely, market, policy, capital, talent, culture and professional support, which are the "gold standard" for EE. Feld (2012) considered that EE consists of eight elements like capital, network, government, leadership, talent, companies, support services and engagement. Theodoraki et al. (2017) believed that EE contains seven factors including formal and informal network, physical infrastructure, culture, support entities, public & private funding agencies, research organizations and business consortiums.

Evaluation System of Entrepreneurial Ecosystem

With the deepening of EE research and the need to measure the health of EE, scholars began to study the evaluation system of EE.

Vogel (2013) introduced a three-level evaluation framework for EE, suggesting that the effectiveness of EE should be studied from micro, medium and macro levels, including 1. Basic factors: infrastructure, management and policy, market and innovation. 2. Organizational environment factors: financial services, entrepreneurship education, cultural atmosphere, network services, entrepreneurship support, openness and 3. Personal factors; entrepreneurs (individual or team). ANDE (Aspen Network of Development Entrepreneurs) selected eight key factors to measure the ecosystem: finance, social support, policy, market, human capital, infrastructure, research and development, culture, and designed evaluation indicators and questionnaires. GEM (Global Entrepreneurship Monitor) evaluated EEs at the national level in terms of general conditions (the foundation and environment of enterprise development) and entrepreneurial conditions (the foundation and environment of entrepreneurial activities), measuring aspects like openness, government, financial market, technology, research and development, infrastructure, management, labor force and institutions.

Lack of Existing Research

In recent years, the academic research on the evaluation system of EE has been deepening. The definition of EE is relatively clear. The research on element analysis and structural model is increasing and the research on the index evaluation system is gradually emerging. However, due to the limited research time period, there exist restrictions and deficiencies in the existing literature.

First of all, the construction of EE evaluation system is mainly aimed at the national level (BEEP, GEM etc.) and there exists a lack of relevant research on the vitality of EE at the regional level within the country. Entrepreneurial activities are subject to the interaction of complex economic, market and institutional environment (Acs et al., 2014), and the gap among the levels of entrepreneurial activities between regions in China is becoming more and more obvious. Depending on whether enterprises are located within a country or in different countries, entrepreneurial activities show marked differences in terms of start-ups or expansion. Some regions are more conducive to entrepreneurship than others (Audretsch et al., 2018). How EE explains this characteristic difference between regions depends heavily on an evaluation method to measure the relative importance of the links between regions (Meshram & Rawani, 2019). Currently, however, there is a lack of such evaluation system. Hence, the study on the evaluation system of regional EE vitality can provide theoretical basis for improving the unbalanced development of regional entrepreneurship in China.

In addition, there is a lack of continuous data tracking in existing studies, which is obvious because of the fact that most of the current evaluation indicators rely on questionnaire and other forms to obtain indicators related data. Most existing studies quantify qualitative problems through surveys and rarely use statistical data to design the evaluation system, resulting in the lack of simple numerical representation for evaluation of EE vitality.

This paper, therefore, aims to solve these problems and build an evaluation system according to the characteristics of regional EE to promote regional entrepreneurial activities.

ESTABLISHMENT OF AN EVALUATION SYSTEM FOR ENTREPRENEURIAL ECOSYSTEM VITALITY

Due to the complexity of EE, the construction of EE vitality evaluation system needs to be divided into several levels. Among them, the first level is the goal to be achieved *i-e* to evaluate the vitality of regional EE. The second level is the evaluation of the characteristics of the target level, which is mainly composed of the support standards for the vitality of the regional EE. The third level is the index which can obtain data for quantitative representation and to be set as the index level. Through the setting of target layer, feature layer and index layer, it reflects the composition of the index system of regional EE vitality.

Index Formation

To achieve the goal of intuitively reflecting EE vitality and the characteristics of regional entrepreneurial activities and entrepreneurial environment, this paper selects three characteristic layer indicators to reflect EE vitality based on the existing research of EE characteristics, namely density, connectivity and diversity.

Density

The density reflects the intensity of entrepreneurial activities in the region. For most regions, the purpose of the development of EE is to improve the entrepreneurial density, which includes creating more entrepreneurial enterprises in the region, cultivating more entrepreneurs, and providing more employment opportunities through entrepreneurship. The selected indices of density feature layer are as follows:

1. Start-up density: For the regional EE, the core of any activity is the entrepreneurial activity itself, although the role of the environment cannot be ignored, the center is still a direct participant in EE-entrepreneurs and startups (Acs et al, 2014; Stam, 2015). To measure the density of EE in a region, we should first measure the number of entrepreneurs and entrepreneurial enterprises in the region. Compared with the number of entrepreneurs, the number of entrepreneurial enterprises is more convenient in the statistical level. Moreover, entrepreneurs carry out entrepreneurial activities through entrepreneurial enterprises. Therefore, measuring entrepreneurial enterprises is more in line with the interpretation of entrepreneurial density. The number of new enterprises is an intuitive expression of the number of regional entrepreneurial activities.
2. Employment density of individual entrepreneurs: Under the policy background of "mass entrepreneurship and innovation", individual entrepreneurship can

better reflect the regional entrepreneurship vitality under the current state. Individuals establish enterprises and carry out entrepreneurial activities through their own capital, technology, interpersonal relationship and other resources, providing a large number of regional employment opportunities. One of the significance of building a regional EE is to improve the regional employment rate, create a virtuous cycle of growth and prosperity, and improve the quality of life of regional citizens. By observing the employment impact of individual entrepreneurship, we can find whether EE successfully provides employment opportunities for individuals in the region. The density of entrepreneurial energy should include all the people involved in the entrepreneurial activities of these companies, not just the entrepreneurs. So, another way to measure density is to measure employment density of individual entrepreneurs in a region.

3. High-tech enterprise density: There are some specific subjects which play an important role in ecosystem development in business ecosystem theory. In the area of regional entrepreneurship, scientific and technological entrepreneurship play an important role in promoting technological innovation and other aspects. At the same time as high-tech enterprises are developing, they are also forming a more suitable entrepreneurial environment, which has a significant spillover effect on enterprises in other industries. The entrepreneurial success of technology enterprises has a positive impact on attracting external scientific and technological talents in the region (Needleman, 2012).

Diversity

Diversity is an important feature of EE. There are various types of participants in EE, including entrepreneurial enterprises, universities and other scientific research institutions, governments and intermediate institutions, etc. In addition to the diversity of subjects, there also exist diversity of the same type of subjects. For example, entrepreneurial companies belonging to different industries have different resources and focus on providing different products and services (Zahra, 2011). Generally speaking, the higher the diversity of EE, the richer the types of subjects they have. It plays different functions in different positions of different industries or industrial chains, which is conducive to the development of the ecosystem (Isenberg, 2011). The indicators selected by the diversity feature layer are as follows:

1. Economic diversity: For economic development, no city or region should be overly dependent on a particular industry. Research shows that a single industrial structure is not conducive to the development of regional innovation and entrepreneurship. Although the development of a single industry will bring economies of scale, this paper is not to replace specialization with diversity,

but to consider the diversity of specialization on the basis of recognizing specialization. That is to say, compared with those regions that only focus on one or two industries, cities and regions focusing on multiple economic fields will enjoy greater entrepreneurial achievements and will have greater entrepreneurial vitality.

2. Policy diversity: Building a sustainable EE requires a sound policy, environment, financial, educational and other support (Nadgrodkiewicz, 2013; Soto-Rodríguez, 2014), especially in the domestic context, this entrepreneurial boom largely comes from policy guidance. The various policies provided by the government help enterprises to identify opportunities and allocate resources, thus promoting the development of entrepreneurship, ensuring the prevalence of EE environment (Li & Gransey, 2014), and enhancing the vitality of the ecosystem. Government policies which play a positive role in promoting regional innovation and entrepreneurship vitality support entrepreneurial systems in various aspects, such as the financial support for entrepreneurial enterprises, investment in scientific research funds and human capital. The policy support needed for entrepreneurial activities is also all-round and diversified. Single and unbalanced investment will not generate higher entrepreneurial vitality.

For the selection of indicators at the policy level, this paper draws on the foreign classic evaluation index research on entrepreneurial ecological environment factors and according to the domestic situation and the support of these factors or not, it selects the support policies for new enterprises, scientific research investment policies, entrepreneurial talent training policies and entrepreneurial network building policies as the measurement dimension of policy diversity. This paper focuses on the diversity of the input of EE factors at the policy level and measures the balance in the degree of the investment in the above four aspects at the policy level which can reflect the diversity of EE at the policy level.

3. Enterprise diversity: Entrepreneurial enterprises have great differences in EE of a region because of the direct participants of entrepreneurial activities. In addition to the differences in the same industry, enterprises in different industries or in different positions in the industry also play different roles. Empirical research shows that enterprises in similar industries will have agglomeration effect, while enterprises in different industries can obtain a positive spillover effect through merger. This kind of enterprise diversity will help ease the negative impact of economy and conducive to the healthy development of the ecosystem (Boschma & Iammarino, 2009; Frenken et al., 2007). Therefore, this paper measures the enterprise diversity index *i-e* whether the number of

enterprises in different industries is balanced or not, so as to judge the vitality of regional EE.

Connectivity

Connectivity is based on the symbiosis between subjects in an ecosystem. The relationships between EE components, which engage in common activities based on common goals (starting a new business, etc.), form an interconnected network (Roundy et al., 2017). A dynamic EE is not an isolated subject, but a collection of different subjects. Avram and Avasilcai (2014) also reveal the two-way relationship between subjects, reflecting the connectivity between subjects. Well-developed social networks in the ecosystem benefit entrepreneurs by improving the transfer of information between the EE participants and those outside the EE (Roundy, 2017). The connectivity between subjects also helps to form a system network and provide a platform for entrepreneurial learning, which is more conducive to the development of the ecosystem (Pierce, 2009). The indicators selected by the connectivity feature layer are as follows:

1. Movement of population: Population movements are a way of upsetting the balance of ecosystems, encouraging "collisions" between individuals, a key source of ideas. Meanwhile, the trend of population movement reflects the flow of high-quality talents who can enhance the capabilities of core entrepreneurs to seize opportunities and build successful enterprises. Population flow is very important for regional innovation and entrepreneurship activities (Li et al, 2016). Therefore, the population flow within the region is taken as the vitality indicator to indicate the connectivity of regional EE.
2. Foreign investment: The existing research in China shows that foreign investment has obvious spillover effect on regional development, and the direct investment of the former can significantly promote the improvement of regional innovation and entrepreneurship ability (Roundy & Fayard, 2019). Foreign direct investment enterprises improve the level of science and technology in the region, bring more advanced management methods, and promote market competition, so as to enable local enterprises to carry out improvement and innovation activities, strengthen the links of enterprises in the region and enhance the connectivity and vitality of the regional EE.
3. Intermediary service: Intermediary service is an important indicator to measure the sustainable vitality of regional entrepreneurship. They mainly provide convenient services for enterprises to obtain capital, technology, market, site and other conditions. Generally speaking, intermediary service providers include crowd innovation space such as incubator, lawyers and

accounting firms, science and technology centers and so on. Makerspaces may contribute to the development of more user innovations and therefore more user entrepreneurs (Van Holm, 2015), which provides start-up enterprises with entrepreneurial space and infrastructure services, thus reducing the cost of start-up enterprises, accelerating the growth of enterprises, and promoting the transformation of scientific and technological achievements. The science and technology center provides technical support and high-quality talents to promote the development of enterprise innovation. Intermediary services play a key role in the development of entrepreneurial activities and even economic development.

Selection of Empirical Measurement Data

According to the evaluation content of regional EE indicators and considering the scientific nature and accessibility of data selection, this section selects corresponding representation data for the index layer of the evaluation system.

Data Selection for Measuring Density

Startup density is measured by the number of newly founded enterprises in a certain area for a certain period of time. However, because the enterprise survival rate is low, many newly founded enterprises may face the plight of bankruptcy. Therefore, the number of newly founded enterprises alone cannot represent the vitality of regional ecosystem and we take the net increase of enterprises in one year as the basis for judging the number of new enterprises.

Employment density of individual entrepreneurs is a measure of the employment opportunities provided by the self-employed, which is reflected in the employment of private enterprises including private limited liability companies, corporations, partnerships and sole proprietorships in the region. At the same time, there are still a large number of individual proprietorship enterprises in China, which is very common in entrepreneurial activities. The number of private enterprises and individual proprietorship enterprises employment reflects the participation of regional citizens in entrepreneurial activities. Therefore, this paper takes the number of private enterprises and individual employment as the data to measure the employment density of individual entrepreneurship.

The data of high-tech enterprise density should reflect the technological level of regional high-tech enterprises and measure the contributions of these enterprises to the regional development. We select the annual output value of high-tech enterprises in the region as a measure of the density of high-tech enterprises.

Data Selection for Measuring Diversity

Diversity mainly measures the equilibrium degree of different elements under corresponding indicators. This paper adopts the entropy measurement method proposed by Palepu (1985) to measure diversity. The calculation formula of entropy measurement is:

$$D = \sum_{i} \left[P_i \times \ln \left(1 / P_i \right) \right]$$

D is the diversity index, and P_i is the proportion of category i in the population.

Economic diversity measures the equilibrium degree of contribution of different types of industries to regional economy. According to the classification required by China's *Regulations on the Division of Three Industries*, this paper measures economic diversity by GDP of each year.

As for policy diversity, this paper measures the equilibrium degree of the number of policies issued by regional governments in four aspects, namely, support for new enterprises, scientific research, cultivation of entrepreneurial talents and establishment of entrepreneurial network. In view of the possibility of data acquisition, we select the number of policies by various governments in the region to measure the diversity of policies.

Enterprise diversity measures the balance in the distribution of enterprises in the regional EE. In accordance with the *Industry Classification of National Economy* formulated by China's statistics bureau, this paper calculates the diversity index through the number of enterprises in 20 categories of the industry.

Data Selection for Measuring Connectivity

Population flow statistics aim to clear regional population changes over a period of time. The number of net immigrant population may reflect the expectations of citizens for the regional development level. In general, the individuals always migrate to areas with high development expectations. In this paper the net population inflow is used to represent the population flow index data. The calculation method is as follows:

$$\begin{aligned} &\textit{Net population in flow} = \textit{year-end population} \\ &\times \left(\textit{population growth rate} - \textit{natural population growth rate} \right) \end{aligned}$$

For foreign investment, this paper selects the number of enterprises with foreign direct investment as the index data.

Intermediary services are measures of support for entrepreneurial activity in a region. We select the regional science and technology business incubators in number as the index data. Business incubator is an important booster that reflects the entrepreneurial atmosphere and promotes the growth of entrepreneurial enterprises. Comparing with other intermediary service providers, incubators which reflect the role of entrepreneurial ecosystems in promoting entrepreneurial activity are easier to access to the data.

According to the selection method of indicator layer data set in this section, data and sources of regional EE evaluation system are summarized as shown in Table 1.

Table 1. Measurement and sources of EE evaluation system

Characteristics of the Layer	Index Layer	Indicators to Measure	Source
	Start-up density	Number of new enterprises	China Statistical Yearbook
	Employment density of individual entrepreneurs	The number of private enterprises and individuals employed	China Statistical Yearbook
	High-tech enterprise density	Output value of high-tech industry	China Statistics Yearbook on High Technology Industries
Diversity	Economic diversity	Calculate the diversity index according to the output value	China Statistical Yearbook
	Policy diversity	Calculate the diversity index by policy category	Regional government websites
	Enterprise diversity	Calculate the diversity index according to the number of enterprises	China Statistical Yearbook
Connectivity	Population flow	Net migration	China Statistical Yearbook
	Foreign investment	Number of foreign-invested enterprises	China Statistical Yearbook
	Intermediary service	Number of incubators	Torch Center of the Ministry of Science and Technology of China

VITALITY EVALUATION OF ENTREPRENEURIAL ECOSYSTEM IN LIAONING PROVINCE

Index Weighting

In this paper, AHP is used to build a hierarchical model according to the evaluation system (Saaty, 1990). Because the decision-maker's attitude can reflect the final decision-making and the decision-maker can examine different scenarios related to the final decision-making by adjusting the weight of preferences, the weight of indicators is determined by the decision-maker (Sitaridis & Kitsios, 2019). In the form of questionnaire, we invite seven experts from Liaoning Province Social Science and Technology Federation, universities and government institutions in the field of entrepreneurship research to allocate the weight of each layer of the hierarchy model. According to the assignment, the AHP operation process is completed to obtain the final regional EE evaluation system weight value.

Table 2. Weights of EE evaluation system

The Target Layer	Characteristics of the Layer	The Weight	Index Layer	The Weight	The Total Weight
Regional entrepreneurship ecosystems are vibrant	Density	0.40	Start-up density	0.33	0.132
			Employment density of individual entrepreneurs	0.19	0.075
			High-tech enterprise density	0.48	0.195
	Diversity	0.18	Economic diversity	0.31	0.055
			Policy diversity	0.45	0.080
			Enterprise diversity	0.24	0.043
	Connectivity	0.42	Population flow	0.40	0.170
			Foreign investment	0.18	0.075
			Intermediary service	0.42	0.175

Calculation of Vitality Score of Entrepreneurial Ecosystem in Liaoning Province

Index Data Conversion Score

The evaluation index system of the collected data of 31 provinces in mainland China, constitute the index data set, and the provinces of index data divided by the size of population, it indicates that the index data of regional entrepreneurial values per capita, thereby eliminating data in different provinces population difference, through the way with a maximum data column to properly adjust data range is less than 1, as indicators of the revised data set and the score with the formula of efficacy coefficient method, the formula is as follows:

$$y_i = \left(x_i - x_{min}\right) \div \left(x_{max} - x_{min}\right) \times 40 + 60$$

y_i is the evaluation score of index i, x_i is the corrected data of index i of Liaoning province, and x_{max} and x_{min} are the maximum and minimum values of index i in the corrected data set.

Calculation and Comparison of Vitality Scores of Entrepreneurial Ecosystem in Liaoning Province

According to the weighted index and transformed index score, the vitality score of the EE of Liaoning province was calculated. The characteristic score of Liaoning province and the highest score of each characteristic layer were shown in the Table 3.

Table 3. Vitality scores and comparisons of EE in Liaoning province

The Target Layer	Characteristics	Index Layer	Liaoning Province Index Score	Liaoning Province Characteristics of the Score	Maximum Characteristic Component
Regional entrepreneurship ecosystems are vibrant	Density	Start-up density	68.53	66.13	97.72(Jiangsu)
		Employment density of individual entrepreneurs	69.4		
		High-tech enterprise density	63.19		
	Diversity	Economic diversity	88.06	90.25	91.76(Hubei)
		Policy diversity	89.93		
		Enterprise diversity	93.68		
	Connectivity	Population flow	74.62	69.75	84.14(Shanghai)
		Foreign investment	64.26		
		Intermediary service	67.47		

The comprehensive evaluation value of EE vitality in Liaoning province is:

0.40*66.13+0.18*90.25+0.42*69.75=71.95,

and it is evaluated ‘general’.

CONCLUSION

Analysis of Evaluation Results

Through the analysis results of the evaluation system, we found the following four problems in EE of Liaoning province:

First, EE of Liaoning province lacks entrepreneurial activities and entrepreneurial atmosphere. The evaluation value of density characteristic of Liaoning EE is the lowest among the three characteristic levels, which directly reflects the lack of entrepreneurial subjects and entrepreneurial activities in Liaoning province. In terms of new enterprises, the number of new legal entities in Liaoning province in 2016 was 44,046, lower than the domestic average of 79,425. In terms of individual entrepreneurship, the number of people employed by private enterprises and individuals in Liaoning province accounted for 19.90% of the total population in 2016, largely different from 49.35% in Shanghai, 48.17% in Beijing and 45.90% in Zhejiang. Opportunities for entrepreneurship constructed by entrepreneurs (Shane, 2012) do not exist objectively and do not precede the consciousness and atmosphere of entrepreneurs. The lack of entrepreneurial atmosphere of Liaoning province can be an obstacle to its development.

Second, the transformation of scientific and technological achievements is slow and the capacity for scientific and technological innovation is low. As the index with the highest weight in the evaluation system, the density of high-tech enterprises in Liaoning province only got 63.19 points. The number of high-tech enterprises in Liaoning province was 460, and the high-tech output value was 1,459.2 billion yuan. The number of enterprises, the total output and the average output of enterprises are obviously lagging behind the southeast coastal areas, indicating that there are certain problems in Liaoning province in the aspects of scientific and technological innovation and achievements. (Guangdong's high-tech output reached 3,776.52 billion, with 6,570 enterprises; Jiangsu province's high-tech output was 30,707.9, and the number of enterprises was 5,007)

Third, the construction of soft environment lags behind and the establishment of entrepreneurship support service system has not taken shape. In terms of intermediary services, Liaoning province only scored 67.47. The number of entrepreneurial intermediary service platforms in Liaoning province is small with weak service awareness, and the service level of workers engaged in entrepreneurial activities is uneven. Also, there exist few entrepreneurial institutions which can provide comprehensive services for entrepreneurs from the beginning to maturity. Despite the efforts of governments at all levels to construct a service environment conducive to innovation and entrepreneurship in recent years, the weak foundation of original entrepreneurial intermediary services has not shown any significant improvement since it has been quite a short period of time. Fourth, there can be a problem in policy of Laioning province related to talent attraction and training because it suffers from serious brain drain. As mentioned above, the population flow reflects the trend of talent flow, and the high net migration means the region has a strong talent attraction ability, which is helpful to improve the level of regional entrepreneurship. However, the net migration of population in Liaoning province appears to be negative. For example, the net migration of population in 2016 is -36,100, which reflects the lack of attractiveness and competitiveness of the talent policy in Liaoning province. In addition to the shortage of talents, the construction of relevant professional disciplines of entrepreneurship such as training and education is relatively lagging behind, the cultivation of entrepreneurship talents is insufficient at college level education, the popularization of entrepreneurship courses is not comprehensive and the syllabus taught at primary and secondary level schools doesn't focus on the courses related to entrepreneurship. There also exists a certain contradiction between the rigid classroom teaching and the innovation and entrepreneurship concept. Students have little participation in entrepreneurship practice and lack of innovation ability.

Policy Suggestions

In view of the evaluation and analysis of the vitality of EE and the existing problems in Liaoning province, combined with the entrepreneurship policies of the regions with the best characteristic indices in the evaluation system, this paper puts forward the following targeted suggestions:

Density-Based Policy Recommendations: A Case Study of Jiangsu

1. Improve the efficiency of the transformation of scientific and technological achievements and increase support for science and technology enterprises.

In order to improve the level of regional scientific and technological innovation, Jiangsu province has issued the "management measures of new and high technology entrepreneurship service center" and other policies to promote the construction of innovation and entrepreneurship carrier. It also encourages the development of high-tech enterprises by a combination of industry, education and research. Keeping in view the steps taken by the Jiangsu province, Liaoning province should increase investment to encourage technology holders to setup their own businesses and the government should provide preferential policies and more financial support for high-tech start-ups to help them establish new industries and commercialize scientific and technological achievements in the region. Besides, cooperation, close co-ordination and linkages between enterprises, universities and scientific research institutions should be established. The development of enterprise science and technology should be promoted through the forms of practice bases, entrepreneurship competitions and derivative enterprises, so as to help the application of high-tech projects in universities and scientific research institutions and improve the efficiency of achievement transformation.

2. Improve education system with a special focus on innovation and entrepreneurship and foster a culture of encouraging the establishment of entrepreneurship in the province.

Jiangsu province vigorously promotes the innovation and entrepreneurship education reforms, establishes the "Innovation and Entrepreneurship College", capacitates the entrepreneurship education teachers, and prepares for supporting syllabus and teaching materials with increased proportion of credits regarding entrepreneurship practices and learning for college students. As a result, educational institutions in Jiangsu province have become the model for China's innovation and entrepreneurship education. Keeping in mind the above steps taken by Jiangsu province, Liaoning province should promote the extensive development of entrepreneurship education. First, equip and capacitate the teachers with improved trainings regarding entrepreneurship education and consult or cooperate with universities and enterprises to improve the level of research and to teach entrepreneurship. Second, education regarding entrepreneurship should be included in the syllabus at the primary and secondary education systems in order to introduce entrepreneurship right in the roots of education system. Awareness regarding entrepreneurship should be created in the society by introducing community awareness centers, conducting free seminars, open court sessions and through print and electronic media publications in order to mobilize community members towards entrepreneurship. Competitions among college students should be arranged to encourage young people to be creative in floating new ideas and innovations regarding entrepreneurship.

Policy Suggestions Based on Diversity: Take Hubei as an Example

1. Formulate the general plan of entrepreneurship policy and introduce policy of talent introduction.

Since 2015, Hubei province has provided policies to guarantee business activities, such as "one hundred plan", "I choose in Hubei province" and "science and technology entrepreneurship ten" policy. Entrepreneurship policy has obvious stages and pertinence. Hubei province will adjust the policy in time according to the actual situation, at the same time, it will pay attention to the introduction of talent and provide entrepreneurial talent with the household registration, housing, money and so on. Considering these steps, the Liaoning provincial government should formulate explicit entrepreneurship policy planning, set clear goals, and make overall planning for the deployment of entrepreneurship resources at all levels. At the same time, it should encourage non-local residents to settle down by providing household registration application for non-local personnel, especially technical personnel, and taking specific measures for them to buy and invest in property.

2. Simplify the examination and approval process and include entrepreneurship in the performance assessment.

The general environment for entrepreneurs should be improved in Liaoning province. The start-up work should be included in the local and county performance assessment. The approval process should be simplified, and the approval time should be shortened, so that the promotion plan of entrepreneurs can be completed on time. Liaoning province should also strengthen education and supervision. Relevant policies related to entrepreneurship should be developed regarding the capacity building of government officials and public servants at all levels in order to improve business trainings and education. At the same time, researchers like us should improve the evaluation system of government officials related to entrepreneurship, and link the implementation of entrepreneurship activities with the assessment of government officials related to entrepreneurship. For entrepreneurial activities, the government should also streamline administration procedures and delegate power, so as to enhance entrepreneurial vitality, open up a "fast track", simplify procedures, improve efficiency, and create an efficient and convenient government environment.

Policy Recommendations Based on Connectivity: A Lesson From Shanghai

1. Introduce high-quality foreign-invested enterprises and attract high-end entrepreneurial resources.

Shanghai has the highest proportion of foreign-invested enterprises around the world, which provides Shanghai with a large number of international high-end innovation and entrepreneurship resources, thus enhancing market competition and driving force for local enterprises to improve and innovate. Liaoning province should also take steps to attract high-quality foreign-invested enterprises, provide preferential tax policies for these enterprises, provide land, factories and other resources, build Dalian, Panjin and other ports, and strive to create an inclusive business environment.

2. Improve the entrepreneurship service system.

Shanghai has a large number of research and development centers for public service platforms and those of affiliates and for entrepreneurs to engage in entrepreneurial activities to provide a good foundation support. Based on this, Liaoning province should integrate all kinds of social resources to guide or set up a comprehensive platform of enterprise services, to help start-ups grow, and to provide enterprises with funds, personnel, project, technology, market factors, etc. At the same time, they should encourage all walks of life to participate in the development of entrepreneurial enterprises, boost the development of legal, financial and other necessary intermediary service institutions, and attract competent service institutions to Liaoning to improve the level of various special services.

REFERENCES

Acs, Z., & Armington, C. (2004). Employment Growth and Entrepreneurial Activity inCities. *Regional Studies*, *8*(8), 911–927. doi:10.1080/0034340042000280938

Acs, Z., Autio, A., & Szerb, L. (2014). National Systems of Entrepreneurship: Measurement ssues and policy implications. *Research Policy*, *43*(3), 476–494. doi:10.1016/j.respol.2013.08.016

Audretsch, D., Mason, C., Miles, M. P., & O'Connor, A. (2018). The dynamics of Entrepreneurial ecosystems. *Entrepreneurship and Regional Development*, *30*(3-4), 471–474. doi:10.1080/08985626.2018.1436035

Audretsch, D. B., & Belitski, M. (2017). Entrepreneurial ecosystems in cities: Estabilshing the framework conditions. *The Journal of Technology Transfer*, *42*(5), 1030–1051. doi:10.100710961-016-9473-8

Avram, E. G., & Avasilcai, S. (2014). Symbiosis proccss in business ecosystem. *Advanced Materials Research*, *3483*(1036), 1066–1071. doi:10.4028/www.scientific.net/AMR.1036.1066

Boschma, R., & Iammarino, S. (2009). Related variety, trade linkages, and regional growth inItaly. *Economic Geography*, *85*(3), 289–311. doi:10.1111/j.1944-8287.2009.01034.x

Bruton, G. D., Ahlstrom, D., & Li, H. L. (2010). Institutional theory and entrepreneurship: Where are we now and where do we need to move in the future? *Entrepreneurship Theory and Practice*, *34*(3), 421–440. doi:10.1111/j.1540-6520.2010.00390.x

Cohen, B. (2006). Sustainable valleyentrepreneurial ecosystems. *Business Strategy and the Environment, 15*(1), 1–14. doi:10.1002/bse.428

Feld, B. (2012). *Startup Communities: Building an entrepreneurial ecosystem in your city.* John Wiley & Sons.

Frenken, K., Van Oort, F., & Verburg, T. (2007). Related variety, unrelated variety and regionaleconomic growth. *Regional Studies, 41*(5), 685–697. doi:10.1080/00343400601120296

Isenberg, D. (2010). How to start an entrepreneurial revolution. *Harvard Business Review, 88*(6), 40–50.

Isenberg, D. J. (2011). *The entrepreneurial ecosystem strategy as a new paradigm for economic policy: Principles for culti- vating entrepreneurship.* Presentation at the Institute of International and European Affairs.

Li, J., Strange, R., Ning, L., & Sutherland, D. (2016). Outward foreign direct investment and domestic innovation performance: Evidence from China. *International Business Review, 25*(5), 1010–1019. doi:10.1016/j.ibusrev.2016.01.008

Li, J. F., & Garnsey, E. (2014). Policy-driven ecosystems for new vaccine development. *Technovation, 34*(12), 762–772. doi:10.1016/j.technovation.2014.07.002

Mack, E., & Mayer, H. (2016). The evolutionary dynamics of entrepreneurial ecosystems. *Urban Studies (Edinburgh, Scotland), 53*(10), 2118–2133. doi:10.1177/0042098015586547

Mason, C., & Brown, R. (2014). *Entrepreneurial ecosystems and growth oriented entrepreneurship.* Final Report to OECD.

Meshram, S. A., & Rawani, A. M. (2019). Understanding entrepreneurial ecosystem international. *Journal of Social Ecology and Sustainable Development, 10*(3), 103–115. doi:10.4018/IJSESD.2019070107

Moore, J. F. (1993). Predators and prey: A new ecology of competition. *Harvard Business Review, 71*(3), 75–86. PMID:10126156

Nadgrodkiewicz, A. (2013). Building entrepreneurial ecosystems. *Economic Reform Features Services, 12*, 18–21.

Neck, H. M., Meyer, G. D., Cohen, B., & Corbett, A. C. (2004). An entrepreneurial system view of new venture creation. *Journal of Small Business Management, 42*(2), 190–208. doi:10.1111/j.1540-627X.2004.00105.x

Needleman, S. E & Fletcher, O. (2012). A start-up ecosystem forms in Chicago. *Wall street Journal*, *259*(61), 3-5.

Palepu, K. (1985). Diversification strategy, profit performance and the entropy measure. *Strategic Management Journal*, *6*(3), 239–255. doi:10.1002mj.4250060305

Pierce, L. (2009). Big losses in ecosystem niches: How core firm decisions drive complementary product shakeouts. *Strategic Management Journal*, *30*(3), 323–347. doi:10.1002mj.736

Roundy, P. T. (2017). Small town' entrepreneurial ecosystems: Implications for developed and emerging economies. *Journal of Entrepreneurship in Emerging Economies*, *9*(3), 238–262. doi:10.1108/JEEE-09-2016-0040

Roundy, P. T., Brockman, B. K., & Bradshaw, M. (2017). The resilience of entrepreneurial ecosystems. *Journal of Business Venturing Insights*, *8*, 99–104. doi:10.1016/j.jbvi.2017.08.002

Roundy, P. T., & Fayard, D. (2019). Dynamic capabilities and entrepreneurial ecosystems: The micro-foundations of regional entrepreneurship. *The Journal of Entrepreneurship*, *28*(1), 94–120. doi:10.1177/0971355718810296

Saaty, T. L. (1990). How to make a decision: The analytic hierarchy process. *European Journal of Operational Research*, *48*(1), 9–26. doi:10.1016/0377-2217(90)90057-I

Shane, S. (2012). Reflections on the 2010 AMR decade award:Delivering on the promise of entrepreneurship as a field of research. *Academy of Management Review*, *37*(1), 10–20. doi:10.5465/amr.2011.0078

Sitaridis, I., & Kitsios, F. (2019). Competitiveness analysis and evaluation of entrepreneurialecosystems: A multi-criteria approach. *Annals of Operations Research*, *2019*, 1–23.

Soto-Rodríguez, E. (2014). Entrepreneurial ecosystems as a pathway towards competitiveness: The case of Puerto Rico. *Competition Forum. American Society for Competitiveness*, *12*(1), 31–40.

Spiegel, B. (2015). The relational organization of entrepreneurial ecosystems. *Entrepreneurship Theory and Practice*, *41*(1), 49–72. doi:10.1111/etap.12167

Spilling, R. (1996). The entrepreneurial system: On entrepreneurship in the context of a mega-event. *Journal of Business Research*, *36*(1), 91–103. doi:10.1016/0148-2963(95)00166-2

Stam, E. (2015). Entrepreneurial ecosystems and regional policy: A sympathetic critique. *European Planning Studies*, *23*(9), 1759–1769. doi:10.1080/09654313.2015.1061484

Suresh, J., & Ramraj, R. (2012). Entrepreneurial ecosystem: Case study on the influence of environmental factors on entrepreneurial success. *European Journal of Business and Management*, *4*(16), 95–101.

Theodoraki, C., Messeghem, K., & Rice, M. P. (2017). A social capital approach to the development of sustainable entrepreneurial ecosystems: An explorative study. *Small Business Economics*, *51*(1), 1–18.

Van Holm, E. J. (2015). Makerspaces and contributions to entrepreneurship. *Procedia: Social and Behavioral Sciences*, *195*, 24–31. doi:10.1016/j.sbspro.2015.06.167

Vogel, P. (2013). The employment outlook for youth: Building entrepreneurial ecosystems as a way forward. *G20 Youth Forum*.

Zahra, S., & Nambisan, S. (2011). Nambisan S. Entrepreneurship in global innovation ecosystems. *AMS Review*, *1*(1), 4–17. doi:10.100713162-011-0004-3

Chapter 2
Research on the Operation Efficiency of Science and Technology Innovation Incubator Under Different Leading Modes

Meng Zhang
https://orcid.org/0000-0003-1159-2606
Shandong Normal University, China

Liyao Pan
https://orcid.org/0000-0003-0637-8488
University of Texas at San Antonio, USA

Xiaomin Du
Yingkou Institute of Technology, China

ABSTRACT

The incubator of scientific and technological innovation plays an important role in leading scientific and technological innovation, accelerating the transformation of scientific and technological achievements, and promoting industrial upgrading and transformation. The Chinese economy is in the transition stage, so the research on the operating efficiency of the incubator of scientific and technological innovation based on the Chinese context has its unique value. In this study, combined with Chinese context, the business incubator is divided into two main modes: government and private. By using DEA research method, this chapter analyzes a series of problems, such as the overall difference and difference grade of the operating efficiency of

DOI: 10.4018/978-1-7998-3495-3.ch002

incubators among the four major economic zones of China, the comparison of the operating efficiency of different modes between Northeast and Western regions, and the gap between private-led incubators in eastern China and private-led incubators in Northeast and Western China.

INTRODUCTION

In recent years, the incubator of scientific and technological innovation has become an important means to promote the development of scientific and technological innovation and enhance the vitality of regional economy (Bergek & Norrman, 2008; Schwartz & Göthner, 2009; Özdemir & Şehitoğlu, 2013; Bruneel, Ratinho, Clarysse, & Groen, 2012; Merigó, Gil-Lafuente & Yager, 2015; Ratinho & Henriques, 2010). In addition, incubators with good operating efficiency are also conducive to the development of regional entrepreneurship (Jamil, Ismail & Mahmood, 2015). Since the incubator of scientific and technological innovation needs to achieve the maximum output under the given conditions of input, the research on the incubation mechanism and operating efficiency has been paid attention by scholars, government and business (Aernoudt, 2004; Barbero, Casillas, Ramos, & Guitar, 2012). However, most of the existing researches on incubators are concentrated in developed regions such as the United States and the United Kingdom, whose incubators have formed a good incubation mechanism. Research on emerging areas where incubator projects are being developed is urgent and necessary (M'Chirgui, Lamine, Mian & Fayolle, 2018). As one of the rapidly developing emerging countries, China has become the third largest country in the world in the field of the incubator projects of scientific and technological innovation (Jamil, Ismail & Siddique, 2016). Therefore, it is of great value for incubator research to study the current situation of operating efficiency development of incubators in China.

As an important carrier of innovation, entrepreneurship and industrialization of scientific and technological achievements, the incubator of scientific and technological innovation have sprung up rapidly in China in just over a decade (Shannxi, 2015). Especially, the "mass entrepreneurship and innovation" policy proposed by the Chinese government in recent years has further stimulated the development of the incubator of scientific and technological innovation. Although China has ranked among the largest and fastest growing economies in the world (Johnson & Tellis, 2008), the economic developmental level of various regions in China is still uneven, and the operating efficiency of incubators is greatly different due to different local government policies and restrictions (Lindelöf & Science, 2002). Under the existing research system, there are studies on the operating efficiency of Chinese incubator of scientific and technological innovation, but it is very rare to systematically study the operational efficiency differences caused by the differences between specific regions and regions, or even the types of incubators under regional characteristics (Hochberg, 2016). In addition, Chinese incubator of scientific and technological innovation was initially established by the government to guide scientific and technological innovation, and its initial incubator mode tends to be a single government-led form. However, due to the lack of competition, the government-led incubators are short of the consciousness of independent innovation (Wplniak & Grebski, 2017). Therefore, the Chinese government began to encourage other demand subjects to join the construction of incubators, and the incubator of scientific and technological innovation led by private subjects emerged (Chandra & Chao, 2011). However, under the special situation of China, the government still plays an important role in leading social scientific and technological innovation, and government-led incubators of scientific and technological innovation still account for a large part, but the research on the advantages and disadvantages of government-led incubators and private-led incubators is still vague. Therefore, it is of great value to study the difference of operating efficiency of incubators of scientific and technological innovation under different dominant modes in China.

According to the actual situation of China's economic and social development, the Chinese government divides the country into four major economic regions: the eastern region, the northeast region, the central region and the western region. Based on this, this study firstly analyzes the regional differences in the operating efficiency of incubators of scientific and technological innovation in the four economic regions of China through macro comparison, and finds out the development problems of incubators of scientific and technological innovation in the northeast and western regions. Secondly, analysis specific development issues of operating efficiency of the incubator of scientific and technological innovation in Northeast and Western China from the perspective of internal microcosmic; Finally, this paper divides incubators of scientific and technological innovation into government-led incubators and private-led incubators and analyzes their operating efficiency by classification, revealing the difference in operating efficiency between the two types of incubators in northeast China and western China, as well as the difference in operating efficiency of private-led incubators between northeast and western regions and eastern region.

DEA is applied to analyze the comprehensive efficiency, pure technical efficiency and scale efficiency. The conclusion shows that, first of all, the operating efficiency of business incubators in western region is generally ineffective, while in northeast China, compared with the central and eastern regions, although it is overall effective, there is a serious shortage of investment. Secondly, although the incubators in northeast China are effective as a whole, there are more than half of invalid incubators, and the pure technical efficiency difference between incubators is very big, with low economic benefits. In western region, incubators are ineffective as a whole, and about half of the incubators inside are ineffective in operating efficiency. Moreover, non-effective scale efficiency is the main reason that affects the operating efficiency of incubators in western regions, and the incubation capacity is weak. Finally, generally speaking, the operating efficiency of private-led incubators in northeast China and western China is better than that of government-led incubators, which is mainly reflected in the pure technical efficiency, but there is still a big gap with private-led incubators in central and eastern China. Based on this, the innovative incubators in northeast and western regions need two steps: one is to reduce the proportion of state-led incubators and transform them into private-led incubators; the other is that private-led incubators in northeast and western regions need to learn from the operating experience of private-led incubators in central and eastern regions.

LITERATURE REVIEW

Research on Operating Efficiency of Incubator of Scientific and Technological Innovation

As an important link of regional innovation ecosystem, business incubator plays an important role in the emerging knowledge economy (M'Chirgui, 2012; Apa, Grandinetti & Sedita, 2017; Mian, Lamine & Fayolle, 2016). However, as a booster for the growth of start-ups (Bruneel et al., 2012), whether they can effectively use limited resources to achieve their own goals and promote the growth of incubated enterprises is still highly uncertain (Lewis, 2001; Bhabra-Remedios & Cornelius, 2003). At present, the research on the operating efficiency of incubator of scientific and technological innovation mainly focuses on the two core elements of input and output, and measures the effectiveness of incubator of scientific and technological innovation from the perspective of rigid indexes. When measuring the two core elements, different countries and regions can adopt indicators that reflect local conditions and characteristics, and the selection criteria may not be consistent (Burnett & McMurray, 2008). Existing research generally measures the input with people, money and goods, and measures the output with social benefits, economic benefits and incubation capacity. Generally, the accepted DEA research method is adopted in evaluation. Therefore, in terms of index selection and measurement methods, there are consistent conclusions within the academic circle. In addition, from the perspective of research purposes and conclusions, the results also focus more on exploring the differences in operating efficiency of incubators in different regions of China, as well as the overall problem of operating efficiency in specific regions . At the same time, in terms of exploring regional differences, the research also gradually covers northeast or northwest region with special situations and points out the degree of regional differences. Compared with the previous research on the single level of cognition, in fact, the operation of the incubator is more complex, and it is necessary to take into account based on multiple level (Baraldi & Havenvid, 2016). However, most of the above studies tend to point out the present situation and shortcomings of operating efficiency of incubators from the macro or overall level, and the research that can explore the specific reasons for the operation efficiency from the micro aspect is still rare. More specifically, when using DEA research method to evaluate the operating efficiency of the incubator of scientific and technological innovation, the research often draws a holistic conclusion because of the specific value of efficiency index, but sometimes this conclusion is not universal, nor can it fully reveal the essence of operating efficiency of incubators, which is also the aspect that needs to be broken through in the present research.

To sum up, the following two problems generally exist in the current evaluation research on the operating efficiency of incubator of scientific and technological innovation. First, few literatures can explore the differences caused by different specific conditions of incubators of scientific and technological innovation, including regional specificity, policy specificity and entrepreneurial environment specificity. In fact, there are still unbalanced regional development and ineffective policies at the local level in China. Therefore, it is very important to analyze problems from the perspective of contingency. Second, most existing studies use macro data to summarize the operating efficiency of business incubators from a holistic perspective, and the research conclusions are not targeted. For example, from a holistic perspective, the overall operating efficiency of incubator of scientific and technological innovation in northeast China is effective, but at the micro level, the number of ineffective incubators is still large, and systematic studies on the combination of macro and micro are rare.

Research on the Classification Incubator of Scientific and Technological Innovation With Different Dominant Modes

At present, there are two main models for the classification of incubator of scientific and technological innovation: one is based on the functions and value-added services provided by incubators; the other is based on the perspectives of founders and property owners. Different dividing methods correspond to different research purposes. The former mainly focuses on how different models of incubators can achieve performance, for example, exploring the difference between profit patterns of different functional incubators such as comprehensive type, investment promotion type or professional type and how to carry out problems (Hughes, Ireland & Morgan, 2017). While the latter paid more attention to the impact of different legal or governance structures on the operational model of incubator of scientific and technological innovation, which includes what operating modes of joint operations or different types of independent property rights of different legal persons and the unique differences in their operating modes, for example, to explore the differences between the university business incubators and the business incubators, as well as the operational characteristics of the business innovation center (Grimaldi & Grandi, 2005; Von Zedtwitz & Grimaldi, 2006). Of course, some studies directly classified the types of incubator of scientific and technological innovation based on the state-owned and private sectors, collected sample data through questionnaires, and the regulating effect of the two kinds of ownership nature on the relationship between corporate social capital and innovation performance. This research paradigm is of great significance to reveal whether there are significant differences between state-owned enterprises and private enterprises in regions with regional characteristics. However, at present, there is still a lack of systematic comparative studies on the two dominant modes from the perspective of input and output, and detailed studies on operational efficiency factors of incubator of scientific and technological innovation under different dominant modes (Tang, Lee, Liu & Lu, 2014).

In fact, as a product of multi-party cooperation, incubator of scientific and technological innovation will be greatly influenced by different owners and participants on its operating process and decision-making mechanism, and eventually lead to significant operational efficiency differences. Especially for incubator of scientific and technological innovation in China, because the government still plays an important role in market economy and leading scientific and technological innovation, the proportion of state-owned incubator of scientific and technological innovation is still large, which is quite different from other regions in the world, and this difference has become a special situation. Therefore, in China, based on the classification of state-owned and private, it is of great research value to explore the advantages and disadvantages of operational efficiency of the two leading models of incubator of scientific and technological innovation and the differences between the two types of incubator of scientific and technological innovation in different regions.

RESEARCH DESIGN

Research Methods

This study needs to analyze the operating efficiency of Chinese incubator of scientific and technological innovation. However, it is difficult to construct a production function and efficiency function with a clear and unified form because of the unique heterogeneity of incubator, the inconsistency of definition, the scope of evaluation criteria for defining the effectiveness of incubator and the difficulty of selecting factors that affect the incubation of successful enterprises. Therefore, it is extremely difficult to measure the operating efficiency of incubator effectively. Data envelopment analysis (DEA) has significant advantages in evaluating decision making units with multiple inputs and outputs: (1) it is not necessary to know the specific forms of production function and efficiency function. (2) it can process different types of data, and do not need to carry out a unified dimensional processing of all indicators; (3) the weight of DEA method is the de-optimal weight calculated by the actual data of the decision unit, rather than the weight set subjectively. (4) the correlation between various input or output indicators does not affect the evaluation result of DEA method. Therefore, data envelopment analysis (DEA) was used to evaluate the operating efficiency of Chinese incubator of scientific and technological innovation.

Since the return to scale of incubator of scientific and technological innovation is variable, this paper chooses the BCC model with variable return to scale to evaluate its operating efficiency. In this paper, incubator of scientific and technological innovation is taken as a decision-making unit, and it is easier to adjust the input amount of resources than to control the output. The input-oriented model is a model that measures the proportion of factor input that can be reduced when the output is maintained. Therefore, this paper chooses input-oriented BCC model and super efficiency model to evaluate the operating efficiency of Chinese incubator of scientific and technological innovation.

Selection of Evaluation Indicators

The selection of input-output indicators is an important factor affecting the calculation results of DEA method, so the selection of indicators is crucial. The input-output indicators in this paper are as follows.

1. Input index: The normal operation of incubator of scientific and technological innovation requires the input of human resources, financial resources and material resources. First of all, the entrepreneurship service talents with high-quality and professional management ability are the important input factor to improve the incubation ability of incubator of scientific and technological innovation. This paper measured it by the total number of active personnel in the incubator. Secondly, incubator of scientific and technological innovation provide financing support for incubated enterprises through their own incubation funds, government financial subsidies and venture capital from various social parties. Considering the availability of data, this paper takes the total amount of incubation funds of incubator of scientific and technological innovation as the evaluation index of financial input of incubators. Finally, the site condition

of the incubator of scientific and technological innovation is the hardware infrastructure of incubating science and technology enterprises, and the field area of the incubator is the material input of the incubator of the science and technology enterprise.

2. Output index: According to the previous research literature, the output index of this paper has three factors: incubation ability, economic benefit and social benefit. First, based on the research on the output performance of incubators by Allen & McCluskey (1991), Hisrich & Smilor (1988), and McMullan, Long & Graham (1986), this paper takes the incubation capacity as the factor layer to evaluate the operating efficiency output index of science and technology business incubators, and takes the cumulative number of graduated enterprises and annual graduation rate as the index layer (Allen & Levine, 1986; Hisrich & Smilor, 1988; McMullan et al., 1986). Secondly, referring to the research of Allen et al., Hisrich et al., Smilor et al., this paper takes economic benefit as the factor layer to evaluate the efficiency output index of incubator operation, and takes the number of intellectual property rights approved by incubated enterprises, the average income of incubated enterprises upon graduation and the total income of incubators as the index layer (Allen & Levine, 1986; Hisrich & Smilor, 1988; Smilor, 1987; Allen & Rahman, 1985). Finally, based on the research of McMullan et al. (1986), Bollinger, Hope, & Utterback, and Miller, Miller & Cote (1987) this paper takes social benefits as the factor layer to evaluate the operating efficiency and output index of technology enterprises, and takes new jobs as the index layer (McMullan et al., 1986; Bollinger et al., 1983; Miller & Cote, 1987). The input-output indicators set in this paper are shown in Table 1.

EMPIRICAL ANALYSIS

Macro Analysis of Operating Efficiency of Incubator of Scientific and Technological Innovation in Four Regions of China

To explore the overall development situation of Chinese incubator of scientific and technological innovation, we use the BBC input orientation model in DEA data envelopment analysis to analyze the operating efficiency of national incubators in four economic regions of China (eastern region, central region, western region and northeast region), this part of the data comes from the < China Torch Statistical Yearbook 2015-2017>.

Table 1. Input and output index table of incubator of scientific and technological innovation

Index	Factors Layer	Index Layer	The Required Data
Input index	Human input	Total number of employees in the incubator (person)	Total number of employees in the incubator (person)
	Financial input	Total incubation fund of the incubator (yuan) Investment in public technical service platforms (1000 yuan)	Total incubation fund of the incubator (yuan) Investment on public technical service platforms (1000 yuan)
	Material input	Incubator area (m^2)	Incubator area (m^2)
Output index	Incubation ability	Cumulative number of enterprises graduated(number), annual graduation rate (number of enterprises graduated in that year/number of incubated enterprises in that year)	Cumulative number of graduated enterprises(number) Number of enterprise graduates in that year (number) Number of incubated enterprises in that year(number)
	Economic benefits	Number of intellectual property rights approved by incubated enterprises (item), average income of incubated enterprises upon graduation (yuan), total income of incubators (yuan)	Number of intellectual property rights approved by incubated enterprises (item) Average income at graduation of incubated enterprises (yuan) Total income of incubator (yuan)
	Social benefits	New jobs (number of employees in incubated enterprises + number of personnel in incubators)	Number of employees in incubated enterprises (person)

As can be seen from Table 2, from 2014 to 2016, except for the western region, the comprehensive efficiency of national incubators in the other three regions was 1, indicating that the operating efficiency of incubators in the three regions was all effective, while the comprehensive efficiency of incubators in the western region was less than 1, indicating that the operating efficiency of incubator of scientific and technological innovation in the western region was relatively ineffective.

Due to the defects of the basic DEA model in the model, the efficiency value of the calculated DEA effective decision-making unit can only be 1, so it is no longer possible to further compare and analyze the decision-making unit that is also DEA effective (efficiency value is 1). Therefore, Andersen et al. proposed a super-efficiency DEA model, compared with the basic DEA model, the reference set constructed by the super-efficient DEA model does not contain the evaluated decision making unit itself, so for those decision making units whose efficiency value is 1 in the basic DEA model, the efficiency value calculated by the superefficient DEA model may be greater than 1, so the comparison problem between the DEA

Table 2. Operating efficiency of the four regions from 2014 to 2016

Region	Year	The Comprehensive Efficiency	Pure Technical Efficiency	The Scale Efficiency	Scale Reward
The eastern region	2016	1.000	1.000	1.000	-
	2015	1.000	1.000	1.000	-
	2014	1.000	1.000	1.000	-
The central region	2016	1.000	1.000	1.000	-
	2015	1.000	1.000	1.000	-
	2014	1.000	1.000	1.000	-
The western region	2016	0.926	0.929	0.997	irs
	2015	0.989	1.000	0.989	drs
	2014	0.896	0.898	0.997	irs
The northeast region	2016	1.000	1.000	1.000	-
	2015	1.000	1.000	1.000	-
	2014	1.000	1.000	1.000	-

Note: in the scale reward, the "drs" indicates decreasing returns on scale, and the "irs" indicates increasing returns on scale, and the "-" indicates invariable returns on scale.

efficient decision making units is effectively solved. In order to further analyze the operational efficiency differences of incubators among the eastern region, the central region and the northeast region, this paper uses EMS1.3 software and BBC input-oriented model to calculate DEA super efficiency in the three regions. The super-efficiency value represents the significance that these incubators can still remain effective if they are scaled up according to a certain proportion.

As can be seen from Table 3, the average super-efficiency values of the eastern region, the central region and the northeast region are all more than 1, and the average super-efficiency value in the eastern region is 130.68%, indicating that the incubator in the eastern region can still keep DEA relatively effective by increasing the input by 30.68%, and the incubator in the central region can still keep DEA relatively effective by increasing the input by 23.92%. However, in northeast China,

Table 3. Super-efficiency value and ranking of national incubators in the four regions from 2014 to 2016

Region	2014	2015	2016	The Mean Value
The eastern region	176.96%	109.95%	105.12%	130.68%
The central region	127.02%	108.61%	136.14%	123.92%
The northeast region	480.84%	231.55%	103.31%	271.9%

an additional 171.9% of investment can still keep DEA relatively effective. Therefore, compared with the eastern region and the central region, the incubator in northeast China still has a lot of room for improvement, and it is necessary to increase the input of incubator elements in northeast China.

To sum up, from 2014 to 2016, the overall operating efficiency of incubators in western China was not effective, while in northeast China, although overall effective, there was still a lot of room for improvement, and more investment in incubators was needed. In order to find out the crux of the incubator operating efficiency in northeast China and western China, this paper analyzes the operating efficiency of incubators in the two regions from a microscopic point of view.

Micro-Analysis of Operating Efficiency of Incubators in Northeast China and Western China

This part continues to use the BBC input-oriented model in DEA data enveloping analysis to measure the operating efficiency of incubators of scientific and technological innovation in northeast and western China. This part of the sample data is from <China Torch Statistical Yearbook 2013>. In 2012, 45 incubators of scientific and technological innovation in Northeast China were selected as national incubators, and 60 incubators of scientific and technological innovation in the western region were selected. Excluding the incubators with incomplete data, 32 samples of incubators of scientific and technological innovation in Northeast China and 43 valid samples of incubators of scientific and technological innovation in the western region were obtained.

1. analysis results of operating efficiency of incubators of scientific and technological innovation in northeast and western China

It can be seen from Table 3 and 4 that, first of all, the input of incubators of scientific and technological innovation in northeast China should not be increased blindly. As many incubators in northeast China have diminishing returns on scale, the scale of these incubators should be controlled and the input should be reduced. On the contrary, there are a large number of incubators with increasing returns on scale in the western region, so we should increase their investment in factors; Secondly, the research found that the operating efficiency of incubators of scientific and technological innovation in northeast China was effective from a macroscopic perspective, while the microanalysis found that the operating efficiency was less than half effective, which indicated that the macro-analysis had some limitations and the microanalysis was necessary. In addition, about half of the incubators of scientific and technological innovation in the western region operate efficiently, so the macro and micro conditions are not good. Finally, pure technical efficiency of incubators in the northeast region are very different from each other, the pure technical efficiency values of ineffective incubators are between 0.3-0.99, which indicates that the development of operating capacity of these ineffective incubators is very uneven. Therefore, improving the operating ability of incubators is an effective way to improve the operating efficiency of ineffective incubators in Northeast China, rather than simply expanding the scale and increasing investment. However, 38.2% of incubators in western China have no pure technical efficiency, while 51.2% have no scale efficiency, indicating that ineffective scale efficiency is the main reason that affects the operating efficiency of incubators in western China.

To further explore the internal problems of incubator development in Northeast and West China, this article divide the selected incubator of scientific and technological innovation into two categories: the government-led incubators and private-led ones, explore the internal development differences of operating efficiency of incubators between the two regions by classification analysis, and identify the crux of the problem affecting the development of the incubator. Among them, government-led incubators refer to incubators established by central or local governments, and private-led incubators refer to incubators established by citizens or enterprises. Based on this classification, this paper observes the operating efficiency of 32 national incubators in northeast China and 43 national incubators in western China. I_1-I_{16} in Table 4 are private-led incubators, G_1-G_{32} are government-led incubators, W_1-W_{23} are government-led incubators and W_{24}-W_{43} are private-led incubators. The summary is as follows:

According to Table 4, 5, 6, the pure technical efficiency of private-led incubators is obviously better than that of government-led incubators in northeast China and western China, while the scale efficiency of private-led incubators is slightly worse than that of government-led incubators. The comprehensive efficiency of 56.25% private-led incubators in northeast China are 1, while that of only 37.5% government-led incubators are 1. Meanwhile, the technical efficiency of 60.7% government-led incubators in western China are effective and also lower than that of 65% private-led incubators. In addition, the comprehensive efficiency value and technical efficiency value of most invalid private incubators in Northeast China are concentrated near the effective value 1, while the distribution of comprehensive efficiency value and technical efficiency value of government-led incubator is scattered, which indicates that the overall difference of comprehensive efficiency and technical efficiency between incubators is very great, and the operating efficiency of government-led incubators still have a lot of room to improve.

In addition, the northeast region should control the resource input of government-led incubators and increase the input of private-led incubators. In the private-led incubators with ineffective operating efficiency in northeast China, 57.14% of the

Table 4. Results of operating efficiency analysis of national incubators in northeast China

Organization Code	The Comprehensive Efficiency	Pure Technical Efficiency	The Scale Efficiency	Scale Reward	Organization Code	The Comprehensive Efficiency	Pure Technical Efficiency	The Scale Efficiency	Scale Reward
I_1	1.000	1.000	1.000	-	G_{17}	0.308	0.497	0.620	drs
I_2	1.000	1.000	1.000	-	G_{18}	0.539	0.558	0.967	drs
I_3	1.000	1.000	1.000	-	G_{19}	1.000	1.000	1.000	-
I_4	0.447	0.727	0.615	drs	G_{20}	0.785	1.000	0.785	irs
I_5	1.000	1.000	1.000	-	G_{21}	1.000	1.000	1.000	-
I_6	1.000	1.000	1.000	-	G_{22}	0.769	0.791	0.972	drs
I_7	0.653	1.000	0.653	irs	G_{23}	1.000	1.000	1.000	-
I_8	0.694	0.802	0.865	irs	G_{24}	0.737	0.853	0.864	drs
I_9	1.000	1.000	1.000	-	G_{25}	1.000	1.000	1.000	-
I_{10}	0.514	0.631	0.815	drs	G_{26}	0.873	0.881	0.990	irs
I_{11}	1.000	1.000	1.000	-	G_{27}	0.513	0.635	0.807	drs
I_{12}	0.262	0.359	0.730	drs	G_{28}	0.341	0.559	0.611	drs
1_{13}	0.621	0.776	0.800	irs	G_{29}	1.000	1.000	1.000	-
I_{14}	0.633	0.659	0.960	irs	G_{30}	0.885	0.966	0.916	drs
I_{15}	1.000	1.000	1.000	-	G_{31}	0.664	0.668	0.994	irs
I_{16}	1.000	1.000	1.000	-	G_{32}	1.000	1.000	1.000	-
The mean value	The comprehensive efficiency:0.789			Pure technical efficiency:0.861			The scale efficiency:0.899		

Note: in the scale reward, the "drs" indicates decreasing returns on scale, and the "irs" indicates increasing returns on scale, and the "-" indicates invariable returns on scale.

incubators show increasing returns on scale, while in the government-led incubators with ineffective operating efficiency, 70% of the incubators show decreasing returns on scale. It shows that most private-led incubators in northeast China can further improve the operating efficiency of incubators by expanding the scale of incubators, while most government-led incubators should avoid blindly expanding the scale of incubators, but should focus on improving the operating capacity and the benefit efficiency of input factors.

Table 5. Analysis results of operating efficiency of national incubators in western China

Organization Code	The Comprehensive Efficiency	Pure Technical Efficiency	The Scale Efficiency	Scale Reward	Organization Code	The Comprehensive Efficiency	Pure Technical Efficiency	The Scale Efficiency	Scale Reward
W_1	1.000	1.000	1.000	-	W_{23}	0.967	0.988	0.978	irs
W_2	1.000	1.000	1.000	-	W_{24}	1.000	1.000	1.000	-
W_3	1.000	1.000	1.000	-	W_{25}	0.575	0.945	0.608	irs
W_4	0.679	0.797	0.852	irs	W_{26}	1.000	1.000	1.000	-
W_5	0.826	0.870	0.949	irs	W_{27}	0.463	0.814	0.568	irs
W_6	0.843	1.000	0.843	drs	W_{28}	0.855	0.879	0.973	drs
W_7	0.623	0.626	0.996	drs	W_{29}	1.000	1.000	1.000	-
W_8	1.000	1.000	1.000	-	W_{30}	1.000	1.000	1.000	-
W_9	1.000	1.000	1.000	-	W_{31}	1.000	1.000	1.000	-
W_{10}	0.919	1.000	0.919	irs	W_{32}	1.000	1.000	1.000	-
W_{11}	1.000	1.000	1.000	-	W_{33}	0.923	1.000	0.923	irs
W_{12}	0.498	0.566	0.879	irs	W_{34}	0.685	0.879	0.780	irs
W_{13}	1.000	1.000	1.000	-	W_{35}	0.892	0.909	0.981	irs
W_{14}	0.517	0.727	0.711	irs	W_{36}	1.000	1.000	1.000	-
W_{15}	1.000	1.000	1.000	-	W_{37}	1.000	1.000	1.000	-
W_{16}	1.000	1.000	1.000	-	W_{38}	1.000	1.000	1.000	-
W_{17}	1.000	1.000	1.000	-	W_{39}	0.427	1.000	0.427	irs
W_{18}	1.000	1.000	1.000	-	W_{40}	0.767	0.910	0.842	irs
W_{19}	1.000	1.000	1.000	-	W_{41}	1.000	1.000	1.000	-
W_{20}	0.847	0.958	0.884	irs	W_{42}	0.656	0.702	0.934	irs
W_{21}	0.628	0.670	0.938	irs	W_{43}	0.973	1.000	0.973	irs
W_{22}	0.671	0.694	0.967	irs					
The mean value	The comprehensive efficiency:0.866				Pure technical efficiency:0.929			The scale efficiency:0.928	

2. Analysis of the ineffectiveness of incubators in northeast and western China

According to the principle of data envelopment analysis, this paper not only calculated the comprehensive efficiency, pure technical efficiency and scale efficiency of each decision-making unit, but also calculated the reduced input or

Table 6. Average operating efficiency of two types of incubators in two regions

Region	Operating Efficiency	Private-led Incubators	Government-led Incubators
The northeast region	The comprehensive efficiency	0.802	0.776
	Pure technical efficiency	0.872	0.838
	The scale efficiency	0.902	0.908
The western region	The comprehensive efficiency	0.861	0.870
	Pure technical efficiency	0.952	0.909
	The scale efficiency	0.900	0.953

increased output required of the decision-making unit with relatively non-effective operation efficiency. It can be seen from Table 7 and Table 8 that, in general, there are redundant input and insufficient output in incubators of scientific and technological innovation in the northeast and the western regions., which are mainly manifested as the following three problems:

a. There are a lot of incubators with redundant input in northeast China and western China and there is waste. The input of its elements should be controlled. Except for I_7 and G_{20} in northeast China and W_6, W_{10}, W_{33}, W_{39} and W_{43} in western China, all incubators have problems of redundant space area of incubators, in-service personnel and total investment of incubation funds. Therefore, it is necessary to control the input of the redundant incubators and reduce the waste.

b. For incubators with mismatched scale, the scale should be expanded or reduced according to the actual situation, so as to realize the optimal matching mode and achieve relatively effective comprehensive efficiency. The input redundancy of I_7 and G_{20} in Northeast China, W_{10}, W_{33}, W_{39}, and W_{43} in the western region are all 0, but their comprehensive efficiency is still in an inefficient state, and the pure technical efficiency value is 1, while the scale efficiency is less than 1, which indicates that the ineffective scale efficiency is the main reason for the ineffective comprehensive efficiency. In addition, I_7 and G_{20} in the western region and W_{10}, W_{33}, W_{39}, W_{43} in the northeast region have increasing returns on scale(irs), so should further expand their scale of incubators, while W_6 has decreasing returns of scale (drs), therefore it needs to control its scale, realize the optimal matching mode, thus achieve the comprehensive efficiency that is relatively effective.

c. The overall output of non-effective incubators in northeast China and western China is insufficient. The Table 2 shows that the insufficient output of the incubator in the northeast region is mainly concentrated on the average income at graduation, the total income of incubators, the total number of intellectual property rights approved and the annual graduation rate. Therefore, the inefficient operating efficiency of the non-effective incubator in the northeast is mainly reflected in the weak incubation ability and low economic benefit, and the low economic benefit is especially serious. As can be seen from Table 3, the output insufficiency of incubators in western regions is mainly concentrated on the cumulative number of graduated enterprises, annual graduation rate and average income upon graduation. Therefore, the ineffective operating efficiency of non-effective incubators in western regions is mainly reflected in the weak incubation capacity and low economic benefits, especially the insufficient incubation capacity.

In conclusion, in terms of investment direction, we should not increase the resource input of incubators blindly in the whole northeast and western regions. For incubators with redundant input, resource input should be controlled or reduced, while for incubators with increasing return on scale, resource input should be increased. In addition, in terms of the output efficiency of input resources, both the northeast region and the western region should devote themselves to improving the economic benefits and incubation ability of incubators. Among them, the northeast region should pay more attention to improving the economic benefits of incubators of scientific and technological innovation, while the western region should focus on making up for the insufficient output of incubation ability.

According to the classification, the Figure 2 shows that the non-effective government-led incubators and private-led incubators in the northeast and western regions all have insufficient output that in incubator capacity (annual graduation rate, cumulative graduate companies), economic benefits (through the number of intellectual property rights approved by incubated enterprises, the average income of incubated enterprises upon graduation and the total income of incubators), social benefits(jobs) three aspects, mainly reflected on the weak incubation ability, low economic benefits and the lack of economic output of government-led incubators. From the perspective of the capability of the incubator, the two types of incubators in the two regions have insufficient output in the annual graduation rate, and the government-led incubator is more than the private-led incubator, but the output of the private-led incubator in the cumulative graduation enterprises is higher than that of the government-led incubator. This may be caused by the fact that the duration

Table 7. Input-output adjustment table of operating efficiency of invalid incubators in northeast China

Organization Code	Input Redundancy Value			Insufficient Output Value					
	Site Area (10 m²)	Incubator Staff (person)	Total Incubation Fund (10000 yuan)	Cumulative Number of Graduated Enterprises(number)	Average Income at Graduation (10000 yuan)	Total Income of Incubator (10000 yuan)	Total Number of Approved Intellectual Property Rights (item)	Annual Graduation Rate	Increase Jobs (number)
I_4	-677.215	-13.487	-134.873	85.254	0	242.938	27.457	0.081	0
I_7	0	0	0	0	0	0	0	0	0
I_8	-8.979	-0.739	-15.844	27.126	161.848	198.457	0.933	0.004	185.260
I_{10}	-124.146	-37.098	-1477.844	15.363	136.572	0	16.941	0.023	0
I_{12}	-223.200	-9.920	-1187.056	0	1356.354	0	21.408	0.013	0
I_{13}	-8.821	-1.529	-17.642	46.126	269.092	40.892	0	0.015	0
I_{14}	-34.908	-3.659	-52.278	37.089	0	107.115	8.993	0.037	0
G_{17}	-683.027	-20.996	-317.937	87.241	0	213.323	48.643	0.144	0
G_{18}	-21.680	-1.474	-13.320	113.384	1089.746	754.303	15.127	0.066	461.405
G_{20}	0	0	0	0	0	0	0	0	0
G_{22}	-211.683	-5.243	-82.868	0	35.358	1573.044	114.390	0.005	1507.848
G_{24}	-129.530	-5.524	-82.868	0	0	995.442	0	0.034	42.828
G_{26}	-63.773	-1.071	-252.61	0	88.814	209.900	19.321	0.054	0
G_{27}	-136.527	-5.437	-193.886	0	477.987	210.499	0	0.034	428.669
G_{28}	-496.236	-29.961	-187.259	11.654	234.622	727.795	14.604	0.198	0
G_{30}	-26.887	-1.130	-22255.687	0	457.720	2920.444	62.065	0.029	0
G_{31}	-34.945	-2.089	-55.411	0	284.6	0	19.692	0.023	0

Note: All marked as "0" means that the pure technical efficiency value is 1 and there is no relaxation variable. In addition, all the others have input redundancy and output insufficiency, and input-output relaxation variable is given

of the establishment of the Chinese private-led incubator is shorter than that of the government-led incubator and the size of the incubator is less than that of the government-led incubator. From the perspective of economic benefits, compared with private-led incubators, government-led incubators in the two regions have a prominent problem of insufficient economic benefits, except private-led incubators in western regions have a higher output than government-led incubators in terms of approved intellectual property rights.

Table 8. Input-output adjustment table of operating efficiency of invalid incubators in western China

Organization Code	Input Redundancy Value			Insufficient Output Value					
	Site Area (10 m^2)	Incubator Staff (person)	Total Incubation Fund (10000 yuan)	Cumulative Number of Graduated Enterprises(number)	Average Income at Graduation (10000 yuan)	Total Income of Incubator (10000 yuan)	Total Number of Approved Intellectual Property Rights (item)	Annual Graduation Rate	Increase Jobs (number)
W_4	-1341.36	-3.855	-60.868	0	0	290.215	15.766	0.156	0
W_5	-6343.275	0	0	0	522.249	0	0	0.186	0
W_6	0	0	0	0	0	0	0	0	0
W_7	-3392.72	-7.487	-46936.327	0	0	0	0	0	931.563
W_{10}	0	0	0	0	0	0	0	0	0
W_{12}	-1067.021	-16.716	-984.699	5.278	658.322	131.387	0	0.029	0
W_{14}	-890.885	-8.199	-81.988	66.890	0	0	80.513	0	316.227
W_{20}	-2370.191	-0.54	-20.771	0	4315.182	189.435	36.449	0	0
W_{21}	-10196.443	-6.93	-195.029	0	2129.516	125.295	0	0.165	0
W_{22}	-843.72	-9.388	-5862.714	86.106	302.403	0	0	0.207	0
W_{23}	-27.691	-0.199	-87.584	5.639	811.363	500.379	0	0.078	0
W_{25}	-97.59	-0.985	-16.411	11.271	254.226	0	0	0.034	487.596
W_{27}	-435.378	-3.167	-65.21	10.924	469.993	0	29.809	0.143	0
W_{28}	-2082.216	-3.027	-84.755	49.938	259.643	0	0	0.039	0
W_{33}	0	0	0	0	0	0	0	0	0
W_{34}	-331.523	-2.672	-38.374	30.79	0	0	53.61	0	0
W_{35}	-191.058	-1.45	-142.351	73.657	0	0	32.528	0	0
W_{39}	0	0	0	0	0	0	0	0	0
W_{40}	-302.72	-1.79	-26.853	0	0	0	0	0.064	0
W_{42}	-1750.963	-4.467	-675.752	3.187	0	0	44.657	0	485.567
W_{43}	0	0	0	0	0	0	0	0	0

3. Comparative analysis of private-led incubators in northeast and western regions and eastern regions

In order to compare the development differences between the private-led incubators in northeast and western regions and eastern regions, we randomly selected 15 national incubators of scientific and technological innovation from each region, and calculated their operating efficiency by using the BBC input-oriented model in DEA. This part

Figure 1. A figure of insufficient output of invalid incubators in Northeast China and Western China

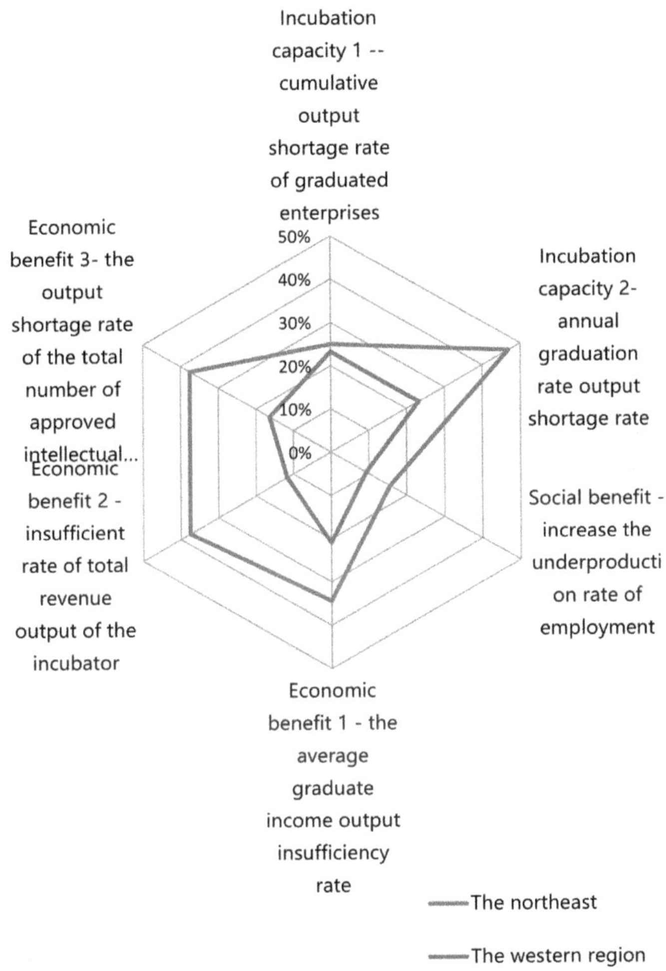

of the data is from <China Science and Technology Statistical Yearbook 2013>. As can be seen from the table 8, the operating efficiency of private-led incubators of scientific and technological innovation in the eastern region is better than that in the northeast region and the western region. Only three private-led incubators in western China have effective operating efficiency, and the average comprehensive efficiency is not high. In addition, although there are 8 incubators in Northeast China and 8 incubators in the eastern region having the effective comprehensive efficiency of the incubators, the average comprehensive efficiency, pure technical efficiency and scale efficiency of 15 incubators in east China are all higher than those in northeast

Figure 2. The pointing graph of the output insufficiency of two types of non-effective incubators in the northeast of China

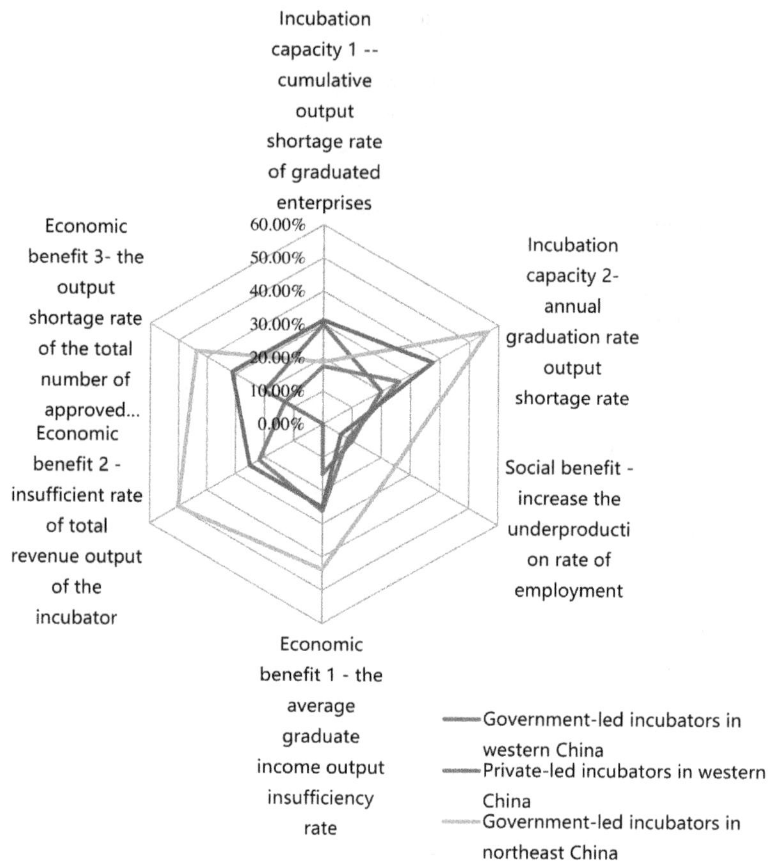

China. Therefore, there is still a gap between the private-led incubators in northeast and western regions and those in the eastern region, so they should learn from the private-led incubators in the eastern region.

CONCLUSION

Through the above studies, this paper can draw the following three main conclusions:

First of all, from the macroscopic level, the results of DEA show that only the operating efficiency of incubators of scientific and technological innovation in the western region is invalid. Although the operating efficiency of incubators of scientific and technological innovation in northeast China is effective as a whole, the

Table 9. Operating efficiency of two types of incubators in three regions

Organization Code	The Comprehensive Efficiency	Pure Technical Efficiency	The Scale Efficiency	Scale Reward	Organization Code	The Comprehensive Efficiency	Pure Technical Efficiency	The Scale Efficiency	Scale Reward	Organization Code	The Comprehensive Efficiency	Pure Technical Efficiency	The Scale Efficiency	Scale Reward
W_1	0.633	0.715	0.855	drs	EN_1	1.000	1.000	1.000	-	E_1	0.634	0.817	0.776	drs
W_2	0.309	0.523	0.592	irs	EN_2	1.000	1.000	1.000	-	E_2	0.994	1.000	0.904	drs
W_3	0.757	1.000	0.757	drs	EN_3	1.000	1.000	1.000	-	E_3	0.699	0.776	0.900	drs
W_4	0.304	0.472	0.644	irs	EN_4	0.593	0.663	0.894	drs	E_4	0.862	1.000	0.862	drs
W_5	0.535	0.669	0.799	drs	EN_5	1.000	1.000	1.000	-	E_5	1.000	1.000	1.000	-
W_6	0.345	0.515	0.670	irs	EN_6	1.000	1.000	1.000	-	E_6	1.000	1.000	1.000	-
W_7	1.000	1.000	1.000	-	EN_7	0.656	1.000	0.656	-	E7	1.000	1.000	1.000	-
W_8	1.000	1.000	1.000	-	EN_8	0.705	1.000	0.705	irs	E_8	0.890	1.000	0.890	drs
W_9	0.668	0.736	0.908	irs	EN_9	1.000	1.000	1.000	-	E_9	0.949	1.000	0.949	drs
W_{10}	0.413	0.565	0.731	irs	EN_{10}	0.62 0	0.671	0.924	irs	E_{10}	1.000	1.000	1.000	-
W_{11}	0.635	0.819	0.775	drs	EN_{11}	1.000	1.000	1.000	-	E_{11}	1.000	1.000	1.000	-
W_{12}	0.526	0.538	0.979	drs	EN_{12}	0.258	0.519	0.497	irs	E_{12}	0.867	0.881	0.995	drs
W_{13}	1.000	1.000	1.000	-	EN_{13}	0.622	1.000	0.622	irs	E_{13}	1.000	1.000	1.000	-
W_{14}	0.367	0.639	0.574	drs	EN_{14}	0.784	0.959	0.818	irs	E_{14}	1.000	1.000	1.000	-
W_{15}	0.517	0.527	0.982	irs	EN_{15}	1.000	1.000	1.000	drs	E_{15}	1.000	1.000	1.000	-
Mean	0.601	0.715	0.818		Mean	0.816	0.921	0.874		Mean	0.926	0.965	0.952	

results of super-efficiency show that compared with the eastern and central regions, there is a serious shortage of overall investment in Northeast China, and there is a lot of room for improvement. Even if the input is increased by 171.9%, DEA can still be kept relatively effective. In addition, in 2016, in spite of the ineffectiveness of the incubator in the western region, it is in a scale-up state. This indicates that northeast China and western China need to increase the investment in incubators as a whole, including attracting more talents, introducing foreign investment funds and further improving infrastructure construction. The above conclusion also indirectly confirms that the old industrial bases in northeast China and western China are faced with serious brain drain and economic depression, etc. Such imbalance in regional economic development is an important challenge in the process of Chinese economic transformation.

Secondly, from the micro level, about half of the incubator of scientific and technological innovation in northeast China and western China are ineffective. The pure technical efficiency of different incubators in northeast China is quite different, and the non-effective scale efficiency is the main reason that affects the operating efficiency of incubators in western China, mainly because of insufficient investment. This conclusion not only shows that the conclusion at the macro level has its limitations, but also indicates that the operating capacity of incubators in northeast China is not developed evenly and there is a big gap between them. In addition, through a separate analysis of ineffective incubators in northeast China and western China, the following three problems can be found: (1) the problem of input redundancy and there is waste. This shows that for incubator of scientific and technological innovation in northeast China and western China, they should not blindly increase investment. On the contrary, ineffective incubators should reduce investment, while effective incubators should increase investment more vigorously. (2) scale mismatch, and there is a gap with the optimal scale. For the incubator with mismatched scale, specific problems should be analyzed, and the scale should be expanded or reduced according to the actual situation, so as to realize the optimal matching mode and achieve relatively effective comprehensive efficiency. Especially in the northeast, many leading state-owned incubators are too large in scale but do not produce efficiency matching their own scale. However, private-led incubators have restrained their own development due to their relatively small scale, which is very serious. Therefore, it is necessary to strictly supervise and control the use of resources of state-owned incubators to avoid excessive waste, while private-led incubators should be given certain policy support; (3) the problem of insufficient output, the economic benefits, social benefits and incubation capacity of northeast and western regions are insufficient. Among them, low economic benefits and weak incubation capacity are the main problems. Low economic benefits are the most important problems in the development of incubators in Northeast China, while the western region is mainly manifested in the insufficient output of incubator capacity. Therefore, the incubator of scientific and technological innovation in the western region needs to redesign and optimize its operation mechanism from the aspects of incubation function and service positioning to improve its incubation ability. The incubator of scientific and technological innovation in the northeast region also needs to improve its business model and improve its profitability. We should not regard the incubator as a simple organization or platform, but pay attention to the cultivation of its market function ang improving its market mechanism.

Finally, through the classification and comparison of the two leading modes, the research shows that the pure technical efficiency of the private-led technological innovation incubators in the northeast and the western regions is better than that of the government-led entrepreneurial incubators, but the scale efficiency of the private-led incubators in the two regions is slightly lower than that of the government-led incubators, which may be due to the long establishment time and many investment factors of the Chinese government-led incubators. In addition, through the comparison of the private-led incubators of scientific and technological innovation in the northeast and the western regions and the eastern region, it is found that the eastern region is obviously superior to the northeast and the western regions. In the development of incubators, regional advantages and their future growth potential should be matched (Schwartz, 2008). Ignoring the advantages of traditional locations may lead to what Aerts, Matthyssens & Vandenbempt (2007) call "incubator vulnerability" (Aerts et al., 2007). Because private-led incubators of scientific and technological innovation in the northeast and the western region are limited by the establishment period, regional economic development level and policies, etc. They need to learn the operational experience of mature private-led incubators in the eastern region, especially the design of business model. So, in the future, incubators of scientific and technological innovation in the northeast and the western region need two steps: the first step is to gradually reduce the proportion of government-led incubators, transforming them to private-led incubators. Secondly, it is necessary to learn operational experience of eastern incubators and improve its market function and operating mechanism, so as to become more mature.

REFERENCES

Aernoudt, R. (2004). Incubators: Tool for entrepreneurship? *Small Business Economics*, *23*(2), 127–135. doi:10.1023/B:SBEJ.0000027665.54173.23

Aerts, K., Matthyssens, P., & Vandenbempt, K. (2007). Critical role and screening practices of European business incubators. *Technovation, 27*(5), 254–267. doi:10.1016/j.technovation.2006.12.002

Allen, D. N., & Levine, V. (1986). *Nurturing advanced technology enterprises: Emerging issues in state and local economic development policy*. Praeger Publishers.

Allen, D. N., & McCluskey, R. (1991). Structure, policy, services, and performance in the business incubator industry. *Entrepreneurship Theory and Practice, 15*(2), 61–77. doi:10.1177/104225879101500207

Allen, D. N., & Rahman, S. (1985). Small business incubators: a positive environment for entrepreneurship. *Journal of Small Business Management, 23*(3), 12.

Andersen, P., & Petersen, N. C. (1993). A procedure for ranking efficient units in data envelopment analysis. *Management Science, 39*(10), 1261–1264. doi:10.1287/mnsc.39.10.1261

Apa, R., Grandinetti, R., & Sedita, S. R. (2017). The social and business dimensions of a networked business incubator: The case of H-Farm. *Journal of Small Business and Enterprise Development, 24*(2), 198–221. doi:10.1108/JSBED-07-2016-0103

Baraldi, E., & Havenvid, M. I. (2016). Identifying new dimensions of business incubation: A multi-level analysis of Karolinska Institute's incubation system. *Technovation, 50*, 53–68. doi:10.1016/j.technovation.2015.08.003

Barbero, J. L., Casillas, J. C., Ramos, A., & Guitar, S. (2012). Revisiting incubation performance: How incubator typology affects results. *Technological Forecasting and Social Change, 79*(5), 888–902. doi:10.1016/j.techfore.2011.12.003

Bergek, A., & Norrman, C. (2008). Incubator best practice: A framework. *Technovation, 28*(1-2), 20–28. doi:10.1016/j.technovation.2007.07.008

Bhabra-Remedios, R. K., & Cornelius, B. (2003). Cracks in the egg: improving performance measures in business incubator research. *16th Annual Conference of Small Enterprise Association of Australia and New Zealand.*

Bollinger, L., Hope, K., & Utterback, J. M. (1983). A review of literature and hypotheses on new technology-based firms. *Research Policy, 12*(1), 1–14. doi:10.1016/0048-7333(83)90023-9

Bruneel, J., Ratinho, T., Clarysse, B., & Groen, A. (2012). The evolution of business incubators: Comparing demand and supply of business incubation services across different incubator generations. *Technovation, 32*(2), 110–121. doi:10.1016/j.technovation.2011.11.003

Burnett, H. H. M., & McMurray, A. J. (2008). Exploring business incubation from a family perspective: How start-up family firms experience the incubation process in two Australian incubators. *Small Enterprise Research*, *16*(2), 60–75. doi:10.5172er.16.2.60

Chandra, A., & Chao, C. A. (2011). Growth and evolution of high-technology business incubation in China. *Human Systems Management*, *30*(1-2), 55–69. doi:10.3233/HSM-2011-0739

Grimaldi, R., & Grandi, A. (2005). Business incubators and new venture creation: An assessment of incubating models. *Technovation*, *25*(2), 111–121. doi:10.1016/S0166-4972(03)00076-2

Hisrich, R. D., & Smilor, R. W. (1988). The university and business incubation: Technology transfer through entrepreneurial development. *The Journal of Technology Transfer*, *13*(1), 14–19. doi:10.1007/BF02371496

Hochberg, Y. V. (2016). Accelerating entrepreneurs and ecosystems: The seed accelerator model. *Innovation Policy and the Economy*, *16*(1), 25–51. doi:10.1086/684985

Hughes, M., Ireland, R. D., & Morgan, R. E. (2007). Stimulating dynamic value: Social capital and business incubation as a pathway to competitive success. *Long Range Planning*, *40*(2), 154–177. doi:10.1016/j.lrp.2007.03.008

Jamil, F., Ismail, K., & Mahmood, N. (2015). University Incubators: A gateway to an entrepreneurial society. *Journal of Economics and Sustainable Development*, *6*(6), 153–160.

Jamil, F., Ismail, K., & Siddique, M. (2016). Business incubators in Asian developing countries. *International Review of Management and Marketing*, *6*(4S), 291–295.

Johnson, J., & Tellis, G. J. (2008). Tellis G J. Drivers of success for market entry into China and India. *Journal of Marketing*, *72*(3), 1–13. doi:10.1509/JMKG.72.3.001

Lewis, D. A. (2001). Does technology incubation work? A critical review. *Reviews of Economic Development Literature and Practice]*, *11*, 48.

Lindelöf, H., & Science, P. (2002). Parks and the growth of new technology-based firms—Academic-industry links, innovation and markets. *Research Policy*, *31*(6), 859–876. doi:10.1016/S0048-7333(01)00153-6

M'Chirgui, Z. (2012). Assessing the performance of business incubators: Recent France evidence. *Business and Management Research*, *1*(1), 62. doi:10.5430/bmr.v1n1p62

M'Chirgui, Z., Lamine, W., Mian, S., & Fayolle, A. (2018). University technology commercialization through new venture projects: An assessment of the French regional incubator program. *The Journal of Technology Transfer*, *43*(5), 1142–1160. doi:10.100710961-016-9535-y

McMullan, W. E., Long, W. A., & Graham, J. B. (1986). Assessing economic value added by university-based new-venture outreach programs. *Journal of Business Venturing*, *1*(2), 225–240. doi:10.1016/0883-9026(86)90016-9

Merigó, J. M., Gil-Lafuente, A. M., & Yager, R. R. (2015). An overview of fuzzy research with bibliometric indicators. *Applied Soft Computing*, *27*, 420–433. doi:10.1016/j.asoc.2014.10.035

Mian, S., Lamine, W., & Fayolle, A. (2016). Technology Business Incubation: An overview of the state of knowledge. *Technovation*, *50*, 1–12. doi:10.1016/j.technovation.2016.02.005

Miller, R. E., & Cote, M. (1987). *Growing the next Silicon Valley: A guide for successful regional planning*. Free Press.

Özdemir, Ö. Ç., & Şehitoğlu, Y. (2013). Assessing the impacts of technology business incubators: A framework for technology development centers in Turkey. *Procedia: Social and Behavioral Sciences*, *75*(75), 282–291. doi:10.1016/j.sbspro.2013.04.032

Ratinho, T., & Henriques, E. (2010). The role of science parks and business incubators in converging countries: Evidence from Portugal. *Technovation*, *30*(4), 278–290. doi:10.1016/j.technovation.2009.09.002

Schwartz, M., & Göthner, M. (2009). A multidimensional evaluation of the effectiveness of business incubators: An application of the PROMETHEE outranking method. *Environment and Planning. C, Government & Policy*, *27*(6), 1072–1087. doi:10.1068/c0897b

Schwartz, M., & Hornych, C. (2008). Specialization as strategy for business incubators: An assessment of the Central German Multimedia Center. *Technovation*, *28*(7), 436–449. doi:10.1016/j.technovation.2008.02.003

Shannxi, P. R. (2015). Snapshot of technology business incubators in China. *International Journal of u-and e-Service. Science and Technology*, *8*(7), 235–242.

Smilor, R. W. (1987). Managing the incubator system: Critical success factors to accelerate new company development. *IEEE Transactions on Engineering Management*, *EM-34*(3), 146–155. doi:10.1109/TEM.1987.6498875

Tang, M. F., Lee, J., Liu, K., & Lu, Y. (2014). Assessing government-supported technology-based business incubators: Evidence from China. *International Journal of Technology Management*, *65*(1-4), 24–48. doi:10.1504/IJTM.2014.060956

Theodorakopoulos, N. K., Kakabadse, N., & McGowan, C. (2014). What matters in business incubation? A literature review and a suggestion for situated theorising. *Journal of Small Business and Enterprise Development*, *21*(4), 602–622. doi:10.1108/JSBED-09-2014-0152

Von Zedtwitz, M., & Grimaldi, R. (2006). Are service profiles incubator-specific? Results from an empirical investigation in Italy. *The Journal of Technology Transfer*, *31*(4), 459–468. doi:10.100710961-006-0007-7

Wplniak, R., & Grebski, M. E. (2017). Functioning of the business incubator centre in Gliwice. *Zeszyty Naukowe Politechnika Śląska. Seria Organizacja i Zarzadzanie*, *105*, 569–580.

Chapter 3
Innovation and Business Sustainability Among SMEs in Africa:
The Role of the Institutions

Lydia Takyi
Schoo of Management, IT and Governance, University of KwaZuLu-Natal, South Africa

Vannie Naidoo
University of KwaZulu-Natal, South Africa

ABSTRACT

Many SMEs lack business competitiveness and sustainability. Their potential for growth and expansion is limited, and they are constrained by institutional challenges (such as high-interest rates and rigid regulatory requirements) which impede their creativity, innovativeness and sustainability. Despite the numerous contributions of the sector to the Ghanaian economy, SME internationalisation in Ghana is at the nascent stage and is bedevilled with a gamut of institutional challenges. Studies of the formal and informal institutional effects on indigenous SME internationalisation in the Ghanaian economy are limited. Furthermore, a stylised framework which serves as a model to aid academics and researchers in investigating the impact of the formal institutions (legal and political) and informal institutions (socio-culture) on Ghanaian-owned businesses is under-canvassed in the Ghanaian entrepreneurial eco-system. Hence, this paper suggests a model for institutions and SME internationalisation to boost their innovativeness and business sustainability.

DOI: 10.4018/978-1-7998-3495-3.ch003

INTRODUCTION

Small and medium enterprises (SMEs) are the lifeblood of many countries and are instrumental in promoting employment and economic growth. SMEs contribute a sizeable income to a country's GDP. For SMEs to continue growing and flourishing within an economy that is marred by the financial crisis and fluctuating economic and political crises, these enterprises need to be innovative. Innovation is, therefore, crucial to SMEs' long-term sustainability and expansion into foreign markets. This chapter explores the various themes connected to SME internationalisation, with specific reference to institutional factors which mitigate or facilitate indigenous Ghanaian SMEs. This paper further highlights and discusses certain crucial factors like social culture and legal and political factors which influence innovation and internationalisation of SMEs in Ghana.

Defining SMEs

There are various definitions of SMEs. In the discussion below, SME will be explored and discussed. National Small Business Act of 1996 defined SMMEs as a separate and distinct entity, including co-operative enterprises and non-governmental organisation, managed by owners or more which include its branches or subsidiaries if any is predominantly carried on in any sector or subsector of the economy. Most countries adopted a quantitative definition based on the categories of enterprises, number of employees and an annual turnover (Berisha, 2015). In Ghana, the most commonly used definition of SMEs is the number of employees of the enterprise. In applying this definition, however, there is some controversy concerning the arbitrariness and cut off points used by the various official records (Dalitso & Peter, 2000). The European Commission (2003) defines SMEs as enterprises which employ fewer than 250 persons and/or have an annual turnover not exceeding EUR 50 million, and/or an annual balance sheet total not exceeding EUR 43 million. Thus, the definition of SME varies and is dependent upon whose point of view (Berisha & Pula, 2015). It is interesting to note that the National Board for Small Scale Industries (NBSSI) in Ghana used both fixed assets and number of employees to define what constitutes SME in Ghana. It defined SME as a firm with not more than nine workers and has plant and machinery (excluding land, buildings and vehicles) not exceeding 10 million Ghanaian cedis, (Kayanula & Quartey, 2000)

Small and medium enterprises are engaged in an economic activity wherein they provide goods or services in the marketplace. Pride, Hughes and Kapoor (2013:10) explain that an enterprise or as others may call it "business", is an organization established by efforts of individuals with the aim of satisfying personal or economic needs and to make a profit. Enterprises are essential because they create jobs, contribute to national income and contribute to sustainable economic development.

Globally, formal businesses are registered by relevant authorities of a concerned government (Dutta, 2009). Small-medium enterprises may take the form of a legal structure that is legislated by the government. Some forms of small and medium enterprises are namely sole proprietorship, partnership, close corporation or companies.

It is interesting to note that the National Board for Small Scale Industries (NBSSI) of Ghana define the constituents of SMEs to include the fixed assets and number of employees. The institution defines SMEs as a firm with not more than nine employees that have plant and machinery (excluding land, buildings, and vehicles) not exceeding 10 million Ghanaian cedis (Kayanula & Quartey, 2000).

Problem Statement

Despite the numerous contributions of the sector to the Ghanaian economy, SMEs' internationalisation in Ghana is at the nascent stage and bedevilled with copious institutional and industrial challenges (ITC, 2016). ITC (2016) asserts that preponderant of SMEs lack business competitiveness, sustainability, growth and expansion, and constraint with institutional challenges (such as high-interest rate, rigid regulatory requirement) which impede their creativity, innovation, and internationalisation. Conversely, with the implementation of appropriate government institutional policies and programmes, government support (financial and non-financial), appropriate internal management of the SMEs, institutional challenges can overcome. Konfidants (2019) affirm the assertion that the indigenous Ghanaian producers and manufacturers will need some assistance from the government and the regulatory bodies, to improve competitiveness for the local market.

Nevertheless, studies on the entrepreneurial institutional antecedent on indigenous SMEs internationalisation is mostly under-researched in the Ghanaian environment. Even in some instances were both empirical and conceptual research are studied, existing literature shows dominance research in entrepreneurship and innovation, entrepreneurial characteristics and business growth etc. For instance, previous studies examine the relationship between entrepreneurial characteristics, business growth and goal achievement (Robson & Obeng, 2008); entrepreneurship and innovation (Robson, Haugh, & Obeng, 2009); entrepreneurial characteristic and small business growth (Obeng, Robson, & Haugh, 2014) another on; institutional antecedent and entrepreneurial environment (Adomako, Danso, & Ampadu, 2015) and; institutions and export relationship among SMEs (Amoako & Lyon, 2014) just to mention a few. Even research on prevailing scholars focus on internationalisation strategies (Seglah & Armah, 2016); entrepreneurship and economic growth (Adusei, 2016) and; environmental influence and new technology ventures (Amankwah-Amoah & Hinson, 2019) with limited emphasis on indigenous firms. Thus, studies on the formal and informal institutional effects on indigenous SMEs internationalisation are limited studies in the Ghanaian economy. In specific, a stylised framework which serves as a model to academics and researchers to aid in investigating the impact of the formal institution (legal and political) and informal institutions (socio-culture) on Ghanaian-owned businesses is under canvassed in the Ghana entrepreneurial eco-system. Hence a model on institutions and SMEs internationalisation is seminal given the impact on Africa firm's internationalisation process. The gap is the focus of this paper.

Government Support for SMEs Sustainability and Internationalisation in Ghana

SMEs Transformational Agenda and Export Earners in Ghana

Over five decades now, most governments have endeavoured to intensify SMEs internationalisation (Tesar & Moini, 1998) due to relevancy of SMEs export and export earners contributions (Michael et al., 2016). SMEs mostly suffer from the limited size and credit accessibility (Michael et al., 2016; Wellalage & Fernandez, 2019) which create numerous challenges when entering the foreign market (Coviello & McAuley, 1999; Martínez-Román, Gamero, Delgado-González, & Tamayo, 2019). The institution and business environs in developing economies and Ghana in specific play an influential effect on individuals and private enterprises, export activity, innovation and internationalisation (Amoako & Lyon, 2014; Love & Roper, 2015; Martínez-Román et al., 2019; Ullah, 2019; Wellalage & Fernandez, 2019); hence require germane institutional policies from the local government in order to boost SMEs growth, expansion and internationalisation.

SMEs have been the key contributor to Ghana's economic development and transformation. Due to the influential role of SMEs to the Ghanaian economy, the Government of Ghana has established germane policies and programmes and implemented structures for an enabling and favourable business atmosphere dedicated to the development, growth and sustainability of the SMEs since the 1960s (Boachie-Mensah & Marfo-Yiadom, 2007). Government programmes and policies have primarily focused on establishing SMEs regulatory institutions and government financial institutional support for SMEs in Ghana. Ghanaian Government SMEs transformation and financial infusion led to the creation of Ministry of Rural Industries (MRI) in 1965 which took over from the Industrial Development Corporation (IDC) (Boachie-Mensah & Marfo-Yiadom, 2007). In 1966, after the change in government, the new government fused the MRI with the

Ministry of Industries to form the Ghanaian Enterprises Development Commission mandated to offer financial assistance to SMEs. The National Board for Small Scale Industries (NBSSI) Act 434 was subsequently established to promote SMEs through the setting up of the Entrepreneurship Development Programme (EDP) and the Business Advisory Center (BACs). The NBSSI later set up the Investment and Credit Department to help ease the financial constraints facing SMEs. Later on, the Business Assistance Fund (BAF), with an initial amount of 10 billion Ghana Cedis, was created to support SMEs financing. In 1997, the BAF funds had already been over-subscribed, and the Government of Ghana replaced it with the Export Development and Investment Fund (EDIF). Later EDIF was replaced with the Export Development and Agricultural Investment Fund (EDAIF) with a mandate to build SMEs export and input substitution (Boachie-Mensah & Marfo-Yiadom, 2007). To further support SMEs export in the non-traditional crop and for making funds available, EXIM Bank replaced EDAIF.

Babatunde (2009) argue that the slow pace of export activity in African countries, compared to other economies in the world, is as a result of 'over export concentration' on traditional products at the detriment of non-traditional exports. To change the institutional and country-level SMEs, GEPA was established to diversify the concentration of Ghana's export on traditional export (such as products of unprocessed minerals, cocoa beans, timber logs and lumber) to non-traditional exports product of processed/semi-processed agriculture, industrial art and craft and export trade-in services (GEPA 2017). The blossoming demand from Ghanaian products in the foreign market and the anticipated market niche in the EU and increased SMEs export earners (Non-Traditional Export) value from $2.55billion in 2017 to $5.3 billion in 2021, whiles expanding the market destination of NTE and create market niche for Smooth Cayenne pineapple in the European Union (EU), necessitates new and effectual strategic moves from the Ghanaian government. The National Export Strategy (NES) has been instituted by the Government of Ghana mainly to accelerate the growth of non-traditional export sector To provide a new paradigm for SMEs in Ghana, the Government of Ghana (GoG) has resourced 11 priority products under the National Export Strategy initiative. Due to the GoG policy and vision to transform the Ghanaian economy into an industrial-based economy, NES for Ghanaian SMEs was expanded to include other essential products with export potential in the various districts and at the regional level under the "One District One Factory" (1D1F) policy, since export is the focal force for firms socio-economic transformation (GEPA 2017), and entry mode of firms internationalisation (Lin & Ho, 2019; Schmidt & Hansen, 2017). Additionally, GOG has introduced policies and programmes such as 'One District, One Factory' (1D1F), 'One Region, One Industrial Park', 'One Constituency, One Million Dollars' and 'Planting for Food and Jobs', to promote and sustain SMEs and; to reduce the unemployment rate in Ghana(GEPA 2017: 13).

Financial Support to SMEs Internationalisation

SMEs capacity building boosts their competitiveness, sustainability and growth rate. Country-level policies, such as national export strategies, made-in Ghana, etc., stimulate local content growth, export activity and SMEs sustainability. In fostering export base activities among Ghanaian exporters, the Ghanaian Government has provided both financial and non-financial support to the agro-processing sector in the Non-Traditional Export products. For example, in 2017, GOG through GEPA provided financial assistance worth GHC1.6 million to cashew farmers to aid the farmers to garner other necessary farming materials and equipment (such as seedlings, herbicides, insecticides). To ensure indigenous SMEs sustainability and foster export growth, the GOG launched the 'Cashew Development Plan' to assist in solving agro-processing challenges (infrastructure) (GEPA 2017).

The Government of Ghana and State-based institution (GEPA) support to non-traditional export products sector yield an excellent and remarkable benefit. As of 2017, cashew, which is the leading agricultural NTE, earned US$262 million, representing 10.28 percent of the total export earnings in the non-traditional export sector (GEPA 2017). Analysts and scholars envisage the contribution of cashew to export earnings increase between US$400million and US$ 500 million (GEPA 2017). Besides, as discussed above, the GOG in association with GEPA support the Ekumfi Pineapple Processing Factory (EPPF) with 3.5 million pineapple suckers.

UNPACKING THEORY ON PERCEPTION OF SMEs INNOVATION AND INTERNATIONALISATION

The underpinning discussion in institutional theory is to ascertain the interplay between organisational performance (both local and international) and business milieu. It implies that SMEs internationalisation is also affected by external institutional factors. The institution determines the direction of actions, and inactions of a firm. Institutions dimension, such as social values, economic and regulatory conditions, degree of regulation to enact and enforce law, models firm's activities (Dana, 2006; Thornton, Ribeiro-Soriano, & Urbano, 2011) and that, country's cultural dynamism (Simón-Moya, Revuelto-Taboada, & Guerrero, 2014; Thornton et al., 2011), makes research on institution critical in the international business (McGaughey, Welch, & Welch, 1997), for business innovation, sustainability and internationalisation. Studies on the influence of institutions on firm (SMEs) internationalisation is copious in the literature (Amoako & Lyon, 2014; Boso, Adeleye, Ibeh, & Chizema, 2019; GEM, 2019; Hoskisson, Wright, Filatotchev, & Peng, 2013; Monticelli, Calixto, Vasconcellos, & Garrido, 2017; Morais & Ferreira, 2019; Omokaro-Romanus, Anchor, & Konara, 2018). The general discourse evolving from these researches is the impact of institution on the pace (Oviatt & McDougall, 2005), and firms (SMEs) internationalisation (Adomako et al., 2015) and that the firm (SMEs) entrepreneurial activities, actions and export are culturally embedded (Amoako & Lyon, 2014; Muralidharan & Pathak, 2017; Roxas, Lindsay, Ashill, & Victorio, 2007). The central discourse on the effect of institutions suggests that institutional dimension (both formal and informal) either positively (facilitate) or negatively (impede) SMEs internationalisation process and agenda. Due to the social context phenomenon and cultural embedded activity of entrepreneurship and export, scholars such as (Dau & Cuervo-Cazurra, 2014; Fritsch & Storey, 2014; Misati, Walumbwa, Lahiri, & Kundu, 2017; Monticelli et al., 2017; North, 1990; Roxas et al., 2007; Urbano & Alvarez, 2014) have emerged in elucidating the changes in entrepreneurship dimensions between nations.

Several theories have elucidated the internationalisation trajectory of a firm, many models expound on the internationalisation decision, actions and dynamic processes' (Zapletalová, 2015) of firms'. For example, from classical trade theories to product life-cycle in international trade theories, to neo-institutional theories of institutional entrepreneurship and, finally to the firm's internationalisation theories of Uppsala model, innovation-related theories, network theories, institutional-based theory and Neo-institutions reveal the varied models of internationalisation. Economic scholars argue for two models of institutions: the exogenous propounded by (North, 1990) and endogenous by (Aoki & Hayami, 2001; Greif, 1994). Critical analysis on (Aoki & Hayami, 2001) institutions indicates that institutions are an outcome of a set of plans and beliefs that are mutually consistent and repeatedly executed. (North, 1990) however argues that institutions are the canons, standards and imposition idiosyncratic which inhibit or facilitate human cooperation and, (Scott, 1995) consist of laws, values and believes of legitimate concern that direct, limit or free a national domestic trade transaction. That is institutions are both exogenous (the rule of the game) or endogenous (an outcome of the game).

This study draws support form (North, 1990) definition of institutions and elucidates institutions as a set of laws, regulations, standards and beliefs that determine the acceptable standards of behaviour for a particular group of people. The focus of this paper and the research setting makes it apt to adapt (North, 1990) institutional perspective. The reason being that, in Ghana, whereas the judicial system (legal) implements the formal laws, the social and culture way of living enforces the informal standard laws (Adomako et al., 2015). According to (North, 1990), economic uncertainty hinders business transaction, which this paper affirms that the actions of the player of the institutions foster or impede SMEs internationalisation. Northian opines that institutions comprise the formal and the informal dimension which set the rules of the game in the form of formal laws, informal norms and beliefs and their operating standard (North, 1990). These context-based institutional characteristics (such as the laws and norms) tend to proffer impediment and motivations in the entrepreneurial environment (North, 1990), and internationalisation activities of SMEs (Jafari Sadeghi, Nkongolo-Bakenda, Anderson, & Dana, 2019). Others researchers affirm the perspective (Amoako & Lyon, 2014; Love & Roper, 2015; Ullah, 2019). Nyame-Asiamah, Amoako, Amankwah-Amoah, and Debrah (2020) further stipulate that "government bureaucracy, corruption and weak legal system" are the institutional impediment to businesses. The preponderance of the studies on the formal institutional strands includes the political and legal factors, financial and non-financial support, economic factors and government policies and procedures (Gnyawali & Fogel, 1994; Jafari Sadeghi et al., 2019; Monticelli et al., 2017). For instance, current studies on institutions contend that restrictions from the political and legal environment, like embargoes and sanctions, inhibit firm global market operations (Sadeghi, Nkongolo-Bakenda, Anderson, & Dana, 2019). In Ghana, literature reviews that weak legal system, particularly the judiciary and state support institutions, and administrative bottleneck are the formal institutions constraining entrepreneurship and export activities (Amoako & Lyon, 2014; Djankov, Miguel, Qian, Roland, & Zhuravskaya, 2004a; Johnson, McMillan, & Woodruff, 2002).

Further, recent research identifies "lack of access to financial credit, inadequate infrastructure and human capital as the country-level institutional factors constraining business, (Amankwah-Amoah and Hinson, 2019: 294), and internationalisation. Alternatively, informal institutions connote the generally accepted shared cultural value, social standards and appropriate behaviour which evolve from agreed practices, norms, beliefs of a society or group of people (Scott, 1995; Stephan & Uhlaner, 2010). According to North (2005), informal institutions are rules, customs and practices that develop from the traditions of a group of people. These codify norms and beliefs are embedded in society and shape individual behaviour. Accordingly, the embedded and implied code of conduct creates and communicates socially accepted shared practices and attitudes of a group of particular people in a given society (Adomako et al., 2015; Takyi-Asiedu, 1993; Yeboah-Assiamah, Muller, & Domfeh, 2017). In Ghana, informal institutions have a significant effect in determining and patterning the country- level entrepreneurial activities than the formal institutions (Adomako et al., 2015). Thus, the shared and unwritten but implied code of conduct, socio-cultural beliefs, practices and customs of a particular group of people, directly and indirectly, influence and pattern country-level entrepreneurship, entrepreneurial activity and firm internationalisation. Accordingly, the cultural embedded and implied attitudes of informal institutions proffer germane opportunities and determine the level of acceptability and legalisation of entrepreneurial activity of a society which may thwart blossoming and budding entrepreneurs and obstruct their internationalisation ambitions. Therefore the interplay of the formal and informal institutions on SMEs internationalisation cannot be underestimated.

Socio-Cultural Impact on SMEs Internationalisation

Extensive studies have shown the effect of institutional factors on business internationalisation (Muralidharan & Pathak, 2017; Oviatt & McDougall, 2005; Peng, 2003; Peng & Luo, 2000).

(Oviatt & McDougall, 2005) asset, the pace of internationalisation is effect by environmental factors, industrial factors, entrepreneur and forces of competition and that, (Muralidharan & Pathak, 2017) informal institutions increases the degree of business internationalisation. Scholars opine that informal institutions display the values, beliefs, norms and cannons of a group of people (Adomako et al., 2015; Golesorkhi, Mersland, Randøy, & Shenkar, 2019) which are synonymous to the socio-cultural activities of the people (Golesorkhi et al., 2019). According to (Shane, 2003), socio-cultural institutional terrains consist of social and cultural norms and beliefs. (Scott, 1995; Stephan & Uhlaner, 2010) contend that informal institutions refer to the shared cultural values, socially accepted expectations and appropriate behaviour based on generally accepted practices, norms, and beliefs of a society or group of people. (Adomako et al., 2015; North, 2005) expressed similar views. The extant literature suggests that informal institutions are the embedded an implied code of conduct, which create and communicate socially accepted shared practices and attitudes of a group of particular people in a given society (Adomako et al., 2015; Takyi-Asiedu, 1993; Yeboah-Assiamah et al., 2017).

From the above views on dimensions of socio-cultural institutional, it appears the outcome of socio-cultural factors on firms (SMEs) internationalisation is dual: it shapes country-level entrepreneurship activity, innovation and export activity and foreign market business and; proffer germane entrepreneurship opportunities, entrepreneurship desirability and innovation, creativity and sustainability. Accordingly, the culturally-embedded and implicit attitudes of informal institutions can proffer germane opportunities and determine the level of acceptability and legalisation of entrepreneurial activity of a society which may thwart blossoming and budding entrepreneurs and obstruct their internationalisation ambitions and vice versa. Thus, the context situated and time-specific phenomena of informal institutions (Adomako et al., 2015; Helmke & Levitsky, 2004), but also the ensuing challenges of bringing together investigation of social and cultural influence on entrepreneurship (Thornton et al., 2011), necessitate researchers parsimonious heed when canvassing on the socio-cultural effect on entrepreneurship. In other words, studies on socio-cultural influence on entrepreneurship must be sparingly studied: due to the complexity and challenges associated with socio-cultural issues and; because socio-cultural issues are situational-influenced and country-based phenomena. Deducing from the discussion as mentioned earlier, the entrepreneurial strategic proclivity, growth and expansion expectation are the consequences of a particular cultural climate which reflects the cultural environs of the firm and influence internationalisation approach.

Dimensions of Socio-Culture Institutional Elements

Albeit, there has been an extensive study on formal institutions, research on informal institutions is relatively limited, and that conceptual and empirical study in the extant literature is scant (Adomako et al., 2015; Muralidharan & Pathak, 2017; North, 2005).

Various studies on the constituents of country-level informal institutions influence (Adomako et al., 2015; Chiles, Bluedorn, & Gupta, 2007; Gnyawali & Fogel, 1994; North, 1990; Omokaro-Romanus et al., 2018) and internationalisation (Muralidharan & Pathak, 2017; Omokaro-Romanus et al., 2018) are copious in the prevailing studies. Whereas Muralidharan and Pathak (2017) considers performance orientation, self-expression and social desirability(Peng, 2003; Peng & Luo, 2000 argues on strategic government connections with key bureaucrats. Others (Adomako et al., 2015), in their studies on the institutional structure of entrepreneurial climate in Ghana, postulate that informal institutions include socio-cultural factors such as social and cultural norms and beliefs of a society. In specific, the authors argued that the informal institutions of an entrepreneurial climate constitute an informal network, family support, social acceptance and socio-cultural elements (Adomako et al., 2015).

Elucidating further on the strands of socio-cultural institutional factors, (Nikolaev, Boudreaux, & Palich, 2018) opine that, societal desirability of entrepreneurship, such as risk-taking and independent thinking, impact on the internationalisation of SMEs. Additionally, (Eijdenberg, Thompson, Verduijn, & Essers, 2019; Khavul, Bruton, & Wood, 2009) contend that cultural specific informal network system, like support from affiliated associations and clubs, political and business ties; family social support (Eijdenberg et al., 2019) and; the extend of societal acceptance and approval of entrepreneurship (Adomako et al., 2015; Shane, 2003), influence SMEs internationalisation. Thus, it is unambiguous that the idiosyncratic nature of a country culture depicts the dimension of informal institutions which may include: the societal attitude and desirability of entrepreneurship; informal network system; informal social support system (family) and; the societal acceptance of entrepreneurship. Below is a brief explanation of each dimension.

Societal Attitude and Desirability of Entrepreneurship

Societal context depicts behaviour, beliefs, values and way of life. Cultural values indicate the extent to which a particular society considers entrepreneurial behaviour to be desirable (Nikolaev et al., 2018). Societal desirability of entrepreneurship connotes the societal perception of entrepreneurship as a career choice (Bosma & Kelley, 2019; Busenitz, Gomez, & Spencer, 2000; Koellinger, 2008). The value society place on entrepreneurship may influence the rate of new business formation (Busenitz et al., 2000; Reynolds, Carter, Gartner, & Greene, 2004); nature of business (Muralidharan & Pathak, 2017), and entrepreneurial reward such as risk-sharing, social capital support and provision of valuable information (Adler & Kwon, 2002; Fukuyama, 2001), necessary for business expansion and sustainability. Bosma and Kelley (2019) expound on the social desirability of entrepreneurship in border sense to include high societal status for entrepreneurs, positive media representation of entrepreneurship and entrepreneurs and the ease of doing business. Other studies in Ghana have also taken into account socio-cultural elements influencing firm internationalisation. (Langevang, Gough, Yankson, Owusu, & Osei, 2015), basing their argument on the 2010 GEM report, identified two critical measures as influencing entrepreneurial activity in Ghana: attitudes toward entrepreneurship such as whether entrepreneurship is a desirable career choice and the status attributed to entrepreneurs and; the perceived capabilities of potential entrepreneurs, such as the belief in having the knowledge and skills to start a business, perceived opportunities and the fear of failure. GEM (2019) concludes the positive societal view of entrepreneurship has resulted in 74.5 of African admiration for entrepreneurs in their society and, preponderant percentage (76.2%) of Africans desire entrepreneurship as a right career choice. In Ghana, for example, nine out of ten Ghanaians (both business owners and non-business owners) consider entrepreneurship as an appropriate career choice and hold successful entrepreneurs in high esteem (Langevang et al., 2015). Thus, inferring from the discussion, the positive societal attitude and desirability for entrepreneurship translate into positive respect for SMEs operating in the global market. Moreover, if national attitudes toward entrepreneurship are positive, they can generate social support, financial support, and networking benefits for businesses (Ács et al., 2018). Consequently, a nation with high desire emphasis on entrepreneurship as a career choice encourages burgeoning and blossoming entrepreneurs (SMEs) to take advantage of any opportunities in the environment, adopt and implement particular entrepreneurial activity (export and innovation activity) and business strategy in order to grow locally, expand and internationalise. Therefore, a receptive attitude to entrepreneurship, and entrepreneur's products or services, impact on the business innovation and export activity, business strategy adoption and internationalisation.

Informal Social Network

Societal attitude and desirability of entrepreneurship is a proclivity to the social network. Existing literature argues that social desirability of entrepreneurship exhibit the kind of social network entrepreneurs have (Asler & Kwon 2002; Fukuyama 2001) and that socially embedded nature of entrepreneurial activity foster networking relationship, which serves as the source of accessing information to the small businesses (Carlsson, 2002; Kingsley & Malecki, 2004). The social relationship among firms (exporters) is influential in SMEs internationalisation (Hilmersson, 2014). In some instances, for example, the informal network system is used as a mitigating strategy against institutional constraints such as indiscriminate enforcement of rules, excessive bureaucratic policies (Eijdenberg et al., 2019; Khavul et al., 2009). Additionally, ability to develop strong informal network relationship (political and business ties) aid access to government and political leaders intervention policies and programmes to businesses, facilitate and intensify the degree of internationalisation and improve firm's technological knowledge in the domestic and international market (Monticelli et al., 2017; Omokaro-Romanus et al., 2018; Zhang, Ma, Wang, Li, & Huo, 2016).

For instance, research in Asian tigers and China (Zhang et al., 2016) reveals that albeit the Chinese government encourage innovation among firms by giving out land, bank credits and tax subsidies to SMEs, it is however only accessed by the SMEs with strong political links and that, political connections and ties have strong positive relationship with firm internationalisation than business links. Congruent studies affirm that social and business networks support firms to over the difficulties related to foreign market entry and help to garner access to the global market (John, Sek Hong, & Christine, 2002).

Recent studies on four Nigeria firms reveals that network-based relationship (business ties) played an influential role in Alpha internationalisation (Omokaro-Romanus et al., 2018).

According to the authors, because the majority of Alpha management decision team are Indian ethnic groups, it aids in Alpha international expansion to Nepal. In Ghana, for example, the collectivistic culture allows the extended and general community members opportunity to perform a considerable role in the activities and lives of the individual members and organisations (Adomako et al., 2015). In some instances, opinion leaders, like the chiefs, kings and religious leaders are very seminal in gaining resources and proffering valuable and necessary information to businesses (Adomako et al., 2015; Amoako & Lyon, 2014). In some extreme case of institutional weaknesses, Ghanaian SMEs exporters resort to the kinship, religious leaders and friendship to continue their export business (Amoako & Lyon, 2014). Thus, albeit the power and authority (formal political system) reside in the government bureaucrats, the power, authority and leadership in the informal political system rest on the kings, chiefs (Adomako et al., 2015) and friendship (built trust) (Amoako & Lyon, 2014).

Interestingly, despite the focal role of informal social network play in the firm's internationalisation trajectory, there is a low network-based relationship among Africa entrepreneurs as compared to other continents. For example (GEM, 2019) acknowledge low (12%) personal affiliation with entrepreneurs in Africa (Egypt) with the Middle East (Saudi Arabia) recording the highest rate (79%). Therefore, albeit unfavourable (favourable) institutional elements hamper (foster) firm innovation, business strategy and internationalisation, a strong informal interplay, such as political and business ties can aid SMEs to mitigate the institutional challenges for domestic growth and international expansion and allay the impending consequences on SMEs internationalisation.

Informal Social Support

Another key informal institutional factor that can influences SMEs internationalisation is the social support system, which refers to a personal assessment and viewpoint on how he or she is loved, cared by others, valued, respected and part of the supportive, informal social network (Taylor, 2011). Relatively well researched is on the interplay between the informal social support system and SMEs internationalisation. The family is the primary social institutions in every society, which form the basic structure on which every society's customs, rights and responsibilities are based (Adomako et al., 2015).

It implies that family is the fundamental institutions on which individual seek financial and non-financial support. According to (U.S. Census, 2000: 20), a family refers to "two or more persons living together and related by blood, marriage, or adoption" (Edelman, Manolova, Shirokova, & Tsukanova, 2016). (Ardayfio-Schandorf, 1994) however opinion, a family is a group of individual bond either by kinship or hereditary in which the elderly family members take responsibility of the younger ones.

Scholars (Adomako et al., 2015; Bika, 2012; Eijdenberg et al., 2019; Sørensen Jesper, 2007) posits that a strong family support plays a significant role in entrepreneurial activities and some cases, (Beehr & McGrath, 1992) provide solution to a problem and Davidsson and Honig (2003) impact on business establishment (small businesses). Other researchers opine that the informal social support serves as primary institutional structures (Adomako et al., 2015); mitigation strategy against institutional impediment (Amoako & Lyon, 2014); institutional enabler (Khavul et al., 2009) and; source of receiving and giving information and credit facility (Amoako & Lyon, 2014). For instance, Eijdenberg et al. (2019) studies in Tanzania demonstrate that, many entrepreneurs seek financial assistance from relatives and family members when faced with economic challenges and that, family still serve as' institutional influencer' and a 'social safety net' in proffering financial support and labour assistant to the entrepreneur whenever the institution is unfavourable. Congruent outcome pertains in Ghana. According to (Adomako et al., 2015), SMEs (small businesses) in Ghana usually consider borrowing from families and friends as the most suitable and 'lender of last resort', generally, small business receive diverse support to engage in small business enterprise, farm project and trade (Ardayfio-Schandorf, 1994)

Similarly, the social support system (family) in Ghana also serves as the basic mitigation strategy for SMEs in export when constraints by the weak institution. According to (Amoako & Lyon, 2014) studies on alternative strategy in the event of weak institutions sequel that, SMEs in export mostly rely on the relationship with their family, kinship and friendship to export to the West African countries. The authors surmise that "*SMEs exporters in Ghana are more likely to rely upon personalised relationships built on trust to address their problems and grievances. The relationships, e.g. close working relationships with partners based on credit provision, shared religion or intergenerational ties, are compared to strong ties based on family or kinship and friendships*" (Amoako and Lyon 2014: 126). Consequently, if the social support system is seminal in SMEs foreign market business, then it is imperative to garner a comprehensive understanding of how these social network system impact SMEs internationalisation.

Social Acceptance of Entrepreneurship

Another socio-cultural influence to SMEs internationalisation is the extent to which society approves entrepreneurship (SMEs export activity). Extant Literature demonstrates that social acceptance of entrepreneurship tends to influence the taste of national and buying preference (Adomako et al., 2015) and new venture creation (Shane, 2003). Thus, societal lifestyle affects entrepreneurship, entrepreneurial activities, taste and preference and ultimately SMEs internationalisation. Despite the blossoming internationalisation of Africa businesses (Adusei, 2016; Boso et al., 2019; Omokaro-Romanus et al., 2018; Sadeghi et al., 2019) firms in the continents (international ones) are bedevilled with numerous challenges such as 'winning the hearts and minds of African consumers' (Boso et al., 2019). The liability of Africanness has resulted in low taste and preference for African products. For example, according to (Adomako et al., 2015) there is low social acceptance of Ghanaian produced goods compare to the goods from western countries (e.g. the UK and North America). Cultural erudite like (Ojaide, 2018) and others (Adomako et al., 2015) add (Ngwu et al., 2015) contend that most Africans high preference for western countries food and foreign brands, in relations to low taste for Africa goods, were as a result of globalisation, burgeoning number of middle class in Africa, colonisation, high deficit trust-related issues and constant stereotypes.

Conversely, a canonical specialist (Shimp & Sharma, 1987) alludes that lack of patronising, as a result of low taste and preference for locally produced goods, maybe reduce through internationalisation or interact with other foreign national. (Gnyawali & Fogel, 1994; Spencer & Gómez, 2004) argues; entrepreneurial awards and mentioning of small or new ventures name in speeches may enhance societal attitude towards entrepreneurship and improve societal acceptance of entrepreneurship. Current research (Boso et al., 2019) and (Transparency International, 2017) argue that for Africa firms in international business to overcome the ability of Africanness, there should be strongly built trust relationship among African countries and tenacious attempts by other African countries, as done Ghana, Rwanda, South Africa Botswana, Senegal and Nambia, to exit the bottom of corruption perception surveys.

Accordingly, high social approval of entrepreneurship boost individuals entrepreneurial orientation spirit and create favourable conditions in the home country environment, encourage existing entrepreneurs to improve, grow and expand their business whiles taking opportunities in the favourable institutions to move to proximate or distant countries. Conversely, where there is an unfavourable informal institution, in this case, low social acceptance of entrepreneurship, then entrepreneurs in such an uncertain and unfavourable country will target other markets, possibly foreign market to sell their products and to seek other sources of revenue.

Legal and Political Aspects of SMEs Internationalisation

SMEs internationalisation is influence by both the formal and informal entrepreneurial institutional milieu (Amoako & Lyon, 2014; Love & Roper, 2015; Ullah, 2019). The legal aspect of institution form part of the formal institutional structure, and that, the legal and political elements are among the most mentioned strands of formal institutions (Adomako et al., 2015). Scholars (Akimova & Schwodiauer, 2005; Amoako & Lyon, 2014) argues that the legal aspect of formal institutions guarantees adherence to a contractual agreement among parties. Extant literature also confirms weak entrepreneurial institutions such as legal enforcement system, administrative hindrances and legal fees charges hamper entrepreneurship and SMEs export activity (Amoako & Lyon, 2014; Djankov, Miguel, Qian, Roland, & Zhuravskaya, 2004b; Johnson et al., 2002).

Conversely, one can postulate that unfavourable legal and political institutions context, like high legal charges, delayed legal system, which may spur judicial/ legal corruption and inefficiency hence thwart SMEs internationalisation growth and agenda. Research demonstrates that in Ghana, key institutional constraints to business is the high cost associated with legal (court) settlement coupled with an undue delay in the legal system (Abor & Quartey, 2010).

Proposed Conceptual Framework of Institutions on SMEs Internationalisation

The paper proposes a conceptual framework of SMEs internationalisation by drawing support from institutional theory (North, 1990), resource-based theory (Barney, 1991; Wernerfelt, 1984), neo-institutional theory and entrepreneurial institutional context (Gnyawali & Fogel, 1994). The researchers parsimoniously classify the various institutional factors based on (Law, Wong, & Mobley, 1998) classification, (Roxas et al., 2007) recommendations and (Jabareen, 2009) insight. Figure 1 shows that both the formal (limited to legal and political) and informal institutions affect SMEs internationalisation trajectory and that, institutional structure encourage as well as restrain SMEs internationalisation agenda. We further contend that, in Ghana, the institutional context of SME in export business is a function of social-cultural, political and legal environs and mainly rooted in the socio-cultural issues. The paper argues that the socio-cultural (informal institutions) SMEs environment constitute the level of societal desirability, societal acceptance, informal social network system and informal social support system, while the legal and the political SMEs in export terrain includes the legal and the court system, government SMEs sustainable support programmes (financial and non-financial incentives). Theoretically, the conceptual framework aims to proffer a comprehensive understanding of the institutional impact on SMEs internationalisation. For example, this framework serves as an essential guide into how the formal (legal and political) and the informal (socio-culture) affect indigenous SMEs internationalisation which research is under explore in Ghana.

Figure 1.
Source: Author composition, 2020

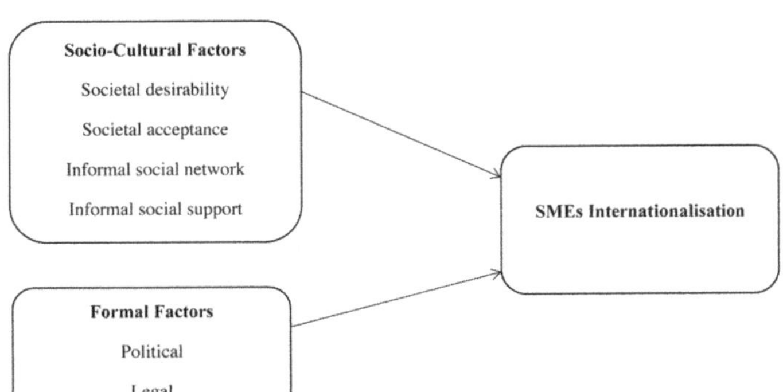

CONCLUSION

In this chapter, it has become clear that SMEs are crucial mechanisms that can help sustain world economies. Innovation and creativity are essential ingredients that add value to SMEs and ensure their continued growth and sustainability in these trying financial times. Despite global recessions, political instability, turbulent economic fluctuations and changing social dynamics, SMEs will continue to assist countries in providing jobs and contributing to a country GDP. Each country has to invest in training its young minds to be creative, innovative, and entrepreneurial-minded. A robust, secure and favourable governmental, social and cultural support that develops and maintains the entrepreneurial and innovation spirit, business sustainability and possible internationalisation processes must be stimulated within the country in support of SMEs.

Future Research Areas

This chapter requires additional future research to be conducted in developing economies on how innovation in SMEs can add to a country's economic sustainability. Further studies on the challenges facing the development and implementation of entrepreneurial strategies in SMEs across sectors and different economies can help shed more light in this area. Empirical studies on internationalisation on SMEs in Ghana and Africa as a continent can also be useful in unpacking gaps and making recommendations in how countries like Ghana, South Africa and Africa can improve on internationalising their SME sector in the future.

REFERENCES

Abor, J., & Quartey, P. (2010). Issues in SME development in Ghana and South Africa. *International Research Journal of Finance and Economics*, *39*(6), 215–228.

Adomako, S., Danso, A., & Ampadu, E. (2015). Institutional outlook of the entrepreneurial climate in Ghana. *International Journal of Social Economics*, *42*(6), 566–582. doi:10.1108/IJSE-09-2013-0206

Adusei, M. (2016). Does entrepreneurship promote economic growth in Africa? *African Development Review*, *28*(2), 201–214. doi:10.1111/1467-8268.12190

Akimova, I., & Schwodiauer, G. (2005). 10. The effect of trust in courts on the performance of Ukrainian SMEs. *Trust and Entrepreneurship: A West-East Perspective*, 156.

Amankwah-Amoah, J., & Hinson, R. E. (2019). Contextual influences on new technology ventures: A study of domestic firms in Ghana. *Technological Forecasting and Social Change*, *143*, 289–296. doi:10.1016/j.techfore.2019.01.019

Amoako, I. O., & Lyon, F. (2014). 'We don't deal with courts': Cooperation and alternative institutions shaping exporting relationships of small and medium-sized enterprises in Ghana. *International Small Business Journal-Researching Entrepreneurship*, *32*(2), 117–139. doi:10.1177/0266242613484778

Aoki, M., & Hayami, Y. (2001). *Communities and Markets in Economic Development*. Oxford: Oxford University Press. doi:10.1093/0199241015.001.0001

Ardayfio-Schandorf, E. (1994). *Family and Development in Ghana: Proceedings of International Training and Research Workshop Held at the University of Ghana, Legon on 14th-18th December, 1992*. Ghana Universities Press.

Babatunde, M. A. (2009). Export performance in sub-saharan Africa: An explanation. *Journal of Economic Theory*, *3*(3), 41–52.

Barney, J. (1991). Firm resources and sustained competitive advantage. *Journal of Management*, *17*(1), 99–120. doi:10.1177/014920639101700108

Beehr, T. A., & McGrath, J. E. (1992). Social support, occupational stress and anxiety. *Anxiety, Stress, and Coping*, *5*(1), 7–19. doi:10.1080/10615809208250484

Bika, Z. (2012). Entrepreneurial sons, patriarchy and the Colonels' experiment in Thessaly, rural Greece. *Entrepreneurship and Regional Development*, *24*(3-4), 235–257. doi:10.1080/08985626.2012.670915

Boachie-Mensah, F., & Marfo-Yiadom, E. (2007). *Entrepreneurship and small business management*. Accra, Ghana: Ghana Universities Press.

Bosma, N., & Kelley, D. (2019). *Global Entrepreneurship Monitor 2018/2019 Global Report.* Global Entrepreneurship Research Association.

Boso, N., Adeleye, I., Ibeh, K., & Chizema, A. (2019). The internationalization of African firms: Opportunities, challenges, and risks. *Thunderbird International Business Review*, *61*(1), 5–12. doi:10.1002/tie.21977

Busenitz, L. W., Gomez, C., & Spencer, J. W. (2000). Country institutional profiles: Unlocking entrepreneurial phenomena. *Academy of Management Journal*, *43*(5), 994–1003. doi:10.5465/1556423

Carlsson, B. (2002). Institutions, entrepreneurship, and growth: Biomedicine and polymers in Sweden and Ohio. *Small Business Economics, 19*(2), 105–121. doi:10.1023/A:1016235022728

Chiles, T. H., Bluedorn, A. C., & Gupta, V. K. (2007). Beyond creative destruction and entrepreneurial discovery: A radical Austrian approach to entrepreneurship. *Organization Studies, 28*(4), 467–493. doi:10.1177/0170840606067996

Ciszewska-Mlinaric, M. (2018). Export Intensity, Geographic Diversification and the Role of Public Support: The Evidence from Old and New Europe SMEs. *Entrepreneurial Business and Economics Review, 6*(2), 45–69. doi:10.15678/EBER.2018.060203

Coviello, N. E., & McAuley, A. (1999). Internationalisation and the Smaller Firm: A Review of Contemporary Empirical Research. *MIR. Management International Review, 39*(3), 223–256.

Dalitso, K., & Peter, Q. (2000). *The policy environment for promoting small and medium-sized enterprises in Ghana and Malawi*. Manchester: Institute for Development Policy and Management, University of Manchester.

Dana, L.-P. (2006). *Entrepreneurship and SMEs in the Euro-Zone: towards a theory of symbiotic entrepreneurship*. London: Imperial College Press. doi:10.1142/p445

Dau, L. A., & Cuervo-Cazurra, A. (2014). To formalize or not to formalize: Entrepreneurship and pro-market institutions. *Journal of Business Venturing, 29*(5), 668–686. doi:10.1016/j.jbusvent.2014.05.002

Davidsson, P., & Honig, B. (2003). The role of social and human capital among nascent entrepreneurs. *Journal of Business Venturing, 18*(3), 301–331. doi:10.1016/S0883-9026(02)00097-6

Djankov, S., Miguel, E., Qian, Y., Roland, G., & Zhuravskaya, E. (2004). *Who Are Russia's Entrepreneurs*. Washington, DC: The World Bank.

Edelman, L. F., Manolova, T., Shirokova, G., & Tsukanova, T. (2016). The impact of family support on young entrepreneurs' start-up activities. *Journal of Business Venturing, 31*(4), 428–448. doi:10.1016/j.jbusvent.2016.04.003

Eijdenberg, E. L., Thompson, N. A., Verduijn, K., & Essers, C. (2019). Entrepreneurial activities in a developing country: An institutional theory perspective. *International Journal of Entrepreneurial Behaviour & Research, 25*(3), 414–432. doi:10.1108/IJEBR-12-2016-0418

Fritsch, M., & Storey, D. J. (2014). *Entrepreneurship in a regional context: Historical roots, recent developments and future challenges*. Routledge.

GEM. (2019). *Global Entrepreneurship Monitor 2018/2019 Global Report* (0046-5070). Retrieved from https://www.gemconsortium.org/report/gem-2018-2019-global-report.pdf

GEPA. (2017). *Report on Analysis of 2017 Non-Traditional Export statistics*. Accra, Ghana: Ghana Export Promotion Authority.

Gnyawali, D. R., & Fogel, D. S. (1994). Environments for entrepreneurship development: Key dimensions and research implications. *Entrepreneurship Theory and Practice*, *18*(4), 43–62. doi:10.1177/104225879401800403

Golesorkhi, S., Mersland, R., Randøy, T., & Shenkar, O. (2019). The performance impact of culture and formal institutional differences in cross-border alliances: The case of the microfinance industry. *International Business Review*, *28*(1), 104–118. doi:10.1016/j.ibusrev.2018.08.006

Greif, A. (1994). Cultural Beliefs and the Organization of Society: A Historical and Theoretical Reflection on Collectivist and Individualist Societies. *Journal of Political Economy*, *102*(5), 912–950. doi:10.1086/261959

Helmke, G., & Levitsky, S. (2004). Informal institutions and comparative politics: A research agenda. *Perspectives on Politics*, *2*(4), 725–740. doi:10.1017/S1537592704040472

Hilmersson, M. (2014). Experiential knowledge types and profiles of internationalising small and medium-sized enterprises. *International Small Business Journal*, *32*(7), 802–817. doi:10.1177/0266242612458443

Hoskisson, R. E., Wright, M., Filatotchev, I., & Peng, M. W. (2013). Emerging multinationals from mid-range economies: The influence of institutions and factor markets. *Journal of Management Studies*, *50*(7), 1295–1321. doi:10.1111/j.1467-6486.2012.01085.x

ITC. (2016). *SME Competitiveness in Ghana: Alliance for Action*. Geneva: International Trade Centre.

Jabareen, Y. (2009). Building a Conceptual Framework: Philosophy, Definitions, and Procedure. *International Journal of Qualitative Methods*, *8*(4), 49–62. doi:10.1177/160940690900800406

Jafari Sadeghi, V., Nkongolo-Bakenda, J.-M., Anderson, R. B., & Dana, L.-P. (2019). An institution-based view of international entrepreneurship: A comparison of context-based and universal determinants in developing and economically advanced countries. *International Business Review*, *28*(6), 101588. doi:10.1016/j.ibusrev.2019.101588

John, C., Sek Hong, N., & Christine, W. (2002). Psychic Distance and Internationalization: Evidence from Hong Kong Firms. *International Studies of Management & Organization*, *32*(1), 36–56. doi:10.1080/00208825.2002.11043656

Johnson, S., McMillan, J., & Woodruff, C. (2002). Property Rights and Finance. *The American Economic Review*, *92*(5), 1335–1356. doi:10.1257/000282802762024539

Khavul, S., Bruton, G. D., & Wood, E. (2009). Informal family business in Africa. *Entrepreneurship Theory and Practice*, *33*(6), 1219–1238. doi:10.1111/j.1540-6520.2009.00342.x

Kingsley, G., & Malecki, E. J. (2004). Networking for competitiveness. *Small Business Economics*, *23*(1), 71–84. doi:10.1023/B:SBEJ.0000026022.08180.b7

Koellinger, P. (2008). Why are some entrepreneurs more innovative than others? *Small Business Economics*, *31*(1), 21–37. doi:10.100711187-008-9107-0

Konfidants. (2019). *A Survey of Made in Ghana Goods sold in Ghana's leading supermarkets*. Retrieved from http://www.konfidants.com/2019/07/01/research-reveals-only-18-of-goods-sold-in-ghanas-leading-supermarkets-are-made-in-ghana/

Langevang, T., Gough, K. V., Yankson, P. W., Owusu, G., & Osei, R. (2015). Bounded entrepreneurial vitality: The mixed embeddedness of female entrepreneurship. *Economic Geography*, *91*(4), 449–473. doi:10.1111/ecge.12092

Law, K. S., Wong, C.-S., & Mobley, W. M. (1998). Toward a taxonomy of multidimensional constructs. *Academy of Management Review*, *23*(4), 741–755. doi:10.5465/amr.1998.1255636

Lin, F.-J., & Ho, C.-W. (2019). The knowledge of entry mode decision for small and medium enterprises. *Journal of Innovation & Knowledge*, *4*(1), 32–37. doi:10.1016/j.jik.2018.02.001

Love, J. H., & Roper, S. (2015). SME innovation, exporting and growth: A review of existing evidence. *International Small Business Journal*, *33*(1), 28–48. doi:10.1177/0266242614550190

Martínez-Román, J. A., Gamero, J., Delgado-González, M. L., & Tamayo, J. A. (2019). Innovativeness and internationalization in SMEs: An empirical analysis in European countries. *Technological Forecasting and Social Change*, *148*, 119716. doi:10.1016/j.techfore.2019.119716

McGaughey, S., Welch, D., & Welch, L. (1997). *Managerial influences and SME internationalisation*. Academic Press.

Michael, M. S., Saban, G., & Abdurahman, A. Z. A. (2016). Factors affecting non-exporting small and medium enterprises' intention to export: Resource based approach. *Procedia: Social and Behavioral Sciences*, *224*, 199–206. doi:10.1016/j.sbspro.2016.05.441

Misati, E., Walumbwa, F. O., Lahiri, S., & Kundu, S. K. (2017). The Internationalization of African Small and Medium Enterprises (SMEs): A South-North Pattern. *Africa Journal of Management*, *3*(1), 53–81. doi:10.1080/23322373.2016.1275940

Monticelli, J. M., Calixto, C. V., Vasconcellos, S. L., & Garrido, I. L. (2017). The influence of formal institutions on the internationalization of companies in an emerging country. *Revista Brasileira de Gestão de Negócios*, *19*(65), 358–374. doi:10.7819/rbgn.v0i0.3040

Morais, F., & Ferreira, J. J. (2019). SME internationalisation process: Key issues and contributions, existing gaps and the future research agenda. *European Management Journal*. doi:10.1016/j.emj.2019.08.001

Muralidharan, E., & Pathak, S. (2017). Informal institutions and international entrepreneurship. *International Business Review*, *26*(2), 288–302. doi:10.1016/j.ibusrev.2016.07.006

Neagu, C. (2016). The importance and role of small and medium-sized businesses. *Theoretical and Applied Economics, 23*(3), 331-338.

Nikolaev, B. N., Boudreaux, C. J., & Palich, L. (2018). Cross-country determinants of early-stage necessity and opportunity-motivated entrepreneurship: Accounting for model uncertainty. *Journal of Small Business Management*, *56*, 243–280. doi:10.1111/jsbm.12400

North, D. C. (1990). *Institutions, institutional change, and economic performance*. Cambridge Univ Press.

North, D. C. (2005). Understanding the Process of Economic Change. Princeton University Press.

Nyame-Asiamah, F., Amoako, I. O., Amankwah-Amoah, J., & Debrah, Y. A. (2020). Diaspora entrepreneurs' push and pull institutional factors for investing in Africa: Insights from African returnees from the United Kingdom. *Technological Forecasting and Social Change*, *152*, 119876. doi:10.1016/j.techfore.2019.119876

Obeng, B. A., Robson, P., & Haugh, H. (2014). Strategic entrepreneurship and small firm growth in Ghana. *International Small Business Journal*, *32*(5), 501–524. doi:10.1177/0266242612463946

Omokaro-Romanus, C., Anchor, J. R., & Konara, P. (2018). The internationalization of Nigerian firms: Motivations and location patterns. *Thunderbird International Business Review*, *61*(1), 75–88. doi:10.1002/tie.21962

Osei, B., Baah-Nuakoh, A., Tutu, K., & Sowa, N. K. (1993). Impact of structural adjustment on small-scale enterprises in Ghana. In *Small Enterprises and Changing Policies: Structural adjustment, finance policy and assistance programmes in Africa* (pp. 51–70). Practical Action Publishing. doi:10.3362/9781780445908.004

Oviatt, B. M., & McDougall, P. P. (2005). The internationalization of entrepreneurship. *Journal of International Business Studies*, *36*(1), 2–8. doi:10.1057/palgrave.jibs.8400119

Peng, M. W. (2003). Institutional transitions and strategic choices. *Academy of Management Review*, *28*(2), 275–296. doi:10.5465/amr.2003.9416341

Peng, M. W., & Luo, Y. (2000). Managerial ties and firm performance in a transition economy: The nature of a micro-macro link. *Academy of Management Journal*, *43*(3), 486–501.

Reynolds, P. D., Carter, N. M., Gartner, W. B., & Greene, P. G. (2004). The prevalence of nascent entrepreneurs in the United States: Evidence from the panel study of entrepreneurial dynamics. *Small Business Economics*, *23*(4), 263–284. doi:10.1023/B:SBEJ.0000032046.59790.45

Robson, P. J., Haugh, H. M., & Obeng, B. A. (2009). Entrepreneurship and innovation in Ghana: Enterprising Africa. *Small Business Economics*, *32*(3), 331–350. doi:10.100711187-008-9121-2

Robson, P. J., & Obeng, B. A. (2008). The barriers to growth in Ghana. *Small Business Economics*, *30*(4), 385–403. doi:10.100711187-007-9046-1

Roxas, H. B., Lindsay, V., Ashill, N., & Victorio, A. (2007). An institutional view of local entrepreneurial climate. *Journal of Asia Entrepreneurship and Sustainability*, *3*(1), 1–28.

Sadeghi, V. J., Nkongolo-Bakenda, J.-M., Anderson, R. B., & Dana, L.-P. (2019). An institution-based view of international entrepreneurship: A comparison of context-based and universal determinants in developing and economically advanced countries. *International Business Review*, *28*(6), 101588. doi:10.1016/j.ibusrev.2019.101588

Schmidt, A., & Hansen, M. W. (2017). Internationalization Strategies of African Firms: A Survey of 210 Food Processing Firms from Tanzania, Kenya and Zambia. Academic Press.

Scott, W. R. (1995). Introduction: institutional theory and organizations. *The Institutional Construction of Organizations*, 11-23.

Seglah, S. K., & Armah, S. E. (2016). *Going regional: internationalisation strategies of Ghanaian service companies within the ECOWAS market*. Academic Press.

Shane, S. A. (2003). *A general theory of entrepreneurship: The individual-opportunity nexus*. Edward Elgar Publishing. doi:10.4337/9781781007990

Shimp, T. A., & Sharma, S. (1987). Consumer ethnocentrism: Construction and validation of the CETSCALE. *JMR, Journal of Marketing Research, 24*(3), 280–289. doi:10.1177/002224378702400304

Simón-Moya, V., Revuelto-Taboada, L., & Guerrero, R. F. (2014). Institutional and economic drivers of entrepreneurship: An international perspective. *Journal of Business Research, 67*(5), 715–721. doi:10.1016/j.jbusres.2013.11.033

SørensenJesper, B. (2007). Closure and Exposure: Mechanisms in the Intergenerational Transmission of Self-employment. In R. Martin & L. Michael (Eds.), *The Sociology of Entrepreneurship* (Vol. 25, pp. 83–124). Emerald Group Publishing Limited. doi:10.1016/S0733-558X(06)25003-1

Spencer, J. W., & Gómez, C. (2004). The relationship among national institutional structures, economic factors, and domestic entrepreneurial activity: A multicountry study. *Journal of Business Research, 57*(10), 1098–1107. doi:10.1016/S0148-2963(03)00040-7

Steel, W., & Webster, L. (1990). *Ghana's Small Enterprise Sector: Survey of Adjustment Response and Constraints' Industry Series Paper 41*. Washington, DC: World Bank, Industry and Energy Dept.

Stephan, U., & Uhlaner, L. M. (2010). Performance-based vs socially supportive culture: A cross-national study of descriptive norms and entrepreneurship. *Journal of International Business Studies, 41*(8), 1347–1364. doi:10.1057/jibs.2010.14

Storey, D. (1994). *Understanding the Small Business Sector. Routledge.*

Takyi-Asiedu, S. (1993). Some socio-cultural factors retarding entrepreneurial activity in sub-Saharan Africa. *Journal of Business Venturing, 8*(2), 91–98. doi:10.1016/0883-9026(93)90013-U

Taylor, S. E. (2011). Social support: A review. In *The handbook of health psychology* (pp. 189–214). New York: Oxford University Press.

Tesar, G., & Moini, A. H. (1998). Longitudinal study of exporters and nonexporters: A focus on smaller manufacturing enterprises. *International Business Review, 7*(3), 291–313. doi:10.1016/S0969-5931(98)00011-0

Thornton, P. H., Ribeiro-Soriano, D., & Urbano, D. (2011). Socio-cultural factors and entrepreneurial activity: An overview. *International Small Business Journal, 29*(2), 105–118. doi:10.1177/0266242610391930

Ullah, B. (2019). Firm innovation in transition economies: The role of formal versus informal finance. *Journal of Multinational Financial Management, 50*, 58–75. doi:10.1016/j.mulfin.2019.04.004

Urbano, D., & Alvarez, C. (2014). Institutional dimensions and entrepreneurial activity: An international study. *Small Business Economics, 42*(4), 703–716. doi:10.100711187-013-9523-7

Volchek, D., Henttonen, K., & Edelmann, J. (2013). Exploring the role of a country's institutional environment in internationalization: Strategic responses of SMEs in Russia. *Journal of East-West Business, 19*(4), 317–350. doi:10.1080/10669868.2013.851140

Wellalage, N. H., & Fernandez, V. (2019). Innovation and SME finance: Evidence from developing countries. *International Review of Financial Analysis, 101370*, 101370. doi:10.1016/j.irfa.2019.06.009

Wernerfelt, B. (1984). A resource-based view of the firm. *Strategic Management Journal, 5*(2), 171–180. doi:10.1002mj.4250050207

Yeboah-Assiamah, E., Muller, K., & Domfeh, K. A. (2017). Institutional assessment in natural resource governance: A conceptual overview. *Forest Policy and Economics, 74*, 1–12. doi:10.1016/j.forpol.2016.10.006

Zapletalová, Š. (2015). Models of Czech companies' internationalization. *Journal of International Entrepreneurship, 13*(2), 153–168. doi:10.100710843-015-0145-9

Zhang, X., Ma, X., Wang, Y., Li, X., & Huo, D. (2016). What drives the internationalization of Chinese SMEs? The joint effects of international entrepreneurship characteristics, network ties, and firm ownership. *International Business Review, 25*(2), 522–534. doi:10.1016/j.ibusrev.2015.09.001

Chapter 4
Research on Cross-Border Entrepreneurial Path of Core Enterprise Based on Ecological Advantage

Dake Jiang
Business School, Dalian University of Technology, China

Hong Zhang
Business School, Dalian University of Technology, China

Lei Wang
Law School, Civil Aviation University of China, China

Jin Liu
Business School, Dalian University of Technology, China

Linlin Chang
Dalian University of Technology, China

ABSTRACT

In the business ecosystem, the core business niche is not occupied by a structural position; its objectives and strategies are easily dispersed, while the core business can't coordinate the business ecosystem elements. Therefore, the ecological advantages obtained by core enterprises in the process of self-organization evolution are not sustainable. To solve this problem, a possible way is to explore how core enterprises consolidate and form new ecological advantages from the perspective of cross-border business. However, the academic community has not discussed the evolution path of cross-border entrepreneurship in detail. For this reason, based on the perspective

DOI: 10.4018/978-1-7998-3495-3.ch004

of ecological advantages, this chapter discusses the strategic path of cross-border entrepreneurship of core enterprises and constructs an interaction model between ecological advantages and core enterprises' cross-border entrepreneurial paths. The study broadens the understanding of the relationship between corporate strategies and business ecosystems, then provides theoretical value for subsequent research.

INTRODUCTION

Strategic positioning has always been one of the heated issues in the field of enterprise management, and the ecological advantage of enterprises is the core of strategic positioning. As the external environment becomes more complex and variable, how to build an ecological advantage becomes the top priority of the core enterprises in the business ecosystem. As a platform-based enterprise that plays a leading role in the commercial ecosystem, the construction of the core enterprise's ecological advantages will not only affect the upgrading, improvement, evolution and innovation of the entire commercial ecosystem, but also the smooth transformation of the entire industry. However, the core business can only passively accept the evolution of self-organizing business ecosystems choice, but cannot take the initiative to occupy the structural position, it cannot be able to purposefully get heterogeneous resources and the strategic objectives and their ability to match resources. Therefore, the advantages that core enterprises have in the process of self-organization and evolution of the business ecosystem are temporary and incomplete, rather than the ecological advantage in a continuous and complete sense. Then, what kind of strategy should the core enterprises that are dominant in the commercial ecosystem adopt to be able to consolidate and further form new ecological advantages?

For the problem above, a possible solution is to explore how the core enterprises can consolidate and form new ecological advantages from the perspective of cross-border entrepreneurship. First of all, cross-border entrepreneurship makes core enterprises promote the integration and reconstruct the business ecosystem, thus occupy a new key niche and further expand the ecological advantage. The penetration of corporate entrepreneurship into organizational strategy encourages companies to act in an innovative and pioneering manner which continuously optimize and restructure the company's existing business ecosystem through a series of activities initiated by the company, and seek opportunities to construct ecological advantages in the process.

Second, cross-border entrepreneurship can assist core enterprises integrate ecological advantages from different sources. The ecological advantage comes from the heterogeneous resources of the external environment in the commercial ecosystem. The core enterprises need to coordinate and optimize the partnership within the business ecosystem. Cross-border entrepreneurial activities of core enterprises have great influence on acquiring heterogeneous resources and reconstructing niche which helps enterprises integrate competitive advantages from different sources, consolidate and form new ecological advantages beyond the past.

Third, the construction of ecological advantages is vital to the entire business ecosystem. The core enterprise plays a leading enterprise that provides the internal niche and platform for the system, it is also an important force to incite the original business ecosystem at the same time.

Therefore, in a complex and ever-changing industrial environment, cross-border entrepreneurial activities of core enterprise are necessary processes for enterprise to maintain and consolidate their ecological advantages and thus achieve industrial upgrading.

However, the current academic research on cross-border entrepreneurship is not sufficient, the evolution path of cross-border entrepreneurship has not been discussed too much. Therefore, focusing on the core companies in the business ecosystem, this paper returns to the perspective of ecological advantages to explore the strategic path of core enterprises' cross-border entrepreneurship. At the same time, this article broadens the academic community's understanding of the relationship between corporate strategy and business ecosystems, portrays a wider range of strategic boundaries, and encourages more scholars to focus on issues of ecological advantage construction and cross-border entrepreneurship.

BUSINESS ECOSYSTEM AND RELEVANT CONTENT

Business Ecosystem

The concept of a business ecosystem originated from the ecosystem concept proposed by British ecologist Tansely. Within a certain time and space, between a variety of organisms and between biomes and their immersive environment, a unified whole that interacts through energy flow and material circulation (Tansley,1935). Moore (1999) creatively applied the concept of ecosystems to enterprise level and defined business ecosystem as an economic union based on the interaction of organizations and individuals.At product level, companies in business ecosystem achieve co-evolution and continuous innovation through cooperation and competition, then continuously develop new products that meet consumer needs. From the perspective of industry and system, business ecosystem spans multiple industries and experiences four stages of birth, development, dominance, self-renewal or extinction.

Based on Moore's research, Iansiti et al. (2004) summarized the basic concepts, structural features and functional effects of the business ecosystem. They introduced the concept of niche in the natural ecosystem to the commercial system. It's believed that the niche is not only the sum of the degree of environmental adaptation and resource utilization, but also the differentiation of different corporate strategies in the commercial ecosystem.

Some scholars think from the network point of view that the business ecosystem is a network organization formed by the interconnected enterprises in the process of interaction. Zahra (1996) pointed out that the network organizations is formed by long-term interaction between enterprises and surrounding organizations, which can provide the resources, market information and partners needed for their development. Pierce (2008) complemented this concept by thinking that business systems are networks that organizations share through formal contracts and interdependence.

In summary, this paper believes that the business ecosystem is based on heterogeneous enterprises and organizations, interacting under the mutual benefit of mutual benefit, mutual benefit, and tends to build a network system based on the development direction of one or more core enterprises.

Ecological Niche

How to choose the right niche based on the technological innovation and market characteristics of products is the key to the growth of a company from a general enterprise to a core enterprise.

The concept of enterprise niche originates from the ecological position of biology. The enterprise niche is an n-dimensional volume within a certain time and space, including physical, biological, and social aspects that limit or promote organizational performance (Brunsman & Sharfman., 1993). Hannan (1977) introduced the niche concept into corporate research for the first time, A population and all other populations compete for occupying a specific resource space. The specific resource space occupied by the enterprise population is called the basic niche, and each enterprise within the population actually occupies part or all of the basic niche, which is called the real niche. The aggregate of the same population, that is, the specific resource space occupied by an industry, is the basic niche, and the specific resource space occupied by the enterprises in the industry can be understood as the actual niche. The specific resource space (enterprise niche) occupied by enterprises interacts with innovation. Smith (2012) believed that breakthrough path-dependent innovation creates a protected space for enterprises, effectively protecting the transformation process of enterprises, and has the characteristics of shielding, cultivating and empowering.

Two species can not occupy the same niche for a long time. Hannan (1983) proposes the use of concepts such as Niche Separation, Niche Overlap and Niche Width to describe the relationship between population competitions. Excessive competition leads to the separation of niches, and diversity is a way for species to avoid competition. If the niche does not provide sufficient spatial resources for the species to survive, the niche will tend to overlap, which will create competition. Similarly, if two companies occupy the same resource or environmental variable for survival and development, their corporate niche will overlap. Intense competition and mutual exclusion will happen between two companies with identical niches. Enterprises with niche separation have greater chances of success than companies with overlapping niche.

The niche breadth of enterprises affects the degree of niche separation and overlap between enterprises, which in turn leads to changes in competition intensity. In natural ecosystems, biological diversity is related to the niche breadth of the species. If the resources actually used are only a small part of the total resources, the niche of this species is narrower; if a species can utilize a wide variety of resources in a continuous sequence of resources, it has a wider niche. Similar to the biological world, Peter (2007) pointed out that the position of a single enterprise within a population, its position in the niche of the population, and the actual niche breadth it occupies determine the number of competitors and the intensity of competition faced by the enterprise. For example, the more intense the market competition of enterprises, the more likely the market resources will be fully utilized; the competitive elimination mechanism will make the number of enterprises lower than the maximum capacity of the market environment, reduce the intensity of competition among enterprises, and allow more enterprises to overlap.

There are many perspectives on the research of enterprise niche, mainly focusing on strategic niche management (SNM). SNM emphasizes the importance of space protection and user engagement as a new way to develop new technologies to create alternatives to existing unsustainable technologies (Kemp, René, Schot, & Hoogma, 1998; Hegger & Vliet, 2007). SNM is an evolutionary approach to nurture, protect, support and control innovations with sustained benefits, a fundamental technological innovation and a tool to overcome systemic lock-in.

For the development of enterprise niche theory, important concepts such as technology niche, market niche, strategic niche management theory, time niche, spatial niche and industrial niche are extended. The technology niche is the protection space for new technologies. New technologies have various problems and shortcomings in the research and development stage. They cannot compete with their mature technologies. Enterprises or organizations build a space for their research and development of new technologies, that is, technology niche, so that new technologies can continue to mature and go to market. The market niche is a market state in which new technologies are gradually matured. Under this state, new technologies do not require special protection from enterprises or organizations, can freely participate in market competition, and better meet consumer needs through subtle changes. At the same time, consumers can directly identify, evaluate or share products or services produced by the technology. Strategic niche management is the construction of a protected space (technical niche) by enterprises or organizations. Through continuous experimentation and learning by developers, new technologies are improved and optimized, so that they gradually mature and enter the market, providing consumers with more. The management process of large-scale products and services, the process of developing new technologies from the technological niche to the market niche.

The strategic niche management theory is a bridge between the technology niche and the market niche, and provides theoretical support for the transformation of enterprise technology into the market. The temporal niche and spatial niche reflect the chronological and geographical location of an enterprise in the ecosystem, while the functional niche has a greater relationship with the position in the industrial chain or supply chain, mainly reflecting the role of enterprises in material, capital, human, technology and information flow. The industrial niche is an industry that interacts with other related industries within a certain period of time and within a certain industrial ecosystem. It is a niche concept from the industrial level, not a single enterprise.

From Competitive Advantage to Ecological Advantage

Competitive Advantage

How to acquire and maintain competitive advantage has always been a research hotspot in the field of strategic management. Since Porter creatively proposed the concept of competitive advantage, the academic community has different opinions on its definition. In general, the theory can be summarized into three main points.

The first is the concept of performance advantage. This view holds that competitive advantage is equal to excess financial performance. For example, Foss et al. (1995) defined competitive advantage directly as excess return. However, it was later questioned by scholars. Petreaf et al. (2003) believed that the equalization of competitive advantage and excess return would confuse the interpretation of performance differences from different perspectives. Today, scholars generally tend to view competitive advantage as an intermediate variable that leads to excess financial performance. They argue that equating competitive advantage with excess returns confuses the interpretation of performance differences from different perspectives. Nowadays, scholars generally tend to view competitive advantage as an intermediate variable that leads to excess financial performance.

The second is the concept of value advantage. Scholars who hold such views define competitive advantage as the difference between the value of the enterprise in delivering value to customers or creating value. It's believed that the competitive advantage is the difference between the cost of the product offered by the company and the cost of the product offered by the competitor (Ghemawat, 1995.); If a company creates more economic value in its product market than its marginal competitors, it could be considered a competitive advantage.

The third is the concept of ability advantage. This view is complementary to the above view, which is generally considered to be a resource or capability that creates excess financial performance for the enterprise. Carpenter et al. (2015) directly define competitive advantage in their work as the ability of firms to use their heterogeneous ways to create value.

In summary, we can understand the competitive advantage as the ability of companies to use their heterogeneous approach to their opponents to create excess financial performance

For the source of competitive advantage of enterprises, there are two viewpoints of exogenous theory and endogenous theory. Exogenous theory studies competitive advantage from the perspective of the external environment of enterprises, including competition strategy theory and modern industrial organization theory. Porter (1990) is a representative of exogenous theory. His five forces model establishes five sources of competition, but he overemphasizes the role of the external environment of the enterprise. The endogenous theory starts from the enterprise's own resources and capabilities, and believes that the competitive advantage of the enterprise is based on the establishment of internal heterogeneity, including resource-based theory, enterprise growth theory and core competence theory. Barney (1991) believes that the company's own heterogeneous resources are the source of competitive advantage; Penroes (1995) adopted the analysis paradigm of resource-capability-growth to further demonstrate that the company's competitive advantage mainly comes from the resources and capabilities of the enterprise itself. In short, the exogenous theory ignores the influence of the internal factors of enterprises on the competitive advantage. The endogenous theory ignores the role and promotion of internal heterogeneous resources to the external environment.

After entering the Internet era, the business environment and the competition methods have been significantly different. The traditional competitive advantage theory can no longer explain the advantages of enterprises in the new environment. In addition, users have developed into one of the important strategic resources of the enterprise, and the classic competitive advantage theory often only starts from the supply end, ignoring the role of the demand side. How to develop competitive advantage theory can better explain the business environment will become a new problem in the research field.

Ecological Advantage

Ecological advantage comes from the concept of dominant species and ecological niche in biology. The dominant species refers to the dominant species in the community. It includes the species with the largest number, the largest volume, and the largest impact on habitats in each layer of the community. For the first time, Iansiti et al. (2004) introduced the concept of niche in natural ecosystems into commercial systems. It is believed that the niche is not only the sum of the degree of enterprise adaptation to the environment and the degree of resource utilization, but also the differentiation of different business strategies in the business ecosystem. Due to the limited resources and market saturation, the ecological niche of enterprises in the same ecosystem will overlap. After continuous competition and evolution, corresponding dominant species will be generated and corresponding ecological advantages will be obtained.

In the case of traditional competitive advantage theory facing challenges, entrepreneurs need to rethink the source and strategic choice of competitive advantage from an ecological perspective. Chinese scholars proposed the concept of ecological advantage in business. Under the concept of ecological advantage, enterprise advantage not only comes from the activity optimization and resource capacity accumulation of the internal value chain of the enterprise, but also from the effective use of external resources. Then they further supplemented the concept of ecological advantage and defined it as the core of the business ecosystem to incite and utilize the internal and external resources and capabilities of the enterprise. This will create a new competitive advantage with heterogeneity, embedding and reciprocity.

Ecological advantages can be divided into two dimensions: state level and potential level. The state level mainly reflects the resources and capabilities of the core enterprises in the business ecosystem. It is the result of the accumulation of the core enterprises under the interaction of the self-organization evolution process and the environment, and represents the overall strength of the enterprise. The potential level mainly reflects the degree of adaptation of core enterprises in the commercial ecosystem to the external environment. It is the continuous power of the core enterprise to the external environment, and represents the exchange of materials, energy and information between the enterprise and the external environment.

Compared with traditional competitive advantage theory, ecological advantages combine exogenous and endogenous theories to make better answers to complex environmental changes. The biggest difference between ecological advantage and traditional advantage is that traditional advantage theory focuses more on independent enterprises, mainly on the internal factors and evolution process of enterprises. The ecological advantage theory focuses on the interaction between the enterprise and the business ecosystem, and explores the synergy between the external environment and the enterprise. In the ecological advantage theory, enterprises are no longer individuals who are single-handedly fighting, and more are playing a cluster effect, which maximizes the consolidation and expansion of competitive advantage through cooperation with external enterprises.

Existing researches focus on the system characteristics, system operation mechanism, and strategic selection and evolution of the business ecosystem. Since ecological advantage is an emerging concept, there are still few research literatures related to ecological advantages in business. Research on this aspect can help us better understand the behavior of enterprises in the ecosystem to obtain competitive advantages and promote the collaborative development of enterprises in the system. Since the concept of ecological advantage integrates exogenous theory and endogenous theory, the change of environment makes ecological advantage and the source and formation path of traditional competitive advantage completely different. Therefore, the construction and formation path of ecological advantage is a hot research field. In general, the current academic research on the ecological advantages still remains in the construction process and path formation, but the role and influence mechanism of ecological advantages have not been extensively demonstrated.

Core Enterprise

According to the role in the business ecosystem, four categories are divided: Keystone, Dominator, Hub landlord, and Niche. Keystone enterprises, also known as backbones, are often the core of the business ecosystem, create value for the business ecosystem and provide effective ways to create value by providing a platform for value creation; Dominator enterprises are responsible for controlling the value creation of most key locations in the system. Hub landlord enterprise is usually in the central position of the system, and ignores the healthy development of the entire system, trying to capture the greatest value. The niche enterprises are scattered in the system and occupy most of the space, which constitutes the main body of the system and is also a bridge linking the systems. On the basis of this doctrine, scholars generally believe that the core enterprise is the fundamental type or the mixture of the cornerstone and the dominant type, constantly creating value in the platform provided by it, and firmly grasping the head resources. At the same time, it provides services and support for gap-type enterprises, and continuously attracts new SMEs into the business ecosystem.

For the definition of core enterprises, the academic view is generally enterprise in the network center. Lorenzoni et al. (1995) consider the core enterprise to be a strategic center with high coordination and resilience. From the perspective of technical capabilities, Gay (2005) believed that only companies with core technologies that do not have or have high imitation barriers in other networks can be regarded as core enterprises. Some Chinese scholars hold the view that core enterprise is defined as a leading enterprise of core competence of one or several kinds that can supply core products and services for business ecosystem and bring great value to the final consumer (Wei & Xing, 2010). Based on the existing research, this paper defines an integrated nature of the core enterprise: If a company has a core technology capability of high imitation barriers in the business ecosystem because of its core position in resources and strategy, providing a platform for the system and continuously creating value, it can be called a core enterprise.

Core companies are responsible for decision-making, organizing, and innovating functions in the business ecosystem. Seizing the opportunity in a timely manner is essential for a core company with organizational and leadership capabilities. Leverage the benefits of core enterprise features for business marketing. The level of core business decision-making has a significant impact on the development or failure of the business ecosystem. The core enterprise is the builder of the business ecosystem that recruits members in the system. This is a specific role that is reflected in the formation, operation and dissolution of the business ecosystem.

The concept of a core enterprise is widely used in many fields, especially in the field of supply chain finance. Scholars focus on the evolution of core enterprises in the network, as well as the symbiotic structure of core enterprise and business ecosystem. Most of the existing researches on core enterprises are to explore how to build a healthy business ecosystem and its evolution mechanism around it, and there is little research on cross-border entrepreneurship of core enterprises.

Cross-Border Entrepreneurship

Under the trend of deepening the development of information technology, adaptive innovation based on multi-team collaboration and cross-industry cooperation has gradually become an important form for companies to break through industrial boundaries and realize new value combinations (Zhu, 2019). At present, although cross-border entrepreneurial research has described the phenomenon of cross-border entrepreneurship, there is no recognized definition to define cross-border entrepreneurship. Therefore, in order to understand cross-border entrepreneurship in a deeper way, we must first grasp the term cross-border. Cross-border activities are the reorganization of existing technologies and resources to infiltrate and integrate elements of different fields. Some scholars have studied the unique thinking patterns embodied in the cross-border entrepreneurial process and attributed them to cross-border thinking. Cross-border thinking refers to a way of thinking that rediscovers and establishes the inherent logical connection between things by translating the original concept, category and attributes of things. The cross-border thinking mode is formed by association, inspiration, prejudgment and insight on the basis of comprehensive understanding of things (stereoscopic thinking) and mastering the internal laws of things (reverse thinking).

Specific to the connotation of cross-border entrepreneurship, many scholars study cross-border entrepreneurship from the perspective of different industries and different fields. For example, Jacobides et al. (2007) believe that it is necessary to integrate entrepreneurial research into industry boundary theory research to understand the evolution of industry boundaries. Some scholars believe that at present, there are boundaries between industries and disciplines, and getting rid of the original knowledge path dependence is an effective way to enhance the motivation of innovation and enhance the level of creativity. Cross-border entrepreneurial activities differ from the industry evolution models in previous studies, not in the traditional model, which always focuses on continuous or destructive changes within the same industry. Burgleman et al. (1996) saw Apple as a cross-border disruptor of great change, and believed that its cross-border entrepreneurial activities have had a huge impact on neighboring industries and define such cross-border entrepreneurs.

Based on the existing research results and the practice of cross-border entrepreneurial activities, this paper defines cross-border entrepreneurship, that is, cross-border entrepreneurship refers to the use of entrepreneurial opportunities discovered or created by the organization to integrate existing knowledge and resources to enter its current location. In the process, companies may even transform due to the transfer of business centers.

MODEL DESIGN

Cross-Border Entrepreneurship of Core Enterprise

In order to introduce a new perspective of ecological advantages in the study of cross-border entrepreneurial paths, the analysis of the framework is mainly to solve two problems: First, whether the cross-border entrepreneurial path of enterprises can enable enterprises to obtain and maintain competitive advantage; Second, is the ecological advantage of the enterprise affecting the cross-border entrepreneurial strategy choice of the enterprise? The former answered the question Why should we conduct cross-border entrepreneurship (Why), and the latter answered the question How the ecological advantage plays a role in the cross-border entrepreneurial path (How).

The Necessity of Cross-Border Entrepreneurship in Core Enterprises

From the current research progress, ecological advantages are not a constant concept. In the commercial ecosystem formed by self-organization evolution, enterprises gain competitive advantage based on the separation of overlapping niches, but this advantage is not the whole of ecological advantages. Generally, the ecological advantages obtained by core enterprises in the commercial ecosystem in the process of self-development are short-lived and incomplete. There are three main reasons for this.

First, the niche occupied by core enterprises in the process of self-organization evolution is not necessarily a structural position. Some scholars proposed that the self-organization evolution process of the commercial ecosystem is essentially a process in which the results of competition between enterprises are stable under the environment selection. Due to the differences in the resources and capabilities of the enterprise, the heterogeneous enterprises are separated by niche in the external environment, and the core enterprises occupy the niche. However, the advantage brought about by the degree of matching between its own ability and the external environment is easy to form organizational rigidity. Once the environment changes, the advantages no longer match the environment, so the niche acquired by the core enterprises in the process of self-organization evolution is not necessarily the structural position.

Second, the goals and strategies of core enterprises are easily dispersed. In the early days of the business ecosystem, core enterprises were often driven by product management logic. In this stage of the business ecosystem, the dominant relationship is still the supply and demand relationship between upstream and downstream enterprises. The core enterprises only play a bridge role, so the heterogeneous resources they obtain are determined by upstream and downstream enterprises rather than themselves. Core enterprises need to take the initiative to continuously expand their influence in the business ecosystem, accelerate the absorption of heterogeneous resources, and selectively and purposely receive more heterogeneous enterprises into the entire business ecosystem.

Third, core enterprises do not have enough coordination of elements in the business ecosystem. According to the perspective of ecological advantages, the ecological advantages obtained by core enterprises in the process of organizational evolution mainly come from the elements in the combined business ecosystem and the coordination and optimization of contractual enterprise relationships. However, in the process of self-organization evolution, the core enterprise only integrates its internal elements and does not coordinate and integrate external elements. Therefore, through the effective use of external elements and internal integration, core enterprises can create new capabilities and technologies to adapt to the changing environment, thus consolidating their ecological advantages.

In summary, the ecological advantages obtained by the core enterprises are not long-term, absolute ecological advantages in the self-organization evolution process of the business ecosystem. In the self-organizing evolution of the business ecosystem, first, the core enterprise cannot occupy a structural position, second, the goals and strategies are easily dispersed, and third, there is no coordination and integration of elements in the business ecosystem. Therefore, in the process of constructing ecological advantages, core enterprises need to implement more advanced mechanisms than self-organization evolution processes, and build new ecological advantages that simultaneously satisfy structural features, centralized strategies and objectives, and coordination and integration mechanisms.

After combing the theory of business ecosystem and the theory of corporate entrepreneurship, we can see that the entrepreneurial spirit of the company, that is, the spirit of the pioneer and the spirit of adventurers, and entrepreneurial activities based on entrepreneurial spirit provide a new source of power for consolidating ecological advantages. By infiltrating the strategic level of the enterprise, entrepreneurship can help core enterprises to continuously search, identify and seize opportunities, and increase the effective utilization of external resources by the core enterprises in the business ecosystem. At the same time, the core enterprise's entrepreneurial activities continue to expand the organizational boundaries and value creation foundation of the entire business ecosystem by bridging the gap-type enterprises in the commercial ecosystem, It has improved the richness of heterogeneous resources in the commercial ecosystem and laid a material foundation for the emergence of ecological advantages.

The Process and Principle of Cross-Border Entrepreneurship

Cross-border entrepreneurship has to undergo three stages: opportunity identification, cross-border search, and strategic choice. Opportunity identification is the process by which an enterprise uses its own resources and capabilities to identify opportunities for entrepreneurship. Cross-border search is the behavior of enterprises to acquire new knowledge and new technologies of partners through resource search across borders. Strategic choice is the strategic decision-making process after the core enterprise identifies the entrepreneurial opportunity and uses the resources to self-upgrade. In general, opportunity identification is a starting point for its own ecological advantages and is a preparatory stage for cross-border entrepreneurship. Cross-border search is a self-upgrading based on ecological advantages and belongs to the development stage. Strategic choice is a means of consolidating ecological advantages and belongs to the implementation stage.

Cross-Border Entrepreneurship Based on Ecological Advantages

Using Ecological Advantages to Conduct Cross-Border Entrepreneurship

Ecological advantages can be divided into two dimensions: state level and potential level. Based on the existing theory, two indicators are extracted from the state level, namely knowledge resources and technology accumulation. Extract an indicator from the potential level, that is, social relations.

In the field of modern strategic management, the academic community generally believes that there are three main entrepreneurial strategies: centralization, differentiation, and diversification. In the cross-border search phase, core enterprises supplement their heterogeneous knowledge to achieve their own cognitive upgrades to better conduct cross-border entrepreneurial strategic decisions and drive core enterprises to implement diversification strategies. By searching for the most advanced technology accumulation, in order to prepare for technological innovation, drive core enterprises to implement differentiated strategies. By searching for a range of individuals and institutions that provide funding, technology, etc. for cross-border entrepreneurship in core businesses, enterprises reorganize and construct social networks to meet the needs of enterprise development and achieve a win-win situation, driving core enterprises to implement centralized strategies.

Thus, it can be concluded that the ecological advantage plays a role in the cross-border entrepreneurial path of core enterprises: after the opportunity identification of the core enterprises on the basis of ecological advantages, the core enterprises will implement strategic decision-making through the upgrading of ecological advantages, and consolidate and form new ecological advantages.

Building an Advantage in Cross-Border Entrepreneurship

In the process of cross-border entrepreneurship, core enterprises started from their own ecological advantages to conduct cross-border search under different dimensions according to the difference of advantages, then complete the active or passive upgrade of enterprises and drive enterprises to implement different cross-border strategies. As a result, they maintain and further expand its ecological advantages.

After the implementation of the diversification strategy, the core enterprises in the business ecosystem will also increase the channels for information acquisition and improve the business ecosystem, which will make the knowledge resources of the enterprises more diversified and of higher quality. After implementing the differentiation strategy, the company further expands its technical potential, so the technology accumulation will continue to be updated and maintain a leading position in the industry. After implementing the centralized strategy, companies can continue to reduce the cost of resource acquisition and information integration, thereby expanding the social network and enriching the entrepreneurial resources of the entrepreneurs themselves.

Core Model

In the process of cross-border entrepreneurship, core enterprises need to experience three stages: opportunity identification, cross-border search, and strategic choice. From the perspective of the two dimensions of ecological dominance and potential, the core enterprises in the commercial ecosystem are based on their own knowledge resources, technology accumulation and social relations. Complete active or passive upgrades and implement specific corporate cross-border strategies to maintain and expand ecological advantage.

After the above research on the role of ecological advantages in the cross-border entrepreneurship of core enterprises and the necessity of cross-border entrepreneurship to maintain the ecological advantages of core enterprises, this paper proposes the model shown in Figure 1.

Figure 1. Interaction model between core enterprise ecological advantage and cross-border entrepreneurial activity

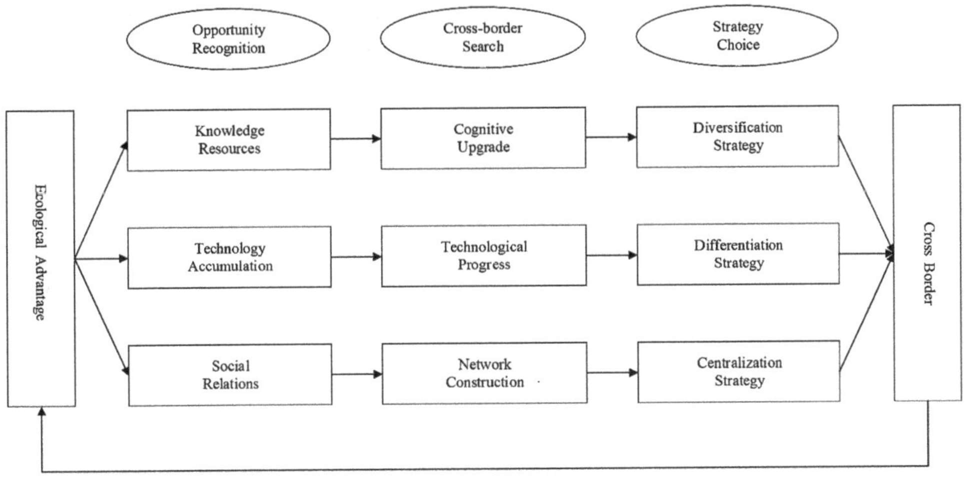

Knowledge resources are part of corporate resources. The transfer, sharing, and common use of knowledge and other resources have caused complex changes in the iterative innovation model of enterprises. Technology accumulation is an enterprise resource that is different from knowledge resources. Knowledge resources emphasize the theoretical level, while technology accumulation emphasizes the process of knowledge landing. In terms of social exchange, companies in the ecosystem can build social relationships and acquire certain social resources through ecological advantages. Depending on the resources obtained, the focus of the enterprise in the cross-border search process is also different. Through the model above, we can find that the enterprises in the ecosystem obtain specific resources through ecological advantages. According to the differences in acquired resources, there will be a certain focus in the cross-border search process, and the most appropriate strategy will be adopted based on existing resources. For example, we can conclude that the core enterprises in the business ecosystem identify entrepreneurial opportunities mainly based on the knowledge resources of the ecological dominance level in the cross-border entrepreneurial activities. They complete cognitive upgrades in the cross-border search process, and ultimately driving the company to implement a diversification strategy. The core enterprises in the business ecosystem will gain a certain technological accumulation through ecological advantages. The continuous maturity of new technologies will further promote the development and progress of other technologies. Due to the novelty and advancement of technology, such core companies will adopt differentiated strategies to guide the next development. The core enterprises in the business ecosystem will obtain certain social relationships through ecological advantages, which are the guarantee of cross-border entrepreneurship. Through the ecological advantages, core enterprises have established social relationships related to core enterprises, and established a single social relationship into a more complex social network, thereby playing a better role in ensuring the development of core enterprises. Due to the scale and scope of the relationship network, such core companies can implement a centralized strategy at a lower cost when starting a cross-border venture.

CASES

Based on the theoretical sampling principle and replication logic of the multi-case research method (Graebner, 2007), select the enterprises suitable for the research topic in the Internet field, and formulate specific case screening criteria:

1. Satisfy the status of the core enterprise and proactively deploying the business ecosystem;

2. All have completed the leap from a single field to a multi-ecological field;
3. Continue to maintain and expand competitive advantage through cross-border entrepreneurial activities;
4. data and its accessibility

According to the above criteria, the three most representative enterprises of Tencent, Xiaomi and Alibaba were selected as the multi-case research objects. The case is briefly introduced as follows

- Tencent: The largest Internet integrated service provider in China, after the 3Q war with 360, focused on improving the core competitiveness of the company and building a diversified ecosystem spanning social, communication, news, games, and life services. In 2017, it became the highest listed company in China.
- Xiaomi: The intelligent hardware company founded by Jinshan CEO Lei Jun, who focused on electronic product development in the early stage, began to lay out the Xiaomi intelligent ecological chain, and moved from the mobile phone field to TV and smart home. Xiaomi successfully listed in 2018 and became the largest Internet of Things platform in China.
- Alibaba: China's largest B2B service provider, Taobao.com, the predecessor of Taobao.com, was the first portal site at that time. After 2010, Ant Financial and Alibaba Cloud were established to establish a B2B business ecosystem with Taobao as the core. It was listed on the New York Stock Exchange in 2014 and became the Internet company with the highest market value in the country.

The Role of Ecological Advantages in Cross-Border Entrepreneurial Activities

Knowledge Resources: The Foundation of Cross-Border Entrepreneurial Activities

It is no longer a controversy that we live in a globalized world characterised by fast information transfer across large geographic areas by means of the Internet. The consequence of this globalization is the emergence of knowledge-based economies where importance is placed on effective management of human capital to ensure that workers continue to create the right value for the economy.

Nowadays, organizations no longer compete solely on the basis of financial capital and strength, rather knowledge is the new competitive advantage in business. Cross-border teams face a highly complex and uncertain internal and external environment.

Among them, knowledge is the foundation of innovation, and knowledge sharing, integration and absorption are the paths for organizations to achieve innovation (Jiang, 2018). Under the traditional theory of competitive advantage, knowledge resources are the basic conditions for enterprises to maintain competitive advantage. From the perspective of ecological advantages, knowledge resources are the prerequisite for enterprises to achieve cross-border entrepreneurship, and can bring long-term and considerable economic advantages to enterprises. In the business ecosystem, if the core enterprises occupying the dominant position want to conduct cross-border entrepreneurial activities, then the importance of knowledge resources is self-evident. If there is no knowledge resource as a support, the enterprise does not have enough understanding of the cross-border field and ventures into a new field, the expected economic benefits will not be guaranteed. At the same time, core enterprises cannot fully utilize their own resource advantages, and may lose the dominant position gained in the self-organization evolution process of the commercial ecosystem.

From the three business cases selected in this paper, knowledge resources play a fundamental role in their cross-border entrepreneurial activities. From a micro perspective, the knowledge resources of an enterprise are mainly reflected in the cognition and experience of the decision-making level of the enterprise.

When the development of QQ business reached saturation, Zhang Xiaolong prepared to enter the field of mobile communication. Before WeChat, QQ mailbox gave him a full experience, that is, knowledge resources. This kind of knowledge resource has laid a solid foundation for the transformation of Tencent from platform social to mobile social in the form of academic sharing.

Lei Jun worked for Jinshan Software Company for ten years before setting up Xiaomi Technology. During his tenure at Jinshan, Lei Jun had a clear-cut ability and solid management skills, and then gained certain knowledge resources. It is precisely because of this that Xiaomi Technology can find the right positioning, successfully build the Internet of Things, and become an Internet giant with Tencent and Ali.

Knowledge resources also include failed experiences. Chen Hang, the founder of Ali's nail team, started his search business in the Ali Yitao business unit and then moved to the coming and going business unit. Although these two experiences were not successful, they also saved valuable experience for him. The nail that was born in the exploration of the failure experience has robbed Ali of the golden position of corporate socialization.

From a micro perspective, knowledge resources can be equated with entrepreneurial cognition and experience, which is the basis for realizing cross-border entrepreneurial activities.

Technology Accumulation: The Core Driving Force of Cross-Border Entrepreneurial Activities

Technology accumulation is an enterprise resource that is different from knowledge resources. Knowledge resources are often reflected in the theoretical level, while technology accumulation is implemented on the practical level. For core enterprises, heterogeneous technology accumulation determines the degree of differentiation of products and services provided by enterprises, which is often the core of the company's survival. In cross-border entrepreneurial activities, heterogeneous technology accumulation is the key to success. If a core business in a business ecosystem wants to achieve significant results in cross-border entrepreneurial activities, it must have technology that is different from other companies. The non-replicability of core technologies determines the upper limit of the company's development. In cross-border entrepreneurial activities, core enterprises must achieve the heterogeneity of products through technological potential differences, and provide enterprises with a place in cross-border competition.

After researching the three case companies in this paper, it is found that technology accumulation plays a central role in its cross-border entrepreneurial activities. The core of Tencent's ability to sit firmly on the Internet is based on its monopoly in the social field. From WeChat to QQ, Tencent is often able to take the lead in launching products before all competitors. The technical advantage makes Tencent often occupy a huge market share in cross-border competition. However, Tencent is not always in a leading position in technology. For example, in the short video war, Tencent's long-sighted micro-vision has no technical advantage compared with the industry leader. Relying on Tencent's huge social foundation, it was finally defeated in this round of fighting.

The rise of Xiaomi Technology will bring the technological advantages to the forefront. Xiaomi can stand out from the competition between many domestic mobile phone brands and foreign giants, mainly because of its attractive price/performance ratio. Among the mobile phones of the same price, the performance of Xiaomi is undoubtedly the most powerful. From technology companies to the Internet of Things Ecology, a solid technical foundation is the only rule for Xiaomi to win in cross-border competition.

Alibaba's success also depends on core technology. From the B2B giant to the multi-ecology, technical support is undoubtedly the most critical. Ant Financial Services took the lead in entering the domestic mobile payment market with Alipay, and the perfect functions and services are the most reliant for users. Tencent, which has an absolute dominant position in technology, can stand up to it with WeChat payment. The rest, even traditional banks such as CCB, have no technical advantage in the Internet field, so they lost their opportunities in this round of competition.

Heterogeneous technology accumulation determines the degree of differentiation of products and services provided by enterprises, which is the core driving force for achieving cross-border entrepreneurial activities.

Social Relations: The Guarantee Conditions for Cross-Border Entrepreneurial Activities

Social relations are the relationship between the roles of the business and the business ecosystem. It reflects the ability of core enterprises in the business system to extract resources from the external environment. Generally speaking, social network can be divided into two aspects: social network scale and social network strength. The scale of social networks mainly refers to the extent of the collection of membership relationships among entrepreneurs. Generally speaking, the larger social network scale often has more smooth information flow, more cross-border entrepreneurial recognition opportunities and greater resource support. The strength of social networks mainly emphasizes the position of entrepreneurs in the social network and the number of structural holes occupied. Entrepreneurs with high social network strength can obtain high-quality, heterogeneous information and resources at a lower cost, and are more relaxed in terms of resource acquisition and resource integration, thereby enriching the social capital of enterprises. In the cross-border entrepreneurial activities of core enterprises, the larger social network scale and higher social network intensity are important guarantees for cross-border entrepreneurial activities of core enterprises in the business ecosystem.

In the three business cases selected in this paper, the role of social relations in the cross-border entrepreneurial activities of enterprises is very obvious. The rise of Tencent not only depends on Ma Huateng's personal decision and the technological advantages of his leading competitors, but also depends on the rich network resources of the top management. Lei Jun, CEO of Xiaomi Technology, relies on his own network of people who have been crawling in Jinshan for more than ten years, and has built a network of relationships closely related to corporate development. Efficient resource acquisition and information integration capabilities also allow Xiaomi to avoid many detours in the development process. Ma Yun's interpersonal relationship circle is more complicated. Although he is a teacher, the experience of Cheung Kong Graduate School of Business has allowed him to accumulate a large amount of alumni resources and provide protection for Ali's rise in the future.

Good social network construction can effectively reduce the cost of resource acquisition and information integration, which is the guarantee for realizing cross-border entrepreneurial activities.

Cross-Border Entrepreneurial Model Selection Based on Ecological Advantages

In the previous article, through the case analysis of Tencent, Xiaomi and Alibaba, we explored the role of ecological advantages in the cross-border entrepreneurial activities of enterprises. The three corporate cases also show that ecological advantages have an important impact on cross-border entrepreneurial activities. However, the mechanism of the ecological advantage for the cross-border entrepreneurial model is still unknown. In this section, this paper will discuss the different strategic choices that enterprises take under the ecological advantage.

From Knowledge Resources to Cognitive Upgrading: Diversification Strategy

Cognition belongs to the category of psychology. It mainly refers to the acquisition of knowledge through the formation of psychological activities such as concept, perception, judgment or imagination. It also refers to the process of processing individual information by individual thinking. Entrepreneur as a key person in the enterprise, its cognitive update and upgrade will also restrict the development of the enterprise. To achieve the conditions of cognitive upgrading, it usually requires a solid knowledge reserve and a wealth of practical experience. When knowledge reserves and experience accumulation reach a critical value, entrepreneurs' awareness of themselves will also escalate. In the cross-border entrepreneurial activities, due to the solid knowledge reserve and rich experience accumulation, the core enterprises have targeted and actively selected the external knowledge required for the development of the enterprise. Therefore, core enterprises often implement diversification strategies in the process of cross-border entrepreneurship driven by ecological advantages.

In the three business cases of this paper, the cross-border entrepreneurial activities of core enterprises are affected by the cognitive upgrade of entrepreneurs. In the three business cases of this paper, cross-border entrepreneurial activities of core enterprises are affected by the cognitive upgrade of entrepreneurs. Tencent's evaluation in the early years was not good. The company has always lacked core competitive technology,which is partly due to Ma's experience being limited by the experience accumulated in the early development of Tencent. However, after experiencing the 3Q war with Zhou Hongwei 360, Ma Huateng completed the cognitive upgrade, realizing that the development of core competitiveness is the key to the development of the enterprise, and proceeded to lay out the multicultural industry, and ruled the Internet industry with the crushing trend.

Entrepreneurs complete cognitive upgrades through knowledge reserves and experience accumulation, drive core enterprises to implement diversification strategies, and complete the transition from single field to multi-field, from single-handed to commercial ecosystem

From Technology Accumulation to Technological Innovation: Differentiation Strategy

The core technology is the lifeblood of the development of the enterprise. The advancement of technology is not only the fundamental way to promote the transformation of the country's economic growth mode, but also the core path for the core enterprises to achieve leap-forward entrepreneurial innovation and development. In general, there are two ways to achieve technological advancement: technology introduction and technological innovation. Because of the technical potential difference, the core enterprises in the business ecosystem are easy to gain a competitive advantage in competing with their peers in cross-border entrepreneurial activities. However, the old core technologies in the new field are likely to be unacceptable, and often require technology introduction or technological innovation to achieve the company's differentiated strategic goals, thereby enhancing the company's innovation capability and core competitiveness. Both technology introduction and technological innovation are basically the same in terms of results and objectives. They are all aimed at realizing the company's differentiated strategic goals and thus updating the technology. However, the process is slightly different: the former is often the core enterprise using the mature technology of other enterprises to realize the technology. The latter is to complete self-iteration through their own efforts. In the cross-border entrepreneurial interaction driven by ecological advantages, the differentiation strategy is often the key strategy to determine the life of the core enterprise.

Judging from the cross-border entrepreneurial process of the three case enterprises in this paper, technological innovation and technology introduction are not only the strategic goals of the company, but also provide a quick channel for enterprise development. After experiencing the credibility crisis of the 3Q war, Tencent discovered its own core competitiveness. Therefore, Ma Huateng recruited Zhang Xiaolong, the legendary product manager. The research and development of WeChat provided Tencent with a monopolistic flow advantage in the industry chain layout of the second decade of the 21st century. Although Xiaomi has excellent software development experience in the head of Lei Jun, there is no technical advantage in multiple fields before the layout of the business ecosystem. Therefore, Xiaomi introduced Liu De, director of the Department of Industrial Design of Beijing University of Science and Technology, responsible for Xiaomi's industrial design and supply chain management. The strong investment in the R&D team has also made Xiaomi's core technology more and more mature. In many hardware fields, the company has seized the market from various fields with its unique technological advantages, and completed the ecological layout of Xiaomi's Internet of Things. The reason why Alibaba can keep pace with Tencent, which is monopolized in the social field, is mainly because it leads the domestic cloud computing capabilities. In 2009, Ma Yun realized that the Internet was about to enter the era of big data, and mastered the core of development by mastering information processing capabilities, so Aliyun was established. In 2018, Alibaba Cloud accounted for 13.2% of the market, followed by the cloud service market leader AWS, higher than Microsoft's 8.7% and Google's 7.3%. It is also the only Chinese company among the top 5 cloud service providers in the world. The common point of summarizing these three case enterprises is to lay out the business ecosystem around 2010, relying on technology introduction or technological innovation to achieve industrial upgrading and achieve differentiated strategic goals.

In summary, core enterprises have achieved closer to differentiated strategic goals through technology introduction and technological innovation. The heterogeneous technology potential has become the key to cross-border entrepreneurial activities of core enterprises.

From Social Relations to Social Network Reconstruction: Centralized Strategy

The social relationship network includes two dimensions: social network scale and social network strength. The status of core enterprises in the social relationship network and the scale of the social network they contain will affect the cross-border entrepreneurial activities of enterprises to varying degrees. The larger the social network is, the higher the social network strength is, and the stronger the enterprise's resource acquisition ability and information integration ability. Building a reasonable social network is also related to organizational trust, personal relationships and other factors. Organizational factors generally refer to the level of trust at the organizational level, such as good business reputation, organizational background, etc., which allows core enterprises to focus more on cross-border entrepreneurial activities and reduce opportunity costs. Personal relationships include the entrepreneurial network and the public's recognition of the company's products, which determines the initial cost of the company's cross-border entrepreneurial activities. Therefore, building a social relationship network leads to a reduction in the social cost of the enterprise, driving the company to implement a centralized strategy to obtain a greater cost advantage.

From the perspective of three case companies, the social relationship network plays an important role in ensuring the smooth progress of initial cross-border entrepreneurial activities. The smooth development of Tencent after its entry into 2010 is largely due to the construction of a multicultural industry chain. The smooth development of Tencent after its entry into 2010 is largely due to the construction of a multicultural industry chain.

Ma Huateng used Tencent's huge network of social relationships accumulated in the early days to accurately grasp market demand, actively respond to national policies, and bring the company's development direction closer to the country's strategic layout. Therefore, it also obtained a certain degree of industrial support. In the short period of 10 years since its establishment, Xiaomi has become an Internet giant comparable to BAT. This is due to the support of the Internet of Things ecosystem. The resources that Lei Jun accumulated during the CEO of Jinshan also played an extraordinary role. In addition to benefiting from the pre-emptive B2B business ecosystem, Alibaba's rise depends on Ma Yun's image of a conscience entrepreneur, which has enabled the masses to maintain a high reputation for Ali products. These three case enterprises ensure the scale and scope of the social relationship network through the layout of the business ecosystem, and then implement the centralized strategy to obtain a greater cost advantage.

Core enterprises use organizational trust, personal relationships and other factors to ensure the scale and scope of the social network, allowing core companies to implement centralized strategies at lower cost to obtain greater cost advantages.

The Iterative Effect of Cross-Border Entrepreneurship on Ecological Advantages

After the previous analysis and the argumentation of the three case enterprises, the paper summarizes the impact of ecological advantages on the cross-border entrepreneurship of core enterprises and its mechanism of action. So cross-border entrepreneurial activities will have an impact on the company's ecological advantage? The answer is yes. Driven by different ecological advantages, enterprises will also make different strategic decisions, and these strategic decisions all guarantee that enterprises will continue to gain ecological advantages. The core enterprises in the business ecosystem implement the diversification strategy, enrich the channels of information acquisition, and improve the construction of the business ecosystem, so that the knowledge resources of the enterprise will be more diverse and higher quality. By implementing the differentiation strategy, we will further expand our technological potential and continuously update our technology accumulation to maintain a leading position in the industry. By implementing a centralized strategy, we will continue to reduce the cost of resource acquisition and information integration, thereby expanding the social network and enriching the entrepreneur's own network of resources.

Throughout the three cases of Tencent, Xiaomi, and Alibaba, they all occupy the core position of the Internet ecology. All three companies are good at using their own ecological advantages to complete the iterative upgrade of enterprises, they realize the expansion of new fields through the strategic choices of cross-border entrepreneurial activities, and build a more complete network of business ecosystems to achieve sustainable development. After the social market became saturated, Tencent turned its attention from the PC side to the mobile side, and entered the mobile communication field to develop WeChat, and then relied on QQ and WeChat to form a monopoly in the social field. The success of WeChat has enabled Tencent's vision, technology accumulation and social network to rise to the next level, and then complete the iteration of ecological advantages through the layout of multiple ecological networks. Xiaomi has occupied a large market share in the low-end mobile phone market through precise market positioning and technological advantages. After that, Lei Jun took the initiative to expand into the smart home industry in order to seek a broader development space. After the success of Xiaomi Ecology, Xiaomi's own ecological advantage It has been consolidated and strengthened in all aspects. The field positioning of Xiaomi Mobile Phone Market has gradually moved from the low-end machine to the mid-range machine. Alibaba has also fallen into a short-term bottleneck after B2B is the largest in the country. After that, Ma Yun took the initiative to change and transformed Alibaba into an integrated Internet service provider. Through the strong performance of cloud computing and financial services, Alibaba's The corporate image has been greatly improved, and the ecological advantages of Alibaba have been expanded in all aspects.

The cross-border entrepreneurial activities of core enterprises enable enterprises to complete self-upgrading, consolidate and expand ecological advantages, and build a more complete business ecosystem.

Model Testing

After the above analysis and discussion of the case, the cross-border entrepreneurial activities of each case enterprise were sorted out, and the model was established under different conditions.

It can be seen from Table 1 that Tencent, Xiaomi and Alibaba, three representative typical enterprise cases, can well support the interaction model of ecological advantages and cross-border entrepreneurial activities constructed in the previous article under the replication logic of multi-case studies.

In the cross-border entrepreneurial activities, the core enterprises in the business ecosystem identify the entrepreneurial opportunities based on the knowledge resources of the ecological dominance level, complete the cognitive upgrade in the cross-border search process, and finally drive the enterprise to implement the diversification

Table 1. Specific activities of the three case enterprises in the process of cross-border entrepreneurship

		Tencent	Xiaomi	Alibaba
The role of ecological advantages in the process of cross-border entrepreneurship	Knowledge resource	Zhang Xiaolong's success in developing QQ mailbox before WeChat	Lei Jun served as CEO of Jinshan for ten years before setting up Xiaomi, he has excellent management experience and research and development skills.	Ma Yun has a solid B2B entrepreneurial foundation before building the Ali ecosystem and studied at Cheung Kong Graduate School of Business.
	Technology accumulation	Be the first one to complete the research and development of WeChat, the products are irreplaceable	Use technology advantages to create high cost performance	Strong cloud computing capability is the key to the ecological layout of Ali products
	social relationship	Build a multi-diversity network that spans social, news, film, games, etc.	Building the ecological layout of the Internet of Things in Xiaomi Home	Establish a B2B ecological cluster based on Taobao and transform into an integrated service provider
The Mechanism of Ecological Advantages on Cross-border Entrepreneurial Activities	Implement a diversification strategy through cognitive upgrades	After the 3Q war, Ma Huateng focused on forming the core competitiveness of the company.	Lei Jun divides the development of the Internet into three phases. Xiaomi is close to the Internet company by technology companies.	Ma Yun recognizes the gap in the field of Internet finance and expands the vertical layout of B2B to the upstream and downstream of the supply chain.
	Implementing a differentiated strategy through technological advancement	Ma Huateng recruited Zhang Xiaolong to maintain a leading position in technology research and development	Xiaomi hired Liu De, director of the design department of Beijing University of Science and Technology, to supervise industrial design and supply chain management, and increase investment in research and development.	Ma Yun increased the investment of Alibaba Cloud to ensure the technological advantages in the Internet era.
	Implementing a centralized strategy through the construction of a social network	Ma Huateng used the early Tencent social dividend to complete the multi-ecological layout and actively responded to national policies.	Lei Jun's network of resources accumulated during his tenure as CEO in Jinshan provides the basis for Xiaomi's IoT layout.	Ma Yun's image of a conscience entrepreneur has made the public's acceptance of Ali products higher.
The iterative effect of cross-border entrepreneurship on ecological advantages		The success of WeChat allowed Tencent to gain advantages in knowledge resources, technology accumulation, and social relations, and further expand the ecosystem layout.	The layout of the Internet of Things has enabled Xiaomi's technical potential to continue to improve, and mobile phone positioning has gradually shifted from the low end to the mid-end machine.	Alibaba gradually moves closer to Internet integrated service providers. The support of cloud computing and ant finance makes Taobao triumphant all the way.

strategy; based on the ecological dominance The level of technology accumulation after the identification of entrepreneurial opportunities, and the cross-border search stage through technological introduction and technological innovation to achieve technological progress, drive companies to implement differentiated strategies; based on the ecological advantages of the social relationship to identify entrepreneurial opportunities, and cross-border search In the process, a social relationship network is constructed to drive the enterprise to implement a centralized strategy.

CONCLUSION

In an increasingly complex industrial environment, the traditional competitive advantage theory is no longer perfectly applicable. Core companies need to focus on building new ecological advantages to maintain their core competitive position. Based on the perspective of ecological advantages, this paper gathers the cross-border entrepreneurial activities of core enterprises and selects three companies that have successfully deployed the business ecosystem in the Internet field to conduct case studies. The main research conclusions include the following points

The ecological advantage can be simply understood as the competitive advantage that the core enterprise gains based on its advantageous position in the business ecosystem. The main difference between it and the traditional competitive advantage is that the traditional competitive advantage is often limited to the enterprise itself, and the ecological advantage emphasizes the synergy between the enterprise and the external environment. In the perspective of ecological advantages, companies are no longer alone, but develop together.

Cross-border entrepreneurship of core enterprises is mainly through the stages of opportunity identification, cross-border search and strategic selection. Based on their own ecological advantages, the core enterprises identify entrepreneurial opportunities, complete active or passive upgrades through cross-border search, and implement cross-border entrepreneurial strategies that are consistent with the dimensions of ecological advantages.

Ecological advantages have a guiding role for cross-border entrepreneurship, and cross-border entrepreneurial activities make ecological advantages complete iteration in turn. Under the advantage of knowledge resources, core enterprises complete cognitive upgrades and choose to implement diversification strategies, which will further expand their knowledge resources advantages. Under the advantage of technology accumulation, complete technological progress, choose to implement differentiated strategy, make technology constantly updated, and ensure the leading position in the industry. Under the advantage of social relations, actively construct a social relationship network, choose to implement a centralized strategy, continue to reduce the cost of resource acquisition and information integration, and maintain the advantages of social relations.

The theoretical significance of this research is to clarify the new concept of ecological advantage and enrich the theory of competitive advantage. The definition, source and connotation of ecological advantage are explained, and the differences between ecological advantage and traditional competitive advantage are discussed in the article, which further enriches the theory of competitive advantage. Through case studies of three representative companies, following the replication logic and theoretical sampling rules of multiple case studies, a detailed analysis of the cross-border entrepreneurship of a particular type of company, a core company, and discussion of both ecological advantages and cross-border entrepreneurship The circular logical relationship between them has expanded the academic circles' research on the advantages and entrepreneurial relationships.

Regarding practical contributions, the cross-border entrepreneurial activities of core companies are the key to obtaining ecological advantages. In the face of a complex and changing business environment, core companies in the business ecosystem want to take the lead in cross-border entrepreneurial activities and must make full use of their own ecology advantage.

For core companies in the business ecosystem, it is necessary to complete the transformation from knowledge resources to cognitive upgrade based on knowledge reserve and experience accumulation, and then approach the strategic goal of diversification; complete technology through technology introduction and technological innovation Upgrade and move closer to the strategic goals of differentiation; by building a network of social relationships, practice a centralized strategy to gain a greater cost advantage.

REFERENCES

Barney, J. B. (1991). Firm resources and sustained competitive advantage. *Advances in Strategic Management*, *17*(1), 3–10.

Brunsman, K. J., & Sharfman, M. P. (1993). Strategic choices and niche movements: a probabilistic model of organizational selection and mortality. *Academy of Management Annual Meeting Proceedings, 1993*(1), 2-6. 10.5465/ambpp.1993.10315156

Burgelman, R. A., & Grove, A. S. (1996). Strategic dissonance. *California Management Review*, *38*(2), 8–28. doi:10.2307/41165830

Burgelman, R. A., & Grove, A. S. (2007). Cross-boundary disruptors: Powerful inter-industry entrepreneurial change agents. *Research Papers*, *1*(3-4), 315–327. doi:10.1002ej.27

Carpenter, M., Sanders, G., & Education, P. (2015). Strategic management: pearson new international edition: concepts and cases. *Long Range Planning, 29*(6), 907-908.

Foss, N. J., Knudsen, C., & Montgomery, C. A. (1995). An Exploration of Common Ground: Integrating Evolutionary and Strategic Theories of the Firm. *Resource-Based and Evolutionary Theories of the Firm: Towards a Synthesis*.

Friesen, P. H., & Miller, D. (2007). A mathematical model of the adaptive behaviour of organizations. *Journal of Management Studies*, *23*(1), 1–25. doi:10.1111/j.1467-6486.1986.tb00932.x

Gay, B., & Dousset, B. (2005). Innovation and network structural dynamics: Study of the alliance network of a major sector of the biotechnology industry. *Research Policy*, *34*(10), 1457–1475. doi:10.1016/j.respol.2005.07.001

Ghemawat, P. (1995). Competitive advantage and internal organization: Nucor revisited. *Journal of Economics & Management Strategy*, *3*(4), 685–717. doi:10.1111/j.1430-9134.1995.00685.x

Graebner, E. M. E. (2007). Theory building from cases: Opportunities and challenges. *Academy of Management Journal*, *50*(1), 25–32. doi:10.5465/amj.2007.24160888

Hannan, M., & Freeman, J. (1977). *The population ecology of organizations*. Social Science Electronic Publishing. doi:10.1086/226424

Hegger, D. L. T., Vliet, J. V., & Vliet, B. J. M. V. (2007). Niche management and its contribution to regime change: The case of innovation in sanitation. *Technology Analysis and Strategic Management*, *19*(6), 729–746. doi:10.1080/09537320701711215

Iansiti, M., Levien, R., Iansiti, M., & Levien, R. (2004). The keystone advantage: What the new dynamics of business ecosystems mean for strategy, innovation, and sustainability. *Future Survey*, *20*(2), 88–90.

Iansiti, M., Levien, R., Iansiti, M., & Levien, R. (2004). The keystone advantage: What the new dynamics of business ecosystems mean for strategy, innovation, and sustainability. *Future Survey*, *20*(2), 88–90.

Jacobides, M. G., & Winter, S. G. (2007). Entrepreneurship and firm boundaries: The theory of a firm. *Journal of Management Studies*, *44*(7), 1213–1241. doi:10.1111/j.1467-6486.2007.00726.x

Jiang, Y., & Chen, C. C. (2018). Integrating Knowledge Activities for Team Innovation: Effects of Transformational Leadership. *Journal of Management, 44*(5), 1819–1847. doi:10.1177/0149206316628641

Kemp, R., Schot, J., & Hoogma, R. (1998). Regime shifts to sustainability through processes of niche formation: The approach of strategic niche management. *Technology Analysis and Strategic Management, 10*(2), 175–198. doi:10.1080/09537329808524310

Lorenzoni, G., & Baden-Fuller, C. (1995). Creating a strategic center to manage a web of partners. *California Management Review, 37*(3), 146–163. doi:10.2307/41165803

Moore, J. F. (1999). Predators and prey: A new ecology of competition. *Harvard Business Review, 71*(3), 75–86. PMID:10126156

Penrose, E. T. (1995). The theory of the growth of the firm. Oxford, UK: Oxford University Press.

Peteraf, M. A., & Barney, J. B. (2003). Integrating management and economic perspectives on corporate strategy unraveling the resource-based tangle. *Managerial and Decision Economics, 24*(4), 309–323. doi:10.1002/mde.1126

Pierce, L. (2008). *Big losses in ecosystem niches: how core firm decisions drive complementary product shakeouts*. Ssrn Electronic Journal.

Porter, M. (1990). Competitive advantage of nations. *Competitive Intelligence Review, 1*(1), 14-14.

Smith, A., & Raven, R. (2012). What is protective space? reconsidering niches in transitions to sustainability. *Research Policy, 41*(6), 1025–1036. doi:10.1016/j.respol.2011.12.012

Tansley, A. G. (1935). The use and abuse of vegetational concepts and terms. *Ecology, 16*(3), 284–307. doi:10.2307/1930070

Weifeng, J., & Xinghua, D. (2010). Research on core enterprise's knowledge flow-coupling control in technological innovation network. *Science Research Management*.

Zahra, S. A. (1996). Goverance, ownership, and corporate entrepreneurship: The moderating impact of industry technological opportunities. *Academy of Management Journal, 39*(6), 1713–1735. doi:10.5465/257076

Zhu, C. (2019). Big data as a governance mechanism. *Review of Financial Studies, 32*(5), 2021–2061. doi:10.1093/rfs/hhy081

Chapter 5
The Evaluation of Financial Ecological Environment and Optimization Research in Liaoning Province:
Based on the Empirical Research With Factor Analysis and Panel Threshold 2008-2014

Yu Wang
Dalian University of Technology, China

Haoyang Gao
Dalian University of Technology, China

Haomin Du
Dalian University of Technology, China

Kaifeng Wu
Dalian University of Technology, China

Yuqing Chen
Dalian University of Technology, China

DOI: 10.4018/978-1-7998-3495-3.ch005

ABSTRACT

This chapter constructs a system of financial ecological environment that is based on the multiple indicators: economic foundation, financial development, and institutional environment of 14 cities in Liaoning Province from 2008 to 2014. In addition, it supplements a measurement of influence of financial quality and uses the factor analysis method and panel threshold model to explore the dynamic evolution characteristics and optimization route of financial ecological environment. The empirical study shows that (1) the whole trend performs as an inversed U shape with the characteristics of rising at first and then declining and its influential mechanisms are disparate in different periods; (2) the financial ecological environment qualities of coastal cities rank in the upper and middle reaches of the overall rankings, while the qualities of inland cities comparatively fall behind; (3) the impact of urban financial ecological environment on economic growth in Liaoning Province presents as a non-linear single threshold, and the threshold values are 0.48, 0.52, 0.46, and 0.41, respectively.

INTRODUCTION

Facing the downward pressure on the new normal of China's economy growth, the economy of the Northeast China has experienced a cliff fall. This "New Northeast Provinces Phenomenon" arouses people's wide concern. The economy of Liaoning Province, in particular, fell from the seventh largest in 2014 to the tenth in 2015. According to the work report on the government in 2016, the growth rate of GDP in Liaoning Province in 2015 increased by 3% over the previous year, which was lower than the national average of 6.9%, which also ranked the last, compared with the GDP growth rate of other 30 provinces, and it was 0.1 percentages lower than the GDP growth rate of Shanxi Province. The reasons for the gap: i) most industries in Liaoning Province are excessively concentrated on resource-based industries which depend on coal, electricity and oil. On the basis of regional industrialization, the poor development of the service industry is obvious, especially in high-tech industries; ii) from another perspective, financial constraints are the core issues that restrict the development of regional high-tech industries. A well-functioning financial ecological environment can help release the pressure of financing constraints of enterprises, and government governance, economic basis, financial development and institutional culture, to some extent, can have a beneficial influence on constituting the financial ecological environment. However, based on the current situation of Liaoning Province's financial ecological environment, from one aspect, the government's improper intervention in finance still exists, the relationship between banks and enterprises is uncoordinated, and the general competitive power of financial institutions is not tight. On the other aspect, the present model of financial development which focuses on quantity rather than quality in Liaoning Province can not significantly play its role in promoting economic growth. Besides, there is a dilemma of increasing the quantity and quality of finance simultaneously. Therefore, taking the view of Liaoning Province's financial ecological environment as a starting point, it is logical to build a reasonable indicator evaluation system and then control the impact of different levels of financial ecological environment indicators on economy development, providing policy references for seeking for the optimization of Liaoning Province's financial ecological environment.

Overview of Financial Ecological Environment

Financial ecological environment is an ecological-like concept. The content of using ecological methods to study financial system is relatively broad, while there is no recognized definition so far. Most of the existing studies define the connotation and extension of this concept from a special or a general perspective. The special sense of financial ecological environment theory includes social credit system, policies and laws. For example, Zhou Xiaochuan (2004) contends that financial ecology environment is a micro-level financial environment, including laws, social credit system, accounting and auditing standards, intermediary service system, the progress of enterprise reformation and the relationship between banks and enterprises (Xiaochuan 2004). Suning (2005) contends that financial ecology is a metaphor. It is not a representation of the internal operation of the financial industry, but a concept of ecology to describe the external environment of the financial industry Suning (2005). This perspective mainly emphasizes the connotation of financial ecological environment and its influence on the behavior and operation results of financial institutions from a static point of view. The general financial ecological environment theory includes cultural environment, economy environment, legislative environment and so on. Wang Laixi (2012) illustrates that financial ecology is an environmental condition which is consisted of politics, society, culture, ideologics, institutions, policy constraints, micro-foundation, laws and regulations, traditional customs and other factors, what financial structure and financial activities need to face. It has a variety of constraints and influences on the behavior and performance evaluation of financial institutions (Laixi, 2012). In addition, some research defines the financial ecological environment from the perspective of dynamic balance of system theory. Xu Noojin (2005) summarizes the financial ecology as a dynamic equilibrium system with certain structural characteristics and functions which is formed by division of labour and cooperation in order to survive and develop in the long process of close relationship and interaction with various financial environment and internal financial organizations (Noujin 2005). Jin Xinxue and Xie Bangchang (2014) pointed out that the financial ecology was a dynamic and balanced system of interdependence and restriction formed between financial subjects and the internal and external environments in which they lived and developed (Xinxue and Bangchang 2014).

As the concept of the financial ecological environment has received more and more attention, many scholars have begun to study its formation direction and practical impact. Han Hongben (2019) pointed out that the development of the financial ecosystem was closely related to the attractiveness of cities. The development of China's economy has gradually formed a regional "aggregation effect", and a core area of economic development unique to the region has been formed around key cities. This created a financial environment with regional characteristics and formed a financial ecosystem. The level of regional economic development and the operating efficiency of the financial industry are largely affected by the quality of the regional financial ecological environment. In this regard, it becomes necessary to establish a reasonable evaluation index system (Hongben 2019). Zhao Chengjing (2019) proposed the financial ecological cycle system, and pointed out that in order to realize the benign cycle of the entire financial ecological environment of the city, it was necessary to find the shortcomings and deficiencies in it to optimize the financial development environment. She redefined the financial ecological environment and clarifies that a comprehensive financial ecosystem was complex and high-risk, just like the natural ecosystem. It needs to keep on advancing, innovating, and evolving, except that companies remain active in the market The government and intermediary agencies should also provide a high degree of cooperation (Chengjing 2019). Tang Caixia (2019) studied the impact of financial ecological environment on companies. She proposed that the development of the financial ecological environment would not only reduce the cash flow sensitivity of listed companies, alleviate the pressure on financing, but also made the existing cash of the company which had a higher marginal value. The level of corporate governance has greatly affected the functioning of the financial ecological environment (Chengjing 2019).

The significant differences in the understanding of financial ecological environment among existing studies are as follows: (1) Evaluation indicators. Xu Xiaolin (2005) measured the quality of financial ecological environment in three cities by the rate of economic return on capital (Xiaolin 2005). Chen Zheming (2006) believes that the evaluation indicator should at least include the level of economic development, financial development, social credit and financial ecological security system (Zheming 2006) .The research group of Luoyang Branch of the People's Bank of China has given 127 quantitative and qualitative evaluation indicators (Research Group 2006). Huang Guoping (2007) assessed the quality of financial ecological environment of all provinces and municipalities in China from three dimensions: the current situation of financial system, the financial ecological environment and the efficiency of financial ecological system. He believed that the financial ecological environment of Fujian Province was better (Guoping and Yuhui 2007). Zhou Jing et al. (2012) assessed the financial ecological environment of 31 provinces and municipalities in China based on four first-level indicators: economic basis, financial resources, government finance and social credit (Jing and Peijia 2012). (2) Evaluation methods Wang Zujie (2006) and Huang Guoping (2007) respectively used Analytic Hierarchy Process (AHP) to construct the indicator system for evaluating regional financial ecological environment. Zhang Ruihuai (2007) established a comprehensive evaluation model of rural financial ecological environment by introducing BP Artificial Neural Network (ANN). Hubin (2009), Xie Taifeng (2010) and Zhang Xiaofeng (2012) used factor analysis method to establish their financial ecological environment evaluation models respectively (Bin 2009; Taifeng and Lu 2010; Xiaofeng 2012). Jin Jie (2009) used SWOT analysis method to analyze the advantages, disadvantages, opportunities and challenges of financial ecological environment in Liaoning province and their relationship with economic development from both qualitative and quantitative perspectives, and formed a reasonable understanding of financial ecological environment in Liaoning province (Jie 2009). Zhang Jun et al. (2014) evaluated the financial ecological environment of 29 provinces and municipalities in China with the principal component analysis method, and found that Fujian province scored 2.6 points, ranking 14th (Jun 2014). Ni Jiajin (2018) used a genetic algorithm-based projection tracking method to model 15 indicators extended from the economic foundation and financial resources, and obtained the relationship between financial ecological development and an analysis of the impact of the financial ecological environment on economic growth.

Research on the Optimization of Financial Ecological Environment

After the era of post-crisis, financial capital is affected by risk differences of regional finance and the trend from high-risk areas to low-risk areas is increasingly significant,.The financial ecological environment is directly related to the sustainable development of local enterprises, so each region is more committed to optimizing the financial ecological environment. Pan Jun (2015) analyzed the impact of financial ecological environment on corporate financing constraints and government debt financing costs, and believed that a good financial ecological environment can reduce government debt financing costs and ease corporate financing constraints (Jiajin 2018). Li Yuanyuan (2019) analyzed the impact of financial ecological environment on state-owned enterprises and non-state-owned enterprises, and pointed out that non-state-owned enterprises are more sensitive to changes in financial ecological environment. Xiang Lin (2010) pointed out that the optimization mode of financial ecological environment by constructing the measurement indicator of financial ecological environment and the econometric model of economic growth, indicating that only by improving regional economic development and people's living standards, and strengthening dwellers' education of culture and specialized knowledge, then the financial ecological environment can be fundamentally improved (Chao 2010). Ji Minghui et al. (2011) pointed out that the level of social credit determines the quality of financial ecological environment. Financial ecological environment reflects the overall level of social credit. Supported by the construction of moral culture and guaranteed by the construction of legal culture, it can enhance the credit awareness of the whole people. The main ways include improving credit evaluation mechanism, system and methods, doing a good job in propaganda of credit culture (Wei 2011). Wei Zhihua (2014) pointed out that the financial supervision mechanism should be improved, the risk of financial institutions should be assessed timely, comprehensively and accurately, and the critical level of risk of financial institutions should be determined. To achieve this goal, the establishment and improvement of a unified and sound accounting system, risk measurement of the assets of financial institutions, pre-approval and in-process supervision and real-time supervision, actively promoting the interaction and cooperation between financial regulators are all indispensable.

Research Review and Innovation

First of all, in the establishment of evaluation indicator system, scholars generally choose several indicators:economic basis, financial development status, legal environment and credit level,and evaluate the regional financial ecological environment. However, in the design of sub-variable indicators of regional financial development level, which is an important factor affecting the financial ecological environment, there is usually a lack of financial efficiency indicators reflecting the development degree of regional financial quality, and most of them remain in the determination of financial quantitative indicators. Secondly, the current literature mostly evaluates and ranks the financial ecological environment of different regions based on the cross-sectional data of specific years, and seldom reveals the dynamic change process of regional financial ecological environment. Thirdly, Ye Chusheng, (2005)believes that due to the rootlessness of financial development theory, the evaluation of regional financial development usually needs to be carried out by means of the research idea of economic growth model. Therefore, the exploration of the optimization path of regional financial ecological environment cannot be carried out without the fact that the function of regional financial development support real economic growth. This paper concludes that the impact of financial ecological environment on economic growth in Liaoning Province is characterized by a nonlinear single threshold, which can be exceeded by three main ways: improving economic basis, financial development and institutional environment. Besides,

The possible innovations of this paper: (1) Adding a financial efficiency variable can reflect financial quality in the construction of financial ecological environment indicator system. (2) Based on the time series variables of 2008-2014, this paper constructs and evaluates the financial ecological environment indicator of Liaoning Province, and then reveals its dynamic evolution characteristics. (3)The threshold model is used to couple the financial ecological environment indicator and economic growth indicator of Liaoning Province, and then to explore the reasonable optimization interval.

CONSTRUCTION AND EVALUATION OF FINANCIAL ECOLOGICAL ENVIRONMENT INDICATOR IN LIAONING PROVINCE

Construction of Evaluation Indicators System

Following the 15 indicators of three aspects: regional economic foundation, financial development and institutional environment, this paper constructs the overall evaluation indicator system of financial ecological environment in Liaoning Province (Xiangyou, 2015), further supplements the financial efficiency indicators reflecting the development of financial quality in the sub-indicators of financial development level (Čihák, 2013), as detailed in Table 1. Economic basis refers to the sum of production relations determined by the productivity of a certain stage of social development. It is the foundation on which the financial industry exists and develops, and is an important part of the financial ecological environment. Financial development is the process of increasing the size of financial transactions and the heightening of the financial industry, leading to continuous improvement in financial efficiency. The higher the level of financial development is, the better the financial ecological environment is. The institutional environment is a set of basic political, social, and legal foundational rules that establish the basis for production, exchange, and distribution. It is an important component of the external operating environment of the financial industry and the basis for the orderly operation of the financial industry.

For the measurement of regional financial efficiency indicators, this paper uses three-stage DEA model proposed by Fried et al (2002) to calculate the financial efficiency indicators of Liaoning Province and the data is refined into the level of prefecture-level cities (Fired and Lovell 2002), using the financial efficiency indicators to reflect the perfection of regional financial quality. The model not only evaluates the efficiency of decision making units better, but also effectively eliminates the influence of uncontrollable factors such as environmental factors and random factors on the efficiency of the system itself. In the first stage, use the traditional non-parametric Malmquist indicator model to calculate the total factor productivity from the perspective of financial input-output; in the second stage, use the SFA model to decompose the input relaxation in the first stage; and in the third stage, use the DEA model with financial inputs that has been adjusted.

Specifically, DEAP 2.1 and Frontier software were used to calculate the financial efficiency changes of cities in Liaoning Province. In the data selection, the financial value added of each city in 2008-2014 was used as the output variable, and the fixed capital stock as well as the number of employees were used as input variables (Li Cangshu, 2014). Jin Chunyu (2013) select regional economic development level (per capita GDP), change in the wealth of residents and enterprises (deducting the fiscal revenue in GDP/GDP in the current year), industrial structure (the ratio between service industry output and GDP), people's living standards (1 minus Engel

Table 1. Financial Ecological Environment Evaluating Indicators

Target Level	Domain Level	Indicator Level
		X1: Regional GDP growth rate (%)
		X2: GDP growth rate per capita (%)
		X3: Growth rate of fixed asset investment (%)
	Economic Basis	X4: Financial revenue (100 million yuan)
		X5: Total retail sales of consumer goods (100 million yuan)
		X6: Actual use of foreign direct investment (US$10,000)
Financial Ecological		X7: The number of listed companies (home)
Environment		X8: Regional financial efficiency
	Financial Development	X9: Per capita disposable income of urban residents (yuan)
		X10: Year-end loan balance growth rate of financial institutions (%)
		X11: Growth rate of financial institutions' year-end deposit balance (%)
		X12: Number of law firms (number)
	Institutional Environment	X13: Total population at the end of the year (10,000 people)
		X14: Household consumption level (yuan/person)
		X15: Total import and export (100 million yuan)

coefficient) and deposits of regional financial institutions (bank deposits/GDP) as environmental variables (Chunyo, Zhe, Haobo 2013). Each input and output indicator data comes from Liaoning Statistical Yearbook (2009-2015), Liaoning Financial Statistical Yearbook (2009-2015) and Liaoning City Yearbook (2009-2015).

Evaluation Method

In order to ensure the validity and reliability of the evaluation indicators, it is necessary to establish a multi-level and multi-indicator financial ecological environment evaluation system. Since the traditional analytic hierarchy process has obvious subjectivity when determining weights, this paper uses a more objective factor analysis method to evaluate indicators. By analyzing the relationship between those variables, we can classify the closely related variables into one class and find some common factors that can represent the original variables, so that they can reflect most of the information of the original variables.

There are n variables $x_1, x_2, \ldots, x_n$. If these variables can be represented by a linear combination of m(m<n) factors $f_1, f_2, \ldots, f_n$, you can get the expressions of these n variables based on factor analysis:

$$\begin{cases} x_1 = a_1 f_1 + a_2 f_2 + \ldots + a_{1m} fm + \varepsilon_1 \\ x_2 = a_2 f_1 + a_2 f_2 + \ldots + a_{2m} fm + \varepsilon_2 \\ \ldots \\ x_n = a_{n1} f_1 + a_{n2} f_2 + \ldots + a_m fm + \varepsilon_n \end{cases} \tag{1}$$

The matrix expression of equation (1) can be converted to $X=FA+\varepsilon$, F is a factor, which is also called the common factor because it appears in the linear expression of each original variable. $A=(q)$, $i=1,2,\ldots,n$; $j=1,2,\ldots,m$, is the factor load matrix, while $\varepsilon \sim N(0,1)$ is a special factor which is the part of the original variable that cannot be explained by the factor.

Evaluation of Financial Ecological Environment Indicators

Data Standardization

In order to accurately reflect the impact and impact direction of each financial ecological environment influencing factor, the selected indicators must be standardized first to eliminate the differences caused by different measurement units. The common method of standardization is the Z-score method, and the 15 variables

Table 2. Statistics of Financial Ecological Environment Indicator

	Period	Min	Max	Prob	Std
Zx1	7	-1.76938	1.11527	.0000000	1.00000000
Zx2	7	-1.79408	1.10150	.0000000	1.00000000
Zx3	7	-1.67995	1.24765	.0000000	1.00000000
Zx4	7	-1.40001	1.04891	.0000000	1.00000000
Zx5	7	-1.29058	1.44638	.0000000	1.00000000
Zx6	7	-1.58207	1.05046	.0000000	1.00000000
Zx7	7	-1.38286	1.14236	.0000000	1.00000000
Zx8	7	-1.21550	1.32525	.0000000	1.00000000
Zx9	7	-1.20852	1.52453	.0000000	1.00000000
Zx10	7	-.96748	1.89182	.0000000	1.00000000
Zx11	7	-1.46374	1.43306	.0000000	1.00000000
Zx12	7	-1.25637	1.57006	.0000000	1.00000000
Zx13	7	-1.52962	1.23159	.0000000	1.00000000
Zx14	7	-1.25845	1.39068	.0000000	1.00000000
Zx15	7	-1.42751	1.09137	.0000000	1.00000000

after standardization are named as $zx_1, zx_2, \ldots, zx_{15}$. Table 2 shows the descriptive statistics of the financial ecological environment indicators of Liaoning Province after standardization.

Through standardization, the absolute values of correlation coefficients among the indicators of Financial Ecological Environment in Liaoning Province are all above 0.3, demonstrating that the data is suitable for factor analysis method. The chi-squared value of the standardized data through Bartlett's test of sphericity is 327.409 and the probability is 0.000; the Kaiser-Meyer-Olkin measure of sampling adequacy value is 0.549, indicating that the correlation coefficient matrix of the standardized data is not a unit matrix, and consequently factor analysis method is feasible.

Extraction of Common Factors

Extraction of common factors is a vital part of factor analysis. Table 3 gives three common factors which affect the Financial Ecological Environment of Liaoning Province and their variance contribution rate.

The cumulative variance contribution rate of the three common factors is 97.466%. It shows that the three common factors contain 97.466% information of 15 original

Table 3. Common Factor and Variance Contribution

Component	Initial Eigenvalues			Extraction Sums of Squared Loadings			Rotation Sums of Squared Loadings		
	Total	% of Variance	Cumulative %	Total	% of Variance	Cumulative %	Total	% of Variance	Cumulative %
1	12.737	84.914	84.914	12.737	84.914	84.914	6.507	43.377	43.377
2	1.355	9.037	93.951	1.355	9.037	93.951	4.509	30.063	73.440
3	.527	3.516	97.466	.527	3.516	97.466	3.604	24.027	97.466

variables, which can better replace the original variables and can reasonably evaluate the Financial Ecological Environment of Liaoning Province. In order to make the common factor better explain the original variables, by rotating factors, the factor loading matrix can be obtained.

Table 4 shows that the load on the first factor of 8 indicators, which reflect the economic foundation of Liaoning Province, exceeds 0.6, the total variance contribution rate exceeds 84%. It is known that the economic base is the most important factor affecting the financial ecological environment of Liaoning Province. A total of 6 indicators reflecting the level of financial development in Liaoning Province have

Table 4. Rotating Component Matrix

	Components		
	1	2	3
Zx1	-.477	-.660	.563
Zx2	-.458	-.674	.564
Zx3	-.451	-.875	-.047
Zx4	.878	.369	-.302
Zx5	.717	.590	-.353
Zx6	.916	.334	-.216
Zx7	.825	.450	-.274
Zx8	.740	.544	-.387
Zx9	.681	.621	-.375
Zx10	-.182	-.213	.929
Zx11	-.580	-.644	.418
Zx12	.688	.635	-.336
Zx13	-.319	-.060	.907
Zx14	.732	.569	-.366
Zx15	.754	.426	-.482

a load of more than 0.5 in the second factor quotient, the total variance contribution rate exceeds 9%, indicating that the level of financial development is an important factor influencing the financial ecological environment of Liaoning Province. The load on the third factor of 4 indicators, which reflect the credit situation of Liaoning Province, exceeds 0.5, and the total variance contribution rate is about 3%, indicating that the regional credit situation has a certain impact on the financial ecological environment.

Common Factor Score

Using the regression method of factor analysis, a matrix of common factor score coefficients as shown in Table 5 can be obtained. According to Table 5, linear combinations of standardized variables are used to express common factors, and the scoring function of common factors is

$$\begin{cases} f_1 = 0.254zx_1 + 0.282zx_2 + ?+ 0.213zx_{15} \\ f_2 = -0.326zx_1 - 0.358zx_2 + ?- 0.173zx_{15} \\ f_3 = 0.151zx_1 + 0.155zx_2 + ?- 0.058zx_{15} \end{cases} \quad (2)$$

Table 5. Score coefficient matrix of Common Factor

	Factor				Factor		
	f1	f2	f3		f1	f2	f3
Zx1	0.254	-0.326	0.151	Zx9	0.012	0.132	0.01
Zx2	0.282	-0.358	0.155	Zx10	0.243	0.002	0.499
Zx3	0.302	-0.671	-0.239	Zx11	0.11	-0.238	0.039
Zx4	0.419	-0.324	0.076	Zx12	0.016	0.147	0.038
Zx5	0.076	0.067	0.029	Zx13	-0.014	0.294	0.468
Zx6	0.504	-0.387	0.134	Zx14	0.104	0.028	0.023
Zx7	0.311	-0.18	0.09	Zx15	0.213	-0.173	-0.058
Zx8	0.126	-0.01	0.009				

Substituting the factor score coefficients in Table 5 into equation (2) can calculate the scores of the three common factors. Then use the variance contribution rate of each common factor as the weight, through formula (3):

$$f = \frac{\lambda_1}{\lambda_1 + \lambda_2 + \lambda_3} f_1 + \frac{\lambda_2}{\lambda_1 + \lambda_2 + \lambda_3} f_2 + \frac{\lambda_3}{\lambda_1 + \lambda_2 + \lambda_3} f_3 \quad (3)$$

The comprehensive factor scores of the financial ecological environment of Liaoning Province from 2008 to 2014 can be obtained (see Figure 1). Where λ is the initial eigenvalue of each common factor, Table 3 shows λ_1=12.737, λ_2=1.355, λ_3=0.527.

As shown in line Graph 1, in the view of time line, the financial ecological environment of Liaoning Province generally shows a inverted U characteristics of rising and then decreasing. First of all, from 2008 to 2012, the financial ecological environment of Liaoning Province is optimized year by year. Although the financial crisis has caused severe deterioration on the world economy, the national economy quickly emerges from the shadow of the crisis because of the benefit from the country's overall proactive fiscal policy and the quantitative easing of monetary policy by injecting a large amount of liquidity into the economy. It is obvious that there has also been a marked improvement in the economic recovery of Liaoning Province. Therefore, from the perspective of economic base, the policy has a major positive impact on the improvement of the financial ecological environment in Liaoning Province. During this period, the government began to strengthen the supervision of the financial industry and the control of non-performing loans and venture capital of banks; from the perspective of the macro-legal system environment, it is also conducive to upgrading the financial ecological environment of Liaoning Province. Considering the core factor, financial development, there are different ways to improve the ecological financial environment from the quantitative and quality levels. Wang Yu (2017) pointed out that during 2008-2011, China's financial industry's total factor productivity indicator showed a downward trend (although it rebounded slightly in 2009), while the technological progress indicator of financial industry continued to decline. However, during this period, due to the impact of quantitative easing monetary policy, the scale efficiency indicator of the financial industry showed an upward trend. This shows that although the technological progress of the Liaoning financial industry slowed down or even regressed in the post-crisis period, the continuous expansion of the financial scale avoided the substantial decline in the overall efficiency of the financial industry. Secondly, from 2012 to 2014, the financial ecological environment in Liaoning Province has deteriorated again. From the perspective of the impact of financial development, with the gradual withdrawal of quantitative easing policy, the development of the scale of the financial industry is steadily weakening as a means of adjustment and assistance to mitigate external shocks. From the perspective of economic fundamentals, the main reason is the correction of the economic data fraud in Liaoning Province and the negative

Figure 1. Financial Ecological Environment Indicator 2008-2014

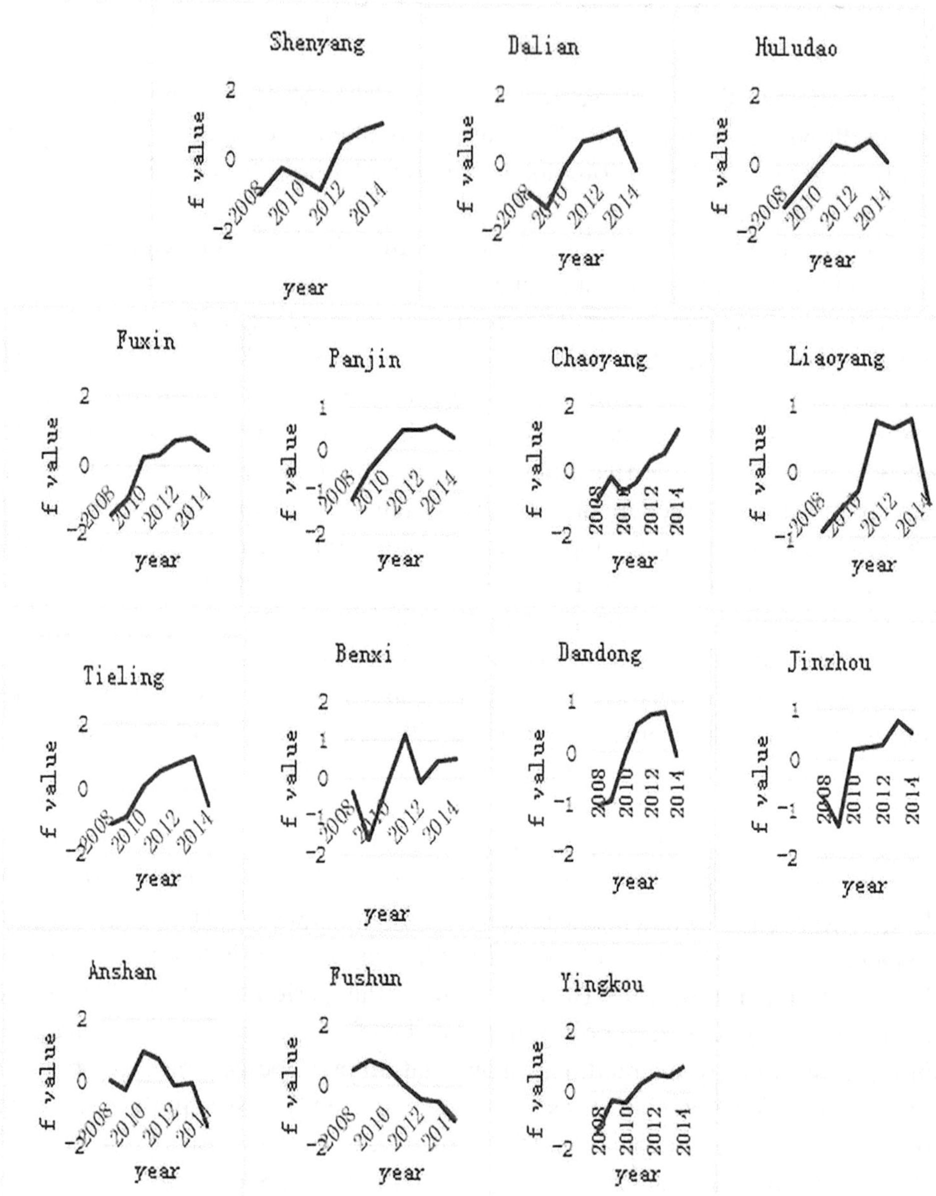

growth of regional GDP and the double-digit decline of fiscal revenue. The amount and proportion of fake revenues data has increased year by year from 2011 to 2014. The added value of Liaoning's industrial enterprises that are above designated size fell by 11.1%, which is the main factor dragging down the negative GDP growth in Liaoning. These two factors together led to a decline in the financial ecological environment indicators in Liaoning Province.

Financial Ecology Environmental Assessment Based on City Segmentation

Following the above research methods, financial eco-environmental indicators were carried out for 14 prefecture-level cities in Liaoning Province (Shenyang, Dalian, Huludao, Fuxin, Panjin, Chaoyang, Liaoyang, Tieling, Benxi, Dandong, Jinzhou, Anshan, Fushun, Yingkou). The construction and calculation of the system, and the following trends in the financial ecological environment of each city are shown in Figure 2.

Figure 2. Financial Ecological Environment of every city in Liaoning Province

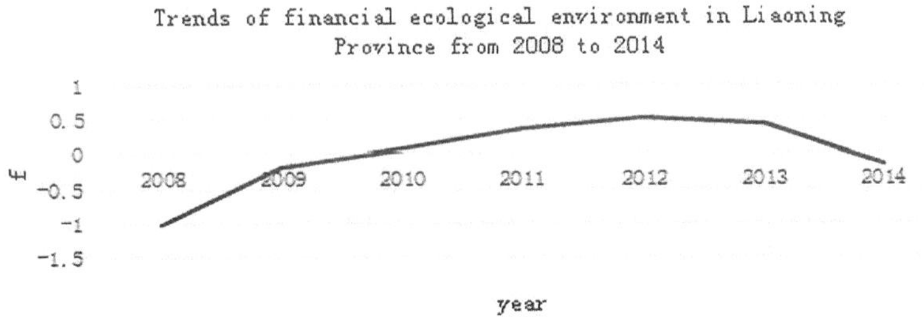

Through analyzing the financial ecological environment of 14 cities in Liaoning Province (Shenyang, Dalian, Huludao, Fuxin, Panjin, Chaoyang, Liaoyang, Tieling, Benxi, Dandong, Jinzhou, Anshan, Fushun and Yingkou) with factor analysis method, it is capable to draw the trend map of the financial ecological environment of each city from 2008 to 2014. In order to determine the regional differences of the financial ecological environment quality in Liaoning Province, the quality of 14 cities in Liaoning Province was ranked. The results are shown in Table 6. The ranking is based on the arithmetic average of the financial ecological environment assessment scores of each city from 2012 to 2014.

According to the evaluation results of the financial ecological environment quality of each city, Shenyang ranks first steadily and there is a significant gap between it and the second place. There is no doubt that the leading position is closely related to

Table 6. Ranking of Financial Ecological Environment 2012-2014

Rank	City	f
1	Shenyang	0.8343
2	Chaoyang	0.7292
3	Fuxin	0.6442
4	Yingkou	0.6325
5	Jinzhou	0.5491
6	Dalian	0.5120
7	Dandong	0.4879
8	Huludao	0.4327
9	Panjin	0.4317
10	Tieling	0.4286
11	Liaoyang	0.3257
12	Benxi	0.3131
13	Anshan	-0.4928
14	Fushun	-0.6980

the status of its provincial capital. It is clear to see that coastal cities (like Yingkou, Jinzhou, Dalian, Dandong, Huludao, Panjin) are all in the upper and middle of the financial ecological environment quality ranking among all the cities in Liaoning due to the convenient transportation brought by their ports and the economic benefits brought by the coastal industries developed therefrom, while inland cities (Anshan, Fushun, Benxi, Liaoyang, Tieling) rank in the lower reaches. Relatively speaking, the quality of financial ecological environment in these cities is poor.

Next, this paper focuses on the specific analysis of Yingkou and Anshan, two cities with the polarization of the trend of financial ecological environment, and Shenyang, the capital of Liaoning Province.

1. Shenyang is the capital of Liaoning Province, the regional central city of Northeast China, the vice-provincial city, and the core city of Shenyang Economic Zone in the national experimental area for comprehensive reform of new industrialization, is the political, economic, financial, cultural, transportation, information and trade center of Northeast China, the base of advanced equipment manufacturing industry in China, and also the national historical and cultural city.

According to the ranking, Shenyang's overall financial ecological environment has absolute advantages over other cities. From the trend of development in recent years, although the trend of Shenyang's financial ecological environment has fluctuated a little in recent years, it is also gradually optimized and perfected as a whole. From the perspective of economic basis, the financial crisis in 2008 also brought heavy losses to the economic development in Shenyang, which is also a heavy industrial city. However, under the "new normal" economy, GDP of Shenyang has been higher than the national average. Employment rate and disposable income have increased compared with previous years; from the perspective of financial development, financial support for the real economy is further strengthened. Credit funds positively support the construction of key infrastructure and major industrial projects in the city as well as strongly support the development of regional economy and small and medium-sized enterprises. By the end of December 2015, the balance of domestic and foreign currency deposits of Shenyang banking financial institutions was 1403.5 billion yuan, an increase of 10.4% over the previous year. The balance of domestic and foreign currency loans of banking financial institutions was 1158.1 billion yuan, with an increase of 12.8% over the same period last year, and the increase of loans was the top in the province. The financial industry is relatively safe, and its development has been relatively stable, and its contribution to the economy is gradually increasing. From the perspective of institutional environment, the municipal government attaches great importance to optimizing the legal environment for economic development, and further improves the legal service guarantee system for Shenyang's economic development. In addition, the credit environment has been significantly improved since the start of the "Credit Shenyang" construction. At present, the overall level of credit construction is in the forefront of the province.

2. The trend map of Yingkou's financial ecological environment shows that the financial ecological environment of Yingkou City is improving day by day from 2008 to 2014, and the development of the financial industry is in a good environment. The overall trend is more prominent and effective in 14 municipal areas of Liaoning Province.

From the aspect of economic basis, Yingkou has rich magnesite resources, plenty of private enterprises and good general development trend. Yingkou port is the second largest port in northeast China and one of the most important strategic resources to revitalize the "Five Points, One Belt" economic belt of northeast China in Liaoning province. Despite of the geographical advantages, it plays an important strategic support role in the economic development of Yingkou region. From the perspective of financial development, in the context of the national" the Belt and the Road" strategy, the provincial government approved the establishment of Yingkou port financial innovation pilot zone in order to give better play to the financial support for ports, and encouraged greater innovation efforts in port financial system mechanism, organization mode, products and service industry, regulatory means and other aspects. In 2015, the number of banks in Bayuquan economic development zones, where Yingkou port is located, reached 19. From the perspective of institutional environment, the financial development of Yingkou port is still in the initial stage. In order to make the port play a bigger role in promoting the financial development, the government should strengthen the construction of credit environment and establish a multi-level capital market, so as to achieve the goal of simultaneous development of the financial industry and the port construction.

3. Anshan ranks second to last among the 14 cities in Liaoning Province, and its financial ecological environment has been declining almost all the time, which indicates that its financial ecological environment is deteriorating and needs to be improved urgently. From the economic base level, the ability of sustainable development is weak. Anshan city's economic development started from heavy industry, which inevitably formed a traditional economic model that emphasized economic growth and ignored ecological environmental protection. With the target of maintaining the foundation of natural resources necessary for economic developments, yet Anshan is still in a period of transition in which its long-term economic model cannot fully adapt to the sustainable development of ecological environment or the coordination of its economy and society. From the perspective of financial development, financing channels are single and the supply and demand of funds are unbalanced. The main financing method of enterprises is bank loan, which is a great demand for credit funds. However, it is difficult to apply for bank loan, and the financing means of Anshan city still needs to be developed. From the perspective of institutional environment, the government's excessive intervention in the construction of financial ecological environment violates the general rules of financial ecosystem construction and destroys the leading role of financial ecosystem in resource allocation. In the meantime, as a result of the imperfect credit system, the construction of social credit system needs to be strengthened.

EMPIRICAL STUDY ON FINANCIAL ECOLOGICAL ENVIRONMENT OPTIMIZATION INTERVAL IN LIAONING PROVINCE

Construction of Empirical Model

The non-independence of financial development theory determines the non-independence of studying the optimization of financial ecological environment. Relevant researches that emphasize the impact of financial development on economic growth have been facing the "optimal level of financial development constraint", which is also called the financial possibility boundary (Barajas, 2012). Enrico (2012) found that there was a non-linear relationship between financial development and economic growth. Only when the ratio of domestic credit to GDP was between 90% and 110% could financial development significantly promote economic growth. Beck (2014) found in his research on different developed and developing countries that only financial development within a certain boundary range can promote economic growth, while financial underdevelopment without reaching the minimum boundary or excessive financial development beyond the maximum boundary may even negatively affect economic growth. Cecchetti (2012) found that the characteristic of how financial development influences economic growth is a inverted u-shaped "threshold effect", in the other words, there is an efficient frontier in the phenomenon of financial development promoting economic growth and the author gives an image analogy: just like eating too much can cause a person diarrhea, excessive expansion of financial system also acts as a deterrent to economic growth. The complications of finance plunder the resources of the real need in real economic growth.

What mentioned above gives this paper a new inspiration for an optimization path of financial ecological environment in Liaoning Province: the differences of regional financial ecological environment in Liaoning Province may affect economic growth in the characteristics of nonlinear threshold, which means searching for optimal path needs to use economic growth model to determinc thc rcgional financial ccological environment of the reasonable development of Liaoning Province.

For the study on the optimization of financial ecological environment in Liaoning Province, the reasonable optimization interval of financial ecological environment can be found quantitatively by constructing the threshold panel model. The framework of empirical model is shown in equation (4).

$$Y_{it} = \beta_0 + \beta b_{it} + \theta_1 D_{it} \cdot I\left(a_{it} \le \gamma_1\right) + \theta_2 D_{it} \cdot I\left(a_{it} > \gamma_1\right) + \varepsilon_{it} \tag{4}$$

In equation (4), \ is the coefficient of threshold variable, $I(\bullet)$is the indicator function, γ is the specific threshold value, and qit is the threshold variable. When $q_{it}\leq\gamma$, $I(q_{it}\leq\gamma)=1$; $q_{it}>\gamma$, $I(q_{it}>\gamma)=1$. β represents the coefficient vector of control variable, Yit represents economic growth, FDit represents financial eco-environmental indicators, and controlit represents dummy control variables, including regional and time dummy variables.

Model Test

For the above threshold panel model, if γ is known, the corresponding parameter value can be obtained by ordinary panel regression. If γ is unknown, Hansen(1999) proposed that each value of the threshold variable should be used to carry out the regression in the model, and the value corresponding to the minimum residual squared value should be obtained as the threshold estimation value. When the threshold value is estimated, it is necessary to test whether there is threshold effect in the model. The hypothesis test is H_0:θ_1=θ_2; H_1:$\theta_1\neq\theta_2$, and then F statistic is constructed under the original hypothesis for statistical test. Under the condition that the original hypothesis is valid, γ cannot be recognized, and the F statistic is not subject to χ^2. Hansen (1999) used Bootstrap to capture its asymptotically effective P value.

According to the principle of panel threshold model estimation, this paper respectively estimates the measurement model under the assumption that there is no threshold effect, has a threshold, and has two thresholds, with a significance level of 1%, 5%, and 10%. The threshold effect test is performed on the interpreted variables, and the results of the threshold effect test are shown in Table 7. The results show that there is a single threshold in the 99% confidence interval, that is, the financial ecological environment has a nonlinear impact on economic growth. In addition, there are three sub-indicators in the financial ecological environment, including the economic basis, financial development, and institutional environment. There are different parameter estimates for economic growth on both sides of the threshold.

Table 7. Test of Threshold Effect

Variable	Financial Ecological Environment		Economic Basis		Financial Development		Political Environment	
	I	II	I	II	I	II	I	II
F value	5.51	2.25	4.23	2.91	4.81	2.88	9.12	2.52
P value	0.02	0.08	0.04	0.06	0.03	0.09	0.00	0.06
Numerical value	0.48		0.52		0.46		0.41	

Empirical Analysis

According to the regression results in Table 8, when the regional financial ecological environment indicator is lower than the threshold value of ©1, it has no significant negative impact on economic growth; when the regional financial ecological environment indicator is higher than the threshold value ©2, it has a significant positive impact on economic growth. This shows that only when the financial ecological environment is improved to a certain level (threshold value of 0.48) can achieve the purpose of promoting economic growth, thus correspondingly finding the target optimization interval of the regional financial ecological environment. Further, it can be found that improving the financial ecological environment can be achieved through three effective ways. Firstly, consolidating the regional economic base can include adjusting the industrial structure, promoting the transformation of the economic system, giving full play to the advantages of the Northeast Heavy Industry Base, encouraging the development of a low-carbon economy, a circular economy, nurturing emerging industries, and promoting economic growth and efficiency to make it cross the minimum. The threshold of 0.52 is the basic way to improve the regional financial ecological environment. Secondly, improving the level of regional financial development, including broadening financing channels, improving asset allocation efficiency, providing financial guarantee for enterprise development and industrial growth, and forming a benign interaction mechanism that promotes and interdepends financial and real economy. The problem worthy of attention in this process is that we must reasonably expand the regional financial scale (of course, the financial scale should be controlled within the optimal range of constraints, otherwise it will be prone to economic financialization) and then improve the level of financial efficiency and ensure financial development. It is necessary to continuously improve from the two dimensions of quality and quantity, which is also the core way to improve the financial ecological environment, so that it exceeds the minimum threshold of 0.46. Thirdly, the improvement of the institutional environment plays an important supporting role in improving the financial ecological environment, including improving the construction of credit information system and the credit environment. Improving the credit evaluation mechanism, system and method and promoting credit culture can finally guarantee that the threshold value exceeds 0.41.

In summary, the impact of the financial ecological environment on the economic growth of Liaoning Province presents a non-linear single-gate characteristic. By improving the regional economic base, financial development and institutional environment, the three main aspects, can financial ecological environment exceeds the corresponding minimum threshold. The threshold of financial ecological environment may finally exceed 0.48 and we can find a reasonable optimization interval for it

Table 8. Empirical Analysis of Financial Ecological Environment optimization

Variable	Financial Ecological Environment	Economic Basis	Financial Development	Political Environment
fd(q≤©1)	-0.443	-	-	-
	(-1.45)	-	-	-
fd(q>©1)	1.212**	-	-	-
	(2.31)	-	-	-
fd(q≤©1)	-	-0.596	-	-
	-	(-1.55)	-	-
fd(q>©1)	-	1.334**	-	-
	-	(2.47)	-	-
fd(q≤©1)	-	-	-0.412	-
	-	-	(-1.39)	-
fd(q>©1)	-	-	1.295**	-
	-	-	(2.38)	-
fd(q≤©1)	-	-	-	-0.405
	-	-	-	(-1.31)
fd(q>©1)	-	-	-	1.178*
	-	-	-	(1.88)
Regional dummy variable	YES	YES	YES	YES
Time dummy variable	YES	YES	YES	YES
N	98	98	98	98

Note: () is the t-test value; *, **, *** respectively indicate the t-test through the significant level of 10%, 5%, and 1%.

CONCLUSION

This paper uses the data of 14 prefecture-level cities in Liaoning Province from 2008 to 2014 to construct the financial ecological environment system from three aspects, economic foundation, financial development and institutional environment. It also considers the impact of financial efficiency factors on financial development sub-indicators. The factor analysis method and the threshold model are used to empirically analyze the dynamic evolution trend and optimization path of the financial ecological environment in Liaoning Province. The results show that the financial ecological environment in Liaoning Province generally shows a figure of inverted U whose characteristics is rising and then decreasing, and the influence mechanism of different periods is different. The upward trend in 2008-2011 was mainly due to the expansion of financial scale, efficiency improvement and the improvement of the institutional environment. The decline in 2012-2014 was mainly due to the decline of the impact of quantitative easing policy and the correction of economic data in Liaoning Province; The city (Yingkou, Jinzhou, Dalian, Dandong, Huludao, Panjin) is ranked in the middle and upper reaches due to the convenient transportation brought by its port and the economic benefits brought by the coastal industry developed thereby. Inland cities (Anshan, Fushun, Benxi, Liaoyang, Iron) Relatively speaking, the quality of financial ecological environment is relatively poor; the impact of urban financial ecological environment on economic growth in Liaoning Province presents a non-linear single-gate characteristic, and the thresholds of financial ecological environment, economic base, financial development and institutional environment are respectively 0.48. 0.52, 0.46, 0.41, and based on this empirical evidence to find the optimal range of financial ecological environment in Liaoning Province.

Since the financial crisis in 2008, the downward pressure on the domestic economy has continued to increase, especially in Liaoning Province, the largest province with the largest economic pressure in the Northeast region. In the current transition period of new and old growth kinetic energy, the direction of regulation and control has been increased to promote the province. The construction of financial ecological environment ensures the important tasks of completing economic and social development: (1) From the perspective of economic development, efforts are made to promote structural adjustment and strive to improve quality and efficiency. A prominent factor restricting the development of Liaoning Province is the structural problem. The industrial added value of Liaoning Province accounts for 46% of GDP and 87% of the secondary industry. It is necessary to vigorously change the industrial one-column and single-structured industrial system. It is necessary not only to make Liaoning's equipment manufacturing industry bigger and stronger, to speed up the cultivation of strategic emerging industries, to transform and upgrade traditional industries, and to actively develop the private economy. In-depth implementation of innovation-driven development strategy, giving play to the multiplier effect of innovation on driving development; (2) From the perspective of financial development, we need to serve the real economy, focus on solving the practical difficulties of private enterprises in the process of establishing, growing and innovating, makes large enterprises "topping the ground" and small enterprises "overwhelming". Improving financial services and clearing the channels for finance to enter the real economy, especially small and medium-sized enterprises, has made finance an important force for promoting innovation and entrepreneurship, enabling financial institutions to continuously improve financial efficiency in the process of serving the real economy; (3) From the perspective of institutional environmental construction, continuously improve the legal system, further optimizing the business environment, reducing the institutional transaction costs of enterprises and further enhancing the awareness of grassroots service enterprises is indispensable. Strengthening government public service functions, improving the public service capabilities of governments and building a unified credit service platform is also what matters. The government should also equally treat all types of market entities and ensure that all types of market entities earn equal treatment in terms of investment approval, government support, and participation in government investment.

REFERENCES

Barajas, A., Ralph, C., & Seyed, R. Y. (2012). *The Finance and Growth Nexus Re-examined: Do All Countries Benefit Equally?* IMF Working Paper.

Beck, T., Hans, D., & Christiane, K. (2014). Is more finance better? Disentangling intermediation and size effects of financial systems. *Journal of Financial Stability*, *10*(10), 50–64. doi:10.1016/j.jfs.2013.03.005

Bruce, E. (1999). Threshold effects in non-dynamic panels: Estimation, testing, and inference. *Journal of Econometrics*, *93*(4), 345–368.

Cecchetti & Kharroubi. (2012). *Reassessing the Impact of Finance on Growth.* BIS Working Paper.

Chen, Z., & Peng, Y. (2006). Evaluation Indicator System and Model Construction of Regional Financial Eco-environment. *Statistics & Decisions*, (6), 31–35.

Čihák & Demirgüč-Kunt. (2013). *Financial Development in 205 Economies, 1960 to 2010.* National Bureau of Economic Research.

Enrico, B., Ugo, P., & Arcand, J. L. (2012). *Too Much Finance?* IMF Working Papers.

Fried, H. O., Lovell, C A K., Schmidt, S. S., & Yaisawarng, S. (2002). Accounting for Environmental Effect and Statistical Noise in Data Envelopment Analysis. *Journal of Productivity Analysis*, *17*(1), 157–174. doi:10.1023/A:1013548723393

Han, H. (2019). *Evaluation of financial ecological environment of regional center cities.* Anhui University of Finance and Economics.

Hu. (2009). The Assessment and Empirical Study of Regional Financial Ecological Environment. *Economic Management Journal, 2009*(6), 32-37.

Huang & Liu. (2007). An Evaluation System on Chinese Financial Ecologies. *Systems Engineering Theory & Practice, 2007*(6), 52-60.

Ji & Wu. (2011). Assessment and Analysis of Factors Affecting the Financial Ecological Environment in Northeast Area. *Journal of Northeastern University (Social Science), 2011*(9), 410-415.

Jie, J. (2009). *A Study on Relationship of Financial Ecological Environment and Economic Development of Liaoning*. Northeastern University.

Jin, C., Zhe, H., & Zhang, H. (2013). Analysis of Catching-up Effect and Growth Effect of Total Factor Productivity in China's Regional Financial Industry. *Statistics & Decisions*, (3), 162–167.

Jin, X., & Xie, B. (2014). Evaluation and demonstration of regional financial ecological environment. *Statistics & Decisions*, (15): 160–162.

Jing, Z., & Wei, P. (2012). The Study of Provincial Financial Ecological Environment Assessment. *Journal of Northwest University*, *42*(1).

Jun, P., Wang, L., & Shen, X. (2015). Financial Ecological Environment and Local Government Debt Financing Costs: Empirical Test Based on Provincial Urban Investment Debt Data. *Accountability in Research*, *3*, 34–41.

Li & Guo. (2019). Research on the Impact of Capital Structure on Corporate Risk Undertaking-Based on the Dual Perspective of Property Right Heterogeneity and Financial Ecological Environment. *Wuhan Finance, 2019*(12), 44-50.

Li, C. (2014). The Measure and Correspondence Analysis on the Efficiency of China's Financial Industry. *Statistical Research*, *31*(1), 91–97.

Ni, J. (2018). *Research on Comprehensive Evaluation of Financial Ecological Environment and Its Relationship with Economic Growth*. Zhejiang University of Commerce and Industry.

Research Group, Luoyang Central Bank of PBC. (2006). Research on the Evaluation Target System of Regional Financial Ecological Environment. *Journal of Financial Research*, (1), 167–177.

Suning. (2005). Optimizing the Financial Environment and Improving the Financial Ecology. *Financial Digest, 2005*(10), 4-6.

Tang, C. (2019). *Research on Mitigating Effect of Financial Ecological Environment and Corporate Governance on Financing Constraints*. Guangxi University of Science and Technology.

Wang, Z., & Zhang, R. (2006). On the Evaluation Indicator System of Regional Financial Ecological Environment. *Journal of Financial Research*, (5), 167–177.

Wang & Cheng. (2017). The boundary effect of financial development on firms' R&D investment-Based on the HECKIT model of the scale & efficiency threshold. *Studies in Science of Science*, *35*(1), 110–124.

Wang. (2012). Analysis of the Effect of Financial Eco-environment on Financial Industry and Regional Economic Development--Taking the Effectiveness and Problems of Financial Eco-environment in Central Plains Economic Zone as an Example. *Enterprise Economy, 2012*(2), 147-151.

Wei, Z. (2014). Financial Ecological Environment and Corporate Financial Constraints-Evidence from Chinese Listed Firms. *Accountability in Research*, (5), 73–82.

Wu & Chen. (2015). Evaluation and Analysis of Financial Ecological Environment in Fujian. *Journal of Minjiang University, 2015*(1), 26-34.

Xiang, L. L. J. Z. C. (2010). An Empirical Analysis of Factors Influencing Financial Ecological Environment's Optimizing. *Ecological Economics*, (7), 38–42.

Xie & Zhu. (2010). An Empirical Study on Financial Competitiveness of Major Cities in China. *Wuhan Finance Monthly, 2010*(2), 19-22.

Xu, N. (2005). On China's Financial Ecological Environment. *Journal of Financial Research*, (2): 35–43.

Xu, X. (2005). The Assessment of Regional Financial Ecology Environment. *Journal of Financial Research*, (11), 53–62.

Ye, C. (2005). Seeking for the Micro-foundation of Development Theory: Also on the Formation of a Theoretical Paradigm of Development Economics. *Social Sciences in China*, (4), 29–40.

Zhang. (2007). Research on Rural Financial Ecology: An Analytical Framework of New Institutional Economics. *Financial Theory & Practice, 2007*(2), 41-48.

Zhang. (2012). *Research on the Evaluation Target System of Regional Financial Ecological Environment*. Academic Press.

Zhang. (2014). Evaluation and Optimizing Suggestions of Financial Ecological Environment in Yangtze River Delta Region. *Contemporary Economics, 2014*(22), 64-65.

Zhao, C. (2019). *Research on the Evaluation of Regional Sci-tech Finance Ecological Environment*. Anhui University.

Zhou. (2004, Dec. 7). Perfecting the legal system and improving the financial ecology. *Financial Times*.

Chapter 6
Financial Industry Under Entrepreneurial Ecosystem:
Internet Finance, Interest Rate Marketization, and Bank Performance

Xiaomin Du
Yingkou Institute of Technology, China

Xiangxiang Lang
Dalian University of Technology, China

ABSTRACT

Due to the three functions of cost reduction, disintermediation, and information asymmetry, internet finance continues to impact the traditional banking business in the financial industry, posing a new competitive risk for commercial banks. In developing countries such as China, given the imperfect development of the financial market, the government needs to introduce a series of policies, but new policies will bring the risk of market uncertainty. Due to the double uncertainty of the market and the system in developing countries, commercial banks are caught between competitive and new policy risks. Therefore, exploring the impact of these two risks on the performance of commercial banks is very important to allow commercial banks to discern, resist, and respond to risks. This research uses the data of A-share listed banks for the past 10 years. Empirical research shows that internet finance and interest rate liberalization have a negative impact on bank performance. The liberalization of interest rates further increases the negative impact of internet finance on bank performance.

DOI: 10.4018/978-1-7998-3495-3.ch006

INTRODUCTION

In developing countries, the financial industry is still in infancy, and there are dual uncertainties in the market and institutions, including uncertainties around market competition (competition methods, competition rules, etc.) and policy (policy persistence, policy effectiveness, etc.). These two uncertainties create double risks for a commercial banking entity. In particular, the competitive risk between commercial banks is becoming weaker while the burgeoning competition external to the industry is resulting in a greater impact on commercial banks given the diversification of competitive methods. In particular, the emergence of Internet finance presents tremendous operational risks. With the development of the financial industry and the gradual liberalization of the market, banks are facing the impact of various external competition methods, and the development of Internet finance in particular is having a high impact (Hou et al., 2016; Guo and Shen, 2016). Internet finance breaks down the monopoly position and interest rate solidification of commercial banks for offline payments and uses their characteristics of high efficiency, convenience, and low cost to reduce the profits of traditional commercial banks at the deposit and loan and intermediary business levels, thereby affecting the performance level of commercial banks (Yue and Pin, 2018; Ozili, 2018). In addition, policies are not always perfect and may even mask some risks due to the uncertainty of institutions in developing countries. In China, interest rate liberalization is an important measure that was launched by government during the process of economic restructuring (Tannaa et al., 2017). Its purpose is to gradually establish the market interest rate system and formation mechanism based on the central bank interest rates and money market rates for mediation. Interest rate liberalization is determined by the market supply and demand of financial institutions' lending rate and deposit rate levels, which enable the market mechanism to play a leading role in the allocation of financial resources and thus promote the development of the market economy (Barrell et al., 2017). However, interest rate liberalization, a policy introduced by the Chinese government in the preliminary stage of financial industry development, holds an initial risk related to uncertainty, and its effectiveness needs to be explored in depth. Therefore, it is highly important to reveal the impact of interest rate liberalization policies on the performance of commercial banks.

Based on the above discussion for the contemporary Chinese financial industry, especially for commercial banks, it is critical to determine how to respond the double risks of interest rate liberalization and Internet finance [Njikam, 2017; Balogun et al., 2016; Dabo,2012]. Furthermore, the dual forces of national policy and market competition have a significant impact on commercial banks. However, the existing research is not very concerned about how bank performance is affected by the impact of Internet finance and the changes in the context of interest rate liberalization.

Therefore, exploring the law of performance changes of commercial banks under the dual risk of interest rate liberalization and Internet finance is the focus of this study.

Accordingly, this paper uses the data of China's A-share listed commercial banks from 2010 to 2017. First, this paper studies the relationship between Internet finance and bank performance. Then, the research explores the impact of interest rate liberalization on commercial bank performance to reveal the effectiveness of the interest rate liberalization policy. Last, this paper examines the impact of Internet finance on bank performance in the context of interest rate liberalization, namely, how commercial bank performance changes under the double uncertainty risk. The results show that (1) Internet finance has a negative effect on bank performance, (2) interest rate liberalization has a negative effect on bank performance and (3) interest rate liberalization further aggravates the negative impact of Internet finance on bank performance. The above results indicate that the liberalization of interest rates is temporarily in a state of failure in the development of China's current financial industry and that this state will make external forces such as Internet finance more negative to the banking industry. The contribution of this paper is to provide a comprehensive proposal for the development of the financial industry from the perspective of both national policy and a market economy.

LITERATURE REVIEW AND HYPOTHESIS

Internet Finance and Bank Performance

Internet finance is a new, organic, combined financial model of Internet technology and the financial business that has simultaneously had a negative impact on the traditional financial system (Allen et al., 2005; Berger et al., 2009; Werthamer, 1997). At present, China's most representative Internet financial services model mainly includes third-party Internet payments, P2P online lending and crowdfunding (Srivastava, 2014; Huang and Ji, 2017). Third-party Internet payments serve mainly the function of third-party guarantee payments by relying on large portal websites and using the credit of the bank that is cooperating with it as the credit support. P2P network loans cut into the niche market, provide standardized borrowing for small micro enterprises and individual customers, and reduce operating costs by using risk control technology for big data, which creates a unique competitive advantage. Crowdfunding is mainly performed through the use of good communication networks to raise funds from network investors and to simultaneously achieve a publicity effect.

Internet finance implies three core characteristics: cost reduction, information asymmetry reduction and disintermediation. The reduction in transaction costs means that Internet finance can replace traditional financial intermediaries, physical outlets and labor services in the market (such as not requiring outlets for mobile banking), which is a new blow to commercial banks. The reduction of information asymmetry is reflected in the wide use of big data in information processing (a core characteristic of Internet finance). The reduction of information asymmetry means that big data is widely used in Internet finance, which promotes the opening and sharing of information in the financial industry. Disintermediation means that Internet finance promotes eliminating intermediary functions that are not suitable for financial development and replacing them with new non-bank financial institutions or financial instruments. The development of Internet finance will inevitably cause changes to the traditional financial model and gradually, negatively impact the financial industry, especially commercial banks (Zhang, 2015). This impact not only weakens the intermediary role of banks but also makes the profits of the bank's intermediaries decrease and exacerbates the market competition of commercial banks, which reduces the marginal profit of banks (Franklin et al., 2002; Ovidiu et al., 2015).

Based on this discussion, this paper proposes the following hypothesis.

H1: In developing countries, Internet finance as a competitive uncertainty risk will reduce the performance of commercial banks.

Interest Liberalization and Bank Performance

The essence of interest rate liberalization is relaxing interest rate control to eliminate the protection of bank deposits and loan spreads, reflect the scarcity of funds and promote the efficiency of social resource allocation (Alessandra 2018). Theoretically, interest rates are the price of money. Interest rate liberalization promotes the improvement of a bank's operating performance to promote the continuous, stable and healthy development of the banking industry (Hellmann et al., 2000). Interest rate liberalization can improve the efficiency of financial systems and strengthen the economy, but it will increase bank risk as well (Shahrokhi, 2008). A long-term excessively loose low-interest monetary policy will affect the risk accumulation and risk tolerance of financial intermediaries, especially banks, resulting in excessive accumulation of risk in the banking system (Wahyoe et al., 2013). At the same time, interest rate liberalization has affected the bank's enthusiasm for sound operations by intensifying market competition and reducing the marginal revenue of banks and the value of bank concessions (Jadiyappa et al., 2016; Hjortsoe et al., 2018). In addition, interest rate liberalization will also increase market interest rate volatility, exacerbating inter-bank competition and increasing bank operational risk (Ranciere et al., 2016). Interest rates liberalization unquestionably contributes by stimulating the development of the regional financial industry, but for commercial banks, potential risks lurk as well.

Interest rate liberalization is the core of financial system reform in developing countries, but the international environment of economic globalization and financial integration has forced countries to face a more complex external environment while relaxing interest rate controls. In China, bank deposits and loan interest spreads have been protected for a long time, and development retains a monopoly position. But after financial liberalization, as the government's financial regulation is reduced, banks' prudent investments will gradually decrease as risky investments increase under pressure to reduce profits, which will simultaneously increase their operational risk (Borio, 2008). In addition, domestic commercial banks lack the tools to avoid interest rate risk under a long-term interest rate control environment, but under interest rate liberalization, frequent fluctuations in interest rates will increase the pressure on bank risk management (Hellmann et al., 2000).

Based on this discussion, this paper proposes the following hypothesis.

H2: In developing countries, interest rate liberalization as the policy uncertainty risk will improve the performance of commercial banks.

Internet Finance and Bank Performance Under the Background of Interest Rate Liberalization

As a combination of Internet technology and financial business (Repullo, 2004), Internet finance is a third financial financing model that is different from the indirect financing of commercial banks and direct financing in capital markets (Cubillas and González, 2014). As a burgeoning force, Internet finance clearly competes with the traditional banking system (Allen et al., 2002). Internet finance has different risk characteristics from traditional finance, expanding the boundaries of transaction possibilities and serving a large number of people who are not currently covered by traditional finance. Especially in developing countries, Internet finance is more difficult to regulate under policy risks. For example, in China, laws and regulations regulating Internet finance have been recently formulated, but they are still not perfect. This has led to the failure of current regulatory legislation to regulate Internet financial credit risk, which has led to rigid redemption and overreliance on guarantees, exacerbating a range of potential risks arising from information asymmetry (Shahrokhi, 2008).

In most developing countries, especially in China, financial markets have been subject to macroeconomic regulation and control by the government for a long time, and their financial systems have been dominated by banks. This has led commercial banks to pay more attention to competition among peers and neglect external emerging forces. In the context of interest rate liberalization, the traditional deposit and loan benchmark interest rates are shifting towards market-based interest rates (Shen and Pin, 2015), which has greatly stimulated the vigorous development of Internet finance and thus increased the competitiveness of the entire financial industry. Interest rate liberalization and Internet finance development are the inevitable result of economic, social and scientific progress and are conducive to deepening financial market reform, optimizing financial resource allocation, and further promoting the healthy development of the real economy, but they also have an obvious impact on traditional commercial banks.

Based on this discussion, this paper proposes the following hypothesis:

H3: In developing countries, interest rate liberalization will improve the negative impact of Internet finance on bank performance.

RESEARCH DESIGN

Sample Selection and Data Sources

Based on the reliability, availability, and validity of the data, this paper uses the annual data of China's A-share listed commercial banks from 2007-2017 as a research sample. The sources of the data are the annual reports that are disclosed by banks, the Guotai'an database, and Internet financial development data. From the China Financial Network, online home loans and other related research reports were obtained. After excluding the samples with missing data, 126 observations were eventually obtained.

Variable Definitions

1. Explained variables: Bank performance. With reference to the existing research on bank operating performance, this paper selects the ROA(return on assets)) and the ROE (Rate of Return on Common Stockholders' Equity)of commercial banks as a measure of commercial bank operating performance, which can be more fully reflected in a bank's overall performance level.
2. Explanatory variable: Internet finance. This paper selects the ratio of third-party Internet payments to bank assets and the ratio of the transaction scale of P2P lending to bank assets as Internet financial indicators.
3. Adjustment variable: Liberalization of interest rates. China's interest rate liberalization reforms ended in 2015. Therefore, this paper uses dummy variables to measure the index of China's interest rate liberalization, and we

believe that China did not complete the reform of interest rate liberalization in 2015; before this date, the indicator was 0. After 2015, China completed the reform of interest rate liberalization with an index of 1.

4. Control variables. a) Equity asset ratio. This ratio reflects the proportion of shareholders' equity capital in total assets. When the index is larger, the proportion of equity capital is higher, the proportion of liabilities is lower, and the role of the long-term stable development, business expansion and profitability of a bank is more important. b) Total assets turnover. The total assets turnover rate is an important index to comprehensively evaluate the operation quality and utilization efficiency of all assets of a bank. When the turnover rate is greater, a faster turnover of total assets reflects a stronger sales ability. By increasing the turnover of assets, banks can generate an increase in absolute profits. c) Growth rate of bank loans. Commercial banks' operating performance to a large extent depends on the expansion of bank credit scales. It is necessary to study the performance of commercial banks to consider the credit behavior of commercial banks. Bank loan growth is an important variable that reflects the behavior of bank credit. d) Loan asset ratio. When the proportion of loans is higher, banks make more loans, and their profitability is strong.

Table 1. Variable definition

Variable Category	Variable Name	Variable Symbol	Variable Definition
Explained variables	ROA	ROA	Total profit/total assets
	ROE Third party Internet payment	ROE	Net profit/average equity capital
Explanatory variable		TIP	Third-party Internet payment transaction scale/total assets.
	P2P Internet lending	P2P	P2P transaction amount/total assets
Adjustment variable	Liberalization of interest rates	Lib	Dummy variable, with year 0 for 2015 and before, otherwise 1
Control variables	equity asset ratio	EAR	Owners' equity / total assets
	total assets turnover	TTC	Operating income/average total assets
	loan growth rate of bank	LGR	Bank loan growth rate
	loan asset ratio	CAT	Loan/total asset

Model Building

Based on the existing research in China and abroad, this paper establishes a multiple regression panel model. Model (1) is designed to test the impact of Internet finance on the performance of commercial banks. Model (2) introduces market-based adjustment variables to study the relationship between Internet finance and commercial bank performance in the context of interest rate liberalization.

$$\text{Performance} = \alpha_0 + \alpha_1 IF + \beta_i \text{Control}_i + \varepsilon \quad (1)$$

$$\text{Performance} = \alpha_0 + \alpha_1 IF + \alpha_2 MAR + \alpha_3 IF * MAR + \beta_i \text{Control}_i + \varepsilon \quad (2)$$

THE EMPIRICAL ANALYSIS

Descriptive Statistics

The statistical results for the variables in this paper are shown in Table 2.

Analysis of Empirical Results

Because the explanatory variables include bank performance measured by ROA and ROE and considering that the variables TIP and P2P, which measure the Internet finance of commercial banks in the explanatory variables, may be collinear, the empirical tests are divided into the following four submodels. The regression results are shown in Table 3.

From the regression results of Models 1 and 3, the variable TIP is significantly negative, which indicates that third-party Internet payments directly reduce the ROA and ROE of commercial banks. According to the results of Models 2 and 4, the variable P2P is significantly negative, which indicates that P2P online lending plays a negative role in commercial banks' ROA and ROE. The main reason for this negativity is that Internet finance reduces the traditional commercial bank in the middle of the loan and the profits at the business level, which affects the profitability of commercial banks.

Table 4 shows the effect of interest rate liberalization on bank performance. The results show that interest rate liberalization has a negative impact on both the ROA and ROE. This result indicates that the liberalization of interest rates has created pressure on banks' performance. The banking industry has not yet been able to meet the challenges of interest rate liberalization. Accordingly, China's financial market is not yet mature.

Table 2. Variable descriptive statistics

Variables	Observed Values	Mean Values	Standard Deviation	Minimum Values	Maximum Values
ROA	128	0.0132	0.0023	0.0077	0.0182
ROE	126	0.0917	0.0191	0.0538	0.1486
TIP	128	3.5980	4.8602	0.0751	25.1928
P2P	112	0.2722	0.4990	0.0002	2.7178
Lib	128	0.25	0.4347	0	1
EAR	128	0.0640	0.0088	0.0341	0.0856
TTC	126	0.0154	0.0026	0.0110	0.0281
LGR	126	0.1576	0.0602	0.0506	0.5215
CAT	128	0.4711	0.0701	0.2955	0.5987

Note: The relevant ratio data do not include % in the calculation

Table 3. Regression Results for Internet Finance and Bank Performance

	Bank Performance			
	Dependent Variable: ROA		**Dependent Variable: ROE**	
	(1)	**(2)**	**(3)**	**(4)**
TIP	-0.0002***		-0.0009**	
	(-4.04)		(-2.88)	
P2P		-0.0023***		-0.0087**
		(-5.30)		(-3.13)
EAR	0.0273	-0.0032	-1.026***	-1.023***
	(1.19)	(-0.12)	(-7.29)	(-6.04)
TTC	0.199**	0.195**	4.486***	4.733***
	(2.83)	(2.79)	(10.33)	(10.67)
LGR	-0.0041	-0.0042	0.0018	-0.0164
	(-1.19)	(-1.21)	(0.08)	(-0.74)
CAT	-0.0010	0.0030	-0.0330	-0.0322
	(-0.27)	(0.81)	(-1.43)	(-1.37)
cons.	0.0102***	0.0103***	0.107***	0.104***
	(4.31)	(4.58)	(7.32)	(7.23)
R^2	0.2698	0.3573	0.5857	0.6203
Adj R^2	0.2394	0.3269	0.5684	0.6023
N	126	112	126	112

Note: The values in the brackets are t-values. ***, **, and * indicate significant correlations at the 0.01, 0.05, and 0.1 levels, respectively.

Table 4. Regression Results for Interest Rate Liberalization and Bank Performance

	Bank Performance	
	Dependent Variable: ROA	Dependent Variable: ROE
	(5)	(6)
Lib	-0.0034***	-0.0111***
	(-9.27)	(-4.15)
EAR	0.0718***	-0.900***
	(3.69)	(-6.33)
TTC	0.161**	4.303***
	(2.85)	(10.41)
LGR	-0.0075**	-0.0113
	(-2.71)	(-0.56)
CAT	0.0049*	-0.0029
	(2.07)	(-0.17)
cons.	0.0059**	0.0893***
	(3.19)	(6.65)
R^2	0.5164	0.6126
Adj R^2	0.4963	0.5965
N	126	126

Note: The values in the brackets are t-values. ***, **, and * indicate significant correlations at the 0.01, 0.05, and 0.1 levels, respectively.

As seen from Table 5, Internet finance and bank performance have a significant negative correlation, which is consistent with the results in Table 2. In Models 5 and 7, the interaction between third-party Internet payments and interest rate liberalization is significantly positive. In Models 6 and 8, the interaction between the P2P network and the liberalization of interest rate loans is also significantly positive, which shows that the interest rate liberalization reform has intensified the Internet performance of the negative phase relations for financial and commercial banks on the Internet against the background of the financial reform. The interest rate liberalization reform of commercial banks' caused losses by raising interest rates as banks were simultaneously required to maintain quality loan customers and lower lending rates. As commercial banks further narrowed their spreads, the operating performance of commercial banks was further reduced.

Table 5. The Regression Results for Internet Finance and Bank Performance under the Background of Interest Rate Liberalization

	Bank Performance			
	Dependent Variable: ROA		Dependent Variable: ROE	
	(7)	(8)	(9)	(10)
TIP	-0.0001*		-0.0014**	
	(-2.27)		(-2.94)	
P2P		-0.0029**		-0.0268***
		(-3.19)		(-4.10)
Lib	-0.0037***	-0.0036***	-0.0156***	-0.0144***
	(-7.31)	(-7.23)	(-4.26)	(-4.08)
TIP*Lib	0.0001		0.0013**	
	(1.72)		(2.64)	
P2P*Lib		0.0027**		0.0267***
		(2.86)		(3.94)
EAR	0.0850***	0.0673**	-0.760***	-0.682***
	(4.18)	(2.77)	(-5.18)	(-3.96)
TTC	0.164**	0.142*	4.283***	4.553***
	(2.87)	(2.45)	(10.41)	(11.10)
LGR	-0.0061*	-0.0040	0.0014	-0.0045
	(-2.19)	(-1.37)	(0.07)	(-0.22)
CAT	0.0006	0.0033	-0.0395	-0.0460*
	(0.20)	(1.04)	(-1.74)	(-2.06)
cons.	0.0072***	0.0071***	0.0997***	0.0927***
	(3.66)	(3.69)	(7.08)	(6.85)
R^2	0.5367	0.5729	0.6409	0.6868
Adj R^2	0.5092	0.5441	0.6196	0.6657
N	126	112	126	112

Note: The values in the brackets are t-values. ***, **, and * indicate significant correlations at the 0.01, 0.05, and 0.1 levels, respectively.

CONCLUSION

This article selects the 2010-2017 data including the rate of return on total assets and net worth, from Chinese A-share listed commercial banks to measure the commercial bank performance level and then analyzes the influence of the double risks from Internet finance and interest rate liberalization on commercial bank performance. The research results show that:

First, Internet finance has a negative impact on bank performance, which is consistent with the hypothesis in this paper and suggests that Internet finance through its technical superiority impacts the traditional business model of commercial banks. This negative impact is caused by diverting commercial banks' deposits and loans, weakening the bank's function for the settlement of payments with commercial banks that compete directly and causing bank customer growth rates to gradually decrease, which then reduces the performance of commercial banks.

Second, the liberalization of interest rates has a negative impact on bank performance and indicates that China's financial market is not yet mature. The effective implementation of the liberalization of interest rate policy needs to be established based on complete financial markets, and the commercial banks are unable to cope with the current opportunities and challenges that are brought by the liberalization of interest rates. The financial market must be further improved.

Third, interest rate liberalization has aggravated the negative impact of Internet finance on bank performance. With market competition becoming increasingly fierce, the means of competition gradually become diversified, and the liberalization of interest rate policy further aggravates the competition of banking risks, which makes the financial market's main body unable to adjust to unfair competition under customers' guidance. At present, this situation is not good for commercial banks.

Based on the research results of this paper, to respond to and overcome the double risks of policy uncertainty and market uncertainty, we propose the following policy suggestions for the commercial banks in developing countries.

First, in a competitive environment with uncertainty risk, commercial banks should enhance market competitiveness and implement more targeted competitive strategies. Currently, the boundary of competition has become increasingly blurred for the financial industry. The high risk brought by Internet finance has a great impact on commercial banks. Therefore, commercial banks need to improve many aspects of their own competitive strategies. One strategy is the need to increase the level of differentiation. Commercial banks can seek differentiated products to improve the customer service experience, expand online trading and cross-border cooperation to seek win-win cooperation, increase their own differentiated competitive advantage, draw lessons from the Internet financial thinking, and accurately grasp the opportunities that are caused by Internet technology to promote the depth of Internet technology and banking business integration and to realize the healthy development of commercial banks. The second strategy is to introduce products with a lower cost structure. Based on the development of the Internet, the establishment of an independent financial process system has become a development idea of commercial banks. They can try to establish a direct bank business model to make a commercial bank business without management fees, which can reduce the operating costs of banks and provide customers with products with a more favorable price that are independent from and outside of the traditional banking system.

Second, facing serious risk brought by policy uncertainty, at the bank level, banks can increase their ability to integrate the interest rate liberalization policy from two aspects. One aspect is to improve the interest rate system and improve the level of refined management. In the face of the diversification of enterprises and customers, commercial banks should perfect the interest rate stratification system. To correctly evaluate the relationship between the risks and benefits of high-risk clients, banks should provide increasingly more favorable interest rate options to high-quality customers. The second aspect is to raise the level of interest rate pricing and enhance the ability of risk management. Commercial banks should establish a flexible pricing system, improve the response speed for interest rate changes, clear the interest rate risk management objectives, gradually improve the interest rate risk management organizational structure, and pay close attention to the cultivation of the interest rate risk control technology talents to then improve the market competitiveness of the bank.

Third, for the policy to be effective, at the national level, the government in developing countries needs to proceed from three aspects to solve the problem of policy failure in the financial market. The first aspect is to promote the market-oriented interest rate reform step by step. Based on the development stage of financial market, the "one-step approach" and "one size fits all" interest rate liberalization plans are difficult to achieve. The interest rate liberalization reform needs to be gradually carried out. The gradual advancement of reforms will help to prevent and defuse financial risks, maintain the stability of the financial system, and promote the healthy development of the economy. The second policy suggestion is to promote the unification of the "dual track system" of interest rate liberalization. The unification of deposit and loan benchmark interest rates and money market interest rates provides a basis for effective market pricing, which can reduce market price volatility, facilitate the long-term stable development of the financial market, and enable the government to effectively allocate resources through the market price mechanism. The third policy suggestion is to adapt measures to local conditions and make accurate decisions. Developing countries' financial markets cannot fully adapt to the "one size fits all" policy of interest rate liberalization. For regions with different levels of economic development, there should be differences in the interest rate liberalization reforms, which will make financial markets more flexible, increase the autonomy of commercial banks, promote commercial banks, and make these banks integrate into the market and develop in a healthy way.

REFERENCES

Balogun, W., Dahalan, J., & Hassan, S. (2016). Long Run Impacts of Interest Rate Liberalization on Stock Market Development. *Procedia: Social and Behavioral Sciences*, *219*, 126–133. doi:10.1016/j.sbspro.2016.04.053

Barrell, R., Karim, D., & Ventouri, A. (2017). Interest rate liberalization and capital adequacy in models of financial crises. *Journal of Financial Stability*, *33*, 261–272. doi:10.1016/j.jfs.2016.09.001

Berger & Gleisner. (2009). Emergence of financial intermediaries in electronic markets: The case of online P2P lending. *BuR Business Research Journal, 2*(1).

Borio, C. (2008). *The financial turmoil of 2007-? A preliminary assessment and some policy considerations*. Academic Press.

Cubillas, E., & González, F. (2014). Financial liberalization and bank risk-taking: International evidence. *Journal of Financial Stability*, *11*, 32–48. doi:10.1016/j.jfs.2013.11.001

Dabo, Z. (2012). The impact of financial liberalisation on the performance of banks in Nigerian. *Procedia: Social and Behavioral Sciences*, *62*, 548–554. doi:10.1016/j.sbspro.2012.09.091

Dal Colle, A. (2018). The mechanics of commercial banking liberalization and growth. *Journal of Banking & Finance*, *86*, 194–203. doi:10.1016/j.jbankfin.2016.04.014

Dandapani, K., & Shahrokhi, M. (2008). E-finance: Status, innovations, resources and future challenges. *Managerial Finance*.

Guo & Shen. (2016). The impact of Internet finance on commercial banks' risk taking: evidence from China. *China Finance and Economic Review*, *4*(1), 16.

Hellmann, T. F., Murdock, K. C., & Stiglitz, J. E. (2000). Liberalization, moral hazard in banking, and prudential regulation: Are capital requirements enough? *The American Economic Review*, *90*(1), 147–165. doi:10.1257/aer.90.1.147

Herbst, A. F. (2001). E-finance: Promises kept, promises unfulfilled, and implications for policy and research. *Global Finance Journal*, *12*(2), 205–215. doi:10.1016/S1044-0283(01)00028-X

Hjortsoe, I., Weale, M., & Wieladek, T. (2018). How does financial liberalisation affect the influence of monetary policy on the current account? *Journal of International Money and Finance*, *85*, 93–123. doi:10.1016/j.jimonfin.2018.03.015

Hou, X., Gao, Z., & Wang, Q. (2016). Internet finance development and banking market discipline: Evidence from China. *Journal of Financial Stability, 22*, 88–100. doi:10.1016/j.jfs.2016.01.001

Huang, Y., & Ji, Y. (2017). How will financial liberalization change the Chinese economy? Lessons from middle-income countries. *Journal of Asian Economics, 50*, 27–45. doi:10.1016/j.asieco.2017.04.001

Jadiyappa, N., Vanga, N. R., & Krishnankutty, R. (2016). Financial liberalisation and Capital structuring decisions of corporate firms: Evidence from India. *Economics Letters, 149*, 33–37. doi:10.1016/j.econlet.2016.10.004

Njikam, O. (2017). Financial liberalization and growth in African economies: The role of policy complementarities. *Review of Development Finance, 7*(1), 73-83.

Ozili, P. K. (2018). Impact of digital finance on financial inclusion and stability. *Borsa Istanbul Review, 18*(4), 329–340. doi:10.1016/j.bir.2017.12.003

Ranciere, R., Tornell, A., & Westermann, F. (2006). Decomposing the effects of financial liberalization: Crises vs. growth. *Journal of Banking & Finance, 30*(12), 3331–3348. doi:10.1016/j.jbankfin.2006.05.019

Repullo, R. (2004). Capital requirements, market power, and risk-taking in banking. *Journal of Financial Intermediation, 13*(2), 156–182. doi:10.1016/j.jfi.2003.08.005

Shen, Y., & Guo, P. (2015). Internet finance, technology spillover and commercial banks TFP. *Journal of Financial Research, 417*(3), 160–175.

Srivastava, A. (2014). The status and impact of E-finance on developing economy. *Golden Research Thoughts, 3*(11).

Stoica, O., Mehdian, S., & Sargu, A. (2015). The impact of internet banking on the performance of Romanian banks: DEA and PCA approach. *Procedia Economics and Finance, 20*, 610–622. doi:10.1016/S2212-5671(15)00115-X

Tanna, S., Luo, Y., & De Vita, G. (2017). What is the net effect of financial liberalization on bank productivity? A decomposition analysis of bank total factor productivity growth. *Journal of Financial Stability, 30*, 67–78. doi:10.1016/j.jfs.2017.04.003

Wang, Q. (2019). Necessity Analysis and Core Principles of Internet Financial Supervision. *Academic Journal of Business & Management, 1*(2).

Werthamer, N. R., & Raymond, S. U. (1997). Technology and finance: The electronic markets. *Technological Forecasting and Social Change, 55*(1), 39–53. doi:10.1016/S0040-1625(96)00144-8

Xie, P. (2012). Research on Internet financial model. *Journal of Financial Research*, *12*, 11–22.

Yang, D., Chen, P., Shi, F., & Wen, C. (2018). Internet finance: Its uncertain legal foundations and the role of big data in its development. *Emerging Markets Finance & Trade*, *54*(4), 721–732. doi:10.1080/1540496X.2016.1278528

Zheng, Z., Tang, X., & Liu, Y. (2014). Will the Deposit Interest Rate Marketization Increase Bank'Risk Level? Based on an Angle of Narrowed Gap between Deposit and Loan Interest Rate. *Finance & Economics*, *2*, 4.

Zhilai, Z. (2015). The influence of Internet finance of commercial banks—Based on the perspective of the influence of "Internet+" on the retail industry. *Financ Econ*, *5*, 34–43.

Chapter 7
Entrepreneurial Passion, Cognitive Bias, and Technology Commercialization of New Ventures

Biaoan Shan
School of Management, Jilin University, China

Shuanghui Yan
School of Management, Jilin University, China

Xifeng Lu
School of Accounting, Jilin University of Finance and Economics, China

Datian Bi
School of Management, Jilin University, China

ABSTRACT

This chapter utilizes cognitive theory to explain how entrepreneurial passion influences the speed of new venture's technology commercialization and explore the roles of cognitive bias (illusion of control and risk propensity) played in this process. The results show that both entrepreneurial passion and cognitive bias positively impact on the speed of technology commercialization. The authors also find that illusion of control and risk propensity play a partial mediating role in the relationship between entrepreneurial passion and the speed of technology commercialization. This conclusion can make up for the gap of existing theoretical research.

DOI: 10.4018/978-1-7998-3495-3.ch007

INTRODUCTION

Rapidly realizing technology commercialization is an important way for technological firms to gain and sustain competitive advantage. Zahra and Nielsen (2002) pointed out that the high speed of technology commercialization can be utilized to actively challenge competitors and accelerate learning from customers. Especially under Chinese transitional economy context, the external environment changes rapidly. New ventures need to realize technology commercialization successfully in the window of opportunity and quickly transfer new technologies or ideas into products or services to meet customer needs in the market. Therefore, the speed of technology commercialization is the key for new technological ventures to survive in China.

According to existing research, many scholars have focused on how companies successfully commercialize technologies or ideas from the perspectives of government policies, strategic alliances, human capital, resource integration mechanisms, and knowledge management. However, there is a lack of research on the role of emotional and cognitive factors in the process of technology commercialization. New technological ventures are facing more difficulties in the process of technology commercialization, such as limited resources, lack of market experience, high technical uncertainty, and fierce market competition. These all pose great challenges which require passionate founders to make decisions and execute right strategies to achieve. As an important emotional feature, entrepreneurial passion is considered to be a key driver in the difficult situation, which has a positive effect on self-identity, venture growth or performance, technological innovation, and attracting venture capital investment. It's also considered as a key factor in supporting new ventures to make technology commercialization decisions under uncertain environment.

Therefore, it is necessary to address this issue to expand the role of emotional factors played in the technology commercialization of new technological ventures. This paper focuses on the effect of the founder's entrepreneurial passion, a psychological characteristic, on the speed of technology commercialization. Besides, we also discussed the role of cognitive factors. Cognitive bias is viewed as a crucial factor leading to the difference in entrepreneurial decision-making in new ventures. Preview researchers analyzed the effect of cognitive bias on entrepreneurial decision-making such as entrepreneurial opportunity identification and evaluation. However, it still lacks the research on the role of cognitive bias in the process of technology commercialization.

Overall, this study will combine individual emotional factors and cognitive bias, explore the effects of founders' entrepreneurial passion on the speed of technology commercialization based on individual cognitive perspective, and examine the mediating role of cognitive bias in the relationships. We make two main contributions to the entrepreneurship and innovation. Firstly, we extend the understanding of technology commercialization by revealing the effect of founders' entrepreneurial passion on technology commercialization. Secondly, we provide evidences that founders' entrepreneurial passion indirectly influences technology commercialization through cognitive bias.

THEORY AND HYPOTHESES

Entrepreneurial Passion and Technology Commercialization Speed

Entrepreneurial activities always conduct under the environment of high degree uncertainty. Some literature suggested that founder needs to continuously improve entrepreneurial skills with entrepreneurial learning. On the other hand, founder is also required to have unique psychological characteristics that can promote their persistence to cope with these difficulties. Through an in-depth investigation of the individual psychological characteristics of entrepreneurial activities, Baum and Locke (2004) found passion is an important characteristic of successful entrepreneurs, and can greatly stimulate entrepreneurial enthusiasm. Entrepreneurial passion is a salient psychological characteristic embodied in founders, and including three dimensions, namely passion for inventing, passion for founding, and passion for developing (Cardon et al., 2013).

According to the related research on psychological characteristics, founders' entrepreneurial passion is the key factor to impact on their cognition and strategic decision-making behavior. The speed of commercialization will largely determine whether it can launch new products or services ahead of competitors and successfully exploit opportunities and gain competitive advantage. The technology commercialization involves a series of complex activities such as intuitive imagination of technology marketization, cultivating technology to clarify its commercialization prospects, repeatedly testing products or services, promoting the use of technology, and finally achieving continuous commercialization. Zahra and Nielsen (2002) found that that successful technology commercialization stems from the concept of products and requires the technology owned by company to meet customer needs in terms of cost, speed, quality, and novelty. Markman et al. (2005) pointed out that fierce competition, knowledge spillover effects and continuous technological progress make time a scarce resource for technological ventures, requiring companies to quickly utilize technology within the window of time. Therefore, speed is the key to the process of technology commercialization of new ventures.

Founders' entrepreneurial passion will help new ventures make commercial decisions quickly. Strese et al. (2016) also found that the CEO's passion will greatly promote the rapid technological change of company. The commercial application of technology requires a lot of resources and new ventures often face resource limitations. Entrepreneurial passion will enable the founders to use creative ways to solve resource bottlenecks and mobilize social resources, financial resources, and human resources. Passionate founders have a stronger desire to communicate and have a higher ability to acquire new resources. Such individuals are willing to continually invest time and energy in the funding and development of new technological ventures. This kind of goal commitment is crucial for new ventures. It can greatly inspire the founders to persist in the face of difficulties and transfer technology into the market application successfully.

The passion for inventing, funding, and developing will also encourage the founders to learn. For example, the study by Shan (2017) pointed out that passionate entrepreneurs have a stronger willingness to learn and learn about technology and market trends from customers and suppliers by observing and imitating competitors in the industry. This type of positive and strong emotions of founders in entrepreneurship enable the founders and employees to actively communicate, thereby passing on to employees. Breugst et al. (2012) used the theory of emotional contagion and found that entrepreneurial passion is transmitted to employees through social comparison and emotional imitation, thus obtaining employee support. This will help increase the organizational commitment of technology-based ventures' employees, actively invest it in the process of technology utilization, and quickly realize the technology commercialization. Based on the above, we propose the following hypothesis:

H1: Entrepreneurial passion positively impacts on the speed of technology commercialization.

COGNITIVE BIAS AND TECHNOLOGY COMMERCIALIZATION SPEED

Cognitive bias reflects the way individuals (founders) thinking, reasoning, and making decisions. It is also considered to be an important factor in influencing entrepreneurial decision-making. Differences in cognitive bias will trigger variations in perception of internal and external environments among different individuals, thereby impacting on their ability to identify and utilize opportunities. Therefore, it has been used by many researchers to explain why some individuals' entrepreneurial behaviors succeeded while others failed.

Illusion of control and risk propensity are two key cognitive factors that influence entrepreneurial decision-making. Illusion of control represents an individual's self-evaluation of the ability to control or predict outcomes and the extent to which one's skills, abilities, and knowledge conform to a situation. The founders are considered to have a more obvious illusion of control than the ordinary person. Because they always think they have the skills to control, handle, or respond to external environments or events. Therefore, founders of technology-based ventures with high illusion of control tend to view that their technology foundation can match the market and customer needs. At the same time, illusion of control will make the founders more confident, which will actively promote the technology commercialization. This paper proposes the following hypothesis:

H2a: Illusion of control positively impacts on the speed of technology commercialization.

Risk propensity is another important cognitive factor that influences an individual's decision-making. It represents the degree to which an individual tends to take risks. Researchers have found that risk propensity directly impacts on a company's strategic decisions, and founders who have a higher risk propensity and perceive lower risks. According to the research of Busenitz and Barney (1997), founders make strategic decisions more quickly because of their higher risk propensity. The speed of technology commercialization reflects the opportunity of the entry of technological ventures products or services into the market. The decision-making means that the founders must have certain risk tolerance. The study by Tabak and Barr (1999) also emphasized that the implementation of innovative applications involves the introduction of new processes, new products or new services in the organization, especially the risk of radical technology use is higher, so the high-risk tendency of actors will actively improve the efficiency of innovation decision-making. Therefore, we propose the following hypothesis:

H2b: Risk propensity positively impacts on the speed of technology commercialization.

Mediating Effect of Cognitive Bias

The passion of founders has a positive effect on cognitive factors such as setting challenging goals, promising to goals and communication visions, and is more conductive to the subsequent growth of ventures (Entrepreneurial passion also contributes to the cognitive factors of the founders (Drnovsek, Cardon and Patel, 2016; Baum and Locke, 2004). As a positive emotion, entrepreneurial passion will greatly impact on the individual's cognitive bias, which indirectly impacts on the speed of technology commercialization. Therefore, based on the analysis framework of personal characteristics-cognition-behavior/results, we propose that there are strong relationships among entrepreneurial passion, cognitive bias, and the speed of technology commercialization.

As a positive emotion embodied in the entrepreneurial process, entrepreneurial passion is considered to be an important pre-factor of individual cognition. The varying degrees of passion that the founders embody are often accompanied by a corresponding sense of self-efficacy. Individuals who are passionate about entrepreneurial activities tend to be more confident in their skills and knowledge, and believe that they can play a good role in the task of making new ventures successful. Under the influence of this self-efficacy, the founder perceives enough ability to make good use of technology, is confident in the possible outcomes, and ignores the possible risks, which means higher risk propensity and greatly motivates the founder to commercialize potential technologies.

At the same time, the presence of passion prompted the founders to actively scan the external environment. Grichnik, Smeja, and Welpe (2010) use the emotion-as-information theory to discover that these positive emotions can be used as additional information to help individuals understand the difficulties they have in the beneficial aspect. This will greatly reduce the risks perceived by the founders of technological ventures in the process of technology development and commercialization, and let them think that they can control the internal and external uncertain environment and consequences, thereby quickly making corresponding entrepreneurial strategic decisions. Foo (2011) also found that, compared with negative emotions, positive emotions can induce individuals to perceive a more certain environment and own higher control, and effectively reduce perceived risks, which promotes them to quickly make the corresponding decision-making. Therefore, entrepreneurial passion positively impacts on the corresponding decision-making through cognitive bias and improve the speed of technology commercialization of new technological ventures. In light of above reasoning, we propose:

H3a: Illusion of control plays a mediating role in the relationship between entrepreneurial passion and the speed of technology commercialization;

H3b: Risk propensity plays a mediating role in the relationship between entrepreneurial passion and the speed of technology commercialization.

Figure 1. The Theoretical Model

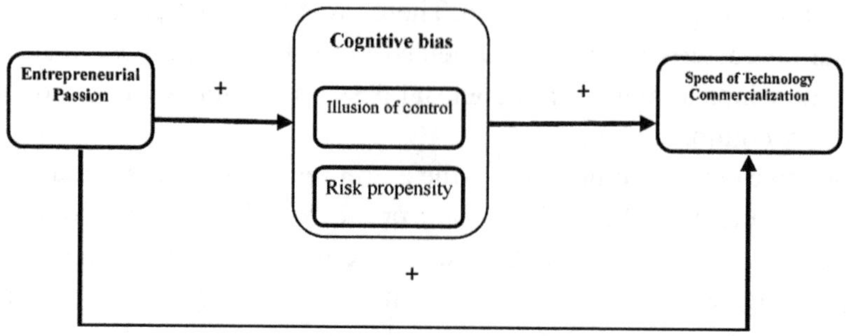

METHODOLOGY

Data Collection and Sample

We sent questionnaires to founders and managers who are familiar with the founders of ventures in the clusters of new ventures in Changchun City, Tangshan City, Zhengzhou City, and the area of surrounding these cities during 2015. According to the research of Milanov and Fernhaber (2009), we view new ventures as the firms registered time no more than ten years (including ten years). Finally, more than 500 questionnaires were distributed, and 141 valid samples were received. The characteristics of the sample are shown below:

In terms of enterprise size, the employee number less than 50 accounts for 85.1% of the total sample and higher than 50 is in14.9% of the samples. In terms of venture age, the creation time no more than 3 years accounts for 63.8% of the samples and more than 3 years is in 36.2% of the samples. In terms of education background, founders who have bachelor's degree account for 43.9% of the samples, have a master's and doctor's degree is in 24.3% of the samples, and founders who have other degree is in 26.8% of the samples,.

MEASURES

Technology commercialization, entrepreneurial passion, and cognitive bias (illusion of control, risk propensity) as the core variables in this paper are measured on 5-point Likert scales and draw on the existing mature measurement scales.

The speed of technology commercialization (TCS). In order to measure the speed of technology commercialization, the method in the research of Chen (2009) is used, and three items (TCS1-TSC3) are adopted. (1) Our firm possessed the competence to initiate the idea of the product in a timely manner; (2) Our firm possessed the competence to develop the product in a timely manner; (3) Our firm possessed the competence to launch the product to the market in a timely manner.

Entrepreneurial passion (EP). For the measurement of entrepreneurial passion, Cardon et al. developed a measurement scale in 2013. According to their study, we adopt fifteen items (EP1-EP15). Two example items: Inventing new solutions to problems is an important part of the life of founder; Founder frequently think about inventing new solutions to business problems.

Control variables. This study sets up several control variables, including age, size, area, education background, prior entrepreneurial experience. (1) The age of venture is measured by the actual establishment years; (2) The firm size (1: The number of employees is less than 20, 2: The number of employees is 20-50, 3: The number of employees is 50-200; 4: The number of employees is above 200); (3) The dummy variable "area" is established according to the location of venture (1: indicates the Zhengzhou area, 0: indicates other areas); (4) Founder education background (1: High school and above; 2: Technical degree; 3 Bachelor's degree; 4 Master's degree and above); (5) Prior entrepreneurial experience is measured based on the experience if fonder had participated in the creation of other ventures before creating this venture (0 did not participate in the establishment of other venture, 1 participated in the establishment of other venture).

VALIDITY

In this study, SPSS 23.0 software is used to test the validity of sample, and analyze the reliability and validity of the questionnaire. Firstly, we conducted KMO and Bartlett tests. The value of KMO is 0.794 and thc statistic of Bartlctt's test of spherical is 1055.18 ($p < 0.001$). Subsequently, this study used the Harman test to put the measurement items of each core variable together for exploratory factor analysis. The results show that the maximum variance is 28%, thus we eliminate the possible common method biases. Confirmatory factor analysis (CFA) was utilized and the results showed (Table 1) that all the values for items are higher than 0.6. The results of Cronbach's alpha also indicate that each value is greater than 0.6. All of these results show that the reliability and validity of the sample have met the requirements of further analysis.

Table 1. Results of reliability and validity

Variables		Measurement Items	Factor Loading	Cronbach's Alpha
Speed of Technology Commercialization		TCS1	.733	.656
		TCS2	.767	
		TCS3	.683	
Entrepreneurial Passion		EP1	.734	.849
		EP2	.773	
		EP3	.698	
		EP4	.701	
		EP5	.637	
		EP6	.684	
		EP7	.653	
		EP8	.617	
		EP9	.645	
		EP10	.632	
		EP11	.670	
		EP12	.786	
		EP13	.653	
		EP14	.621	
		EP15	.667	
Cognitive Bias	illusion of control	IC1	.829	.691
		IC2	.700	
		IC3	.697	
	risk propensity	RP1	.745	.666
		RP2	.754	
		RP3	.697	

Results

Firstly, we carried out the Pearson correlation coefficients among entrepreneurial passion, illusion of control, risk propensity, speed of technology commercialization, and control variables. The results show that all the correlations among variables do not exceed 0.6. Subsequently, the descriptive statistical analysis is conducted (see table 2). The results of mean and standard deviation of each variable show that there is no obvious abnormality, which were within a reasonable range and met the requirements of further analyses.

Table 2. Results of correlations among main variables and descriptive statistical analysis

	1	2	3	4	5	6	7	8	9
Film age	1								
Size	.196*	1							
Area	.541***	.005	1						
Education	-.026	.171*	-.045	1					
Experience	.000	.167*	-.109	.129	1				
EP	.021	.062	-.143	.043	.023	1			
IC	.002	.040	-.163	.249**	-.018	.541***	1		
RP	-.031	.077	-.121	.090	-.028	.444***	.421***	1	
TCS	-.026	.095	-.106	.106	.040	.596***	.495***	.406***	1
Mean	3.05	1.64	.45	2.78	.13	3.51	2.06	3.50	3.42
Standard Deviation	2.52	.84	.49	1.01	.34	.51	.37	.60	.63

Note: *, p<0.05; **, p<0.01; ***, p<0.001; SD, standard deviation.

In order to validate the model and theoretical hypotheses, this study used a hierarchical multiple linear regression and established several regression models (Table 3). Finally, seven regression models were established. Model 1 is the model of the influence of control variables on the speed of technology commercialization. Model 2 is used to verify the influence of entrepreneurial passion on the speed of technology commercialization. Model 3 is used to verify the influence of cognitive bias on the speed of technology commercialization speed. Other models are mainly used to verify the mediating effects of cognitive bias.

According to the results showed in Table 3, the standardized coefficient of the independent variable entrepreneurial passion of this study in Model 2 is 0.593 and is significant at $p < .001$ (Model 2: $\beta = .593$, $p < .001$). Therefore, the results of this analysis indicate that the hypothesis H1 proposed in this study: entrepreneurial passion positively impacts on the speed of technology commercialization is supported by data. That is, H1 is verified.

In the model 3, the standardized coefficient of illusion of control is 0.388, and is significant at the $p < .001$ (model 3: $\beta = .388$, $p < .001$). The standardized coefficient of risk propensity is 0.242, which is significant at $p < .01$ (model 3: $\beta = .242$, $p < .01$). The results show that the mediator variables, both illusion of control and risk propensity have a significant effect on the speed of technology commercialization. Therefore, the hypotheses proposed in this paper H2a: illusion of control positively impacts on technology commercialization speed and H2b: risk propensity positively impacts on the speed of technology commercialization are verified by data.

In order to verify the hypotheses of mediating effects H3a, H3b, this paper follows the procedure of testing mediating effect. Firstly, in order to test H3a, Model 4 and Model 6 are created. The results of model 4 show that the illusion of control has a positive effect on the speed of technology commercialization (Model 4: $\beta = .234$, $p < .01$). At the same time, the coefficient of entrepreneurial passion drops from 0.593 to 0.321. Model 6 is the model that reflects the influence entrepreneurial passion on illusion of control. The result shows that the coefficient of entrepreneurial passion is 0.522 (model 6: $\beta = .522$, $p < .001$), which means entrepreneurial passion positively impacts on illusion of control. Therefore, combined with the above, the mediating effect (partial mediating effect) of illusion of control proposed by this paper is supported by data, which means hypothesis H3a is verified.

Table 3. Results of regression analysis

	The Speed of Technology Commercialization					Illusion of Control	Risk Propensity
	Model 1	Model 2	Model 3	Model 4	Model 5	Model 6	Model 7
Control Variables							
Film age	.009	-.062	-.042	-.071	-.061	.040	-.003
Size	.088	.063	.075	.066	.058	-.009	.028
Area	-.097	.023	.017	.044	.035	-.088	-.064
Education	.088	.071	-.028	.017	.060	.229**	.057
Entrepreneurial experience	-.005	.006	.034	.026	.004	-.089	.009
Independent Variable							
Entrepreneurial Passion		.593***		.321**	.314**	.522***	.436***
Mediator Variables							
Illusion of control			.388***	.234**			
Risk propensity			.242**		.182*		
R^2	.027	.368	.297	.403	.394	.353	.211
ΔR^2	-.010	.339	.259	.371	.361	.323	.175
F	.740	12.6***	7.849***	12.452***	11.977***	11.796***	5.798***

Note:*, p<0.05; **, p<0.01; ***, p<0.001

In order to test H3b, Model 5 and Model 7 are established. Model 5 shows that the coefficient of risk propensity is 0.182 (model 5: $\beta = .182$, $p < .05$), while the coefficient and significance level of entrepreneurial passion are reduced (model 4: $\beta = .314$, $p < .01$). At the same time, it can be seen from Model 7 that the entrepreneurial passion has a positive effect on the risk propensity (Model 7: $\beta = .436$, $p < .001$). Therefore, risk propensity plays a partial mediating role, that is, H3b: risk propensity plays a partial mediating effect in the relationships between entrepreneurial passion and the speed of technology commercialization.

CONCLUSION

Based on the characteristics of new technological ventures, this paper draws on cognitive theory to explain the influence mechanism of entrepreneurial passion on new ventures commercialization speed. The results contribute to the lack of research on the influence of entrepreneurial emotional characteristics on technology commercialization and discuss the role of illusion of control and risk propensity as two cognitive bias factors played in the process. The results show that entrepreneurial passion and cognitive bias (illusion of control, risk propensity) positively impact on the speed of technology commercialization. Illusion of control and risk propensity play a partial mediating effect in the relationships between entrepreneurial passion and the speed of technology commercialization.

Firstly, entrepreneurial passion is a key driver for the rapid realization of technology commercialization for new technological ventures. New technological ventures are faced with the uncertainty of technology and market, as well as a series of dilemmas such as shortage of resources and lack of experience. Also, the founders need to compete with other companies in the industry to achieve a match between technology and market and to commercialize technologies or ideas before competitors in the market. This poses a great challenge to the founders and requires strong emotion to support their persistence. As a result, the founders' passion for inventing, passion for founding, and passion for developing will play a key role. Passionate founders often actively allocated the resources available to them and take creative methods to solve resource dilemmas. At the same time, the important feature of such founders is that they are willing to learn, thus accelerate commercialization of technologies.

Secondly, the study also found that cognitive factors in new technological ventures play an important role in the process of technology commercialization. The market-oriented application of technology involves a series of behaviors and decision-making processes, which requires the founders to quickly make judgments and make decisions based on the special environment. Researchers have pointed out that the founder's decision-making activities are closely related to their cognitive bias. Illusion of control reflects a self-judgment of whether or not to control the external environment or predict the outcomes. A high degree of illusion of control means that individuals have confidence in their abilities, which is crucial for new technological ventures facing the uncertain environment. It helps the founders to be optimistic about potential dilemmas and actively promote the process of technology commercialization. Risk propensity reflects an individual's attitude toward perceived risk. The higher degree of risk propensity he or she owns, the less risk he/she can perceive. New venture transfers technology into market-oriented products or services, and lack of experience take the risks that customers don't accept its products or services. A higher risk propensity, that is, the founder's perceived lower potential risk will motivate him/her to quickly initiate the technology commercialization process.

Thirdly, the empirical analysis of this paper also shows that entrepreneurial passion will indirectly impact on the speed of technology commercialization through cognitive bias. This has important implications for founders and technological ventures. Passion is one of the common characteristics of founders. But the strong passion for entrepreneurial activities does not mean the success of entrepreneurship and the process of commercialization can be carried out smoothly. Achieving the matching of technology and market is a complex process that requires resources, knowledge bases, the founder's assessment of internal and external environments and the founder's courage to make decisions. Passion for inventing, passion for funding and passion for developing can help to increase self-confidence and persistence, reduce the perception of external environmental uncertainty, and positively influence the founder's evaluation of the development of possible outcomes and internal and external environment in the process of technology commercialization.

Therefore, for those founders who are full of entrepreneurial passion, on the one hand, they should actively obtain the required resources through various channels. And on the other hand, they actively promote their illusion of control and risk propensity to quickly achieve technology commercialization. However, cognitive bias in entrepreneurial practice is not always positive. Excessive illusion of control and risk propensity may lead the founders to the trap of advancing, and blindly start technology commercial before they are fully prepared. The direct consequence is that the product or service does not meet market requirements in terms of customer satisfaction, cost or the imitation by other companies due to premature exposure of technical information. Therefore, the successful commercialization of new technological ventures requires passionate founders to cope with possible dilemmas. It should also be based on their resources and knowledge, also with the help of illusion of control and risk propensity.

For new technological ventures, the rapid technology commercialization will help them establish a first-mover advantage in the fiercely competitive environment. This paper has certain theoretical implications for the research of entrepreneurial passion, cognitive bias, and the speed of technology commercialization. Mainly, there are two important contributions. First, this study pays attention to the role of the founder's emotional characteristics in the process of entrepreneurship, and reveals the effect of entrepreneurial passion on the speed of technology commercialization. The role of the founder's emotional factors in entrepreneurial activities has gradually gained attention in recent years. Entrepreneurial activities contain a variety of irrational behaviors, and the development of entrepreneurial decision-making activities are closely related to entrepreneurial passion. Previous studies have focused on the role of this emotional feature in opportunity identification, business performance, entrepreneurial intention, entrepreneurial self-efficacy, entrepreneurial finance, employee behavior, etc. But existing research ignored its influences on innovation activities at the firm level. This paper empirically analyzes the effect of entrepreneurial passion on the speed of technology commercialization and compensates for the lack of theoretical research on emotional factors in the process of technology commercialization.

Second, this paper discovers the role of cognitive factors in the process of technology commercialization, and proposes cognitive biases of illusion of control and risk propensity are the key paths for entrepreneurial passion to influence technology commercialization speed. This study draws on the research logic of emotional characteristics-cognition-behavior/results, deeply explores how entrepreneurial passion impacts on the speed of technology commercialization through two cognitive bias factors, and exploratorily explains the role that entrepreneurial passion plays on the speed of technology commercialization from cognitive perspective.

At the same time, there are still some limitations in this paper. First of all, the emotional characteristics of founders are complex factors. At different time, or be influenced by certain key events, founders may generate various emotions. Therefore, future research needs to measure the stable entrepreneurial passion from multiple perspectives to better verify the theoretical model proposed in this study. Second, in the process of entrepreneurial decision-making, emotional factors and cognitive factors play crucial roles. However, studies have shown that the effects of these factors are not always positive, and may have a negative effect in certain situations. This should be further revealed and tested in future research. Finally, the technology commercialization process of new technological ventures involves learning activities of the founders. Future research can deeply reveal the interaction of entrepreneurial passion and entrepreneurial learning on the speed of technology commercialization.

REFERENCES

Bailetti, T. (2012). Technology entrepreneurship: overview, definition, and distinctive aspects. *Technology Innovation Management Review, 2012*(2), 5-12.

Baum, J. R., & Locke, E. A. (2004). The relationship of entrepreneurial traits, skill and motivation to subsequent venture growth. *The Journal of Applied Psychology*, *89*(4), 587–598. doi:10.1037/0021-9010.89.4.587 PMID:15327346

Breugst, N., Domurath, A., Patzelt, H., & Klaukien, A. (2012). Perceptions of entrepreneurial passion and employees' commitment to entrepreneurial ventures. *Entrepreneurship Theory and Practice*, *36*(1), 171–192. doi:10.1111/j.1540-6520.2011.00491.x

Busenitz, L. W., & Barney, J. B. (1997). Differences between entrepreneurs and managers in large organizations: Biases and heuristics in strategic decision-making. *Journal of Business Venturing*, *12*(1), 9–30. doi:10.1016/S0883-9026(96)00003-1

Cardon, M. S., Gregoire, D. A., Stevens, C. E., & Patel, P. C. (2013). Measuring entrepreneurial passion: Conceptual foundations and scale validation. *Journal of Business Venturing*, *28*(3), 373–396. doi:10.1016/j.jbusvent.2012.03.003

Chen, C. J. (2009). Technology commercialization, incubator and venture capital, and new venture performance. *Journal of Business Research*, *62*(1), 93–103. doi:10.1016/j.jbusres.2008.01.003

Dalborg, C., & Wincent, J. (2015). The idea is not enough: The role of self-efficacy in mediating the relationship between pull entrepreneurship and founder passion–a research note. *International Small Business Journal*, *33*(8), 974–984. doi:10.1177/0266242614543336

De Carolis, D. M., Litzky, B. E., & Eddleston, K. A. (2009). Why networks enhance the progress of new venture creation: The influence of social capital and cognition. *Entrepreneurship Theory and Practice*, *33*(2), 527–545. doi:10.1111/j.1540-6520.2009.00302.x

Drnovsek, M., Cardon, M. S., & Patel, P. C. (2016). Direct and indirect effects of passion on growing technology ventures. *Strategic Entrepreneurship Journal*, *10*(2), 194–213. doi:10.1002ej.1213

Foo, M. D. (2011). Emotions and entrepreneurial opportunity evaluation. *Entrepreneurship Theory and Practice*, *35*(2), 375–393. doi:10.1111/j.1540-6520.2009.00357.x

Galbraith, C. S., DeNoble, A. F., & Ehrlich, S. B. (2012). Predicting the commercialization progress of early-stage technologies: An ex-ante analysis. *IEEE Transactions on Engineering Management*, *59*(2), 213–225. doi:10.1109/TEM.2010.2068050

Grichnik, D., Smeja, A., & Welpe, I. (2010). The importance of being emotional: How do emotions affect entrepreneurial opportunity evaluation and exploitation? *Journal of Economic Behavior & Organization*, *76*(1), 15–29. doi:10.1016/j.jebo.2010.02.010

Kannadhasan, M., Aramvalarthan, S., & Kumar, B. P. (2014). Relationship among cognitive biases, risk perceptions and individual's decision to start a venture. *Decision (Washington, D.C.)*, *41*(1), 87–98.

Keh, H. T., Foo, M. D., & Lim, B. C. (2002). Opportunity evaluation under risky conditions: The cognitive processes of entrepreneurs. *Entrepreneurship Theory and Practice*, *27*(2), 125–148. doi:10.1111/1540-8520.00003

Lin, Y., Wang, Y., & Kung, L. A. (2015). Influences of cross-functional collaboration and knowledge creation on technology commercialization: Evidence from high-tech industries. *Industrial Marketing Management*, *49*, 128–138. doi:10.1016/j.indmarman.2015.04.002

Markman, G. D., Gianiodis, P. T., Phan, P. H., & Balkin, D. B. (2005). Innovation speed: Transferring university technology to market. *Research Policy*, *34*(7), 1058–1075. doi:10.1016/j.respol.2005.05.007

Milanov, H., & Fernhaber, S. A. (2009). The impact of early imprinting on the evolution of new venture networks. *Journal of Business Venturing*, *24*(1), 46–61. doi:10.1016/j.jbusvent.2007.11.001

Murnieks, C. Y., Mosakowski, E., & Cardon, M. S. (2014). Pathways of passion: Identity centrality, passion, and behavior among entrepreneurs. *Journal of Management*, *40*(6), 1583–1606. doi:10.1177/0149206311433855

Nacu, C. M., & Avasilcai, S. (2014). Environmental factors influencing technological entrepreneurship: Research framework and results. *Procedia: Social and Behavioral Sciences*, *109*(2), 1309–1315. doi:10.1016/j.sbspro.2013.12.630

Strese, S., Keller, M., & Flatten, T. C. (2016). CEOs' Passion for inventing and radical innovations in SMEs: The moderating effect of shared vision. *Journal of Small Business Management*.

Tabak, F., & Barr, S. H. (1999). Propensity to adopt technological innovations: The impact of personal characteristics and organizational context. *Journal of Engineering and Technology Management*, *16*(3), 247–270. doi:10.1016/S0923-4748(99)00011-9

Zahra, S. A., & Nielsen, A. P. (2002). Sources of capabilities, integration and technology commercialization. *Strategic Management Journal*, *23*(5), 377–398. doi:10.1002mj.229

Chapter 8
Make Use of the Difference of Failure and Exit to Improve the Operation Efficiency

Yangyang Chen
Hebei University of Technology, China

Weiwei Dong
Tianjin Academy of Social Sciences, China

Dixuan Zhang
Dalian University of Technology, China

Mingwei Jin
Dalian University of Technology, China

ABSTRACT

As business failure is a high probability event that influences the operation efficiency of the entrepreneurial ecosystem, it is necessary to know how to manage business failure experience to promote serial entrepreneurship and improve circulation in the ecosystem. While most scholars agree that it is different between failure and exit, DeTienne suggests that exit could be a way to avoid failure and protect the passion and financial condition of entrepreneurs. Therefore, this chapter analyzes the difference of failure and exit and conducts a model to help entrepreneurs decide whether to exit and how to choose a better way to exit entrepreneurship. In the meantime, this chapter analyzes why entrepreneurial exit can improve the operation efficiency of entrepreneurial ecosystem, and also it would give some ideas about how to bound from failure and benefit from failure to do better next time. After reading this chapter, entrepreneurs have the idea that failure is controllable and exit may be a restart to do business more successfully.

DOI: 10.4018/978-1-7998-3495-3.ch008

OPERATING MECHANISM - MAKE USE OF THE DIFFERENCE OF FAILURE AND EXIT TO IMPROVE THE OPERATION EFFICIENCY OF ENTREPRENEURIAL ECOSYSTEM

As business failure is a high probability event and influence the operation efficiency of entrepreneurial ecosystem, it is necessary to know how to manage business failure experience to promote serial entrepreneurship and improve circulation in the ecosystem. While most scholars agree that it is different between failure and exit, DeTienne(2010)suggests that exit could be a way to avoid failure and protect the passion and financial condition of entrepreneurs. Therefore, this chapter would like to analyze the difference of failure and exit, and conduct a model to help entrepreneurs decide whether to exit and how to choose a better way to exit entrepreneurship. In the meantime, this chapter analyze why entrepreneurial exit can improve the operation efficiency of entrepreneurial ecosystem, and also it would give some ideas about how to bound from failure and benefit from failure to do better next time. We do hope after reading this chapter, entrepreneurs have the idea that failure is controllable and exit maybe a restart to do business more successfully.

1. the operating mechanism of entrepreneurship ecosystem
2. the participants of entrepreneurship ecosystem

When we talk about entrepreneurial ecosystem, we know it involve multi levels and multi subjects. There are a series of interconnected business subjects (e.g. new ventures, investment organization, colleges and so on) and entrepreneurial environment (e.g. policies, culture, and so on), which improve the performance by formal and informal contacts. In this ecosystem, the direct participant are enterprises, while the indirect participants are major industries offered technology and human resource support, government, colleges and research institutions, investment organization (bank and venture capital institutions), intermediary (accounting firm, law office and so on) and cnvironmcnt (c.g. natural cnvironmcnt, culturc, institution and so on).(see fig.1)

The Characters of Entrepreneurship Ecosystem

Most scholars agree that entrepreneurship ecosystem has six key characters, which are diversity, networked, symbiosis, competitiveness, self-sustaining and regional.

1. Diversity. Entrepreneurship ecosystem is composed of many types of participants, such as start-up enterprises, large-scale enterprises, governments, universities, scientific research institutions, investment institutions and

Figure 1. Composition of entrepreneurial ecosystem

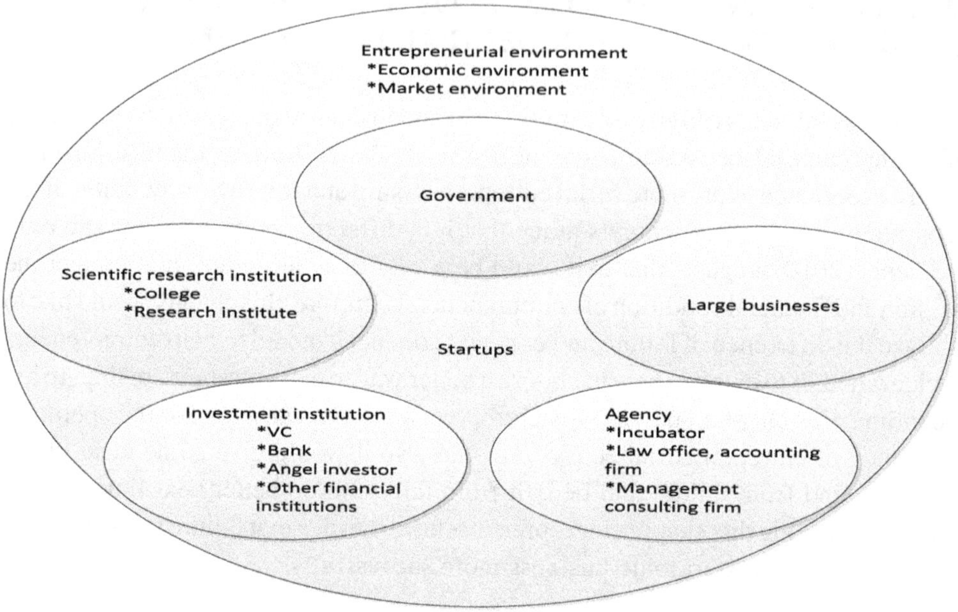

intermediary institutions that provide technology and talents. These subjects play different roles, and drive the development of entrepreneurial ecosystem through cooperation among subjects and complementary resources and capabilities. Actually, even if the same type of entities, such as startups, play different roles in the system. Some enterprises are specialized in technology and mainly focus on technology research and development, while others are good at production and marketing, mainly engaged in production and sales. Correspondingly, there are specialized after-sales service enterprises. They occupy different positions and functions in the value chain and maintain the healthy development of ecosystem.

2. Networked. The entrepreneurial ecosystem contains a variety of participants, each of which is embedded in the network, and the subjects are interrelated and interdependent. In the ecosystem, the subject creates value through interaction and integration and undertakes the work of the system together. Under the network structure of participants, there are complex interactions among them, which can affect the entrepreneurial environment. The improved entrepreneurial environment will attract more subjects to enter, further expand the network between subjects, and finally form a virtuous circle. In the system, there is a certain connection between new enterprises and between new enterprises and mature enterprises, usually in the form of business. With the

development of business, knowledge, technology and opportunities flow with it, resulting in spillover effect. The government and other relevant institutions play a supporting role in providing policy and resource support for start-ups. Through the network relationship among the participants, each of them can interact and work together to promote the construction and development of the entrepreneurial ecosystem

3. Symbiosis. In the ecosystem, the subjects gather together because of the vision of creating value together. By embedding into the complex network, each participant coexists with other subjects and evolves together. Each subject can provide unique products or services, trust each other, follow the common logic, complement each other's functions, depend on each other and create collaboratively, so as to realize symbiosis
4. competitiveness. The resources in the system are limited, which determines the competitive relationship between the participants, especially between the same type. New enterprises often need to compete in order to occupy a certain position in the system, and the enterprises that fail in the competition have to face loss or even failure. Mature enterprises or new start-ups can enhance their competitive advantage through merger and acquisition of other new start-ups. Similarly, new start-ups can choose to be acquired to avoid failure.
5. Self-sustaining. In order to survive and develop, the entrepreneurial ecosystem must be able to achieve dynamic self-sustaining and self -strengthening. The internal main body and elements of the system self-maintain and strengthen through spontaneous organization, so that the internal system becomes orderly, so as to solve the internal contradictions and the unbalanced state caused by environmental stimulation (Cai et al,2016). The entrepreneurial ecosystem is promoted through the interaction of internal subjects and elements. When these elements are perfect enough to complement each other, the system can achieve self-maintenance.
6. Regional. There are some differences in resource base, culture and system elements in different regions. The entrepreneurial process is affected by the interaction of complex economic, social and institutional environment. Therefore, it is necessary to build a suitable entrepreneurial ecosystem according to local resources, geographical location and culture. However, with the continuous development of the Internet, subjects can cooperate with each other through the Internet, so the regional characteristics of entrepreneurial ecosystem will gradually weaken, and cross regional ecosystem may also appear.

The Operation Rules of Entrepreneurship Ecosystem

There are three operation rules of entrepreneurship ecosystem, which are resource aggregation mechanism, value exchange mechanism, and balance regulation mechanism (Lin, 2011).

1. Resource aggregation mechanism. Entrepreneurial ecosystem integrates the resources needed by entrepreneurial enterprises and serves the survival and development of entrepreneurial enterprises. Due to the disadvantages of start-up, the start-up enterprises lack of management experience, customers, capital and other resources, and a well-run entrepreneurial ecosystem can alleviate this problem to some extent. The resources in the entrepreneurial ecosystem are diversified, with different specialties and natures of participants. Only through the orderly flow mechanism within the system, can the resources be gathered in entrepreneurial activities to help the survival and growth of new enterprises.
2. Value exchange mechanism. All subjects in the system are connected with each other to exchange resources and information. This kind of interaction enables both sides to benefit from it, and its essence is the transmission and transformation of value. In fact, when looking at a single startup in the system, we find that whether it's opportunity identification or new project development or product sales, it's the process of exchanging value with other organizations. The value exchange mechanism is centered on entrepreneurial activities, and maintains the operation of the whole entrepreneurial ecosystem by forming the value network within it.
3. Balance regulation mechanism. In a balanced state, entrepreneurial activities in the whole region show the overall characteristics of stable development, and the resource convergence mechanism and value exchange mechanism within the system also run stably all the time, which is conducive to the development of entrepreneurial activities. When new organizations enter, they will inevitably occupy a certain niche and undertake certain responsibilities. When an enterprise exits, its original responsibilities will be decomposed by other enterprises. The regulation mechanism of entrepreneurial ecosystem also means that there is a certain threshold in the entrepreneurial ecosystem. If the business environment deteriorates to a certain extent and the accumulated negative factors in the entrepreneurial ecosystem exceed the threshold, the inherent regulation mechanism will lose its function, which leads to the imbalance of the whole ecosystem.

THE ROLES OF FAILURE AND EXIT IN ENTREPRENEURSHIP ECOSYSTEM

We know the ecosystem can keep self-sustaining and balance, As the entrepreneurial ecosystem is one of the ecosystems, the important characteristic is openness, which means no barriers or low barriers for the new entrants and exit. Only the liquidity can keep the ecosystem full of energy. As we talked before, it is quite common that enterprise fail or perform not well. If these companies do not exit from the system but just keep operation, they would do nothing help but cost resource and lower entrepreneurial passion. What is more, too many zombie enterprises mean low efficiency and unhealthy. If this condition continues for a long time, the environment is not conducive to the development of the new ventures and the system's growth stalls. while potential entrants conduct survey on the environment and operation of the system, the floundering economy dampen entrepreneurs' confidence. Less new ventures are started up, lower levels of activities are. It cannot sustain in a long time. Thus, exit is important to the sustainable development. At the same time, making use of exit is good for reenter and improve the efficiency of ecosystem. It is a longer time for entrepreneur to start a new business than taking over a former company, which can save some time such as the recruiting employees, designing the company structure, arranging the production, and so on. Just like natural ecosystems, there are not only producers (e.g. the new entrants and start-ups), but also decomposers (e.g. exit mechanism). By decomposing those stagnant businesses and failed companies, the entrepreneurial ecosystem keeps benign development. As exit and reenter mean restructuring the available resources in the system, the operation efficiency gets improved. Therefore, it is important to know the concept of entrepreneurial failure and exit and differentiate them.

The Concept of Entrepreneurial Failure and Exit

Entrepreneurial Failure

The most typical character of entrepreneurship is uncertainty which is showed by high failure rate. According to the Forbes (2015), almost 90 percent new ventures ended with failure. Although entrepreneurs and scholars don't agree with the consequences, the optimistic scholars believe up to 44 percent of enterprises are successful (Sarasvathy et al., 2013), which means 56 percent of new ventures are losing. The reason, we argued, was because most research objectives are self-employed, it is hard to separate entrepreneurs from enterprises so that we always treat business failure as entrepreneur failure (Ucbasaran et al., 2013). While there is seriously distinction between them, it is necessary to make illustration at individual level and company level.

1. At individual level

In the perspective of serial entrepreneurship, the failure of new ventures doesn't mean the end of entrepreneurial life of entrepreneurs. Crocker & Wolfe (2001) point out that when entrepreneurs take their self-worth as stake, they feel loss if they lose himself in their self-esteem. Based on experimental data collected from 105 entrepreneurs who have experienced business failure, Khelil (2016) categorize them as confused, supported at arm's length, megalomaniac, dissatisfied lord and big-time gambler, and there is no typical loser to cover all of them. After reviewing existing literature, Jenkins & McKelvie (2016) hold the idea that they can judge the entrepreneur failure from subject and objective aspect. On subject aspect, they think entrepreneur failure is related to return on human capital for optional employment opportunities, while they argue it is based on failure influence and entrepreneurs' feedback, such as finance, emotion, and so on. As mostly entrepreneur failure is based on individual cognitive, this chapter name entrepreneur failure as the situation that entrepreneur can't get their human capital recouped and lose confidence.

2. at firm level

When we talk about business failure, we often care about their financial index, such as debt paying ability, net margin, working capital, and so on. Deakin (1998) take the company which can't afford debts and clear accounts as business failure. From the perspective of contract, Kumar (2001) argue that for the bad operation, the imposed change at ownership and management is business failure. Following traditional business failure theory, entrepreneurial failure is concepted as following, such as bankrupt and liquidation (Zacharakis et al.,1999), the situation in which the company died for having trouble making ends meet (Shepherd, 2003). As entrepreneurship is full of uncertainty, even successful new ventures may have faced unsatisfactory situation and have poor financial performance. Therefore, it is biased to define entrepreneurial failure as the traditional way for not reflecting the character of entrepreneurship. From the perspective of cognitive theory, scholars find at the beginning of starting enterprises, entrepreneurs would set goals for their companies. Based on this, they define entrepreneurial failure as new venture termination for not meeting the goal (McGrath, 1999). This decision about "continuing or termination" depends on the least degree entrepreneurs can accept. They named it threshold, mostly is based on their own judgement (Gimeno et al., 1997). To describe failure better, scholars define it base on attribution theory, for example the closed companies for law issues, partnership dispute and so on. Above all, it is necessary to combine entrepreneurs' understanding and external expressions, then this paper define entrepreneurial failure as the situation in which the new ventures cannot achieve the expect of entrepreneurs and have to be given up.

Entrepreneurial Exit

No matter starting up new business or exit from entrepreneurship, they both are the individual career choice behavior. Thus, entrepreneurial exit is defined as the behavior individual decided to leave self-employed (Dawson & Henley,2013; Beiler, 2017), even the decision individual decide to give up entrepreneurship (Callanan & Zimmerman, 2016). From the perspective of RBV, exit decision is the career choice made for maximize their human capital return (Wennberg et al, 2010). When we treat exit as one component of entrepreneurial process, it means the end of the activity. DeTienne (2010) defines exit as the process that entrepreneurs or venture teams leave the company they found and exit from the ownership and management in different degrees. Combing these concepts, we find when we talk about exit, we care more about the individual or the team than the firm level. Furthermore, it concerns about private business than listed company for the owners of private enterprises have much power and make decisions by themselves. In fact, entrepreneurial exit is a dynamic and multiform phenomenon. Entrepreneurial exit is not only a dynamic process which can be treated as the ending of entrepreneurship, but also a selective behavior made by the owner or team.

The Difference Between Entrepreneurial Failure And Exit

According to the literature review we have done to failure and exit, we find that there are some researches mixed the concept of business closure, discontinuance and failure. In fact, there are some differences and connections and it is necessary to analyze them in detail.

As we talked about before, for the objective we cared are mostly self-employed and private business, entrepreneurs and new ventures often exit at the same time (Akhter et al., 2016). At firm level, there are less researches which mostly treat the conditions exit from the market or organization as exit (Balcaen et al., 2012), such as merger and be acquisition. At individual level, the main difference is the transformation of entrepreneurs' identity.

In many researches on entrepreneurship, organization and strategy management, entrepreneurial exit equals to entrepreneur's failure, which obstruct the research development on exit to some extent. Therefore, it is really important to know the difference between entrepreneurial failure and exit. In the early researches, scholars believe exit is the consequence of poor performance from the perspective of utility maximization5. However, recently researches find that besides the economic factor, entrepreneurs may exit for retirement, education opportunity, and other non-economic factors (Justo et al., 2015). Furthermore, they dividend exit into two forms, which are involuntary exit for financial distress and voluntary exit. When entrepreneurs exit from entrepreneurship for their own issues by their own volition, the company performance may not decrease or even do well. These exit actions are positive but not failure.

While mainstream views of strategy management and organization researches are that the main goals of entrepreneurs are improving the competitiveness of enterprises and wining the profit, exit is negative result and keeping growing is successful result (Wennberg & DeTienne, 2014). Considering failure may lead to exit or continue, the persistence caused by bad company performance, entrepreneurs' disappointment, entrepreneurs' financial and psychology failure is not all positive and successful result7. Actually, the exit for these three reasons could be a way to avoid the real failure happening. Entrepreneurs could use this way to avoid risk and give up those companies with limited growth potential (McGrath, 1999). Thus, entrepreneurial failure doesn't accompany with entrepreneurs' exit and company close. In conclusion, we hold the idea that the differentiation criterion is the financial situation of the enterprise and entrepreneurs' voluntary.

Table 1. the concept of exit and failure

	Individual Level	Firm Level
Entrepreneurial failure	For portfolio entrepreneurs, the percent of the number of failure enterprises to all enterprises created (Ucbasaran et al,.2010)	Business exit for poor performance (Justo et al,.2015); company stopped for not achieving minimum economic viability (Ucbasaran et al., 2013)
Entrepreneurial exit	Give up entrepreneurial career (Stam et al,.2010); retirement (DeTienne, 2010)	Close company with no debt (Headd,2003); sold self-financing company (Amaral et al., 2007)

The Connection Between Entrepreneurial Failure and Exit

Generally speaking, closure is the last form for failure business and exit company. Therefore, there are some connections between entrepreneurial failure and exit.

Entrepreneurial failure is a poignant and destructive experience, which make a big impact on entrepreneurs' finance, psychology and physiology (Cope, 2011). Failure doesn't deserve praise nevertheless, the aim we analyze entrepreneurial failure is getting the idea how to avoid failure and get knowledge to improve subsequent entrepreneurship. In continuous financial system, we can track the financial issues. It is a gradual process from financial stability to loan defaults to bankruptcy or liquidation. Although new ventures do not perform very well in finance, it need some time from the beginning to the real bankruptcy or liquidation. It is a pity that few researches discuss the way to avoid failure and manage the procedure. Considering the concept of failure and exit and the difference between them, we regard exit as a way to avoid failure and reflect the capacity to harvest value, which is the key to realize enterprise value17. Voluntary exiting is much more common for those perform badly than waiting the company going insolvency and bankruptcy (Thorburn K S., 2000). There are three ways to exit, which are financial harvest, stewardship exit and voluntary cessation exit (DeTienne et al., 2015). When entrepreneurs find the possibility of business failure, such as the fluidity of current assets, profitability, and so on, they should analyze the situation, prepare and design the way to exit, which can decrease the failure happening and get part or all the turnover, or even premium. Combing the classification of entrepreneurial failure, we are going to discuss it in two levels.

1. at individual level

According to the survey, over half entrepreneurs think about the exit strategy at the beginning of starting new businesses and nearly all entrepreneurs would finish at least one exit process17. It is a better choice for entrepreneurs to avoid failure by getting financial harvest (e.g. selling company, being acquired by other company) and stewardship exit (e.g. keeping part of management right, MBO or EBO). Financial harvest realizes the company value and get entrepreneurs compensation. Stewardship exit allow entrepreneurs influence company for a long time and get psychological comfort. However, voluntary cessation exit (e.g. liquation and closure) is weaker in financial harvest and psychological compensation, but better than failure cost of involuntary exit. From the concept of entrepreneur failure, when entrepreneurs get their human capital compensation and do not lose confidence, this condition is not so-called failure. In this way, we think these three exit route can avoid the failure happening.

2. at firm level

No matter which way to exit, the ownership and stewardship of the new venture are both change in some degree and different with the original enterprises. This is to say, if the exit is the choice made by entrepreneurs themselves, the company is not failure at least not the original enterprise. In fact, the significance of exit is far from it. The cost of entrepreneurial failure is not only the own capital of entrepreneurs, but also the social resource, capital and benefit. In the hypothesis of revolution door, the number of company exit nearly equals to the amount of new entry in one economic entity (DeTienne & Wennberg, 2016). In this way, the former company which have high failure possibility could exit by changing the ownership and become a new venture to operate and improve the performance.

The internal recycle help new entrants save the preparation timing, which means resource reutilization, and improve the efficiency and turnover rate of resource utilization. It is beneficial for both enterprise and the social environment. To avoid failure, voluntary termination means stopping loss in time and making use of limited resources, furthermore to optimize the entrepreneurial environment and improve the efficiency of entrepreneurial ecosystem.

THE ROUTE TO EXIT FROM ENTREPRENEURSHIP

Following the traditional idea of financial management, existing researches mainly discuss these six exit routes, which are initial public offerings (IPO), mergers and acquisitions (M&A), employee buyout (EBO), family succession, sale and liquidation21. DeTienne and Cardon (2012) do research on entrepreneurial exit strategy according to return on risk, exit complexity and the possibility of participating in company management after exit. IPO and M&A are with high risk and complexity but high return. Although IPO is always seen as way of financing, it is also a way to dilution and exit. M&A is an exit way for both companies and entrepreneurs. EBO is a relative slowly way to transfer the ownership and exit in which the entrepreneurs can participate in business in a long time. Family succession is beneficial to the inheritance of knowledge and improve the value of the enterprise. Sale and liquidation are with low risk and easy to conduct while the benefit is limited. With a view to the state of business, IPO and family succession are fit for the well-run companies. M&A and EBO are suitable for companies with growth potential. Closure and liquation are often found on the poorly developed enterprises and failure business. Thus, we can find choose a suitable exit way important to the enterprises and entrepreneurs, which should be design carefully.

It is said that the exit strategy is formed at the early stage31. This chapter is going to analyze the exit strategy and routes by using the design thinking and science of the artificial. Design thinking is the thinking way of designer, which is the psychological process of designing objectives, service or system. Design thinking includes induction, deduction and abductive reasoning (Dunne & Martin, 2006). While the logic of induction and deduction emphasis on "what it is" and "what should it be" respectively, abductive reasoning underlines "what could it be". Before starting up new businesses, entrepreneurs should not only care about the profits, but also pay much more attention on the development and the whole life of the companies. It begins with opportunity identification. Nascent entrepreneurs pay more attention on starting a new business and running a company than thinking about the whole life cycle. Actually, if the owners do not take all things into consideration, they will be caught in a dilemma sooner or later. Due to liability of newness and the environment dynamic, entrepreneurs have to face the arrested development companies or financial distress. When they have no preparation, they are fear of failure and hesitate to exit. They are likely to try everything to save the company and make it survive. It costs lot but does little to improve the economy. The longer time they spend, the more loss they bear. If they know it inevitable, they would like to prefer "smart failure" and exit to keep their confidence and property. Design thinking works in the life cycle. Entrepreneurs could use the design thinking to do their business plan from the beginning to the end. When they do survey about the environment, they should know it changes all the time and prepare for two eventualities at least. If they admit exit is an indispensable link of the company whole life, they will look this issue objectively, design the exit routes and choose the most suitable one according to the internal and external conditions of the company. Most entrepreneurs start up business for gaining profit while the IPO is the best choice and they do their best to make it. But it is really hard and has high requirement on the companies' finance, regulations, operation and so on. Hence, it should not be the only exit route. Entrepreneurs have to prepare an alternative exit route. M&A require the company have its speciality and have a unique dominant position in the market. Acquiring enterprise get access to complementary resources and achieve a competitive advantage. The acquiree can get cash compensation and the entrepreneurs of it can exit or found next entrepreneurs.

It is a win-win way for both parties. DeTienne et al. (2015) classify IPO and M&A as financial harvest strategy which make entrepreneurs get paid. Family succession require the owner have the successor who has the desire and ability to take over the family business. If they do not have the appropriate candidate, EBO is a good choice. Former employees are familiar with the company and have passion develop it. Both the successor and employees have feelings for the company and are willing to grow the business. These two ways allow entrepreneurs to participate in the management and influence the strategy and decision in a long time. When entrepreneurs reach the target and want to give up the company, sale and liquation are very common. As entrepreneurial enterprises are mainly small and micro enterprises, entrepreneurs have little knowledge of the management, especially the exit knowledge. Their access to information is limited so that they cannot find better way but closure. From the perspective of information service, this chapter construct a model of information process of the choice of entrepreneurial exit routes.

The nature of the choice of entrepreneurial exit route is dominant by the entrepreneur, obtain, analyze and deal with the internal and external information, then finally generate the optional exit route. When entrepreneurs identify other optional opportunity, or find their goal have achieved or have no possibility to achieve, they generate exit intention and begin to obtain information. The exited company, especially those businesses faced possible failure, need to focus on efficiency and pursue success. The information ability of entrepreneurs is generally not good and social networking is limited, which make them difficult to get high quality information. Taking these into account, the information service organization is a good choice. The information service organization is based on the technology layer of information organization and information discovery and resource consolidation layer of information offer and decision support. Through data analysis and intelligence analysis, information service information could provide relevant knowledge about law, finance, company information, M&A, IPO and so on. Information service organization could not only collect the surface message, but also process information to generate knowledge and provide technology analysis and consultation service for entrepreneurs and enterprises. It reduces sunk cost and improve the efficiency of decision-making. Following the information process model, we analyze the information service for exit routes and illustrate the work of each stage of the facilitating agency. When entrepreneurs get message from the environment, policy and the internal of the company and generate exit intention, they entrust information service agency to provide recommendations. We believe management consultancy, law office, accounting firm, asset management company and other service organizations have the ability and channels to fulfill the information process. They can do survey and use their special information channels to collect more effective information. If this commission become the regular business, they will collect and accumulate information in purpose to form their own database, then update in time. When they get next commission, they can search data in the database and match them with the requirement, which is very effective. Information cognition and regeneration are the core of information thinking. Information cognition is a process of dealing with and calculate information to generate knowledge, which transfer the static information (e.g. information in the database, library, and people's brain) into the active power to inform the strategy solving the problem. Information service organization can use modern technology to dispose and analyze the information to protect the purity, availability and security of the information. According to informatics theory and manner, they can identify the information hidden behind the surface, activate information and provide factual basis for decision-making. In this stage, they depend on the information system, which is composed by "hard factors" and "soft factors". The "hard factors" are technical equipment, materials, intelligence officers of the information service institution. The "soft factors" exist in the form of knowledge, such as the intelligence, technological level, management level, decision-making method and so on. When they get clear goals, the information system has the capacity to identify whether the information is good to achieve the goal. They identify the Euclidean distance (the gap) between the information state and target state, and the development tendency by complex analysis. Based on this, they confirm the utility of the information and the standard is formulated by the information service organization according to the entrepreneurs' commission. Information regeneration is the most important stage, which combine the knowledge produced by the cognition and useful information with the exit intention, then choose the entrepreneurial exit route according to the fact. The information service organization has brainpower consist of the specialist and put head together to deal with problems expertly. On the aspect of evaluation model, they design the evaluation index system, evaluate and rank the possible exit routes according to the exit intention and motivation. They would give the optional schemes and recommendations, and illustrate the risk and return. After this, they fulfill their task and do not participate the decision and implementation process. The decision is in the hands of the entrepreneurs. The final stage is information apply-effect. In this step, entrepreneurs need to entrust professional organizations, when they choose financial harvest or stewardship exit route. Unlike the former service, this service is more professional and pointed. They can do help to the execution and make it come true. Entrepreneurs should control and track the operation situation, and lead it to the target, then fulfill the exit process. What is worth mentioning, for habitual entrepreneurs, exit information apply-effect means next turn of opportunity identification.

In conclusion, the model of exit route choice leads by the entrepreneurs, and the information service support the process. It makes the exit, especially the IPO and M&A, come true.

Figure 2. The model of exit route choice

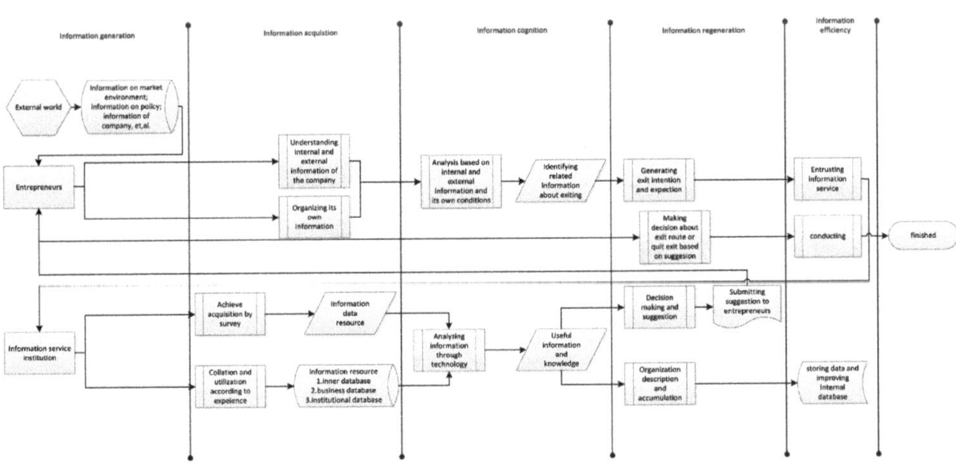

CASE ON EXIT: TAKING THE ENTREPRENEURIAL EXPERIENCE OF SHI YUZHU AS EXAMPLE

In fact, it is not only in theory that we have demonstrated the feasibility of entrepreneurial exit to avoid failure, but also there are numerous cases in practice. Considering that most of the start-ups are small and medium-sized enterprises, the information for public disclosure is limited, especially the information related to failure is more difficult to obtain. Even if the long-term follow-up entrepreneurs are limited by energy and time, it is difficult to obtain first-hand information completely. In this part, we review the experience of Shi Yuzhu, who was once the richest and the most negative entrepreneur in China, to verify the relationship between entrepreneurial failure and exit, and to clarify its significance to the entrepreneurial ecosystem. In order to improve the validity of the research, this paper tries to obtain secondary data through various ways. The data source is divided into two parts, one is "internal data" including biography of Shi Yuzhu, microblog, internal speech documents, personal speech, related videos and other materials; the other is "external data" including relevant media reports, academic literature, biography books and other materials. Focusing on the topic of entrepreneurial failure and exit, data were screened according to the standards of relevance, accuracy and authority, and repeated, non-mutually verified or unverified data were eliminated. Finally, 39 texts about Shi Yuzhu were retained as the main data, including 6 reflexive texts, 5 internal conference speeches, 27 interviews and 1 autobiography.

By combing these materials, we have sorted out the key events in the process of Shi Yuzhu's entrepreneurship, as shown in Figure 3

Figure 3. The chronicle of entrepreneurship events

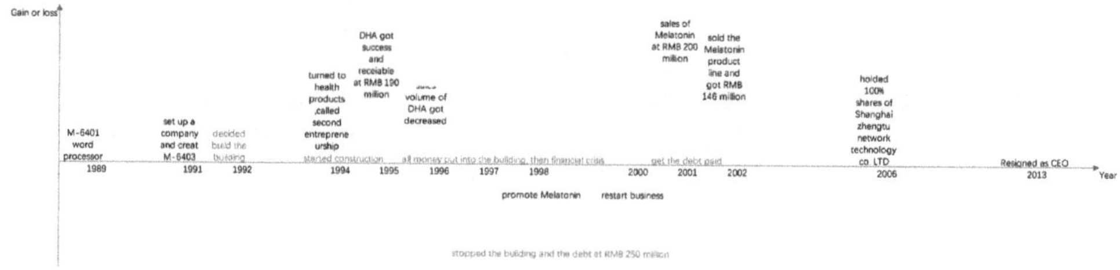

From the first entrepreneurial success of Hanka to the failure of second entrepreneurship, then to the rise of Melatonin and the success of Giant Interactive Group, Mr. Shi realizes the N-type entrepreneurial process, which is a rare and typical case of failure and re-success. After analysis of these contexts, we have three foundings:

1. Entrepreneurial failure does not happen by chance, there is something to be predicted. Half a year before the outbreak of the crisis (i.e. the second half of 1996), the cash flow of Giant Group was not good, from the perspective of financial stability, which is the precursor of failure. But at that time, Shi Yuzhu thought that there were more than 200 million net assets, which was safe, so he did not stop the building. When they found the cash flow of the building was in crisis, they try their best to save it, such as "take this building cooperate with others even with little profit" and finally gave up the building (i.e. failure) until it was "unable to save". Only by identifying the signal of failure can we avoid failure by quitting. Otherwise, when failure is about to break out or has already happened, the behavior of entrepreneurs is mostly futile.
2. It is very important to choose the exit timing and the route to avoid failure. when they start the new venture, they should design the exit way. When they realize the failure may happen, they should do plan about exit route and execute it. Before the failure, not all projects were unprofitable, but he put the funds from these projects into the building, while "the limited funds were firmly tied up, the building led to the financial crisis of the Giant Group". If it is found the company can not afford the building in time, they can seek other cooperation ways or exit ways, which may avoid the failure. when the condition became worse, they choose the way of taking this building cooperate with others even with little profit, but no one took it over for high risk. In other words, the exit route was not appropriate in the circumstance. In the process of cognitive failure and summarizing experience, Shi Yuzhu believes that they should pay attention to the choice of timing and path of exit (i.e. "if we found the trend is not as expected, we should make the decision at once"), or the company would fail (i.e. the funds would be consumed"). From the financial perspective, it can reduce the cost of failure by ending the state of overspending as soon as possible (active or passive). Shi Yuzhu believes "if the media reported the crisis earlier, we might have some money". When faced with possible failure, especially in trouble, it is rarely solved by solving a simple problem or delaying failure, and it needs to "give up decisively". At individual level, affected by the laws and regulations, policy and entrepreneurs' own considerations at that time, entrepreneurs did not separate themselves from the enterprises, especially in terms of assets, which led to them bearing the debts. From the perspective of corporate governance and serial entrepreneurship, this part hold that the separation of individual and corporate debts and the timely withdrawal of individual from the entrepreneurial enterprise can protect entrepreneurs not only on the aspects of assets and their entrepreneurial passion, self-confidence and reputation, which is conducive to promoting subsequent Entrepreneurship.

3. Entrepreneurial exit from the perspective of serial entrepreneurship. At the company level, drawing lessons from failure experience of the building, Shi Yuzhu focused on the products and enterprises more specifically. When he thought the product life cycle of the HJDD toward the end, he sold 75% of the equity and earned the residual value to a great extent which would be used in the subsequent entrepreneurial activities (i.e. investing the CMBC). At individual level, Shi Yuzhu focused on one industry or product management in one period in following entrepreneurship. If necessary, he would exit from the venture by stewardship exit or retiring, and turn his energy to other fields. The energy and ability of entrepreneurs are limited, and continuous entrepreneurs start many times in their life. If they carry out business in parallel or pay attention to the average distribution, it is difficult to succeed, so entrepreneurial exit becomes an inevitable choice.
4. The meaning of exit for entrepreneurial ecosystem. The failure of an enterprise in an ecosystem not only affects its own survival, but also affects the development of its associated enterprises. The failure of the building not only caused the crisis of Giant Group, but also had influence on the financial status of investors and the settlement between suppliers and dealers. When the amount involved is large enough, investors, suppliers and underwriters also failed. If there were many enterprises involved in the system, the operating environment was deteriorating, and the system was in a state of imbalance. If Shi Yuzhu cooperated with others or terminated the building in time, the loss of Giant Group would be greatly reduced and the loss of other related parties would also be descended. Therefore, the impact of the building failure on ecosystem is correspondingly reduced. There is a certain degree of back feeding for the economic environment, and a healthy economic environment will release a positive signal to attract more entrepreneurs to carry out activities, enhance the vitality of the entrepreneurial ecosystem, and promote system upgrading.

THE WAY TO IMPROVE THE OPERATION EFFICIENCY OF ENTREPRENEURIAL ECOSYSTEM

Enterprises are never isolated individuals. They depend on the resource and play roles (e.g. producer, consumer, decomposer and so on) in the system. No matter new entry or exit, they would influence the operation of the system. When new business starts up, it occupies a certain ecological niche, change the original structure, and reshape the inner system division. When enterprise exit from the system, the role it plays in the system and the function need to be undertook or replenished. If the enterprise is so important that the failure and exit may cause ecosystem functional declines and operation efficiency declines. It is essential to illustrate the way of improving the operation efficiency.

We know failure costs a lot, not only the financial loss, but also the psychological cost and physiological cost. It costs much time and energy to recover from failure. While exit could be a way to avoid failure, especially the individual level, it can save the recovery time and be in favor of restarting new business. The new entrants replace the location of previous enterprises in the ecosystem. According to RBV, previous entrepreneurial experience is beneficial to the establishment and development of new ventures. The less time it spends on getting used to environment and system, the more efficiency the ecosystem operates. Business failure happens in the system, which is also a warning and reference for other companies. They can know where the rub is in relative terms. When one company chooses to transfer the ownership or management, the other companies who is more familiar with the business and have the ability to integrate resource are more likely to take over it. Sometimes, the reasons one company does not run well are very complicated. Financing and the ability of entrepreneurs are the main reasons, especially for the new start and the small and micro business. By resource integration, resources get well used and the operation situation gets better. When the owner of a company gets changed, its decision and strategy may change a lot. Maybe it is a new chance for company to take a new lease of life. In the meantime, the ecosystem thrives and fosters more businesses. When the entrepreneurial ecosystem insists on the rule of survival of the fittest and get use of the relationship between exit and reconstruction, the operation efficiency get guarantee.

REFERENCES

Akhter, N., Sieger, P., & Chirico, F. (2016). If we can't have it then no one should shutting down versus selling in family business portfolios. *Strategic Entrepreneurship Journal, 10*(4), 371–394. doi:10.1002ej.1237

Amaral, A. M., Rui, B., & Lima, F. (2007). Entrepreneurial exit and firm performance. *Frontiers of Entrepreneurship Research, 27*(5), 1-15.

Balcaen, S., Manigart, S., Buyze, J., & Ooghe, H. (2012). Firm exit after distress: Differentiating between bankruptcy, voluntary liquidation and M&A. *Small Business Economics, 39*(4), 949–975. doi:10.100711187-011-9342-7

Beiler, H. (2017). Do you dare? The effect of economic conditions on entrepreneurship among college graduates. *Labour Economics, 47*(S1), 64–74. doi:10.1016/j.labeco.2017.05.003

Bruno, A. V., Mcquarrie, E. F., & Torgrimson, C. G. (1992). The evolution of new technology ventures over 20 years: Patterns of failure, merger and survival. *Journal of Business Venturing, 7*(4), 291–302. doi:10.1016/0883-9026(92)90003-A

Cai, L., Peng, X., Satish, N., & Wang, L. (2016). Entrepreneurial ecosystem: Review and prospects. *Jilin University Journal Social Sciences Edition, 56*(1), 5–16.

Callanan, G. A., & Zimmerman, M. (2016). To be or not to be an entrepreneur: Applying a normative model to career decisions. *Journal of Career Development, 43*(5), 447–461. doi:10.1177/0894845316633525

Cope, J. (2011). Entrepreneurial learning from failure: An interpretative phenomenological analysis. *Journal of Business Venturing, 26*(6), 604–623. doi:10.1016/j.jbusvent.2010.06.002

Crocker, J., & Wolfe, C. T. (2001). Contingencies of self-worth. *Psychological Review, 14*(4), 593–623. doi:10.1037/0033-295X.108.3.593 PMID:11488379

Dawson, C., & Henley, A. (2013). Over-optimism and entry and exit from self-employment. *International Small Business Journal, 31*(8), 938–954. doi:10.1177/0266242612445462

Deakins, D., & Freel, M. (1998). Entrepreneurial learning and the growth process in SMEs. *The Learning Organization, 5*(3), 144–155. doi:10.1108/09696479810223428

DeTienne, D. R. (2010). Entrepreneurial exit as a critical component of the: Theoretical development. *Journal of Business Venturing, 25*(2), 203–215. doi:10.1016/j.jbusvent.2008.05.004

DeTienne, D. R., & Cardon, M. S. (2012). Impact of founder experience on exit intentions. *Small Business Economics, 38*(4), 351–374. doi:10.100711187-010-9284-5

DeTienne, D. R., Mckelvie, A., & Chandler, G. N. (2015). Making sense of entrepreneurial exit strategies: A typology and test. *Journal of Business Venturing, 30*(2), 255–272. doi:10.1016/j.jbusvent.2014.07.007

DeTienne, D. R., & Wennberg, K. (2016). Studying exit from entrepreneurship: New directions and insights. *International Small Business Journal, 34*(2), 151–156. doi:10.1177/0266242615601202

Dunne, D., & Martin, R. (2006). Design thinking and how it will change management education: An interview and discussion. *Academy of Management Learning & Education*, *5*(4), 512–523. doi:10.5465/amle.2006.23473212

Gimeno, J., Folta, T. B., Cooper, A. C., & Woo, C. Y. (1997). Survival of the fittest? Entrepreneurial human capital and the persistence of underperforming firms. *Administrative Science Quarterly*, *42*(4), 750–783. doi:10.2307/2393656

Headd, B. (2003). Redefining business success: Distinguishing between closure and failure. *Small Business Economics*, *21*(1), 51–61. doi:10.1023/A:1024433630958

Jenkins, A., & McKelvie, A. (2016). What is entrepreneurial failure? Implications for future research. *International Small Business Journal*, *34*(2), 176–188. doi:10.1177/0266242615574011

Justo, R., DeTienne, D. R., & Sieger, P. (2015). Failure or voluntary exit? Reassessing the female underperformance hypothesis. *Journal of Business Venturing*, *30*(6), 775–792. doi:10.1016/j.jbusvent.2015.04.004

Khelil, N. (2016). The many faces of entrepreneurial failure: Insights from an empirical taxonomy. *Journal of Business Venturing*, *31*(1), 72–84. doi:10.1016/j.jbusvent.2015.08.001

Kumar, R., & Usunier, J. C. (2001). Management education in a globalizing world. *Management Learning*, *32*(3), 363–391. doi:10.1177/1350507601323005

Lin, S. (2011). The concept development and operation mechanism of entrepreneurial ecosystem. *Journal of Central University of Finance & Economics*, *4*, 58–62.

McGrath, R. G. (1999). Falling forward: Real options reasoning and entrepreneurial failure. *Academy of Management Review*, *24*(1), 13–30. doi:10.5465/amr.1999.1580438

Sarasvathy, S. D., Menon, A. R., & Kuechle, G. (2013). Failing firms and successful entrepreneurs: Serial entrepreneurship as a temporal portfolio. *Small Business Economics*, *40*(2), 417–434. doi:10.100711187-011-9412-x

Shepherd, D. A. (2003). Learning from business failure: Propositions about the grief recovery process for the self-employed. *Academy of Management Review*, *28*(2), 318–329. doi:10.5465/amr.2003.9416377

Stam, E., Thurik, R., & Van der Zwan, P. (2010). Entrepreneurial exit in real and imagined markets. *Industrial and Corporate Change*, *19*(4), 1109–1139. doi:10.1093/icc/dtp047

Thorburn, K. S. (2000). Bankruptcy auctions, costs, debt recovery, and firm survival. *Journal of Financial Economics*, *58*(3), 337–368. doi:10.1016/S0304-405X(00)00075-1

Ucbasaran, D., Shepherd, D. A., Lockett, A., & Lyon, J. (2013). Life after business failure: The process and consequences of business failure for entrepreneurs. *Journal of Management*, *39*(1), 163–202. doi:10.1177/0149206312457823

Ucbasaran, D., Westhead, P., Wright, M., & Flores, M. (2010). The nature of entrepreneurial experience, business failure and comparative optimism. *Journal of Business Venturing*, *25*(6).

Wennberg, K., & Detienne, D. R. (2014). What do we really mean when we talk about 'exit'? - a critical review of research on entrepreneurial exit. *International Small Business Journal*, *32*(1), 4–16. doi:10.1177/0266242613517126

Wennberg, K., Wiklund, J., Detienne, D. R., & Cardon, M. S. (2010). Reconceptualizing entrepreneurial exit: Divergent exit routes and their drivers. *Journal of Business Venturing*, *25*(4), 361–375. doi:10.1016/j.jbusvent.2009.01.001

Zacharakis, A. L., Meyer, G. D., & Decastro, J. (1999). Differing perceptions of new venture failure: A matched exploratory study of venture capitalists and entrepreneurs. *Journal of Small Business Management*, *37*(3), 1–14.

Chapter 9
Review of Classical Intention-Based Entrepreneurial Models and Construction of Framework From Combined Perspectives of Entrepreneurial Motivation

Fei Hou
Beijing Normal University, Zhuhai, China

Yu Su
Beijing Normal University, Zhuhai, China

Mingde Qi
Guangdong University of Technology, China

Peixuan Lu
Dalian University of Technology, China

ABSTRACT

An extraordinary proliferation of entrepreneurship education programs has been underway in recent years. One of key purposes of entrepreneurship education is to foster entrepreneurial intention. So how to predict and interpret the process of entrepreneurial intention becomes a dominant topic in academia. Under related entrepreneurial and psychological theories, reasoning and reviewing related classical entrepreneurial intention models, this chapter analyzes the influencing factors and

DOI: 10.4018/978-1-7998-3495-3.ch009

interacting effects and proposes a path-model of entrepreneurial intentions from combined perspectives of entrepreneurial motivation and cognition in order to reveal the underlying psychological mechanism of entrepreneurial intention. The chapter hopes to have added richness to ongoing further researches among academics and discussions among educators and policymakers regarding the importance of entrepreneurial intention in entrepreneurial education.

INTRODUCTION

Discovering and nurturing potential entrepreneurs has been the hot point and eye-catcher for research topic in the fields of related researches on entrepreneurial intentions. Entrepreneurial intentions of potential entrepreneurs have been regarded as a kind of individual psychological process, and factors influencing this psychological process is the core of the researches on entrepreneurial process (Krueger, 2000).

Factors influencing entrepreneurial intentions can fall into internal factors and external factors. Internal factors include individual psychological traits, personal characters as well as cognitions; and external factors are defined as the special situation factors that potential entrepreneurs would be exposed to (Shaver & Scott, 1991; Kickul & Krueger, 2004). Decision-making of potential entrepreneurs would be influenced simultaneously by internal and external factors served as co-pilots role played in the intention-created process.

Individual psychological factors could be regarded as the internal engine for potential entrepreneurs to participate in entrepreneurial activities or launch behaviors related to entrepreneurship. While external situation factors could also affect entrepreneurial intentions through the mediators including individual perceptions and cognitions that would be of prime importance in affecting individual attitudes or beliefs related to entrepreneurial decisions.

Although the inner psychological factors of potential entrepreneurs (such as individual traits, individual characteristics, cognitive) change with external factors (environment) change, but external factors fail to affect entrepreneurial intentions and behaviors directly, while its influencing power has the effects on potential entrepreneurs indirectly through mediating variables (individual internal factors, such as individual cognitive). That is to say, entrepreneurial intentions manifest a certain kind of inner psychological willingness for engaging in entrepreneurial activities, which has been included potential entrepreneurs' overall evaluation and trade-off for individual background factors and external situation factors, and which is why this paper focus on individual internal psychological factors to research on process of entrepreneurial intention.

Based on literature review for researches on entrepreneurial intentions especially in view of internal psychological factors, currently researches on entrepreneurial intentions are almost from perspective of entrepreneurial process (Gelderen et al., 2006; Dimov, 2007; Gruber, 2007; Teece, 2007; Brush et al., 2008; Harper, 2008).

While early researches on entrepreneurial process are mainly from perspectives of individual traits and characteristics to predict and interpret entrepreneurial intentions and behaviors, but the research results are not fully satisfactory (Gartner, 1989). Among current researches on entrepreneurial intentions from perspective of entrepreneurial process, a few factors on the level of individual cognitive are ignored, and there are little researches concerned with entrepreneurial motivation and its role played in the entrepreneurial process, as well as how entrepreneurial motives translate into real entrepreneurial behaviors.

Regarding the study of entrepreneurial intention, scholars have begun to explore the key factors affecting entrepreneurial intention by using internal factors, such as psychological traits, personal characteristics, and the cognition of entrepreneurs, and have analyzed the development mechanism of entrepreneurial intention (Shapero and Sokol, 1982; Scott, 1991; Kickul and Krueger, 2004); however, these studies ignore the impact of external environmental factors on entrepreneurial intention. Later studies have explored environmental factors affecting entrepreneurs, taking into account both internal and external factors when constructing their entrepreneurial intention model (Ajzen, 1991; Shook, 2003). However, the current entrepreneurial intention model ignores the impact of specific situations, as entrepreneurs face specific situations that will inevitably affect their internal factors. That is, entrepreneurial intention is not only influenced by carrier factors (individual factors) but also by specific situational factors. Only when carrier factors and situational factors work together can entrepreneurial intention be stimulated (Elfving, 2008).

Therefore, the study of entrepreneurial intention began from a psychological perspective and then gradually combined with internal factors, such as trait theory, resource view and ability view. The study of entrepreneurial intention has now entered a new stage of research from a situational factor viewpoint. The focus of the present study highlights the role that specific situational factors play in the generation and development of entrepreneurial intention. Thus, different entrepreneurs will exhibit different performances in various specific situations; the entrepreneurs' internal factors and specific situational factors will jointly drive the emergence and development of entrepreneurial intention. However, questions remain: how do these internal and external factors drive entrepreneurial intention, and how do their effects differ? These questions must be explored and interpreted. The paper is organized in the following major sections.

The first part reviews the underground theories based which the research model is built.

The second part reviews and analyzes the current classical intention-based entrepreneurial models.

The third part presents the discuses of foundational models and proposes the research hypothetical model of entrepreneurial intentions from perspectives of entrepreneurial motivation and cognition.

Finally, the last part presents conclusions and implications.

LITERATURE REVIEW

Implications of Entrepreneurial Intention

Shapero & Sokol (1982) proposed another method of entrepreneurial intentions, they introduced a new concept, namely the entrepreneurial event, which includes the following characteristics: (1) initiate business (organizations or individuals to start a new career); (2) integration of resources (organization establishment or structure adjustment so as to realize the goal of the entire organization); 3) organization management (operation by the founder); (4) management autonomy (has certain rights in handling and distribution of resources); (5) risk-taking (founder of shared success or failure). This study is to distinguish between entrepreneurial events and entrepreneurs through this concept, which is to separate a series of entrepreneurial phenomena and the founder of the company. They also set up a model to explain how social and cultural backgrounds, organizational members and other factors influence entrepreneurial events. The cognitive and subjective expectations of entrepreneurship are the product of social and cultural influences, and it is argued that they could determine whether an individual is seriously considering and implementing certain actions. Entrepreneurial expectations could influence entrepreneurial events by individual values, and this values is impacted by individual's social system (peers, family, race, education, and professional background). The perception of feasibility refers to the adequacy of future partners and financial support. Future partners will be able to push forward a new business through capital, labor, moral support, the necessary skills, or risk sharing.

Boyd & Vozikis (1994) extended the theory of entrepreneurial intentions. This study introduces the concept of self-efficacy, which was used to describe the background of entrepreneurial intentions and to explain the process factors that influence people to turn their tendency into action, and also to explain the development of entrepreneurial intentions. Introducing the concept of self-efficacy into the research model of entrepreneurial intentions, it is of important theoretical significance for future researches to investigate the potential influence of entrepreneurial traits on entrepreneurial intentions.

Entrepreneurial intentions refer to the degree of attitudes and willingness of individuals to participate in or engage in entrepreneurial activities. It has a very strong positive correlation with entrepreneurial traits, to a great extent entrepreneurial intentions can reflect entrepreneurs with entrepreneurial characteristics, so researchers could apply entrepreneurial intentions to distinguish entrepreneurs and non-entrepreneurs. Scholars have also studied the entrepreneurial intentions of potential entrepreneurs from a cultural perspective. They believe that cultural factors are the main factors that influence the entrepreneurial intentions of individuals. Culture would be a key factor to judge whether certain area has sufficient environment for entrepreneurial potential entrepreneurial activities, and the final result is the emergence of entrepreneurs. Individual's perception of events and choices of behaviors could be influenced by cultural factors, and also could affect individual's perception of entrepreneurship and subsequent behaviors. Therefore, intensity of entrepreneurial intentions has a profound cultural foundation. In this case, culture could influence entrepreneurship, cultivation, practices and learning of a country or region through entrepreneurial intentions, and further influence its entrepreneurial forms.

This paper considers that the entrepreneurial behavior is planned, purposeful behavior, not a reflection to external stimuli. Based on this definition, it could be stated that entrepreneurial intentions refer to the willingness of the individual to execute the actions in plan. Although behavior is difficult to be observed directly, intentions provide with a better way to understand behaviors (Ajzen, 1991). The underlying logics would be that intentions could tend to predict behaviors, so intentions would be a better way to understand behaviors and actions (Ajzen, 1991). In the model of entrepreneurial intentions, individuals' attitudes towards entrepreneurship are expressed by entrepreneurial willingness and entrepreneurial feasibility, and these two constructs stem from the original model of Shapero & Sokol (1982).

Factors Influencing Entrepreneurial Intention

According to Stein (2004), entrepreneurial intentions could be effectively explained by personal background, including factors such as age, gender, education and work experiences, which have a great influence on entrepreneurial intentions. In addition, entrepreneurial intentions could be considered to be strongly related to entrepreneurial training and self-efficacy. Recently, scholars apply experiment methods to explore factors which could affect the level of entrepreneurship intentions. For example, entrepreneurial intentions of students in Norway is lower than Indonesia students. The reason lies in the fact that Norway belong to countries with lower levels of entrepreneurial enthusiasm, so that students' entrepreneurial intentions at a low state. Therefore, it is obvious that factors of country-context influencing on its residents' entrepreneurial intentions could be their social status and economic returns.

Domestic scholars have done a lot of researches on the factors that could influence entrepreneurial intentions. For example, Fan & Wang (2004) select college students in as the research samples of potential entrepreneurs. Taken student origin region, gender, and major as control variables, the entrepreneurial intention model is constructed to explore the potential influencing factors of entrepreneurship intentions. The results show that personality difference, life attitude, decision making ability, economic conditions and the convenience of obtaining resources are all important factors that influence entrepreneurial intentions. At the same time, in the process of formation of entrepreneurial intentions, the university location is also a key influencing factor.

Dimensions of Entrepreneurial Intention

Entrepreneurial intentions could be divided into two dimensions, including entrepreneurial willingness (perceived desirability) and entrepreneurial feasibility (perceived feasibility). Entrepreneurial willingness refers to the attractiveness of a given behavior by an entrepreneur (becoming an entrepreneur). Entrepreneurial feasibility refers to the extent to which an individual believes that he or she can carry out certain action. The level of entrepreneurship feasibility could be greatly influenced by such factors as entrepreneurial partner, entrepreneurial director, role model and so on. Including sense of responsibility and personal control, entrepreneurial behavior is more likely to be implemented by individuals with high entrepreneurial intentions.

Although a lot of researches on entrepreneurship tendency have appeared, but most studies are based on overall concept of entrepreneurial intentions as variables for research, or entrepreneurial intentions are divided into two components, but fail to identify specific factors influencing on each of two dimensions and distinguish different influencing mechanism. At the same time, scholars come to pay attention to many dimensions of entrepreneurship, but they still fail to figure out how these factors influence it. This paper try to analyze the two dimensions of entrepreneurial intentions, in order to simplify the research model and in-depth explore potential factors influencing entrepreneurial intentions.

1. Related researches on entrepreneurial intentions

Entrepreneurial events are influenced by personal values and entrepreneurial desires, and subjective expectations are influenced by social circumstances such as family, peers, ethnic groups, education, and career background. Murray & MacMillan (1988) study summed up psychological characteristics influencing entrepreneurial intentions are mainly locus of control, risk taking, achievement demand, ability to identify and exploit opportunities, the style of dealing with problems, tolerance of ambiguity, the entrepreneur's personal value choice, which have been widely confirmed.

Bird (1988) uses the model of planned theory to explain entrepreneurial willingness, and points out that research on entrepreneurial intentions is appropriate to rely on the theory of planned behavior, since the establishment of new enterprises need to invest a lot of time to formulate a comprehensive plan. In the framework of the theory of planned behavior (TPB), entrepreneurial willingness depends on three determinants as follows: attitudes, perception of behavior control, and subjective norms. Attitudes represent individual's assessments of behavior, either positive or negative. Ajzen (1991) points out that behavior attitudes could be determined by behavior beliefs and individual subjective value judgments. Perceived behavioral control represents individual perception of controlling behavior. The subjective norm represents external factors influencing individual decisions, and these external factors mainly include expectations of behavior from their spouses, family members, friends, teachers, doctors, supervisors, colleagues and other individuals or groups.

2. Related researches on entrepreneurial feasibility

Fan & Wang (2004) point out that main dimension structure of entrepreneurial intentions include perceived desirability and perceived feasibility. Ajzen (1991) states that the concept of cognition of behavioral control is similar to feasibility cognition, which are related to the existence of the opportunity and the necessity of resources.

Shapero & Sokol (1982) considers entrepreneurial feasibility as a factor associated with potential partner adequacy and financial support. Fan & Wang (2004) also find that there is a significant positive correlation between entrepreneurial feasibility and personal characteristics, including risk-taking, independence, authority, and degree of affinity and innovation. Their research also shows that the influence of maturity, social experience on the feasibility of college students has not been recognized by college students. On the contrary, there will be a negative correlation trend. Entrepreneurial activity is a pioneering activities, which needs more to emphasize daring, dare to face the risk and self-innovation. Undeniably, social experience, maturity would play a certain role, but in certain circumstances, these factors would play the opposite effect. In this case, it would make their own more restraint, indecisive, afraid to take risk and innovation, thus, it would detrimental to the development of entrepreneurship.

By reviewing literatures on the characteristics of entrepreneurs, entrepreneurial process, entrepreneurial ability, entrepreneurial intentions and entrepreneurial motivation, this paper lays the foundation for the establishment of the proposed model.

Through the analysis of the process of entrepreneurship, prior studies only start from a single concept, but they did not explain the relationship between them. Innovation in all aspects of the process or initial stage of an enterprise may emerge in these concepts. Meanwhile, scholars explain the process of entrepreneurship from another aspect, sequence events, and describe it as a simple linear process. We need to note that entrepreneurial activities are nonlinear in practice. This paper assumes the entrepreneurial process as a simple linear process to improve the operability of the research.

Gartne (1985) constructs an important model that explains the entrepreneurial process by organizing four discrete variables, individuals, organizations, environments, and processes. The research introduces three psychological variables, including need to achievement, locus of control and risk taking as well as background, experience, attitude which are related to personal factors, into the research model. Entrepreneurial characteristics play a very important role in the forefront of entrepreneurship research, and it is also an important variable introduced by the early research model. Thus, Gartne (1985)'s model combines entrepreneurs with their environment, which lays a foundation for further exploring the interaction between them.

The definition of entrepreneurial personality is characteristic of the innate personality of an entrepreneur. This article classifies and studies the related research and explores its implications. In addition, most of the researches about the characteristics of entrepreneurs are mostly related to three traits, that is, achievement needs, risk taking and locus of control, which help to further study the connotation of entrepreneurial traits.

Reviewing domestic and foreign related literatures about entrepreneurial intention and the interpretations and research findings of other researches on entrepreneurial intention, which laid the foundation for this definition, a willingness and possibility of entrepreneurial choice for people. In this regard, based on prior researches, this paper divides the entrepreneurial intention dimensions into two dimensions, namely the entrepreneurial willingness and entrepreneurial feasibility. In addition, through literature reviewing, the leading factors of entrepreneurial intention variables are entrepreneurial characteristics, entrepreneurial motivation, entrepreneurial self-efficacy, etc.

FOUNDATIONS OF RELATED ENTREPRENEURIAL THEORIES

Modern entrepreneurial theories have been involved in fields of management, economics, and behavioral sciences. Entrepreneurial theories gradually improved and enriched have laid the foundation for development of research on entrepreneurial intention. First of all, this paper briefly presents the entrepreneurial theories related to construct path-model of entrepreneurial intention.

1. Theory of Resource-Based View (RBV)

According to Barney (1991),Alvarez & Busenitz (2001), Resource-Based View theory could be applied to improve and expense researches and studies on entrepreneurship.

Resource-Based View (RBV) applied in the field of entrepreneurship includes 2 aspects. Firstly, in the aspect of entrepreneurial cognitive, entrepreneurial opportunity identification and opportunity-pursuit act serve as resources. Due to different judgment and assessment by individual entrepreneurs, as well as different designs or ideas for utilization of resources, so these designs or ideas would be taken into action, then entrepreneurial opportunities arises(Kirzner, 1997;Shane & Venkataraman, 2000). Secondly, in the view of entrepreneurial organizing, portfolio of entrepreneurial resources and process of resource composition could be considered as resources. The entrepreneurs defined as individuals gifted with special trait endowments, usually were skilled at apperceiving and developing potential value of untapped resources, putting it in another way that they could perceive entrepreneurial opportunities which is difficult for ordinary people to sense, as well as be good at integrate resources related to entrepreneurial actions and organizing the overall process of entrepreneurial actions so as to seize the entrepreneurial opportunity (Casson, 1982;Kirzner, 1997).

2. Theory of Entrepreneurial Cognitive

Kirzner (1997) refers that cognitive factors play an pivot role in the entrepreneurial researches, and cognitive factors could distinguish entrepreneurs and non-entrepreneurs. Entrepreneurial cognitive researches concern with how entrepreneurs make decisions in accordance with specific cognition, which indicates that entrepreneurial cognition would thus affect entrepreneurial process.

Based on structure of entrepreneurial cognition, characteristics of entrepreneurial cognition can fall into 2 categories.

The first category, related to risk perception, focuses on perceiving and understanding relevant information so as to identify opportunities. Shane & Venkataraman (2000) refers that judgment by entrepreneurs for profits made by new ventures is based on their perception of opportunities. It is indicated that based on risk perception, entrepreneurs' assessment for exposure of risks and opportunities could not only affect their entrepreneurial behaviors, but also ultimately affect the performance of new ventures.

The secondary category, related to entrepreneurial self-efficacy, concern with developing opportunities with cognitive attributes. Krueger (2000) advances that entrepreneurial activities reflect cognitive process of entrepreneurs, which manifests as a kind of planned behavior. Ajzen's Theory of planned behavior (TPB) and Shapero's model of entrepreneurial events state that entrepreneurial self-efficacy is one of important antecedent factors to promote entrepreneurial feasibility, which also is related to pursuit for entrepreneurial behavior, thus further promoting development of entrepreneurial cognition researches.

3. Theory of Planned Behavior(TPB)

According to the Theory of Reasoned Action, which is jointly proposed by Fishbein & Ajzen (1975), individual behavior is not entirely voluntary but under control. Later, on the basis of this theory, a new concept, i.e. Perceived Behavior Control, was added, thus extending the Theory of Planned Behavior, and then developed into Theory of Planned Behavior (TPB).

Fishbein & Ajzen (1975) pointed out that Theory of Planned Behavior focuses on individual behavior tendencies that individual willpower will control individual behavior, and the behavior will be affected by the tendency of non-dynamic factors, such as the resources and opportunities.

On the basis of studies of Shapero (1982), Ajzen (1991) and Katz (1992) and other scholars, Krueger (2000) proposed and modified a model of entrepreneurial intention (see follow-up introduction to the theoretical model of entrepreneurial intention).

To sum up, based on the RBV theory, the new venture's success can be attributed to internal resources. The entrepreneur who has special individual characteristics is an important resource endowment. That is, the entrepreneurs and their inherent qualities can be seen as internal resources, thus contributing to the success of the new venture.

BASIC MODELS OF ENTREPRENEURIAL INTENTION PATH STUDIES

Fishbein & Ajzen (1975)'s Model of Theory of Planned Behavior

Fishbein & Ajzen (1975) improve and develop the theory, on the basis of multi-attribute attitude theory, and put forward the theory of rational behavior. The theory is that behavioral attitudes and subjective norms affect behavioral intention, and behavioral intention is a direct factor in determining behavior. Based on this theory, the theory of planned behavior models structure is built, as shown in Figure 1.

Ajzen noted that actual behavior is driven by behavioral intention, and behavioral intention is based on the joint action of three antecedent variables, namely behavioral attitudes, subjective norms, and perceived behavioral control.

Figure 1. Fishbein & Ajzen (1975)'s Model of Theory of Planned Behavior

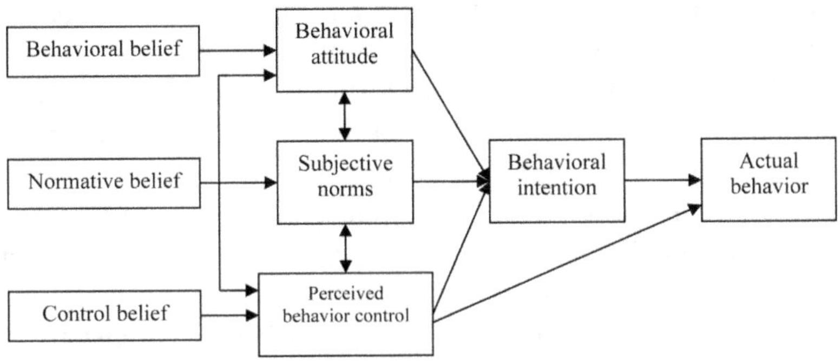

On the basis of cognition and information processing, the Theory of Planned Behavior describes the relationship among attitudes, motivation and behavior and further explores the antecedent variables that affect the behavior tendencies. As can be seen from the model showing the structure of the theory of planned behavior, all factors that can affect the actual behavior are indirect effects on actual behavior by influencing behavioral intention. The impacts of behavioral intention have three factors, which are associated with individual beliefs that linked to external objects.

Krueger & Brazeal's (1994) Model of Entrepreneurial Potential

Krueger & Brazeal (1994) proposed an entrepreneurship model based on Ajzen's theory of planned behavior, and Shapero's entrepreneurship events theory. Entrepreneurial potential as a leading factor, it proposed from a business perspective of risk activities and business development. The model contains three key concepts: subjective expectations, feasibility cognition, and action tendencies.

Figure 2. Krueger & Brazeal's (1994) Model of Entrepreneurial Potential

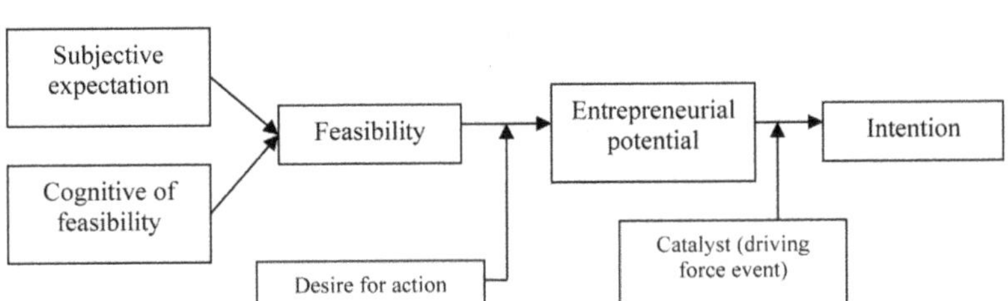

Based on this model, Krueger & Brazeal (1994) describe a process of a potential entrepreneur to develop from subjective expectation and cognition of feasibility, into entrepreneurial intention finally, and put forward proposals that have practical significance. The model highlights the importance of cognition. Support of the surrounding environment, as well as social norms and attitudes, are expected to help potential entrepreneurs to strengthen their subjective perception of viability while potential entrepreneurs' awareness of the viability is more important than reality environment. The model emphasizes the importance of potential entrepreneurs' feasibility cognition, which will directly affect the potential entrepreneurs' assessment of feasibility and will eventually affect entrepreneurial behavior decisions. However, potential entrepreneurs' entrepreneurial self-efficacy is an important variable affecting the cognition of feasibility. The influencing mechanism is not embodied in the model, so this paper will introduce "entrepreneurial self-efficacy" into the study model.

Also shown in the model (in Figure 2) that the two variables—feasibility and desire for action—have important implications for entrepreneurial intention while feasibility of entrepreneurship and entrepreneurial desire have also been proven to be two dimensions of entrepreneurial intention. Meanwhile, the model also indicates that potential entrepreneurs' subjective expectations and cognitive feasibility are important factors affecting the viability of entrepreneurship; but it did not discuss in depth how these individual factors affect entrepreneurial intention' inherent mechanism.

Krueger's (2000) Entrepreneurial Intention Model

Based on the above analysis, Krueger (2000) added the front-end variables that affect feasibility cognition and subjective expectations on the basis of the original model to deepen the entrepreneurial potential model, as shown in Figure 3.

In this model, the individual factors of potential entrepreneurs were refined. It considers influencing factors of individual expectations, cognition of social norms, and subjective sense of self-efficacy, as well as subjective collective efficiency sense, can be divided into individual factors and situational factors. But the models still did not refine individual factors, nor explain how the individual factors affect entrepreneurial intention mechanism. Thus, this paper will refine entrepreneurs' individual factors and incorporate them into the model on the basis of this model, while adding mediating variables namely "entrepreneurial self-efficacy" to explore how potential entrepreneurs' individual characteristics affect entrepreneurial intention mechanism.

Figure 3. Krueger's (2000) Entrepreneurial Tendencies Model

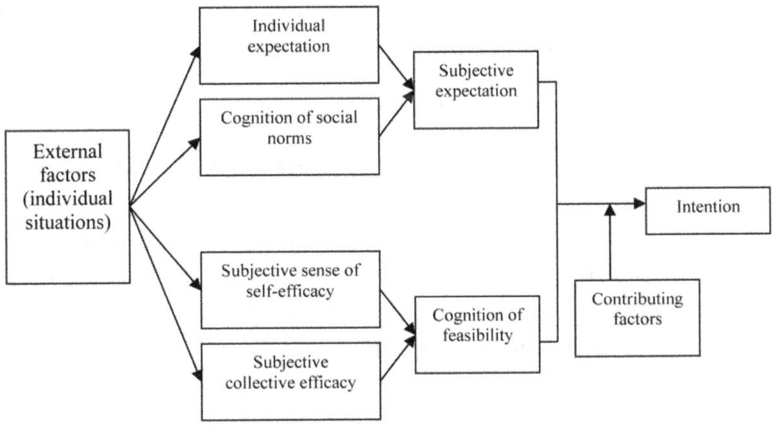

Shapero's (1982) Theory of Entrepreneurial Events and Ajzen's (1991) Theory of Planned Behavior have been used as basic model for Krueger and other scholars. They compared regression analysis results of the two models, and then combine the two models to form a new model of planned behavior theory based on its research purposes, as shown in Figure 4.

Figure 4. Modified Model of Theory of Planned Behavior
(Krueger, 2000)

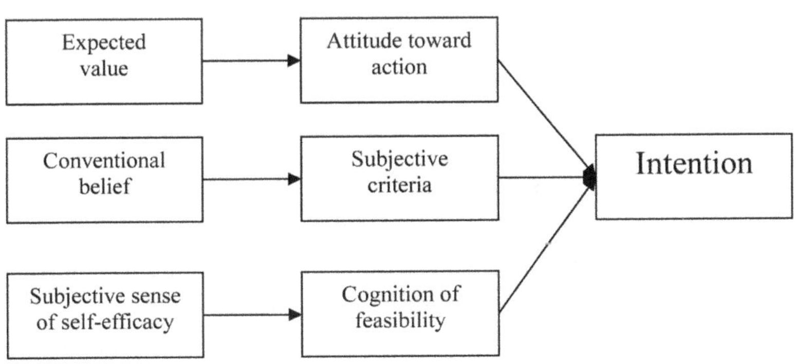

From this model, we can see that potential entrepreneurs' individual factors will affect the attitude of their actions, subjective criteria and the cognition of feasibility, and then ultimately affect entrepreneurial intention. Specifically, the expected value of potential entrepreneurs will affect the attitude of their actions; conventional beliefs will affect their subjective criteria; whereas subjective sense of self-efficacy will affect their cognition of feasibility. Entrepreneurial intention is affected by the attitude of action, subjective criteria and cognition of feasibility, that is, entrepreneurial intention contains dimensions of feasibility cognition and subjective willingness.

Phan et al. (2002)'s Model of Entrepreneurial Tendencies

Phan et al. (2002) investigated Singaporean students as survey samples of potential entrepreneurs, to establish a path model, in which it developed from individual backgrounds, to entrepreneurship attitudes and entrepreneurial beliefs, and finally to the entrepreneurial intention, as shown in Figure 5.

Figure 5. Entrepreneurial Tendencies Model
(Phan et al., 2002)

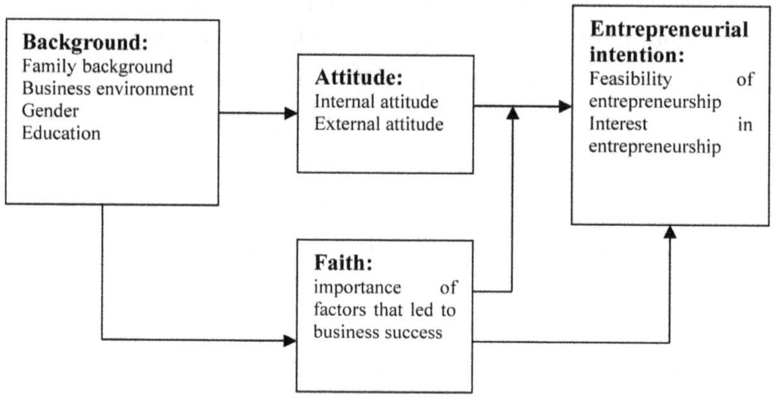

Phan et al. (2002) research drawn four conclusions: first, individual traits and entrepreneurial intention showed a significant positive relationship; second, the high level of education will diminish the potential entrepreneurs' entrepreneurial attitude on account of the assessment of the opportunity cost of human capital; third, entrepreneurial attitude and entrepreneurial intention showed a significant positive relationship; fourth, entrepreneurship attitudes and entrepreneurial beliefs showed a significant positive relationship.

The Model of Entrepreneurial Intentions proposed by Luthje & Franke (2003)

Taking MIT American students with engineering background as research sample of potential entrepreneurs, Luthje & Franke (2003) developed a process model, which begins from personality towards entrepreneurial attitudes, and finally to entrepreneurial intention, as shown in Figure 6.

Figure 6. The Model of Entrepreneurial Intentions
(Luthje & Franke, 2003)

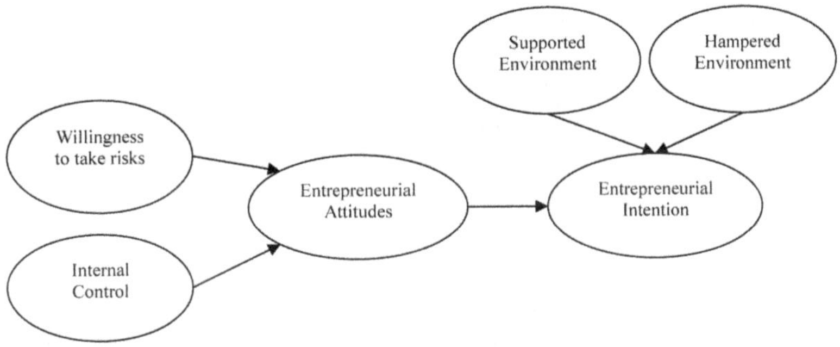

There are three results of Luthje & Franke (2003)'s research: First, supported environment has a significant impact on the entrepreneurial intentions of potential entrepreneurs; Second, entrepreneurial attitudes is another important factor influencing the entrepreneurial intentions; Third, entrepreneurial attitudes are the results of personalities of potential entrepreneurs, which means there are important relationships between the formation of entrepreneurial attitudes and individual personality.

The Model of Entrepreneurial Intentions proposed by Fan & Wang (2004)

Fan & Wang (2004) carried out research on the factors of entrepreneurial intentions and potentials. Taking students as potential entrepreneurs, they deeply analyzed the influence of potential entrepreneurs' personality, personal background, and environmental awareness on entrepreneurial intentions. The Model of Entrepreneurial Intentions was developed in Figure 7.

Figure 7. The Model of Entrepreneurial Intentions
(Fan & Wang, 2004)

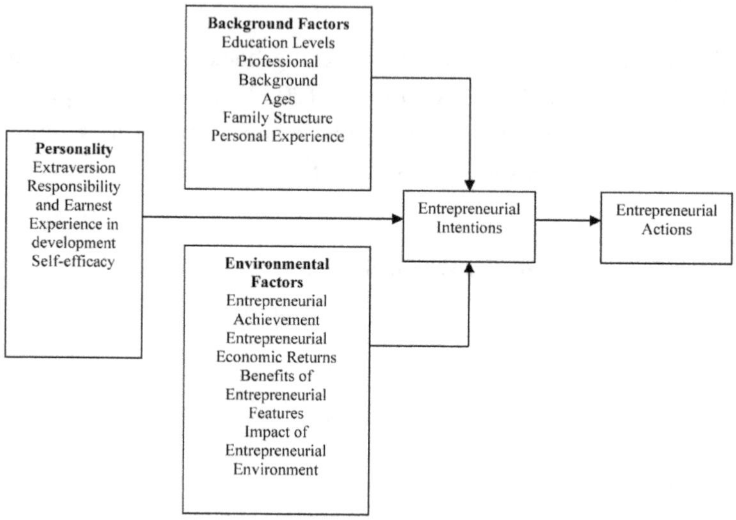

Through research, Fan & Wang (2004) found that, individuals with high levels of tendency for entrepreneurship always show Extraversion, Responsibility and Earnest, Experience in development, and Self-efficacy; each element of Entrepreneurial Intentions and Environmental Factors shows positive correlations; positive correlations also shown between Entrepreneurial Intentions and Background Factors, including Education Levels, Professional Background, Ages, Family Structure, and Personal Experience.

The Model of Influencing Factors to Entrepreneurial Intentions proposed by Guo et al. (2009)

Guo et al. (2009) took undergraduate students as research sample of potential entrepreneurs, and developed the Model of Influencing Factors from the perspective of Entrepreneurship Education Content, which begins from Forward-looking Personality to Entrepreneurship Education, and finally towards the Entrepreneurial Intentions. As shown in Figure 8.

The research shows that, University Experience has a great impact on the Forward-looking Personality; Forward-looking Personality (Personality Traits) has less influence on Entrepreneurial Knowledge, but has much more impact on Entrepreneurial Attitudes; Entrepreneurial Attitudes deeply affects the Entrepreneurial Willingness; there is no significant relationships among Entrepreneurial Knowledge, Entrepreneurial Ability and Entrepreneurial Willingness.

Figure 8. The Model of Influencing Factors to Entrepreneurial Intentions
(Guo et al., 2009)

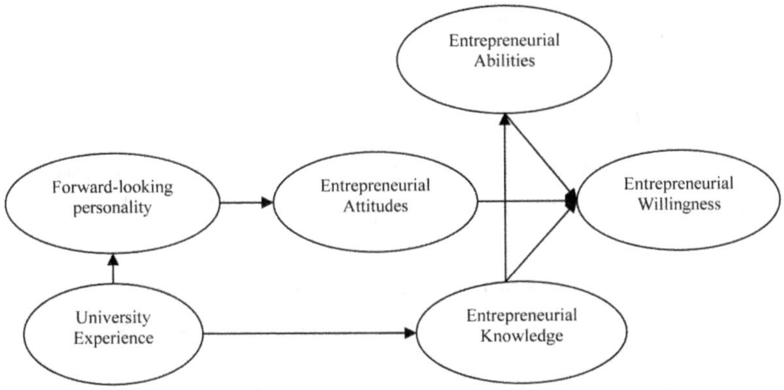

The Model of Entrepreneurial Willingness Proposed by Tang (2009)

Tang (2009) took undergraduate students as research sample of potential entrepreneurs, personal factors (including individual characteristics and individual resources) and environmental factors (including social environment and university environment) as antecedent variables of self-efficacy, and self-efficacy (including five dimensions: entrepreneurial performance / risk tolerance / opportunity identification / relationship coordination / organizational commitment) as mediating variables. The process model was developed, which begins from personal factors and environmental factors to self-efficacy, and finally to entrepreneurial intentions, as shown in Figure 9.

Figure 9. The Model of Entrepreneurial Willingness
Tang (2009)

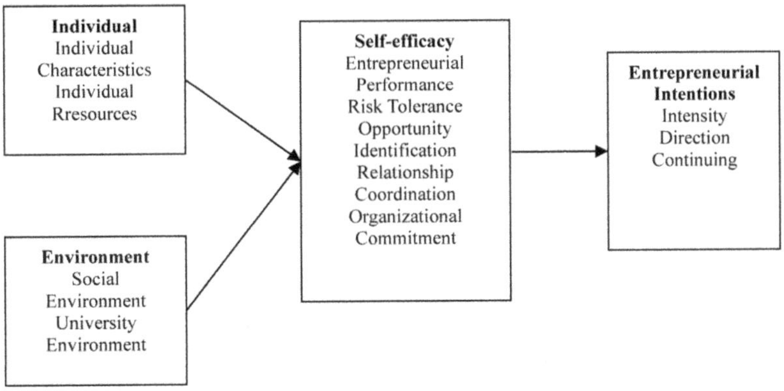

Tang Ming's research shows that, there are positive relations between Individual Characteristics and Individual Resources of potential entrepreneurs and Entrepreneurial Willingness; there are positive relations between Entrepreneurial Environment and Entrepreneurial Willingness; while the variable of Entrepreneurial Self-efficacy (five dimensions) plays an intermediary role in the process.

The Model of Relationships Among Influencing Factors to Entrepreneurial Intentions proposed by Ye (2009)

Ye (2009) took undergraduate students as research sample of potential entrepreneurs, adopted structural equation modeling techniques, and developed the relationship model. The model begins from Individual Personality, Social Resource and Previous Knowledge, through Entrepreneurship Awareness, and finally towards Entrepreneurial Intentions, as shown in Figure 10.

Figure 10. The Model of Relationships among Influencing Factors to Entrepreneurial Intentions
(Ye, 2009)

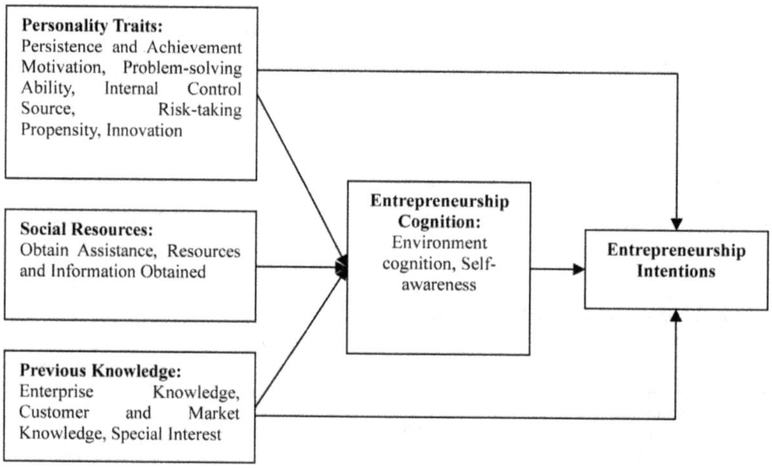

Ye (2009)'s research shows that, Indicator Variables (e.g. potential entrepreneurs' gender, grade level, business practices, entrepreneurial courses received, etc.) and the Entrepreneurial Intentions of potential entrepreneurs have positive relations; while the Personality Traits, Social Resources, Previous Knowledge, and Entrepreneurship cognition of potential entrepreneurs also have positive relations; the Entrepreneurship cognition plays an intermediary role.

MODEL CONSTRUCTION OF ENTREPRENEURIAL INTENTIONS BASED ON ENTREPRENEURIAL MOTIVATION AND COGNITION

As result of review of classical intention-based entrepreneurial models, previous studies provides a foundation for the research model of this paper. On the basis of entrepreneurial cognition theory and the theory of planned behavior, it is designed to construct model of entrepreneurial intentions based on entrepreneurial motivation and cognition.

1. Specific variables to determine the individual characteristics of the entrepreneurs.

According to literature review, entrepreneurial traits that related to entrepreneurial intentions include achievement need, risk-taking, locus of control, innovation, tolerance of ambiguity, etc. In this paper, achievement need, risk-taking, and locus of control were chosen as independent variables based on their frequency, and were included in the study models. As for the external factors that affect entrepreneurial intentions, they also affected entrepreneurial intentions by subjective perception. Potential entrepreneurs will transfer objective effects of the external environment, into their subjective perception, whereas ultimately affect the entrepreneurial intentions.

2. Determine the dimensions of entrepreneurial intentions.

Shapero (1982) presented the entrepreneurship event model. According to the model, individual entrepreneurial intentions are determined by the individual expectations of entrepreneurship, cognition of entrepreneurship feasibility, and the individual's operational capacity.

Krueger (2000) believes that the core element of entrepreneurial intentions models is the strength of entrepreneurship intention, and cognition of entrepreneurial feasibility.

Through literature review, it shows that entrepreneurial intentions contain two dimensions, namely entrepreneurship willingness and cognition of entrepreneurial feasibility.

3. Introduction of entrepreneurial motivation into path model

Entrepreneurial motivation is the key factor to transfer potential individuals into real entrepreneurs. Entrepreneurial motivation of potential entrepreneurs would affect behavior patterns in the entrepreneurial process, which would affect birth and development of new venture, therefore, entrepreneurial motivation is the essential factor influencing entrepreneurial behaviors and intentions (Bird, 1988; Miner et al., 1989; Kuratko & Naffziger, 1997; Robichaud & Roger, 2001). The degree level of entrepreneurial motivation would greatly affect the level of participating in entrepreneurship-related activities, as well as inner willingness to boycott and overcome any obstacles in the process of entrepreneurial activities. So entrepreneurial motivation is the inner engine of entrepreneurial behaviors, which is the core factor to differentiate entrepreneurs from non-entrepreneurs (Herron & Sapienza, 1992; Dimov, 2010).

Therefore, entrepreneurial motivation is introduced into path model of entrepreneurial intentions, due to the fact that motivation of potential entrepreneurs is considered as core inner factor psychologically influencing intentions of entrepreneurship. However, current academic community has a mix definition about entrepreneurial motivation that has be defined as willingness orientation, drive-power orientation, as well as goal orientation. Under the model of IEI (Implementing Entrepreneurial Ideas), personal attention, factors including experiences and behavior oriented to specific goals are of prime important in affecting entrepreneurial intentions.

Entrepreneurial intentions is a kind of psychological state in which intentions would be launched oriented by achievement of entrepreneurial goals, so particular attentions should be paid to study entrepreneurial intentions (Bird,1988). Start-up motivation by which commitment to goals of entrepreneurship would be reflected, is the level of willingness to exert effort in the process of venture creation (Dimov, 2010).

So this paper considers entrepreneurial motivation as specific personal goals of entrepreneurs that should be inner drive power for potential entrepreneurs participating in entrepreneurial activities, and these personal goals would be realized by establishment of new ventures through entrepreneurial activities.

In conclusion, this paper defines entrepreneurial motivation as goal orientation of entrepreneurs, and introduces this variable into path model of entrepreneurial intentions. However, there are little researches or empirical studies on problems related to the relationship between entrepreneurial motivation and entrepreneurial self-efficacy, such as whether or not entrepreneurial motivation served as antecedent variable to entrepreneurial self-efficacy and mediator variable in the path model.

4. Take entrepreneurial motivation (goal orientation) as antecedent variable to entrepreneurial self-efficacy.

Through research on relationship between entrepreneurial motivation and abilities, Locke (1991) states that goal orientation of entrepreneurs has direct impacts on action-efficacy of entrepreneurs. The results of evaluating on entrepreneurs' abilities essential to entrepreneurial success are determined by different goal orientations originated from different entrepreneurial motivations, which would lead to sustainability and intensity of entrepreneurial behaviors.

Pre-concerted tasks and goals are directly associated with entrepreneurial self-efficacy that is defined as entrepreneurs' self-belief and self-confidence about achievement of pre-scheduled tasks or goals with requisite personal abilities and resources. Entrepreneurial motivation (goal orientation) is the inner drive for entrepreneurs participating in venture-creation activities. The more intensity and specificity the entrepreneurial motivation would be, the more clearly and strongly the goal would be, the more strongly the willingness of entrepreneurship would be.

Therefore, it would be lead to the conclusion that entrepreneurial motivation is the psychological antecedent to entrepreneurial self-efficacy through which entrepreneurial motivation would lead to realization of entrepreneurial goals with personal cognitions about abilities needed in entrepreneurial process.

5. introduce entrepreneurial motivation and entrepreneurial self-efficacy as mediating variables into path model

As the entrepreneurial motivation and entrepreneurial self-efficacy are outcome variables in regards to individual characteristics of entrepreneurs, while being predictor variables for entrepreneurship attitudes and cognitions of entrepreneurial feasibility. Thus, entrepreneurial self-efficacy plays an intermediary role between entrepreneurs' individual factors (individual characteristics, entrepreneurial experience, etc.) and entrepreneurial intentions (Boyd & Vozikis, 1994; Chen et al., 1998; Gatewood et al., 2002; Kirkpatrick et al., 2002; Wilson et al., 2007). Although the important role of self-efficacy in entrepreneurial process has been proven, there are no intensive research on how entrepreneurial motivation and entrepreneurial self-efficacy militate between entrepreneurs' traits and entrepreneurial intentions and the relevance between entrepreneurial motivation and entrepreneurial self-efficacy, as well as how all the antecedents would affect the dimensions of entrepreneurial intentions.

Based on the above analysis and referred to related theories, the paper further develops a theoretical model that introduces entrepreneurial motivation and entrepreneurial self-efficacy as mediating variables with aim to study path-mechanism in intention-developing process and how the characteristics of entrepreneurs, entrepreneurial motivation, and entrepreneurial self-efficacy affect on entrepreneurial tendencies, which is shown in Figure 11.

Under entrepreneurial cognitive theory and planned behavior theory, entrepreneurial behaviors of potential entrepreneurs would be triggered co-jointly by entrepreneurial motivation and cognition (Krueger, 2000). Entrepreneurial behaviors are closely linked to entrepreneurial cognitive factors, including knowledge, techniques, as well as capabilities involved in entrepreneurial process. Entrepreneurial

Figure 11. Path Model for Entrepreneurial Tendencies Studies

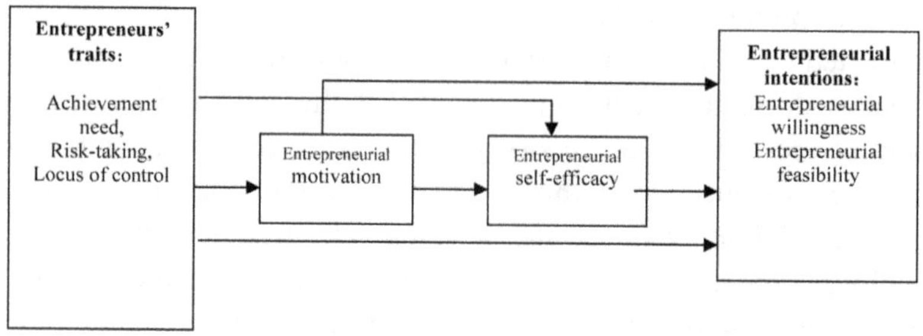

motivation furnishes entrepreneurial behaviors with driving forces, and aid potential entrepreneurs in obtaining cognitive factors (knowledge, technique, capability) in the entrepreneurial process. Therefore, it is a brand-new angle to research entrepreneurial intentions from co-joint perspective of entrepreneurial motivation and cognition, which will strongly contribute to identify and nurture potential entrepreneurs.

As results of literature reviews concerning with entrepreneurial intentions, although studies on fields of entrepreneurial motivation and cognition have been fruitful, there are some flaws as followings:

Firstly, as a new field of research, there is little research on entrepreneurial motivation and how it would have impact on the entrepreneurial process, furthermore, in current literatures related to entrepreneurial motivation, there is no united, clear, and complete definition of entrepreneurial motivation (Shane & Venkataraman, 2000).

Secondly, some researches reveal that entrepreneurial self-efficacy is the core variable to affect entrepreneurial intentions on the basis of entrepreneurial cognitive theory(Bandura, 2001).However, there is little studies on in-depth analyzing how entrepreneurial self-efficacy affects entrepreneurial intentions, including how it affect the dimensions of entrepreneurial intentions and its mechanism of path, as well as further explore the antecedent of entrepreneurial self-efficacy.

Thirdly, current researches related to field of entrepreneurial cognition mainly concentrate on cognitive shortcut, opportunity identification, risk perception, and entrepreneurial decision-making, but there is little research from the combination perspectives of entrepreneurial motivation and cognition. And current most entrepreneurial cognitive researches have only studied single variable and its impacts on entrepreneurial behaviors, but for interaction effects of variables on entrepreneurial behaviors and processes, few studies have been paid attention to. Based on reviewing current models of entrepreneurial intentions, impacts of both entrepreneurial motivation and cognition on entrepreneurial intentions have been ignored, especially little attention paid to the direct relationship between entrepreneurial motivation and entrepreneurial self-efficacy (Kickul & Kruegue, 2004; Elfving, 2008). Krueger

(2000) refers that entrepreneurial self-efficacy, which is defined as perception and evaluation for personal abilities needed to implement entrepreneurial goals, plays a pivotal role in emergence and development of entrepreneurial intentions. How about the relationship between entrepreneurial motivation whose important dimension is goal orientation and entrepreneurial self-efficacy considered as core cognitive variable, and what roles that entrepreneurial motivation (goal orientation) and entrepreneurial self-efficacy would play in the path model, all these issues have failed to be explored and studied.

Based on model reviews, current path models have analyzed the path mechanism between personal traits and entrepreneurial intentions, however, potential psychological and mediators involved in entrepreneurial process have been ignored. Although entrepreneurial attitudes and cognitions have been introduced into path model served as mediating variables, potential antecedents to entrepreneurial attitudes and cognitions have failed to be explored in-depth, as well as how these antecedents have impact on path mechanism.

Under related path models of entrepreneurial intentions, on the basis of related empirical studies, this paper further constructs and develops a theoretical path-model in combined views of entrepreneurial motivation and cognition. The path model of entrepreneurial intentions proposed by this paper has made the following modifications:

Firstly, dimension division of entrepreneurial intentions, to separately compare and analyze the impacts of antecedents on different dimensions of entrepreneurial intentions.

Secondly, introduce entrepreneurial self-efficacy served as core variable of entrepreneurial cognition into path model based on entrepreneurial cognitive theory.

Thirdly, introduce entrepreneurial motivation defined as goal orientation into path model.

Fourthly, take entrepreneurial motivation as antecedent for entrepreneurial self-efficacy, and take both variable as mediators to construct path model based on combined perspectives of entrepreneurial motivation and cognition.

CONCLUSION

Fan & Wang (2004) pointed out that there are three major factors that affect entrepreneurial intentions of individuals: individual background, individual factors, and the environment. The entrepreneurial intentions are determined by the joint action of external environmental factors and internal characteristics of individual entrepreneurs, whereas individual psychological characteristics of entrepreneurs are the inherent driving force of their entrepreneurial intentions. When the external environment meets entrepreneurs' cognitive applicable conditions, entrepreneurial behavior occurs. Therefore, to study the entrepreneurial process, we must study the entrepreneur's own individual inner psychological factors. Based on this analysis, this study focuses on the study of entrepreneurial intentions from inner psychological process, to construct a path model of entrepreneurial intentions based on entrepreneurial motivation and cognition.

Related researches, which analyze influencing factors of entrepreneurial intentions, solely predict and explain the entrepreneurs' behavior and entrepreneurial intentions based on their individual characteristics, obtaining not-very-satisfactory results. As mentioned earlier, the previous models of entrepreneurial intentions analyzed path mechanism from personality traits to entrepreneurial intentions; however, they did not explore in depth the possible intermediate variables of potential entrepreneurs' individual psychological characteristics that may exist in the path models. Recently, some entrepreneurial intentions models introduced entrepreneurial attitude and entrepreneurial cognition as intermediary model variables, but these models have not discussed in depth about the front-end determinants of entrepreneurial attitude and entrepreneurial cognition, as well as their path mechanisms that affect entrepreneurial intentions.

Based on related theories, the paper further develops a theoretical path model of entrepreneurial intentions that introduces entrepreneurial motivation and entrepreneurial self-efficacy as mediating variables with aim to reveal the mechanism of entrepreneurial intention-developing process psychologically and clarify the roles played by entrepreneurial motivation and cognition in the path model.

Implications

The path model proposed and constructed by this paper explores the mechanism of entrepreneurial intentions process in-depth and reveals the psychological process of potential entrepreneurs so as to replenish and enrich entrepreneurial research in view of psychological approach. This paper is one of the first to construct path model of entrepreneurial intentions in combined views of entrepreneurial motivation and cognition. Ultimately, the paper hopes to have added richness to ongoing discussion among academics and educators and policy-makers regarding the importance of entrepreneurial intention in entrepreneurial education.

Future Research

Recently studies built a model of entrepreneurial intention which contains situational variables, and pointed out that these situational variables affected by social norms of the individual's subjective perception, i.e. these situational variables can be measured by the social norms of organizational environment where individual is in, while situational variables would affect an individual's entrepreneurial intention.

In addition to directly affecting entrepreneurial intentions, situational factors could indirectly affect entrepreneurial intentions by influencing other factors, such as situational factors would affect the motivation of entrepreneurs and perception of entrepreneurial feasibility, and then encourage entrepreneurs to produce or abandon entrepreneurial intentions. In addition, as a contingency factor, situational factors might interact with other influencing factors, resulting in development of entrepreneurial intentions. Therefore, situational factors are essential variables for entrepreneurial intentions, which should be introduced into research models in the future studies.

The creation of entrepreneurial intention is also a process. In this process, the entrepreneur needs to measure the weight of each influencing factor, not only to know the growth and decline of the elements, but also to know the relationship between them, in order to determine whether to start a business. The difficulty of research on entrepreneurial intentions is that we have not yet clearly identified the core elements and key activities that affect entrepreneurial intentions. Therefore, future studies should pay close attention to the key factors of entrepreneurial intention and the relationship between these factors, and to explore how these factors interacted and interdepended in the process of evolution of entrepreneurial intentions.

ACKNOWLEDGMENT

This work was financially supported by Guangdong province mutual funds of philosophy and social sciences (GD15XGL01).

REFERENCES

Ajzen, I. (1991). The theory of planned behavior. *Organizational Behavior and Human Decision Processes*, *50*(2), 179–211. doi:10.1016/0749-5978(91)90020-T

Alvarez, S., & Busenitz, L. (2001). The entrepreneurship of resource-based theory. *Journal of Management*, *6*(6), 755–775. doi:10.1177/014920630102700609

Autio, E., Keeley, R. H., Klofsten, M., Parker, G. C., & Hay, M. (2001). Entrepreneurial Intent among Students in Scandinavia and in the USA. *Enterprise and Innovation Management Studies*, *2*(2), 145–160. doi:10.1080/14632440110094632

Bandura, A. (2001). Social cognitive theory: An agentic perspective. *Annual Review of Psychology*, *52*(1), 1–26. doi:10.1146/annurev.psych.52.1.1 PMID:11148297

Barney, J. B. (1991). Firm resources and sustained competitive advantage. *Journal of Management, 17*(1), 99–120. doi:10.1177/014920639101700108

Bird, B. J. (1988). Implementing entrepreneurial ideas: The case for intention. *Academy of Management Review, 13*(3), 442–454. doi:10.5465/amr.1988.4306970

Boyd, N., & Vozikis, G. S. (1994). The Influence of self-efficacy on the development of entrepreneurial intentions and actions. *Entrepreneurship Theory and Practice, 18*(1), 63–77. doi:10.1177/104225879401800404

Brush, C. G., Manolova, T. S., & Edelman, L. F. (2008). Properties of emerging organizations: An empirical test. *Journal of Business Venturing, 23*(5), 547–566. doi:10.1016/j.jbusvent.2007.09.002

Casson, M. (1982). *The entrepreneur.* Totowa, NJ: Barnes and Noble Books.

Chen, C., Greene, P., & Crick, A. (1998). Does entrepreneurial self-efficacy distinguish entrepreneurs from managers? *Business Venturing, 13*(4), 295–316. doi:10.1016/S0883-9026(97)00029-3

Dimov, D. (2007). From opportunity insight to opportunity intention: The importance of person-situation learning match. *Entrepreneurship Theory and Practice, 31*(4), 561–583. doi:10.1111/j.1540-6520.2007.00188.x

Dimov, D. (2010). Nascent entrepreneurs and venture emergence: Opportunity confidence, human capital, and early planning. *Journal of Management Studies, 47*(6), 1123–1153. doi:10.1111/j.1467-6486.2009.00874.x

Elfving, J. (2008). *Contextualizing entrepreneurial intentions.* Abo: Abo Akademi Press.

Fan, W., & Wang, C. M. (2004). The research on factors affecting entrepreneurial intentions. [in Chinese]. *Science of Psychology, 27*(5), 1087–1090.

Fishbein, M., & Ajzen, I. (1975). *Belief, Attitude, Intention and Behavior: An Introduction to Theory and Research.* Addison-Wesley.

Gartner, W. B. (1985). A framework for describing and classifying the phenomenon of new venture creation. *Academy of Management Review, 10*(4), 696–706. doi:10.5465/amr.1985.4279094

Gatewood, E. J., Shaver, K. G., Power, J. B., & Gartner, W. B. (2002). Entrepreneurial expectancy, task effort,and performance. *Entrepreneurship Theory and Practice, 27*(2), 187–206. doi:10.1111/1540-8520.00006

Gelderen, M. V., Thurik, R., & Bosma, N. (2006). Success and risk factors in the pre-startup phase. *Small Business Economics*, *26*(4), 319–335. doi:10.100711187-004-6837-5

Gruber, M. (2007). Uncovering the value of planning in new venture creation: A process and contingency perspective. *Journal of Business Venturing*, *22*(6), 782–807. doi:10.1016/j.jbusvent.2006.07.001

Guo, H., Mao, Y., & Bai, X. (2009). The study on the effects of university education on students' entrepreneurial willingness. [in Chinese]. *Soft Sciences*, *9*, 69–74.

Harper, D. A. (2008). Towards a theory of entrepreneurial teams. *Journal of Business Venturing*, *23*(6), 613–626. doi:10.1016/j.jbusvent.2008.01.002

Herron, L., & Sapienza, H. J. (1992). The entrepreneur and the Initiation of new venture launch activities. *Entrepreneurship Theory and Practice*, *17*(1), 49–55. doi:10.1177/104225879201700106

Katz. (1992). A psychosocial cognitive model of employment status choice. *Entrepreneurship: Theory and Practice*, *16*, 29-37.

Kickul, J., & Kruegue, N. F. (2004). A cognitive processing model of entrepreneurial self-efficacy and intentionally. *Frontiers of Entrepreneurship Research*, *30*(1), 607–619.

Kirkpatrick, S. A., Wofford, J. C., & Baum, J. R. (2002). Measuring motive imagery contained in the vision statement. *The Leadership Quarterly*, *13*(2), 139–150. doi:10.1016/S1048-9843(02)00096-6

Kirzner, I. (1997). Entrepreneurial discovery and the competitive market process: An Austrian approach. *Journal of Economic Literature*, *35*(2), 60–85.

Krueger, N. F. (2000). The cognitive infrastructure of opportunity emergence. *Entrepreneurship*, 185-206.

Krueger, N. F. Jr, & Brazeal, D. V. (1994). Entrepreneurship potential and potential entrepreneurs. *Entrepreneurship Theory and Practice*, *18*(3), 91–104. doi:10.1177/104225879401800307

Krueger, N. F. Jr, Reilly, M. D., & Carsrud, A. L. (2000). Competing models of entrepreneurial intentions. *Journal of Business Venturing*, *15*(4), 411–532. doi:10.1016/S0883-9026(98)00033-0

Kuratko, D. F., & Naffziger, D. W. (1997). An Examination of Owner's Goals in Sustaining Entrepreneurship. *Small Business Management*, *35*(1), 24–33.

Locke, E. A. (1991). The motivation sequence, the motivation hub and the motivation core. *Organizational Behavior and Human Decision Processes*, *50*(2), 288–299. doi:10.1016/0749-5978(91)90023-M

Luthje, C., & Franke, N. (2003). The making of an entrepreneur: Testing a model of entrepreneurial intent among engineering students at MIT. *R & D Management*, *33*(2), 135–147. doi:10.1111/1467-9310.00288

Miner, J. B., Smith, N. R., & Bracker, J. S. (1989). Role of entrepreneurial task motivation in the growth of technologically innovative firms. *Applied Psychology*, *74*(4), 554–560. doi:10.1037/0021-9010.74.4.554

Phan, P. H., Wong, P. K., & Wang, C. (2002). Antecedents to Entrepreneurship among university students in Singapore: Beliefs, Attitudes and Background. *Journal of Enterprising Culture*, *10*(2), 151–174. doi:10.1142/S0218495802000189

Robichaud, Y., & Roger, A. (2001). Toward the Development of a Measuring Instrument for Entrepreneurial Motivation. *Developmental Entrepreneurship*, *6*(2), 189.

Shane, S., & Venkataraman, S. (2000). The promise of Entrepreneurship as a field of research. *Academy of Management Review*, *25*(1), 217–226. doi:10.5465/amr.2000.2791611

Shapero, A. (1982). Social dimensions of entrepreneurship. In The Encyclopedia of Entrepreneurship. Englewood Cliffs, NJ: Prentice Hall.

Tang, M. (2009). *The research on the relationship between entrepreneurial self-efficacy and entrepreneurial intentions* (Dissertation). Zhonglan University. (in Chinese)

Teece, D. J. (2007). Explicating dynamic capabilities: The nature and micro-foundations of sustainable enterprise performance. *Strategic Management Journal*, *28*(13), 1319–1350. doi:10.1002mj.640

Wilson, F., Kickul, J., & Marlino, D. (2007). Gender, entrepreneurial self-efficacy, and entrepreneurial career intentions: Implications for entrepreneurship education. *Entrepreneurship Theory and Practice*, *31*(3), 387–406. doi:10.1111/j.1540-6520.2007.00179.x

Ye, Y. H. (2009). The study on factors affecting undergraduates' entrepreneurial intentions. [in Chinese]. *Educational Studies*, *4*, 73–77.

Chapter 10
The Effects of Opportunity Alertness and Competitive Tension on Organizational Change Strategies

Ao Zhang
School of Accounting, Jilin University, China

Yuehui Cui
School of Economics and Management, Changchun University of Technology, China

Na Li
School of Management, Changchun University, China

Sinan Li
Dalian University of Technology, China

ABSTRACT

Competitive dynamics theory emphasizes that entrepreneurs must be alert to the opportunities, perceiving the tension of competition between firms to implement organizational change strategy. However, empirical studies on the above aspects are very scarce. Based on the literature review, this chapter proposes a research model about opportunity alertness, competitive tension, and organizational change and uses 183 valid questionnaires from the northeast of China to test this model. The empirical results show that opportunity alertness and competitive tension have a significant impact on organizational change strategies respectively, and competitive tension moderates the relationship between opportunity alertness and organizational

DOI: 10.4018/978-1-7998-3495-3.ch010

change strategies. The results show that facing fierce competition, entrepreneurs, who can exert the organizational strategies, should not only improve opportunity alertness, but also strengthen their understanding of the competitive situation among enterprises and the value of competitive tension. Finally, theoretical and practical implications are addressed.

INTRODUCTION

The advent of E-commerce era and global competition make organizational change become the focus of attention for new ventures. The gradual transition from flat organizations to diversified organizations with flexible division of labor is an essential means for organizations to cope with the increasingly fierce market competition (Tang, 2012). How to successfully change and adapt quickly to a changing environment, seize potential opportunities, and gain a favorable market position depends on the perception and control of top executives' awareness of external environmental crisis (Chen & Miller, 2012),which is the main force to promote organizational change. It can be seen that the alertness of top executives will contribute to the successful transformation of the organization.

However, by combing through many well-known management journals in recent years, it can be found that although the study of opportunity alertness shows a growing trend year by year (Shepherd, 2003), especially in the field of entrepreneurial research. However, the research focuses on the analysis of the antecedents of opportunity alertness, the identification and utilization of opportunity alertness, and the relationship between opportunity alertness and the rapid growth of new ventures. From the perspective of opportunity alertness, there are few studies to explain organizational change strategies from the perspective of opportunity alertness (Chen & Miller, 2012). In the current global industry recession situation, organizational change has been seen as the main driving force for economic growth and development. How to recognize and grasp the opportunity and use it to drive organizational strategic change will be a challenge to the cognition of new ventures, and to a certain extent, accelerate the growth and evolution of the organization.

In addition, the external environmental factors of new ventures also have an important impact on organizational change strategy. The view of dynamic competition proposed by Chen et al. (1996, 2007) also proves that if an organization wants to survive in a dynamic competitive environment and continuously improve its performance, it must pay attention to the competitive dynamics of the market. That is, the dynamics and responses of all new ventures competing in the same market (Chen & Miller, 2012). After the organization understands the actions and responses that the opponent may take, and grasps the competitive confrontation between competitors, the organization can effectively implement the organizational change strategy and strengthen the effect of change. Among them, the driving factor that can cause organizations to compete or counterattack is AMC: Awareness-Motivation-Capability. Chen(1996) and Miller(2007), in their research results, call this force that breaks the transient equilibrium of competition and causes the rapid outbreak of competition among new ventures as competitive tension. It reflects the imbalance of temporary equilibrium and reflects the potential pressure on both sides of the competition. Chen (1996) argues that the stronger the competitive tension, the more obvious the organization's intention to adopt competitive confrontation behavior, and the faster its competitive action. Therefore, changes within the organization will also be quickly adjusted to adapt to competition, which in turn leads organizations to adopt a change strategy to match external competition. Thus, the tension of competition has a significant impact on organizational change strategies. At present, some scholars have begun to pay attention to the role of competitive tension in the relationship between alertness and organizational change, but only at the level of qualitative research, lack of corresponding empirical tests (Ardichvili, 2003; Foss & Klein, 2009).

In summary, this study will focus on the influence of opportunity alertness on organizational change strategy, and focus on the influence of competitive tension on the relationship between opportunity alertness and organizational change strategy to deeply explore the deep-acting mechanism of the impact of opportunity alertness on organizational change strategy, and explore the adjustment effect of competitive tension. It can further explain the boundary conditions of opportunity alertness affecting organizational change strategy, deepen the theory of organizational change, and strengthen the recognition of dynamic competition theory. It helps new ventures to adapt to market changes quickly, make sound strategic decisions, and be in a favorable position in the fierce market changes.

LITERATURE REVIEW AND HYPOTHESIS PRESENTATION

Opportunity Alertness

Kirzner (1973) first proposed the concept of "alertness". He believed that alertness is the search, identification and evaluation of information. Venkataraman (1997) believes that at any stage of the development of a new venture, the most important thing is to explain the mining and development of opportunities, and most strategic research scholars believe that the conversion of newly generated technical information into specific commodities is a kind of opportunity (Sarasvathy, 2003), the ability to identify and search for opportunities is an opportunity alertness. Kirzner (1997) states that opportunity alertness is an entrepreneur's sensitivity to opportunities and that information about opportunities is asymmetric, and and if the entrepreneur can identify, evaluate and utilize the opportunity more sensitively, opportunity alertness is high. Shane (2003) believes that opportunity alertness has three characteristics: the ability to perceive the potential economic value of an opportunity, the novelty of an opportunity, and the invisibility of an opportunity. It can be seen that only entrepreneurs with good opportunity alertness can identify, evaluate and take advantage of opportunities. Simsek et al. (2009) argue that opportunity alertness is the ability to proactively capture, process and adapt valuable market information to strategic decisions within an organization. Tang et al. (2012) proposed three levels of alertness, namely, alert scanning and search, alert correlation and link, and assessment and judgment. The first level reflects the entrepreneur's constant scanning of new opportunities in the environment and searching for information that is ignored by others. The second level reflects the combination of different information by entrepreneurs into coherent information and replacing the original information. The three levels reflect that entrepreneurs determine whether their opportunity information can reflect potential business opportunities and profits through evaluation of decisions and judgment of information. For the purposes of this study, the definition and connotation of opportunity vigilance by Tang et al. (2012) will be used for subsequent analysis. Rezvani and Lashgari (2019)developed a new framework for international entrepreneurial alertness in the opportunity discovery ofindividual, group and organizational level.

Organizational Change Strategy

Organizational Change Strategy is a kind of action plan for change (Xue & Klein, 2008), which can point out the goals and directions of change to be achieved by organizational resources and activities. Lee et al. (2017)identify the different types of organizationalchange and quantify them to measure organizational change intensity-severity. Rosenbaum et al.(2018) identify the development of planned organisational change models(POCMs) since Lewin's three-step model and to highlight key linkages between them. Among the many organizational change strategy classifications, Dunphy & Stace's (1992) Contingency model of Organizational Change is closely related to organizational environment and organizational performance. This model is composed of two elements: scale of change and leadership style of change. Moreover, the two are closely related: when the scale of change is small and leadership style of change is collaborative consulting, the organization adopts a participative evolution; when the scale of change is large and the leadership style of change is collaborative consulting, the organization adopts charismatic transformation; when the scale of change is large and the leadership style of change leadership is forced, the organization adopts the dictatorial transformation; when the scale of change is small and the leadership is forced, organization adopts a forced evolution strategy. Regardless of the type of strategy adopted, organizational change strategies will be reflected in both scale and leadership style. This study will carry out analysis accordingly.

Competitive Tension

Tension reflects the transient equilibrium under the constraint of each other, but when the tension increases enough to transform the static relationship between each other into a dynamic interaction, the stable relationship between each other ceases to exist (Chen & Miller, 2012). The reason for the development of the theory of competitive tension lies in that the competitive analysis, such as the competitor strategy group and the competitor group, which emphasized the perceptual orientation research in the past, regarded all the competitors faced by the new ventures as homogeneous, but their essence is heterogeneous. The competitive tension is that competitors continue to exert pressure on their opponents, creating a potential pressure that can break out into open competition and confrontation. Let the opposing sides change from a static relationship to a cumulative pressure of dynamic engagement. Chen et al. (2007) defined "competitive tension" as a tension between competitors that may trigger new ventures to take action against its competitors. If the competitive tension reaches a certain level, the equilibrium will be broken, and competition will become the main melody between the new enterprises. Chen et al. (2007) through the AMC framework of dynamic competition to evaluate and measure the competitive tension between the new ventures and competitors. At the same time, they also integrate previously studies of the characteristics of competitive actions, information processing, competitive actions, the relationship between response and performance, the relationship between competitors' traits and performance, and use these as the basis for competitive tension measurement and application.

Hypotheses Presentation

In the current environment, fine-tuning is no longer a mainstream change strategy. In order to maintain the matching of opportunities and strategies, new ventures must take decisive measures to implement enterprise transformation and actively carry out strategic changes. In the past, many corporate executives' behaviors were based on their understanding of the market or their subconsciousness to achieve the organization's strategic goals. Entrepreneurs who can naturally find opportunities in this way are more alert to opportunities than ordinary people. However, alertness is as natural as learning, and executives with a high degree of alertness will actively examine the match between discovered opportunities and corporate strategy (Kirzner,

1973). However, before alerting to opportunities and making decisions, senior executives will use their abilities and knowledge to assess the right direction and make appropriate organizational size adjustments and leadership style changes. The key to entrepreneurs' success is that entrepreneurs continue to use alertness, use social resources, apply relevant knowledge, absorb relevant information, and explore and evaluate and utilize opportunities to enhance their ability to alert opportunity. And on this basis, make a strategy for organizational change. Gaglio & Katz (2001) believes that opportunity alertness can ensure that high-level executives search for undiscovered opportunities, which will help new ventures speed up internal adjustments. Ko & Butler (2007) explores the impact of opportunistic alertness on organizational strategy from the perspective of social network. In his research, he pointed out that opportunistic alertness has a significant impact on organizational strategic decision-making. Simsek et al. (2009) also pointed out that opportunistic alertness promotes the improvement of entrepreneurship and will drive organizations to adopt a change strategy. Accordingly, this study proposes the following hypotheses:

Hypothesis 1: Opportunity alertness positively influences organizational change strategies.

Competitive tension is very valuable for new ventures because it allows organizations to focus on continuously collecting the needs of target consumers and the performance of competitors. The competitive tension provides organizations with the norm for information sharing and goal achievement. It is a comprehensive organizational value system (Chen & Miller, 2012). Enterprises with competitive tension should understand the reasons for customers' purchases, jointly formulate corresponding strategies and countermeasures, and achieve tasks through communication, so as to grasp the changes in the market and then launch the best adaptation strategy. It can be seen that the competitive tension involves the operation and decision-making process of each part of the new venture. The competitive tension of new ventures requires that the internal executives, human resources, organizational structure, and inter-departmental coordination must match the market information and work together to improve the performance of the new venture. The purpose of competitive tension is to better meet the customer's current and future needs than the competition. This kind of action can provide customers with excess value, such as product service quality, meeting potential demand and reducing customer purchase cost. This will help the organization develop long-term relationships with customers. In order to achieve this goal, the organization must adjust the organization's change strategy based on the competitive tension perception, and strive to organize the change strategy to meet market demand. Accordingly, this study proposes the following hypotheses:

Hypothesis 2: Competitive tension positively influences organizational change strategies.

Dynamic competition theory not only emphasizes the organization's active discovery of opportunities, but also uses the opportunity alertness to adjust organizational strategy, and also emphasizes the impact of competitive tension on organizational factors. The competitive tension reflects the asymmetry of competition among new ventures. This asymmetry requires new ventures to continually increase their opportunity alertness and create a sustainable economic rent, which is the source of long-term competitive advantage. Chen (2008) pointed out that the stronger the competitive tension, the alertness of seeking opportunities through competitive asymmetry will accelerate the speed of organizational change to ensure the market adaptability of the change strategy. In addition, Granstrand (2000) believes that if the innovative behavior of the target company appears in the field of technological superiority of the competitor, it will suffer more obstruction, threats and attacks, which will cause the target enterprise to bear greater pressure. At this time, the top executives with strong opportunity alertness will adjust their organizational strategies and speed up their response. Chen & Miller (2012) believes that competitors can create competitive asymmetry with competitive actions that are difficult to respond or difficult to imitate. On this basis, the competitive tension will strengthen the relationship between opportunity alertness and organizational change. Because of the uncertainty of competition, the strong opportunity alertness of the top management will help them to understand and grasp the external opportunities. While understanding the competitive situation of competitors, they will adjust the internal change strategy. The main objectives of the change are two:one is to seize the opportunity, and the other is to respond to the competitor's competitive behavior. It can be seen that the competitive tension has a moderating effect on the opportunity alertness and the organizational strategic change. Accordingly, this study proposes the following hypotheses:

Hypothesis 3: Competitive tension positively moderates the relationship between opportunity alertness and organizational change strategy.

Figure 1 presents the conceptual model of this study.

Figure 1. The research model

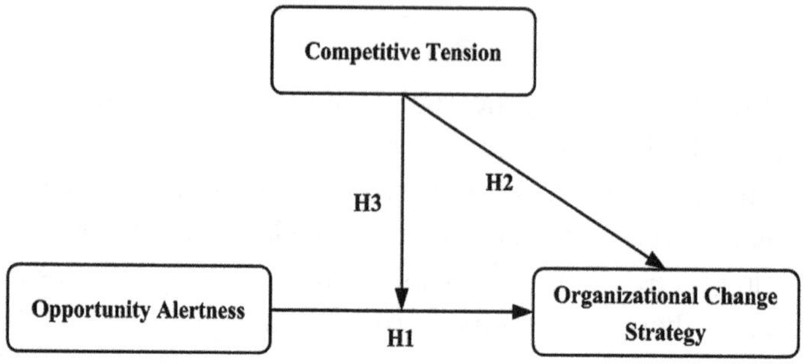

RESEARCH DESIGN

Data and Samples

Before the investigation, the questionnaires including the opportunity alertness, organizational change strategy and competitive tension were compiled according to the literature. In order to ensure the reliability and validity, the questionnaires and items selected in this study are derived from the existing literature to ensure the validity of the content. On this basis, two strategic management scholars were consulted to give feedback and propose revise opinion. Then, 29 new ventures were selected to pre-test the entire questionnaire to test whether the expression of the scale was standardized, and the questionnaire language was easy to understand.

After the completion of the questionnaire, a large-scale investigation was started. The survey is mainly concentrated in the three provinces of Northeast China. First of all, two doctoral students and three master students were trained in the questionnaire, and they sought to understand what the questionnaire should express, and then started the research. The questionnaires were distributed and collected by face-to-face interviews in Dalian, Shenyang, Harbin, Changchun and Siping. Through the acquaintances to get in touch with the responsible persons of the relevant new ventures, they will arrange a time interview after obtaining their consent, and explain the relevant issues in the interview to ensure that the participants understand the meaning of the items and ensure the quality of the questionnaire. According to statistics, a total of 331 questionnaires were distributed in this survey, 212 were collected, and the questionnaires with missing items were excluded. A total of 183 valid questionnaires were obtained, and the effective rate of the questionnaire was 55.29%. The study lasted two months, from September to November 2015.

In order to test Non-response Bias, the study is based on the recommendations of Armstrong & Overton (1977), sorted by the time of questionnaire recovery, and examined whether there were significant differences between the 30% questionnaires collected before and 30% after the survey. The results showed that there was no significant difference in the mean value of the control variables between the two groups ($t=0.744$, $p>0.1$), so it can be judged that the problem of non-response bias in this study questionnaire is not significant. Next, we use the Harman single factor method to solve the common method bias problem. An analysis of the entire questionnaire without rotation revealed that the first factor explained only 21.79% of the variance, no single factor appeared, and both the dependent variable and the independent variable were loaded onto different factors. At the same time, there is no single factor explained the majority of variance. Therefore, the common method deviation problem is not serious. Table 1 presents the characteristics of survey samples.

Table 1. Characteristics of survey samples (N=183)

Characteristics	Sample Size	Percentage	Characteristics	Sample Size	Percentage
Sex			Education		
male	167	91.26%	High school and below	7	3.83%
female	16	8.74%	Secondary school	12	6.56%
Age			Undergraduate	130	71.04%
Under 40	121	66.12%	Postgraduate and above	34	18.57%
41-50years old	42	22.95%	Family Business		
Over 51	20	10.93%	Yes	16	8.70%
Years of Business			No	167	91.30%
1~5years	53	28.96%	Industry		
5~10years	112	61.20%	IT	47	25.68%
More than 10 years	18	9.84%	Biopharmaceutical	32	17.49%
Number of Employees			electronics industry	57	31.15%
1~100	13	7.10%	Service industry	40	21.85%
100~300	74	40.44%	other	7	3.83%
300~500	36	19.67%			
500	60	32.79%			

Variable Measure

Organizational Change Strategy

The study draws on the research results of Dunphy & Stace (1992). This study uses the following five indicators to measure the scale of organizational change: "The scope of organizational changes involves a higher degree of restructuring of the department";"The degree of redistribution of power between departments is higher when organizations change"; "A new organizational unit is usually established and new appointments are made when the organization changes"; "Organization changes often result in changes to the original workflow and coordination mechanisms" and "The work objectives of each department are usually redefined after organizational changes". The Cronbach'α of these indicators is 0.749, and the factor load value distribution range of each test item is between 0.703 ~ 0.821.This study uses the following six indicators to measure the leadership style of change: "I often discuss organizational change decisions with my subordinates"; "Employees are widely involved in organizational changes"; "Organization changes will be assigned according to employee expertise"; "When the organization changes, the staff will be consulted during the work assignment process"; "Organizational changes will not resolve conflicts by order or by exercising formal functions" and"When an organization changes, it does not force employees to accept the resolution that has already been decided". The Cronbach'α of these indicators is 0.759, and the factor load value distribution range of each test item is between 0.634 ~ 0.801.

Opportunity Alertness

The study draws on the research results of Kirzner(2004) and Ardichvili et al. (2003). This study uses the following eight indicators to measure the opportunity alertness: "I always try to find business opportunities from everyday life"; "My business vision comes from digging and insight into everyday work"; "I will spend more time thinking about market changes and managing potential opportunities"; "I use a variety of media to capture and utilize business dynamics"; "I recognize the value of the opportunity that the network brings to the enterprise"; "I understand the situation of competitors and get the necessary information and knowledge"; "When dealing with my daily work, I will try to find new business or methods based on the actual situation of the company" and "When faced with multiple opportunities at the same time, I often choose the best one". The Cronbach'α of these indicators is 0.733, and the factor load value distribution range of each test item is between 0.621 ~ 0.789.

Competitive Tension

The study draws on the research results of Chen et Al. (2007) and Chen & Miller (2012). This study uses the following five indicators to measure the opportunity alertness: "The company will respond quickly to competitive actions in the same industry"; "When the company takes competitive action, we will predict in advance the possible responses of competitors in the same industry"; "The company usually does not respond to competitive actions in the same industry"; "The company keeps abreast of the dynamics of the same industry and moves to adjust the competitive strategy of the company"; "The company will quickly interpret the purpose and impact of certain competitive actions by companies in the same industry". The Cronbach'α of these indicators is 0.774, and the factor load value distribution range of each test item is between0.682~0.829.

In this paper, the age and size of enterprises are used as control variables. For enterprises, their age and size will influence the evolution of the organization, especially the change of organizational change strategy (Chen et all., 2007) . This paper measures the age by the years of the establishment of an enterprise and the size by the number of employees, which are expressed by their natural logarithms. The third control variable is industry, because different industries have different levels of competition, their performance of competitive tension (Chen et all., 2007) and organizational change strategy (Hambrick et all., 1996) will also be different. This study used dummy variables to measure industry. All of the key variables above are measured using the Likert 7 scale.

EMPIRICAL RESEARCH

Correlation Analysis

Before hypothesis testing, the study examined the correlation of variablcs, as shown in Table 2. It can be seen from Table 2 that there is a certain correlation between the coefficients and they are all less than the critical value of 0.7. Moreover, after testing the VIF of the entire questionnaire, it was found that all values were less than 10. In order to eliminate the correlation between variables, the article has done a mean centering on the values.

Examination of Reliability and Validity

In this study, Cronbach's values were used to measure reliability, and structural equations were used to test validity. At first, exploratory factor analysis of the data

Table 2. Correlation matrix and variance inflation factor

Variable	1	2	3	4	5	6
Enterprise Size	N/A					
Industry	0.103	N/A				
Age	0.121*	-0.069	N/A			
Organizational Change Strategy	0.134	0.192**	-0.097	2.31		
Opportunity Alertness	0.236**	0.089	0.224**	0.378***	1.89	
Competitive Tension	0.114	0.152*	0.105	0.441**	0.215*	2.57

*p<0.1;**p<0.05;***p<0.01

shows that the reliability of the questionnaire is good. Through the confirmatory factor analysis of the above variables (as shown in Table 3), we found that the overall fit and validity of each factor meet the requirements, which meet the needs of follow up analysis. Through exploratory factor analysis, it was found that 11 items of organizational change strategy were loaded on two different factors, namely the scale of change and the leadership style of change, and the factor load was higher than 0.6. The results of confirmatory factor analysis also showed that the fit index of each variable scale is better, and The questionnaire has good reliability and validity.

Table 3. Confirmatory factor analysis

Variable	Indicators								
	X^2	df	GFI	NFI	AGFI	CFI	IFI	RMSEA	RMR
Organizational Change Strategy	122.107	75	0.933	0.915	0.907	0.954	0.992	0.047	0.039
Opportunity Alertness	113.261	83	0.952	0.941	0.979	0.987	0.964	0.057	0.037
Competitive Tension	112.373	89	0.954	0.981	0.966	0.972	0.948	0.061	0.052

Hypothesis Test

According to the hypothesis of the study, the hierarchical regression analysis technique is used to test the hypothesis. The results are shown in Table 4.

The empirical results show that there is a significant correlation between the opportunity alertness and the organizational change strategy(β=0.354,p<0.01), and there is also a significant difference between competitive tension and the organizational change strategy (β=0.160, $p<0.05$) in the model 2 . Moreover, R2 and Adj.R2 of model 2 are better than model 1 ($p<0.01$). Therefore, both hypothesis 1 and hypothesis 2 are supported. In the model 3, we add the interaction item of opportunity alertness and competitive tension. The results show that competitive tension significantly positively moderates the relationship between opportunity alertness and organizational change strategy (β=0.214, $p<0.01$). That is, the more obvious the competitive tension is, the higher opportunity alertness will be helpful to the implementation of organizational change strategy. Therefore, hypothesis 3 is supported.

Table 4. Logistics regression analysis summary

Variable	Organizational Change Strategy		
	Model 1	Model 2	Model 3
Age	-0.101	0.086	0.105
Enterprise Size	0.106	0.136	0.107
Opportunity Alertness		0.354***	0.265**
Competitive Tension		0.160**	-0.187
Opportunity Alertness* Competitive Tension			0.214***
R^2	0.251	0.339	0.392
Adj R^2	0.224	0.307	0.357
F-vaule	4.913***	6.481***	9.728***

* p<0.10;** p<0.05;*** p<0.01.

CONCLUSION

Dynamic competition theory emphasizes the impact of the competition situation of new ventures on organizational actions. The development of competitive tension of new ventures to a certain extent will break the short-term equilibrium between enterprises, forcing new ventures to continuously strengthen their opportunity alertness. This will help catalyze competition between new ventures and strengthen organizational change. Based on 183 valid questionnaires, the article explores the relationship between opportunity alertness, competitive tension, and organizational change strategies. The empirical results show that the opportunity alertness and competitive tension have a significant positive impact on the organizational change strategy, and the competitive tension significantly moderates the relationship between the opportunity alertness and the organizational change strategy. This research has obvious theoretical and practical value.

In theory, dynamic competition research lacks an empirical analysis of organizational change strategies from the perspective of opportunity alertness (Chen & Miller, 2012). Therefore, the article further deepens the understanding of the relationship between opportunity alertness and strategic change, increases the empirical experience of dynamic competition theory at the opportunity level, and enriches and strengthens its theoretical foundation. In addition, by studying the impact of competitive tension on organizational change strategies, it not only compensates for the shortcomings of using only competitive tension as a control variable (such as McGrath et al., 1999), but also increases the direct effect of competitive tension and improves its theoretical application. Finally, by studying the moderating effect of competitive tension, it further clarifies the contingency and boundary conditions of the impact of opportunity alertness on organizational change strategy, and deepens the relationship between opportunity alertness and organizational change strategy.

In practice, the impact of opportunity alertness on organizational change strategies indicates that when making organizational changes, new ventures must inspect the daily work norms of the market based on the business opportunities they are searching for, and use market changes to manage potential market opportunities. And on this basis, implement the change strategy, and strive to adapt and match organizational change and potential opportunities. At the same time, entrepreneurs must actively use diversified media networks to capture business dynamics, increase the value of opportunities, and redistribute power between departments based on the value of opportunities. When an entrepreneur finds a new business or method in practice, the organization should establish a new organizational department and conduct new appointments according to business needs, further improve the original working mechanism and process, and achieve the match among the organization, opportunity and external environment. Matching. The impact of competitive tension on organizational change strategy shows that because the short-term equilibrium pattern between new ventures is broken and the organization perceives that the competitive situation in the same industry is changing, then the company should quickly make strategic adjustments and compete against competitors and make bold predictions about the possible responses from competitors. In view of the competition in the same industry, enterprises need to grasp the possible future competition direction at any time, and timely adjust the scale of change and the leadership style of change. Enterprises need to improve their competitive strategies through strategic adjustment to realize the impact of competitive tension on organizational change. The moderating effect of competitive tension on the relationship between opportunity alertness and organizational change strategy shows that the relationship between opportunity alertness and organizational change strategy has a contingency. The regulatory effect of competitive tension not only requires companies to strengthen their opportunity alertness, but also use the awareness of competition to enhance the scale of change and the leadership style of change based on the organization's perception of competitive tension. This will further improve the organizational change strategy and lay a strategic foundation for the development of the organization. In a word, the important premise for entrepreneurs to implement organizational change is to have alertness, so that they can actively acquire, process and utilize valuable market information .On the basis of cognitive competitive tension, we can scan the environment, connect information and judge the situation by enhancing opportunity alertness, so as to implement the correct organizational change strategy.

Research Deficiencies and Future Research Prospects

In order to improve the reliability of the scale, this study adopts the combination of field research and questionnaire distribution. All the questionnaires collected are paper-based. At the same time, the collected questionnaires are evaluated in advance, the incomplete questionnaires are screened and the individual unqualified measurement items are eliminated, and the final measurement scale of this study is obtained. However, due to the limitation of time and ability in this study, the items of the scale may not fully reflect the variables to be measured, so the maturity and reliability of the scale compared with foreign mature scales will still be deficient, and the author will improve it in the future research; the second is the deviation in the survey questionnaire. Although this study carried out pre survey before large-scale survey, and deleted items with poor discrimination. However, some items are not well differentiated, but are caused by the expression problem or the deviation of the respondents' understanding of the expression. In this study, these items will be described twice and tested in future research.

Although all the data in this study have passed the reliability and validity test, and most of the theoretical hypotheses put forward have also been supported by the data, due to the limitations of research time and research funds, only high-tech enterprises and traditional enterpriscs in thc threc northeastern provinces are selected as the research objects in the sample collection scope, while the enterprise development in the three northeastern provinces has regional significant characteristics, although For the underdeveloped areas, the data has certain reference value, but it can not fully represent the development of high-tech enterprises and traditional enterprises in China, not to mention the high-tech enterprises in the eastern developed areas. Therefore, due to the limitation of data, the universality and representativeness of this study still need to be further tested. In view of this result, the author believes that the research area can be expanded in the future research, so that the research results can be more universal; secondly, the data used in this study does not distinguish between high-tech enterprises and traditional enterprises, the data collected is the overall data, which has not been distinguished for comparative analysis, nor for comparative research.

REFERENCES

Ardichvili, A., Cardozo, R., & Ray, S. (2003). A theory of entrepreneurial opportunity identification and development. *Journal of Business Venturing, 18*(1), 105–123. doi:10.1016/S0883-9026(01)00068-4

Armstrong, J. S., & Overton, T. S. (1977). Estimating nonresponse bias in mail surveys. *JMR, Journal of Marketing Research, 14*(3), 396–402. doi:10.1177/002224377701400320

Busenitz, L. W., West, G. P., & Shepherd, D. (2003). Entrepreneurship research in emergence:Past trends and future directions. *Journal of Management, 29*(3), 285–308. doi:10.1016/S0149-2063(03)00013-8

Chen, M. J. (1996). Competitive analysis interfirm rivalry:Toward a theoretical integration. *Academy of Management Review, 21*(1), 100–134. doi:10.5465/amr.1996.9602161567

Chen, M. J. (2007). Competitive dynamics research:An insider's odyssey. *Asia Pacific Journal of Management*, (26), 5–25.

Chen, M. J. (2009). Competitive dynamics research: An insider's odyssey. *Asia Pacific Journal of Management, 26*(1), 5–25. doi:10.100710490-008-9110-7

Chen, M. J., & Miller, D. (2012). Competitive dynamics:Themes,trends,and a prospective research platform. *The Academy of Management Annals*, (6): 1–89.

Dunphy, D. C., & Stace, D. (1992). *Under new management: Australian organizations in transition*. McGraw-Hill.

Eckhardt, J. T., & Shane, S. A. (2003). Opportunities and entrepreneurship. *Journal of Management, 29*(3), 333–349. doi:10.1177/014920630302900304

Foss, N. J., & Klein, P. G. (2009). *Entrepreneurial Alertness and Opportunity Discovery: Origins, Attributes, Critique*. Academic Press.

Gaglio, C. M., & Katz, J. A. (2001). The psychological basis of opportunity identification: Entrepreneurial alertness. *Small Business Economics, 16*(2), 95–111. doi:10.1023/A:1011132102464

Granstrand O. (2000). *The economics of mul-tech:A study of multi-technology corporations in Japan, Sweden and the US*. Background paper submitted to the Dynacom Project.

Hair, J. F., Anderson, R. E., & Tatham, R. L. (1998). *Black, Multivariate data analysis*. Academic Press.

Hambrick, D. C., Cho, T. S., & Chen, M. J. (1996). The influence of top management team heterogeneity on firms' competitive moves. *Administrative Science Quarterly*, *41*(4), 659–684. doi:10.2307/2393871

Kirzner, I. M. (1997). Entrepreneurial discovery and the competitive market process:An Austrian approach. *Journal of Economic Literature*, 60.

Kirzner Israel, M. (1973). *Competition and entrepreneurship*. Academic Press.

Ko, S., & Butler, J. E. (2007). Creativity: A key link to entrepreneurial behavior. *Business Horizons*, *50*(5), 365–372. doi:10.1016/j.bushor.2007.03.002

Lee, K., Lee, K., & Sharif, M. (2017). Procedural justice as a moderator of the relationship between organizational change intensity and commitment to organizational change. *Journal of Organizational Change Management*, *30*(4), 501–524. doi:10.1108/JOCM-08-2015-0139

McGrath, R. G. (1999). Falling forward: Real options reasoning and entrepreneurial failure. *Academy of Management Review*, *24*(1), 13–30. doi:10.5465/amr.1999.1580438

Rezvani, M., Lashgari, M., & Yadolahi Farsi, J. (2019). International entrepreneurial alertness in opportunity discovery for market entry. *Journal of Research in Marketing and Entrepreneurship.*, *21*(2), 76–102. doi:10.1108/JRME-01-2018-0003

Rosenbaum, D., More, E., & Steane, P. (2018). Planned organisational change management: Forward to the past? An exploratory literature review. *Journal of Organizational Change Management*, *31*(2), 286–303. doi:10.1108/JOCM-06-2015-0089

Sarasvathy, S. D. (2003). Entrepreneurship as a science of the artificial. *Journal of Economic Psychology*, *24*(2), 203–220. doi:10.1016/S0167-4870(02)00203-9

Simsek, Z., Heavey, C., Veiga, J. F., & Souder, D. (2009). A typology for aligning organizational ambidexterity's conceptualizations, antecedents, and outcomes. *Journal of Management Studies*, *46*(5), 864–894. doi:10.1111/j.1467-6486.2009.00841.x

Tang, J., Kacmar, K. M. M., & Busenitz, L. (2012). Entrepreneurial alertness in the pursuit of new opportunities. *Journal of Business Venturing*, *27*(1), 77–94. doi:10.1016/j.jbusvent.2010.07.001

Venkataraman, S. (1997). The distinctive domain of entrepreneurship research. *Advances in Entrepreneurship, Firm, Emergence, and Growth*, *3*(1), 119.

Xue, J.-H., & Klein, P. G. (2008). *A Latent-Variables Approach to Entrepreneurship*. Working Paper. Contracting and Organizations Research Institute, University of Missouri.

Chapter 11
Innovation or Imitation in New Ventures?
Contingent Effects of Dysfunctional Competition

Biao Chen
Zhengzhou University, China

Yu Sun
Dalian University of Technology, China

Yuchao Ding
Dalian University of Technology, China

Yang Liu
Dalian University of Technology, China

ABSTRACT

The authors examine the effects of innovation and imitation strategies on new venture competitive advantage during both technological and market turbulence. In turn, they test the moderating effects of dysfunctional competition in these settings. Using data collected from 153 new ventures in China, they find that innovation and imitation strategies have positive effects on new venture competitive advantage. Furthermore, they find that dysfunctional competition increases the positive relationship between imitation strategies and new venture competitive advantage in these settings. However, the negative moderating effects of dysfunctional competition are partly verified. And they find that the consumption attitudes of the younger generation in China may explain why the theory is inconsistent with the empirical results. The theoretical and practical implications of the findings are discussed.

DOI: 10.4018/978-1-7998-3495-3.ch011

INTRODUCTION

Imitation, Innovation, and New Ventures

The economic literature on innovation suggests that imitation can dampen innovation and erode the profits of innovation (Slivko & Theilen, 2014). As a result it is typically argued that new ventures depend on introducing new products ahead of competitors to achieve success (Cai et al., 2014). However, others argue that imitation can improve the market value chain by identifying a superior position and providing improved products to better serve customers that others may not concern, which in turn can reduce the level of R&D investment firms require (Zhou, 2006). Thus, a key decision a firm must make is to be an imitator or an innovator (Slivko & Theilen, 2014). To date, the strategic choice of which strategy, innovation or imitation, generates the best result for firms remains unclear. Scholars have studied this issue from different respective, but they did not reach a consistent conclusion (Zhou, 2006; Naranjo-Valencia et al., 2011; Slivko & Theilen, 2014). This research will, therefore, examine the research question here of whether imitation or innovation generates the best result in what setting.

We argue specifically that there are two main characteristics of environmental change which directs whether a firm chooses imitation or innovation -- technological turbulence and market turbulence (Kohli & Jaworski, 1990; Su et al., 2013; Bodlaj & Čater, 2019). We then also examine the potential for dysfunctional competition to moderate the impact of these two forms of turbulence.

This paper makes two major contributions to the literature. First, we contribute to the entrepreneurship literature by bringing the understanding of imitation/innovation to the domain. Second, previous studies have studied the choice of strategies based on contingency theory, however, they didn't analyze this issue concerning on environmental turbulence and dysfunctional competition simultaneously in new ventures. In this paper, we construct an integration model to empirically analyze new venture strategies. Third, we explain the inconsistent result between theory and empirical results by analyzing the consumption attitudes of the younger generation in China. The finding can complement the theory of strategy choice based on established companies.

Literature Review

Innovation strategies help create new markets, shape consumer preferences, and even change consumers' basic behavior (Zhou, 2006). In contrast, imitation strategies complement the needs of existing markets, improve products to serve existing customers better (Naranjo-Valencia et al., 2011). Theoretically, innovation and imitation strategies can both enable new ventures to gain competitive advantage. However, it is not clear which strategy, imitation or innovation, will generate the best results. To date, the evidence is mixed. Market environment (Zhou, 2006), spillovers and competitive pressure (Slivko & Theilen, 2014) and organizational culture (Naranjo-Valencia et al., 2011) may determine the choice of strategy. However, these researches are based on established companies. Whether they can explain new venture strategies is unknown. So we need to resolve the issue of strategic choice in new ventures.

Research suggests that interaction between strategy and the specific environment may drive the fate of entrepreneurial efforts and provide a better understanding of entrepreneurial success (Aldrich & Martinez, 2001). This would lead to the expectation that the relationship between new venture strategies and competitive advantage may vary under different conditions. Such choices in which strategy works best may be particularly important in environments in which the resources for private firms are limited.Available resources to private firms are scare in a transition economy (Shan et al., 2014). As Li and Zhang argue that in a transition economy, state-owned ventures are founded by the government or its agencies and have great legitimacy and government protection. In contrast, private firms, especially, new ventures, lack legitimacy and government protection. Thus, new ventures may have difficulties in getting resource in China (Li, 2001; Yin, Peng & Peng, 2014).

It has been found that environmental turbulence, both technological and market turbulence, can play a significant role in determining the profitability of a firm (Su et al., 2013). However, most earlier studies have treated technological and market turbulence treat as independent factors (ie., Li & Calantone, 1998; Zhou, 2006; Sheng, Zhou, & Li, 2011; Su et al., 2013). However, according to O'Cass and Sok(2012), developing products and delivering them to customers are the key aim of any firms. Similarly, Haeussler, Patzelt and Zahra (2102) suggest that developing and commercializing products are critical for new ventures. Based on these views, we suggest that new ventures may deal with technological and market turbulence simultaneously, technological and market turbulence may exist and affect new ventures simultaneously. Therefore, it is necessary to construct an integrative framework to examine how these two factors affect the effectiveness of firms' behaviors.

In transition economies, because formal market institutions have not been well developed, dysfunctional competition may affect the effectiveness of new ventures' behavior (Li & Zhang, 2007), which may moderate the relationship between new venture strategies and competitive advantage. As Li and Li (2009) noted, dysfunctional competition can exist in any type of economy, it is more likely to occur in transition economies such as China's. Therefore, we will explore the moderating effects of dysfunctional competition on the relationship between strategies and new venture competitive advantage in different environmental conditions. It may reveal how special conditions affect new venture strategies.

We focus here only on high technological and low market turbulence conditions plus low technological and high market turbulence conditions. As we know, new venture strategies represent an important means to deal with environments (Li, 2001). If the change speed of environment is low, the importance of strategies may be not notable. Compared with established firms, new ventures tend to have relatively limited resources (Shan et al., 2014), and developing and commercializing products can be costly and time consuming (Haeussler, Patzelt & Zahra, 2012). If both technological and market environments change quickly, the survival of new ventures may be impossible because they may not have ability to deal with quick change of technological and market environments simultaneously. Therefore, we do not examine high technological and high market turbulence conditions or low technological and low market turbulence conditions in this paper.

Conceptual Model

Contingency theory suggests that there is no one best way that can be equally effective in all conditions. Extending this assumption to the strategy context, a firm's strategy should match with its internal organizational resources and external environmental conditions (Ginsberg & Venkataman, 1985). As new ventures tend to be relatively small scale and have a simple structure and strong resource constraints (Ruef et al., 2003), their strategies may be mainly influenced by the external environment. In transition economies, the main environmental conditions are environmental turbulence and dysfunctional competition. Therefore, we explore how dysfunctional competition moderates new venture strategies in different environmental turbulence conditions. At the same time, according to strategy management theory, a strategy is a response to the opportunities and threats in the environment (Schendel & Hofer, 1979; Vecchiato, 2019). The aim of a new venture's strategic choice is to exploit these opportunities and resolve the threats, and to gain competitive advantage. We draw on this theory to explain how new ventures achieve growth. We develop our conceptual framework by combining contingency theory with strategic management theory (see Figure 1).

Hypotheses

Innovation Versus Imitation Strategies

Innovation and imitation strategies are theoretically viable, and both can promote competitive advantage (Zhou, 2006; Slivko & Theilen, 2014). The two strategies

Figure 1.

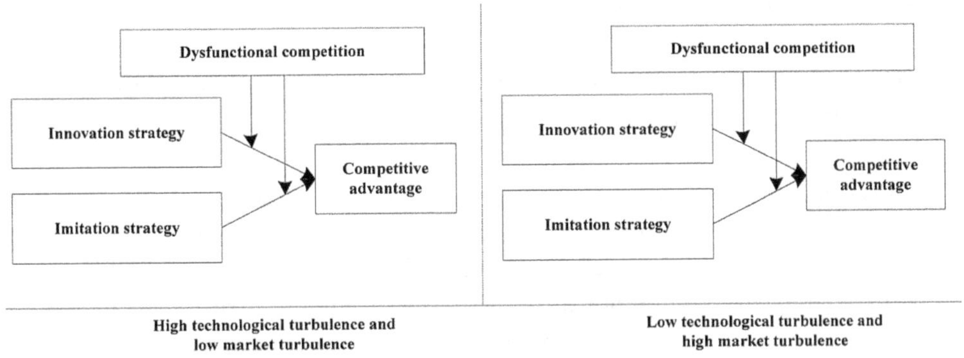

focus on the internal production mode, and function differently. Innovation strategies refer to the degree to which new ventures develop and introduce new products to participate in market activities, and thus gain first mover advantages and improve their productivity and profitability (Li & Atuahene-Gima, 2001; Tsai & Li, 2007; Cai et al., 2017). The strategies focus on the extent and frequency of new product innovations, the number of new products offered, and the rate at which new products are introduced to the market (Li & Atuahene-Gima, 2001). Innovation strategies can move markets toward disequilibrium through creative destruction, and then build more effective behaviors in market activities. First, innovation strategies aim to be the first to bring differentiated products to the market, which has the potential to shape consumer preferences and behavior (Zhou, 2006; Naranjo-Valencia et al., 2011), and construct new value chains. This may prevent rivals from quickly participating in the market. Second, if new ventures emphasize their innovation strategies, they may gain first mover advantages (Tsai & Li, 2007). These strategies can preempt rivals in the acquisition of scarce resources, such as by occupying the most attractive location in advance (Zhou, 2006). New ventures tend to have relatively limited managerial and financial resources, and lack legitimacy (Li, 2001). Therefore, it is difficult for these firms to achieve fair competition with established companies, and innovation strategies can help them construct the new value chains and gain the scarce resources they need to gain competitive advantage.

Furthermore, because of the relatively higher risk and uncertainty inherent in innovation strategies, such innovation processes are fraught with uncertainty with respect to whether the market will accept the new product (Anokhin, Wincent, & Autio, 2011) and whether the new venture can prevent rivals from copying its product, which could lead its output to be below the input. However, the successful implementation of an innovation strategy could move the market toward disequilibrium through creative destruction (Mainela, Puhakka, & Servais, 2014), build more effective behavior, and construct a new value chain, all of which can help new ventures gain competitive advantage. Therefore,

Hypothesis 1: Innovation strategies are positively associated with new venture competitive advantage.

Innovation strategies are resource-consuming, and depend on the resource endowment of the new venture. However, new ventures are characterized as having relatively limited resources, which means that imitation strategies are another option for them. Compared with innovation strategies, imitation strategies emphasize improvements of prior technologies or production processes, and reduce R&D costs and risks (Zott & Amit, 2008; Zheng & Li, 2011). Therefore, imitation strategies may help new ventures to introduce improved products and provide targeted services. First, as imitation strategies emphasize improvements of prior technologies or production processes, existing products can provide relative information, and provide opportunities to identify a superior position and introduce improved products to serve customers better (Naranjo-Valencia et al., 2011). An imitation strategy may promote a new venture's market attractiveness. Second, the existing products already provide an imitation strategy with respect to information, which enables the venture to implement the strategy smoothly (Zhou, 2006). Therefore, new ventures can provide low-cost products and attain cost advantages. Lastly, there are a number of differences between the imitation strategies of new ventures and established companies. In particular, established companies emphasize economies of scale (Zott & Amit, 2008), whereas new ventures focus on imitation, and tend to reduce their R&D investment and risks. The strategies enable new ventures to catch up in terms of technological leadership, and provide a process for accumulating sufficient know-how (Slivko & Theilen, 2014). In short, imitation strategies can identify customer needs, reduce R&D costs and risks, accumulate knowledge, improve the existing value chains, and contribute to gaining competitive advantage.

However, imitation strategies may hinder the promotion of new knowledge and new technology. The strategies focus on improving existing technology and can help new ventures gain market share in the short term; short-term success, however, may lead new ventures to fall into the "success trap" (March, 1991). Imitation strategies may also decrease the motivation and willingness to innovate and thus hinder further development (Politis, 2005). However, because new ventures have only existed for a short time, this "success trap" may not have a significant influence on new ventures (Liu & Li, 2013). Hence, imitation strategies guarantee early survival and short-term business advantages. Therefore,

Hypothesis 2: Imitation strategies are positively associated with new venture competitive advantage.

Contingent Effects of Dysfunctional Competition

Although environmental turbulence encompasses technological and market turbulence, the two types of turbulence function differently (Kohli & Jaworski, 1990; Su et al., 2013). Technological turbulence refers to the speed of change and unpredictability of technology in an industry, whereas market turbulence refers to the rate of change in the composition of customers and their preferences (Sheng et al., 2011; Su et al., 2013). Technological turbulence and market turbulence function in different ways (Kohli & Jaworski, 1990). Technological turbulence creates new product development or imitating opportunities (Sheng et al., 2011), and market turbulence shortens the life cycle of products (Su et al., 2013). In high technological and low market turbulence conditions, new ventures mainly focus on the effects of technological change, and integrate their existing resources to deal with the consequent opportunities and threats. In this case, technological turbulence is referred to as the dominant environment. As the organizational structures of new ventures are relatively simple, there may be few impediments if they want to adapt to new technology. Therefore, they can effectively grasp the opportunities in this condition. In short, if new ventures adopt an innovation strategy, they can grasp the available opportunities through internal R&D that originates from technological change. If they adopt an imitation strategy, they can take advantage of new technology through imitating the innovators. We suggest that innovation and imitation strategies are both conducive to helping new ventures gain competitive advantage in this condition.

However, new venture strategies in technological turbulence dominant environments are likely to be further influenced by dysfunctional competition. Dysfunctional competition refers to the competitive behavior of firms in a market that is perceived as opportunistic, unfair, or even unlawful (Li & Li, 2009), and it may erode the benefits of firms. First, if the institutional frameworks cannot impose severe punishments on unlawful or unethical competitive behaviors, the appropriable value of an innovation strategy will be eroded (Sheng, Zhou, & Lessassy, 2013). Due to the existence of dysfunctional competition, although new ventures allocate substantial resources to R&D, it is difficult for them to gain the expected benefits. For example, piracy of computer software applications is widespread in China (von Krogh & Haefliger, 2007). Because new ventures are also constrained by resources (Shan et al., 2014), they will find it difficult to protect their innovations. In this condition, dysfunctional competition hinders the positive effects of innovation strategies. Second, new ventures may be dependent on underdeveloped institutional frameworks, which allow opportunistic behavior, such as "Shanzhai," to emerge

(Liu & Luo, 2010). Because dysfunctional competition reduces the risks and costs of imitation, it increases the positive relationship between imitation strategies and new venture competitive advantage. Therefore,

Hypothesis 3: In high technological turbulence and low market turbulence conditions, dysfunctional competition negatively moderates the relationship between innovation strategies and new venture competitive advantage, and positively moderates the relationship between imitation strategies and new venture competitive advantage.

In low technological and high market turbulence conditions, new ventures mainly focus on the effects of market change, and integrate their existing resources to deal with the consequent opportunities and threats. In this case, market turbulence is referred to as the dominant environment. Because new ventures lack legitimacy, and are in a risky and vulnerable position in the market (Li, 2001), their products may not be quickly accepted by the market. If customers' preferences change quickly, the possibilities to commercialize the products will also be restricted, and the negative effect of a lack of market legitimacy may be increased. Therefore, changes in customers' preferences not only lead to uncertain demand for firms' products, but also accelerate the obsolescence of the products, which may reduce the economic return of their products (Su et al., 2013). In particular, new ventures are characterized as having limited financial and human resources, and minimal reputation (Robinson, McDougall, & Herron, 1988). Thus, a rapid change in market demand will expand the negative effect of the lack of resources on commercializing new products. Furthermore, the conditions may weaken the stability of the composition of customers and their preferences, and shorten the life cycle of products (Su et al., 2013). Imitation strategies can provide targeted products (Naranjo-Valencia et al., 2011). However, imitators follow innovators, which implies that innovators are the first to bring products to market and have a first-mover advantage. Therefore, it is difficult for late entrants to "compete away" the pioneer's large market share (Zhou, 2006). In particular, the negative effects of imitation strategies are expanded when market turbulence is the dominant environment. We suggest that the survival of new ventures may be more severely challenged in this condition.

However, new venture strategies in market turbulence dominant environments are likely to further influenced by dysfunctional competition. First, new ventures lack legitimacy, which has a negative effect on innovation strategies in this condition, and dysfunctional competition strengthens this negative effect. For new ventures, commercializing new products can be a costly and time consuming process (Haeussler, Patzelt, & Zahra, 2012), and dysfunctional competition in the environment can lead to innovations being imitated or copy by rivals (Li & Li, 2009). Therefore, the value of innovation as a strategy is reduced or even eroded. Although new products can construct new markets, shape consumer preferences, and even change consumers' basic behavior (Zhou, 2006; Naranjo-Valencia et al., 2011), due to the relatively limited marketing capability and lack of legitimacy, the advantage of their innovation strategies will be eroded once they are imitated or copied by rivals. Dysfunctional competition increases the risk of innovations being eroded, and reduces the effect of innovation strategies. Second, dysfunctional competition reduces the negative effects of the lack of market legitimacy on the relationship between imitation strategies and new venture competitive advantage in market turbulence dominant conditions. As the presence of unfair competition (e.g., information disclosure in the bidding process) (Li & Zhang, 2007), new ventures can construct marketing channels to commercialize their imitation products through "unconventional means." Moreover, because there are different degrees of imitation, from pure clones, which represent "me-too" products, to creative imitation, which takes an existing product and improves it (Zhou, 2006), dysfunctional competition can affect the degree of imitation. In developed economies, due to the existence of developed institutional frameworks, firms mainly focus on gradual imitation. In contrast, due to the relatively underdeveloped institutional frameworks in transition economies, "me-too" behavior may emerge. The behaviors of new ventures are especially typical. In this condition, the speed at which the imitators enter the market is accelerated and the "time gap" between imitators and innovators is reduced. Furthermore, this confirms that the role of dysfunctional competition is more notable in transition economies (Li & Li, 2009). Therefore,

Hypothesis 4: In low technological turbulence and high market turbulence conditions, dysfunctional competition negatively moderates the relationship between innovation strategies and new venture competitive advantage, and positively moderates the relationship between imitation strategies and new venture competitive advantage.

METHOD

Sampling and Data Collection

To test the hypotheses advanced in this paper, we collected data from new ventures in China (Changchun, Harbin, and Beijing) using a questionnaire-survey approach. To select new ventures, we used the criterion that a firm had been established no more than eight years (Song et al., 2008). The participants were mainly top managers or employees who had worked at least two years in their firms, which were randomly selected from our sample regions.

We conducted several procedures before formally distributing the survey questionnaire to ensure the reliability of our results. First, the questionnaire was developed using items and concepts drawn from previous studies, and translated multiple times to ensure the Chinese version was consistent with its original meaning. Second, we carried out face-to-face discussions of the scale with firm managers to ensure the translation was accurate. Third, a pilot study was conducted with 30 firms (excluded from the final survey sample). Finally, we trained the investigators about the purpose and content of our research to avoid any ambiguity caused by them.

We removed the incomplete questionnaires and firms that had been established more than eight years. At the conclusion of our survey, 153 firms had returned completed and useable questionnaires. The effective response rate was 34.0%. After further examining the profiles of the firms that provided complete and useable data (as provided in Table 1), we reached the conclusion that the final sample was representative of the study population.

Measures

We used items developed in previous studies to measure the key constructs, and made some modifications during the translation process. Based on Li (2001), we used five items to measure innovation strategy. We sourced the two items measuring imitation strategy from Zott and Amit (2008), Naranjo-Valencia, Jiménez-Jiménez and Sanz-Valle (2011), and Bruton and Rubanik (2002). We used four items to measure dysfunctional competition, building on the work of Li and Zhang (2007) and Li and Li (2009). Finally, we used three items sourced from Walter, Auer and Ritter (2006) to measure new venture competitive advantage.

Table 1. Profile of Responding Firms and Respondents (N=153)

	Percent		Percent
Respondents		**Employees**	
CEO/President	13.6	1-20	47.9
Top Managers	29.5	21-50	26.1
Department Managers	34.8	51-200	18.3
Others	22.1	201and above	7.7
Industry		**Firm Age**	
High Technology	41.7	1-3	46.3
Tradition	58.3	4-6	34.1
		7-8	19.7

The classification criterion of our sample was a firm's perception of the degree of environmental turbulence, including technological turbulence and market turbulence. Following Kohli and Jaworski (1990) and Su et al. (2013), we used eight items to measure environmental turbulence. Four items related to technological turbulence, and four to market turbulence. We included firm age, firm size, and the industry as controls. Firm age was measured by the number of years a firm had been in existence. The number of employees was used to measure firm size. Finally, for industry, we divided the firms into high-tech and traditional types. We set high-tech as 1 and traditional type as 0 in accordance with the setting criterion of virtual variables.

Common Method Bias

As each questionnaire was completed independently by one participant, common methods bias may exist. We used Harman's one-factor test to examine whether common method bias affected the data (Podsakoff & Organ, 1986). Using exploratory factor analysis to examine all of the variables simultaneously, we found that the first factor (representing the amount of CMV) only explained 30.96 percent of the variance in the data. Hence, common method bias did not appear to be present in the data.

Reliability and Validity

We analyzed the reliability and validity of the data using SPSS 16.0, and the results are shown in Table 2. We measured composite reliability using Cronbach's alpha, and all of the alpha values were well above 0.6, indicating good measure reliability. To assess the validity of each construct, five separate confirmatory factor analyses (CFAs) were conducted. As shown in Table 2, the factor loadings were all over 0.7, indicating that the scales had high validity. Overall, the scales had good reliability and validity.

RESULTS

Before carrying out the regression analysis, we first conducted a Pearson correlation analysis. Table 3 presents the descriptive statistics and correlation matrix of the study constructs. The correlation matrix indicates that bivariate associations exist between strategies and competitive advantage, and provides an initial platform to interpret our predicted relationships. We used regression analysis to examine the internal relationships.

Table 2. Factor Analysis and Reliability

Variables	Items (Using Likert's Five Grade Scoring Method)	Descriptive Statistics		Factor Loading	Alpha
		Means	S.D.		
IN	Emphasis on new product /service development	3.60	1.132	0.738	0.818
	Emphasis on extent and frequency of product/ service innovations	3.35	1.100	0.797	
	Emphasis on level of product / service innovation relative to competitors	3.54	1.118	0.741	
	Emphasis on rate of new product / service introduction to market	3.32	1.124	0.784	
	Emphasis on the willing of product / service innovation	3.43	1.160	0.747	
IM	Offering products/services at low prices/prices lower than competitors, as the imitating the product of competitors to reduce R&D cost	2.98	1.036	0.869	0.675
	Minimizing product-related expenditures, as improving process, external operating efficiency and organization operating efficiency	3.31	1.084	0.869	
DY	Unlawful competitive practices such as illegal copying of new products	3.15	1.221	0.821	0.839
	Counterfeiting of your firm's own products and trademarks by other firms	2.87	1.305	0.850	
	Ineffective market competitive laws to protect your firm's intellectual property	2.94	1.166	0.836	
	Increased unfair competitive practices in the industry, as information disclosure in advance	3.21	1.261	0.780	
CO	Advantages in providing targeted service over our competitors,as customized service	3.52	1.101	0.735	0.747
	Advantages in market/ product development	3.37	1.081	0.839	
	Advantages in the value-added products and services	3.49	1.107	0.869	

IN, innovation strategy; IM, imitation strategy; DY, dysfunctional competition; CO, competitive advantages; S.D., standard deviation

The regression analysis was applied to verify the proposed hypotheses, and the results are shown in Tables 4 and 5. First, to verify hypotheses 1 and 2, we carried out a regression analysis on the whole sample. The results are shown in Table 4.

Then, we divided the sample into two parts, high technological and low market turbulence (n=76) and low technological and high market turbulence (n=85), to verify hypotheses 3 and 4. We gradually added the independent variables, a moderator variable, and the interaction of the independent variables and moderator variable. The

Table 3. Descriptive Statistics and Correlation Matrix

Construct	1	2	3	4	5	6	7
1.Enterprise Age	1						
2.Enterprise Scale	0.326**	1					
3.Industry	0.152	-0.029	1				
4.IN	0.083	0.126	-0.154	1			
5.IM	0.012	0.040	0.062	0.172*	1		
6.DY	-0.016	-0.162	0.026	0.034	0.102	1	
7.CO	-0.033	0.107	0.100	0.560**	0.349**	0.102	1
Means	3.837	1.909	0.417	3.452	3.147	3.038	3.459
S.D.	2.596	1.117	0.495	0.856	0.921	1.019	0.893

***p<0.001, **p<0.01 level, *p<0.05 level

results are shown in Table 5. We mean-centred all variables to minimize the threat of multicollinearity in the equations. To check multicollinearity, we calculated the variance inflation factors (VIF). All VIFs were below 3.0, indicating no significant multicollinearity.

The regression model in Table 4 tests hypotheses 1 and 2. It shows a positive relationship between innovation and imitation strategies and new venture competitive advantage. A control variable is added to Model 1, and innovation and imitation strategies are then added to Model 2. Model 2 reveals that innovation strategies

Table 4. Regression Analysis Results of the Overall Sample (N=153)

	Competitive Advantage	
	Model 1	**Model 2**
Enterprise Age	-0.089	-0.098
Enterprise Scale	0.160†	0.089
Industry	0.102	-0.002
Innovation Strategy		0.500***
Imitation Strategy		0.278***
R2	0.030	0.391
Adjusted R2	0.007	0.367
R2 Change	0.030	0.361
F Test Of R2 Change	1.320	37.343***
F value	1.320	16.179***

***p<0.001 level, **p<0.01 level, *p<0.05 level, †p<0.1 level

Table 5. Regression Analysis Results of the Sub-sample (N=153)

	Competitive Advantage					
	High-Technological Turbulence & Low-Market Turbulence (n=70)			**Low-Technological Turbulence & High-Market Turbulence (n=83)**		
	Model 3	**Model 4**	**Model 5**	**Model 6**	**Model 7**	**Model 8**
Enterprise Age	-0.084	-0.205†	-0.201†	-0.155	-0.103	-0.150
Enterprise Scale	0.163	0.154	0.117	0.155	0.097	0.136
Industry	-0.020	-0.012	-0.020	-0.005	-0.095	-0.094
Innovation Strategy (IN)		0.432**	0.499***		0.459***	0.416***
Imitation Strategy (IM)		0.359**	0.141		0.231*	0.212*
Dysfunctional Competition (DY)			0.324*			0.044
IN × DY			-0.315*			-0.093
IM × DY			0.304**			0.241*
R2	0.026	0.392	0.537	0.030	0.303	0.353
Adjusted R2	-0.031	-0.330	0.456	-0.011	0.253	0.274
R2 Change	0.026	0.365	0.145	0.030	0.273	0.049
F test of R2 Change	0.463	14.727***	4.790**	0.739	13.514***	1.679
F value	0.463	6.318***	6.661***	0.739	6.005***	4.493***

***p<0.001 level, **p<0.01 level, *p<0.05 level, †p<0.1 level

has a positive effect on competitive advantage (β=0.5, p<0.001), therefore, H1 is supported. Similarly, H2 is also supported (β=0.278, p<0.001).

The results in Table 5 are to verify hypotheses 4 and 5. According to the table, dysfunctional competition negatively moderates the relationship between innovation strategies and new venture competitive advantage (β=-0.315, p<0.05), and positively moderates the relationship between imitation strategies and new venture competitive advantage (β=0.304, p<0.01) in high technological and low market turbulence conditions. In contrast, dysfunctional competition positively moderates the relationship between imitation strategies and new venture competitive advantage (β=0.241, p<0.05), and the moderating effect on the relationship between innovation strategies and new venture competitive advantage is not significant in low technological and high market turbulence conditions. Thus, H3 is supported, while H4 is partly supported.

CONCLUSION

Innovation and imitation strategies have attracted substantial attention in the literatures. Most studies focus on established companies, yet in comparison, new ventures have relatively limited resources and a simple organizational structure. Hence, as new venture strategies may function differently, it is important to explore the role path of innovation and imitation strategies in new ventures. We aimed to fill this gap in the literature by examining the roles of innovation and imitation strategies in new ventures, and analyzing the contingent effects of dysfunctional competition in different environmental turbulence conditions. We find that innovation and imitation strategies are both viable for new ventures. Innovation strategies can construct new value chains (Mainela et al., 2014); whereas imitation strategies can identify the needs of existing customers (Zhou, 2006) and improve the existing value chains. These strategies help new ventures to gain competitive advantage through different paths, and they are prominent strategic choices for new ventures in China. Hence, we use contingency approaches to provide some insights into understanding why new ventures have different strategic choices.

We divide our sample into two parts: high technological and low market turbulence conditions and low technological and high market turbulence conditions. Based on this, we explain how dysfunctional competition moderates the relationship between the strategies and new venture competitive advantage in different technological and market turbulence conditions. We find that in high technological and low market turbulence conditions, dysfunctional competition negatively moderates the relationship between innovation strategies and new venture competitive advantage, while it positively moderates the relationship between imitation strategies and new venture competitive advantage. In low technological and high market turbulence conditions, dysfunctional competition positively moderates the relationship between imitation strategies and new venture competitive advantage, but has no significant effect on the relationship between innovation strategies and new venture competitive advantage. Our findings suggest that the moderating effect of dysfunctional competition depends on the specific environmental turbulence conditions. In high technological and low market turbulence conditions, innovation strategies can match the demands of the environment, and help new ventures grasp the available opportunities, whereas imitation strategies can help new ventures take advantage of the opportunities that originate from innovators, and reduce their costs and risks. In this condition, dysfunctional competition hinders the positive effects of innovation strategies, particularly by expanding the effects of negative factors. Therefore, the benefits of the innovation strategies are eroded. Moreover, dysfunctional competition reduces the risks and costs of imitation strategies, may increase the speed of "me-too" products, and in particular, reduces the effects of negative factors.

Because new ventures lack legitimacy (Li, 2001), their capacity to commercialize products is constrained in low technological and high market turbulence conditions. Moreover, commercializing new products is time consuming and imitation products are characterized as "time gap," which increases the negative effects of these factors. Dysfunctional competition reduces the negative effect of "time gap" imitation products, but has no significant effect on innovation strategies. We posit one possible explanation for this finding. Previous studies emphasize that commercializing new products is time consuming (Haeussler et al., 2012) and new ventures lack legitimacy (Li, 2001), which ignore the change in consumption attitudes of the younger generation. Thus, the theory is inconsistent with our empirical results. A typical example is the emergence of APP software development firms. The core technology of the product has changed slowly, but consumer preferences have changed quickly. Members of the younger generation in China tend to try new things and accept the concept of "quick consumption." The consumption concept provides an opportunity for new ventures, in that their products can be quickly accepted by the market. Therefore, because innovative products are likely to be accepted and tried by younger consumers, the negative effect of dysfunctional competition may not exist, and the benefits of innovative products may not be eroded. In short, our research reveals that the strategic choices of new ventures depend on the environmental turbulence and dysfunctional competition: the positive effect of dysfunctional competition on imitation strategies is applicable in both environmental conditions, whereas the negative effect on innovation strategies depends on the specific environmental conditions. Overall, our findings provide explanations for the strategic choices of emerging successful new ventures in China.

Limitations and Future Research

In this paper, we construct an integrative framework based on contingency theory and strategic management theory to explain the strategic choices of new ventures in transition economies. Our framework complements the theories of strategic management and entrepreneurship. However, there are some limitations that further research should overcome. First, our sample comes from Changchun, Harbin, and Beijing, and therefore only has a certain degree of representativeness. To enhance the reliability of our research conclusions, future research should expand the study areas to regions such as the southeast coastal areas. Second, new venture strategies are not only influenced by the external environment, but also by the firms' internal resources. Future research should focus on the effects of the resource attributes and capabilities of new ventures on their innovation and imitation strategies. Third, new ventures is the key composition of entrepreneurial ecosystem, which has an incubation function to help new ventures grow as entrepreneurial ecosystem can solve the problems which new ventures face. Hence, we should take intention into the roles that entrepreneurial ecosystem play during the growth process of new ventures. Lastly, as environment turbulence and dysfunctional competition may differ by industry, the new venture strategic choices in different industries could be explored in future research.

REFERENCES

Aldrich, H. E., & Martinez, M. A. (2001). Many are called, but few are chosen: An evolutionary perspective for the study of entrepreneurship. *Entrepreneurship Theory and Practice*, *25*(4), 41–56. doi:10.1177/104225870102500404

Anokhin, S., Wincent, J., & Autio, E. (2011). Operationalizing opportunities in entrepreneurship research: Use of data envelopment analysis. *Small Business Economics*, *37*(1), 39–57. doi:10.100711187-009-9227-1

Bodlaj M, Čater B. (2019). The impact of environmental turbulence on the perceived importance of innovation and innovativeness in SMEs. *Journal of Small Business Management, 57*(sup2), 417-435.

Bruton, G. D., & Rubanik, Y. (2002). Resources of the firm, Russian high-technology startups, and firm growth. *Journal of Business Venturing*, *17*(6), 553–576. doi:10.1016/S0883-9026(01)00079-9

Cai, L., Chen, B., Chen, J., & Bruton, G. D. (2017). Dysfunctional competition & innovation strategy of new ventures as they mature. *Journal of Business Research*, *78*, 111–118. doi:10.1016/j.jbusres.2017.05.008

Cai, L., Hughes, M., & Yin, M. (2014). The relationship between resource acquisition methods and firm performance in Chinese new ventures: The intermediate effect of learning capability. *Journal of Small Business Management*, *52*(3), 365–389. doi:10.1111/jsbm.12039

Cai, L., Liu, Q., Zhu, X., & Deng, S. L. (2014). Market orientation and technological innovation: The moderating role of entrepreneurial support policies. *The International Entrepreneurship and Management Journal*, 1–27.

Ginsberg, A., & Venkatraman, N. (1985). Contingency perspectives of organizational strategy: A critical review of the empirical research. *Academy of Management Review*, *10*(3), 421–434. doi:10.5465/amr.1985.4278950

Haeussler, C., Patzelt, H., & Zahra, S. A. (2012). Strategic alliances and product development in high technology new firms: The moderating effect of technological capabilities. *Journal of Business Venturing*, *27*(2), 217–233. doi:10.1016/j.jbusvent.2010.10.002

Kohli, A. K., & Jaworski, B. J. (1900). Market orientation: The construct, research propositions, and managerial implications. *Journal of Marketing*, *54*(2), 1–18. doi:10.1177/002224299005400201

Li, H. (2001). How does new venture strategy matter in the environment–performance relationship? *The Journal of High Technology Management Research*, *12*(2), 183–204. doi:10.1016/S1047-8310(01)00036-0

Li, H., & Atuahene-Gima, K. (2001). Product innovation strategy and the performance of new technology ventures in China. *Academy of Management Journal*, *44*(6), 1123–1134.

Li, H., & Li, J. (2009). Top management team conflict and entrepreneurial strategy making in China. *Asia Pacific Journal of Management*, *26*(2), 263–283. doi:10.100710490-007-9071-2

Li, H., & Zhang, Y. (2007). The role of managers' political networking and functional experience in new venture performance: Evidence from Chinas transition economy. *Strategic Management Journal*, *28*(8), 791–804. doi:10.1002mj.605

Li, T., & Calantone, R. J. (1998). The impact of market knowledge competence on new product advantage: Conceptualization and empirical examination. *Journal of Marketing*, *62*(4), 13–29. doi:10.1177/002224299806200402

Liu, J., & Li, X. (2013). Imitation or innovation: An empirical study on entrepreneurial opportunity exploitation and entrepreneurial performance. *South China Journal of Economics*, *31*, 20–32.

Liu, M., & Luo, P. (2010). The comparative research on integration innovation mode of brand mobile telephone and modularity innovation mode of mountain fastness mobile telephone based on the long tail theory. *R & D Management*, *22*(4), 1–9.

Mainela, T., Puhakka, V., & Servais, P. (2014). The concept of international opportunity in international entrepreneurship: A review and a research agenda. *International Journal of Management Reviews*, *16*(1), 105–129. doi:10.1111/ijmr.12011

March, J. G. (1991). Exploration and exploitation in organizational learning. *Organization Science*, *2*(1), 71–87. doi:10.1287/orsc.2.1.71

Meyer, K. E., Estrin, S., Bhaumik, S., & Peng, M. W. (2009). Institutions, resources, and entry strategies in emerging economies. *Strategic Management Journal*, *30*(1), 61–80. doi:10.1002mj.720

Naranjo-Valencia, J. C., Jiménez-Jiménez, D., & Sanz-Valle, R. (2011). Innovation or imitation? The role of organizational culture. *Management Decision*, *49*(1), 55–72. doi:10.1108/00251741111094437

Nelson, R. R., & Winter, S. G. (1978). Forces generating and limiting concentration under Schumpeterian competition. *The Bell Journal of Economics*, *9*(2), 524–548. doi:10.2307/3003597

Podsakoff, P. M., & Organ, D. W. (1986). Self-reports in organizational research: Problems and prospects. *Journal of Management*, *12*(4), 531–544. doi:10.1177/014920638601200408

Politis, D. (2005). The process of entrepreneurial learning: A conceptual framework. *Entrepreneurship Theory and Practice*, *29*(4), 399–424. doi:10.1111/j.1540-6520.2005.00091.x

Robinson, R. B., McDougall, P., & Herron, L. (1988) Toward a new venture strategy typology. Academy of Management Proceedings, (1), 74-78.

Ruef, M., Aldrich, H. E., & Carter, N. M. (2003). The structure of founding teams: Homophily, strong ties, and isolation among US entrepreneurs. *American Sociological Review*, *68*(2), 195–222. doi:10.2307/1519766

Schendel, D., & Hofer, C. W. (1979). *Strategic management: A new view of business policy and planning*. Little, Brown.

Schumpeter, J. A. (1934). *The theory of economic development: An inquiry into profits, capital, credit, interest, and the business cycle*. Transaction Publishers.

Shan, B., Cai, L., Hatfield, D. E., & Tang, S. (2014). The relationship between resources and capabilities of new ventures in emerging economies. *Information Technology Management*, *15*(2), 99–108. doi:10.100710799-014-0177-1

Sheng, S., Zhou, K. Z., & Lessassy, L. (2013). NPD speed vs. innovativeness: The contingent impact of institutional and market environments. *Journal of Business Research*, *66*(11), 2355–2362. doi:10.1016/j.jbusres.2012.04.018

Sheng, S., Zhou, K. Z., & Li, J. J. (2011). The effects of business and political ties on firm performance: Evidence from China. *Journal of Marketing*, *75*(1), 1–15. doi:10.1509/jm.75.1.1

Slivko, O., & Theilen, B. (2014). Innovation or imitation? The effect of spillovers and competitive pressure on firms' R&D strategy choice. *Journal of Economics*, *112*(3), 253–282. doi:10.100700712-013-0361-5

Song, M., Podoynitsyna, K., Van Der Bij, H., & Halman, J. I. M. (2008). Success factors in new ventures: A Meta-analysis. *Journal of Product Innovation Management*, *25*(1), 7–27. doi:10.1111/j.1540-5885.2007.00280.x

Su, Z., Peng, J., Shen, H., & Xiao, T. (2013). Technological capability, marketing capability, and firm performance in turbulent conditions. *Management and Organization Review*, *9*(1), 115–138. doi:10.1017/S1740877600003193

Tsai, M. T., & Li, Y. H. (2007). Knowledge creation process in new venture strategy and performance. *Journal of Business Research*, *60*(4), 371–381. doi:10.1016/j.jbusres.2006.10.003

Vecchiato, R. (2019). Scenario planning, cognition, and strategic investment decisions in a turbulent environment. *Long Range Planning*, *52*(5), 843–865. doi:10.1016/j.lrp.2019.01.002

Von Krogh, G., & Haefliger, S. (2007). Nurturing respect for IP in China. *Harvard Business Review*, *85*(4), 23–24.

Voss, G. B., & Voss, Z. G. (2000). Strategic orientation and firm performance in an artistic environment. *Journal of Marketing*, *64*(1), 67–83. doi:10.1509/jmkg.64.1.67.17993

Walter, A., Auer, M., & Ritter, T. (2006). The impact of network capabilities and entrepreneurial orientation on university spin-off performance. *Journal of Business Venturing*, *21*(4), 541–567. doi:10.1016/j.jbusvent.2005.02.005

Zheng, B., & Li, S. (2011). The relationship of competitive strategy, innovation selection, and firm performance. *Science Research Management*, *32*(4), 59–68.

Zhou, K. Z. (2006). Innovation, imitation, and new product performance: The case of China. *Industrial Marketing Management*, *35*(3), 394–402. doi:10.1016/j.indmarman.2005.10.006

Zott, C., & Amit, R. (2008). The fit between product market strategy and business model: Implications for firm performance. *Strategic Management Journal*, *29*(1), 1–26. doi:10.1002mj.642

Zou, H., Chen, X., & Ghauri, P. (2010). Antecedents and consequences of new venture growth strategy: An empirical study in China. *Asia Pacific Journal of Management*, *27*(3), 393–421. doi:10.100710490-009-9157-0

ENDNOTE

1 Data comes from Internet news: http://news.liao1.com/newspage/2012/04/4596474.html.

Chapter 12
The Role of Entrepreneurs in the Entrepreneurial Ecosystem:
Self-Efficacy, Dual Learning, and Performance

Xiu Yang
Guangxi University of Finance and Economics, China

Ting Yang
Guangxi University of Finance and Economics, China

Yi Wang
Shanghai University, China

Qing Wang
Dalian University of Technology, China

ABSTRACT

This chapter introduces entrepreneurial self-efficacy, a psychological cognitive factor, into the context of entrepreneurship, trying to sort out the internal mechanism of entrepreneurial self-efficacy, dual entrepreneurial learning, and entrepreneurial performance and construct a theoretical model. The hypothesis is that entrepreneurial self-efficacy has a positive effect on both dual entrepreneurial learning and new venture performance. Dual entrepreneurial learning has a positive impact on the performance of new ventures and acts as a mediator between entrepreneurial self-efficacy and entrepreneurial performance. The empirical results show that entrepreneurial self-efficacy can promote exploratory entrepreneurial learning and the improvement of new venture performance. Exploratory entrepreneurial learning plays a mediating role in the effect of entrepreneurial self-efficacy on the performance of start-ups, while entrepreneurial learning can't play a mediating role in the process of exploitative entrepreneurial learning.

DOI: 10.4018/978-1-7998-3495-3.ch012

INTRODUCTION

The current social and economic situation has changed. China has set off a wave of self-employment and mass entrepreneurship. The increase of new ventures has made significant contributions to economic growth and development. Entrepreneurs play a decisive role in the process of establishing new enterprises, and their personal entrepreneurial thinking and behavior choices are directly influenced by personal psychological factors, especially the psychological cognitive factor of entrepreneurial self-efficacy, which is considered as one of the prerequisites for successful entrepreneurship (Krueger and Brazeal 1994). Many empirical studies at home and abroad have shown that entrepreneurial self-efficacy has a positive effect on the performance of new ventures. Some scholars believe that entrepreneurial self-efficacy directly affects performance. For example, Khedhaouria, Gurău and Torrès (2015) have confirmed that there is a significant and direct positive relationship between entrepreneurial self-efficacy and enterprise performance through empirical research on 256 small enterprise. Some scholars believe that entrepreneurial self-efficacy indirectly affects entrepreneurial performance by influencing certain behaviors. For example, Su et al. (2018) believe that entrepreneurial decision logic plays an important role between entrepreneurial self-efficacy and entrepreneurial performance, Yi et al. (2018) proposes that risk-taking and action advancement in entrepreneurial orientation promote the improvement of entrepreneurial performance through the influence of entrepreneurial self-efficacy. Although some research on entrepreneurial self-efficacy has achieved some results, there are differences on whether entrepreneurial self-efficacy directly influences new venture performance. Scholars have not paid enough attention to the intermediate process mechanism of entrepreneurial self-efficacy affecting the performance of new venture, and have not reached the same conclusion on the intermediary variables between the two. Therefore, in order to open up the "black box" of the process in which the sense of entrepreneurial self-efficacy influences new venture performance, it is very necessary to deeply explore the mechanism between them.

In recent years, entrepreneurship learning has received extensive attention from scholars in the field of domestic entrepreneurship. Previous studies have shown that in a changeable entrepreneurial environment, entrepreneurship learning is an important factor in explaining the sources of sustainable competitive advantages of new ventures (Liu 2011). Entrepreneurs gradually promote the improvement of entrepreneurial capabilities such as opportunity development and resource integration through the process of entrepreneurship learning, and actively affect the new ventures performance (Cai et al. 2014). Nowadays, the unpredictable economic environment puts forward higher requirements for new ventures with inherent disadvantages. How to effectively learn has become a difficult problem faced by most new ventures. Rea and Carswell (2001) pointed out that entrepreneurship learning is a process of using confidence and self-confidence to drive the use of learning resources to achieve entrepreneurial goals. Psychologists believe that entrepreneurs' personality, cognition and the factors affecting cognition are the decisive factors of entrepreneurial learning, but they do not explain the source and specific process of entrepreneurial learning.

Based on this, this paper follows the logical relationship of "cognition-behavior-result", according to the domestic entrepreneurial situation and taking entrepreneurs as research samples, empirically tests the impact of entrepreneurial self-efficacy on new venture performance, and tentatively introduces dual entrepreneurial learning behavior as an intermediary mechanism, in order to reveal the mechanism process of the effect of entrepreneurial self-efficacy on new venture performance, explore the effective path of transforming entrepreneurial self-efficacy into new venture performance, perfect and enrich the psychological cognitive theory in the field of entrepreneurship, make up for the lack of research on domestic entrepreneurial self-efficacy, and then better guide entrepreneurial practice.

LITERATURE REVIEW

Entrepreneurial Self-Efficacy

Entrepreneurial self-efficacy is a new concept based on Bandura's social cognitive theory of self-efficacy combined with the field of entrepreneurship, refers to the individual's confidence in their ability to successfully play the role of entrepreneur and complete entrepreneurial tasks. This concept was first proposed by Scherer et al. (1989), who defined the sense of entrepreneurial self-efficacy as the degree of individual belief in their ability to successfully complete various entrepreneurial tasks and assume the role of entrepreneurs. Han (2009) argued that the sense of entrepreneurial self-efficacy does not refer to the individual's unique personality traits or entrepreneurial ability itself, but refers to the individual's confidence or belief in undertaking or carrying out entrepreneurial activities based on the judgment and evaluation of his own ability to realize entrepreneurial activities. Chen, Greene and Crick (1998) divide entrepreneurial self-efficacy into five dimensions: market, management, innovation, financial control and risk. Jill and Robert (2005) believe that entrepreneurial self-efficacy is mainly reflected in the four dimensions of opportunity identification efficacy, management efficacy, relationship efficacy and risk tolerance efficacy. Tang et al. (2007) divided entrepreneurial self-efficacy into six dimensions: opportunity identification, strategy, commitment, concept, interpersonal relationship and organization. This paper integrates and refines the above scholars' dimensionality criteria, and examines entrepreneurs' self-efficacy from four dimensions: innovation and change, opportunity identification, relationship coordination, and risk taking.

The sense of innovation and change efficacy refers to the degree of confidence of entrepreneurs in their ability to break the deadlock and innovate and change when facing future uncertain risks and handling problems. The sense of opportunity identification efficacy is defined as the degree of confidence of entrepreneurs in their ability to keenly grasp market changes, identify and utilize new opportunities; Relationship coordination efficacy is used to measure entrepreneurs' confidence in their ability to establish interpersonal relationships. The sense of risk-taking efficacy refers to entrepreneurs' belief that they have the ability to make decisions quickly under pressure, conflicts and complex and changeable environmental conditions and bear the risks brought by decisions (Jill and Robert 2005).

Dual Entrepreneurial Learning

In a complex and changeable external environment, both individuals and organizations need to constantly learn to adapt to the changing situation. Entrepreneurial learning is an individual's process of dealing with entrepreneurial knowledge in entrepreneurial activities, which includes internal knowledge development and external knowledge acquisition (Zhao et al. 2011). The former approach is a low-level learning model, called exploitative entrepreneurial learning, which refers to the learning behavior through refining, screening and practice. It focuses on the depth of knowledge and emphasizes refining and mining existing knowledge and capabilities. The latter approach is a high-level learning model, called exploratory entrepreneurial learning, which refers to learning behavior through search, attempt, change and innovation, emphasizing the expansion of knowledge and challenging existing behavior practices (Xie et al. 2016).

At present, many scholars focus on the relationship between dual entrepreneurial learning and organizational performance at the organizational level, utilizing entrepreneurial learning has an impact on corporate performance by improving the existing capabilities of the company and reducing its operational risks; exploratory entrepreneurial learning is the use of new knowledge acquired from outside companies to develop new technologies or new products, while bringing high returns may come with risks. For example, some scholars believe that both exploratory learning and exploitative learning have positive effects on organizational performance. Some scholars also believe that dual entrepreneurial learning has an inverted U-shaped impact on organizational performance. There are many researches on dual entrepreneurial learning at the organizational level, but few researches on dual entrepreneurial learning at the individual level. Some scholars put forward that individual learning and team learning are the key steps of organizational learning. Organizational learning begins with individual learning, so besides team learning and organizational learning, studying individual learning is also very important to organizational learning and performance. Due to the characteristics of small scale, simple structure and few members in the start-up period of new ventures, how entrepreneurs, as the soul of new ventures, acquire unique knowledge through entrepreneurial learning is an important means to promote the establishment and growth of new enterprises (Cai et al. 2014).

New Venture Performance

New start-ups refer to enterprises that have been established for less than or equal to 8 years and have not yet passed the survival period (Biggadike 1979; Zahra 1993). In many entrepreneurship studies, the performance of new ventures refers to the various results achieved by entrepreneurs (startups) through a series of work behaviors to achieve entrepreneurial goals, is regarded as an indicator to measure the achievements and effects of new ventures, and also an important symbol for the survival and development of new ventures. At present, there are different views on the dimensionality of the performance of new ventures. Some researches believe that the performance of new ventures should be considered from two aspects: financial performance and non-financial performance. Some studies also believe that only by surviving tenaciously can new ventures thrive. They propose to measure entrepreneurial performance in terms of survival and growth. There are also many empirical studies examining entrepreneurial performance from the perspectives of profitability and growth. In recent years, many domestic scholars have adopted Chen's (2009) single dimension of new venture performance for empirical research. In order to study the relationship between the performance of new ventures and other variables, this paper adopts a single dimension and uses Chen's research for reference to measure.

THEORETICAL HYPOTHESES

Entrepreneurial Self-Efficacy and new Venture Performance

Baum and Locke (2004) believe that entrepreneurial self-efficacy can significantly promote the growth and performance of enterprises. Research by Wood and Bandura (1989) shows that people with strong entrepreneurial self-efficacy have more confidence in their ability to complete entrepreneurial tasks. They often set higher and more challenging growth goals in the entrepreneurial process. In order to achieve the goals, they will make continuous efforts, and the results of their efforts will be reflected in their performance. Zhong et al. (2012) pointed out that individuals with high entrepreneurial efficiency will not panic due to unexpected situations, but will firmly believe that they have the resources and capabilities needed to complete the entrepreneurial goals and tasks, and can continue to focus on the entrepreneurial goals and tasks, keep high efficiency in their thinking in complex decision-making scenarios, and choose effective strategies to enable enterprises to achieve the expected results, thus having a positive impact on the performance of enterprises after entrepreneurship. Zhang et al. (2019) believe that network relations can positively affect entrepreneurs' self-efficacy, and entrepreneurial self-efficacy is conducive to entrepreneurs to actively and optimistically invest in entrepreneurial activities and make positive entrepreneurial decisions, thus positively affecting the performance of new ventures. This shows that individuals with higher self-efficacy in entrepreneurship are more confident and optimistic in measuring their own abilities. This confidence enables them to show greater persistence and perseverance in the face of difficulties, to work and study efficiently in a high-pressure environment, and to be more willing to pursue challenging entrepreneurial goals and tasks so as to seize more opportunities and obtain better enterprise performance. Based on this, this paper puts forward the following assumptions:

Suppose H1: Entrepreneurial self-efficacy has a significant positive effect on new ventures performance.

Entrepreneurial Self-Efficacy and Dual Entrepreneurial Learning

Entrepreneurial self-efficacy is the internal driving factor affecting entrepreneurial learning. Murnieks et al. (2014) believe that self-efficacy represents a specific behavioral driving force, which can directly urge individuals to devote their time and energy to a specific activity. Entrepreneurial self-efficacy can mobilize the motivation of entrepreneurs and has a great impact on their innovation and entrepreneurial behavior (Tang and Gu 2016). Entrepreneurs' evaluation of self-efficacy can give a good explanation for their choice, degree of effort and degree of persistence in their efforts (Su et al. 2018). In general, entrepreneurs with similar abilities will choose different entrepreneurial learning behavior patterns due to different entrepreneurial self-efficacy. When evaluating the external environment, individuals with high self-efficacy are full of confidence in their judgment. If entrepreneurs with high self-efficacy believe that the enterprise is in a low-risk situation with controllable expected results, they will carry out exploitative entrepreneurial learning based on the principle of cost-effectiveness. If entrepreneurs with a high sense of self-efficacy, such as innovation, change and risk- taking, believe that the enterprise is in a highly volatile market environment, they tend to adopt exploratory entrepreneurial learning. Entrepreneurs with high self-efficacy have higher risk tolerance than entrepreneurs with low self-efficacy, and are more willing to break the routine and carry out innovation and reform. Exploratory entrepreneurial learning emphasizes the importance of innovation, breaking the existing behaviors and practices to find new fields and new development trends. There is no doubt that entrepreneurs at this time will conduct exploratory entrepreneurial learning based on the principle of opportunity identification and adaptation to changes in external environment. Even if individuals with low entrepreneurial self-efficacy correctly judge the environment in which the enterprise is located, they will still have doubts about their ability to successfully accomplish their goals due to insufficient trust in themselves. Individuals with low self-efficacy are lower than individuals with high self-efficacy in innovation efficiency, risk-taking efficiency, opportunity identification efficiency, etc. They are reluctant to explore areas full of both opportunities and high risks, thus negatively affecting their exploratory entrepreneurial learning. Based on this, this paper puts forward the following assumptions:

Suppose H2a: Entrepreneurial self-efficacy has a significant positive effect on exploitative entrepreneurial learning.

Suppose H2b: Entrepreneurial self-efficacy has a significant positive effect on exploratory entrepreneurial learning.

Dual Entrepreneurial Learning and New Venture Performance

Entrepreneurial learning is an important mechanism for start-ups to face unpredictable environment. It is beneficial for entrepreneurs and organizations to continuously update the adaptability of start-ups and promote the growth of start-ups (Ma et al. 2018). Entrepreneurial learning is a learning process of acquiring, transforming and utilizing knowledge resources. Entrepreneurs can correct strategic decisions by learning new knowledge, and then improve entrepreneurial performance (Yang et al. 2013). The essence of exploitative entrepreneurial learning is entrepreneurs' deeper understanding and application of existing knowledge, rules and strategies. By exploitative entrepreneurial learning, entrepreneurs can strengthen and perfect their existing resource advantages, so that enterprises can focus more on a certain entrepreneurial field, cultivate core competitiveness (Xie et al. 2016), and avoid the risks of technological change in the industry. At the same time, exploitative entrepreneurial learning has the characteristics of low cost and low risk, which to a certain extent promotes the performance of new ventures. Unlike exploitative entrepreneurial learning, exploratory entrepreneurial learning emphasizes that entrepreneurs question and reflect on existing behaviors and paths (Xie et al. 2016), actively think about new strategies, and seek cutting-edge, diverse and refined new knowledge. Therefore, entrepreneurs can provide new insights for their decision-making through exploratory entrepreneurial learning, which can help start-ups to provide customers with different products, services and solutions, so that start-ups can obtain huge competitive advantages and achieve performance improvement (Zhang and Zhao 2017). It can be seen that both exploitative entrepreneurial learning and exploratory entrepreneurial learning are beneficial for entrepreneurs to cope with the uncertain external economic environment, improve entrepreneurial performance and realize sustainable development of enterprises. Based on this, this paper puts forward the following assumptions:

Suppose H3a: Exploitative entrepreneurial learning has a significant positive effect on new ventures performance.

Suppose H3b: Exploratory entrepreneurial learning has a significant positive effect on new ventures performance.

The Mediating Role of Dual Entrepreneurial Learning

At present, a few scholars have studied the relationship between entrepreneurial self-efficacy and entrepreneurial performance. Research shows that entrepreneurial self-efficacy promotes the improvement of entrepreneurial performance. Ye (2006) believes that entrepreneurial self-efficacy as a measure of self-confidence of entrepreneurs, similar to variables such as motivation, is an implicit variable. It needs to affect some entrepreneurial behaviors to affect entrepreneurial performance. For example, Su et al. (2018) have confirmed that entrepreneurial self-efficacy directly affects entrepreneurs' decision-making behavior and affects entrepreneurial performance through the intermediary effect of decision-making behavior. As entrepreneurship is a proccss full of unccrtainty, it rcquires entrepreneurs to have a good adaptability and tolerance to various changes. Previous studies have shown that entrepreneurship learning is an important factor in explaining the source of sustainable competitive advantages of new ventures in a changeable entrepreneurial environment (Liu 2011). Entrepreneurs gradually promote the improvement of entrepreneurial capabilities such as opportunity development and resource integration through the process of entrepreneurship learning and actively affect new ventures performance (Cai et al. 2014).

Entrepreneurial self-efficacy is the internal driving factor affecting entrepreneurial learning. Under the condition of low risk and controllable expected results of entrepreneurship, most entrepreneurs will choose to exploitative entrepreneurial learning based on the principle of cost-effectiveness. Through refining and mining existing knowledge, entrepreneurs will be able to have a deeper understanding of the situation in their fields, thus finding new sub-sectors in their markets, improving their ability to obtain timely opportunities for use (Ge et al. 2016), and ultimately positively affecting new ventures performance. In a complex and changeable environment, for people with high self-efficacy in entrepreneurship, the dynamic nature of the environment means that they are full of opportunities. Entrepreneurs with high self-efficacy in entrepreneurship will be full of confidence in their ability to innovate and change, identify market opportunities, dare to take risks of failure, and acquire resources brought by social relationships. Such confidence will make them willing to innovate, experiment, explore and take risks, thus promoting their exploratory entrepreneurial learning. Obtaining diversified and novel knowledge and strategies from outside can help start-ups to provide customers with different products, services and solutions, so that start-ups can obtain huge competitive advantages and achieve performance improvement (Zhang and Zhao 2017). Therefore, one possible path for entrepreneurial self-efficacy to affect new ventures performance is through the intermediary role of dual entrepreneurial learning. Based on this, this paper believes that dual entrepreneurial learning may be an effective means to transform entrepreneurial self-efficacy into new ventures performance, and puts forward the following hypotheses to be tested:

Suppose H4a: Exploitative entrepreneurial learning has a significant mediating effect between entrepreneurial self-efficacy and new ventures performance.

Suppose H4b: Exploratory entrepreneurial learning has a significant mediating effect between entrepreneurial self-efficacy and new ventures performance.

To sum up, build a conceptual model of the relationship among entrepreneurial self-efficacy, dual entrepreneurial learning, and new venture performance as shown in Figure 1.

RESEARCH AND DESIGN

Data and Samples

This study used questionnaires (came from entrepreneurial ecosystem) to collect receipts. Combined with the existing research, the maturity scale was selected and the initial questionnaire was revised according to the previous research. Then solicit opinions from entrepreneurs and experts to adjust the structure, wording and items of the initial questionnaire, and conduct a pretest for 50 entrepreneurs. Based

Figure 1. Entrepreneurial self-efficacy, dual entrepreneurial learning and new venture performance

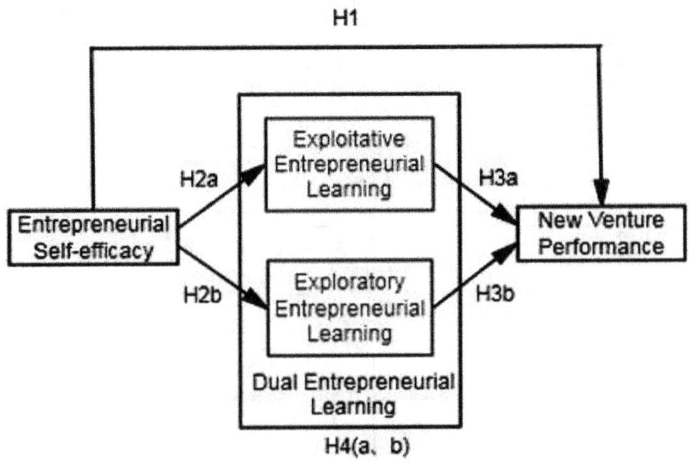

on the results of the pretest, some problems were corrected and finally a formal questionnaire was formed for formal investigation.

In this paper, new ventures are defined as those established within 8 years. The subjects of the questionnaire are independent entrepreneurs or the chief entrepreneurs in the entrepreneurial team. This study is aimed at entrepreneurs in major cities in Guangxi Zhuang Autonomous Region, Guangdong Province, Hunan Province, Zhejiang Province, Jilin Province and other regions. A total of 250 paper and electronic questionnaires were distributed, and 165 were actually recovered, with a recovery rate of 66%. Excluding 39 incomplete and invalid questionnaires, 126 valid questionnaires remained, with an effective rate of 76.36%. See Table 1 for basic information of samples.

Variable Measurement

Variables were measured using a 5-point Likert scale, with 1-5 indicating from "totally disagree" to "totally agree" respectively. Entrepreneurs were required to score truthfully according to the items, their own situation and the actual situation of the enterprise.

Entrepreneurial self-efficacy. According to the previous analysis, entrepreneurial self-efficacy is divided into four dimensions: innovation and change, opportunity identification, risk-taking and relationship coordination. Based on the scale of entrepreneurial self-efficacy developed by Lucas and Cooper (2005), individual measurement items of the scale are modified in combination with sample exploratory

Table 1. Basic distribution of samples

	Sample Size	Percentage (%)		Sample Size	Percentage (%)
1. Gender			**4. Enterprise age**		
Male	71	56.3	£2	49	38.9
Female	55	43.7	3-4	43	34.1
2. Age (years)			5-6	22	17.5
£25	45	35.7	7-8	12	9.5
26-35	50	39.7	**5. Size of the company (employees)**		
36-45	25	19.8	1-20	54	42.9
>45	6	4.8	21-50	47	37.3
3. level of education			51-100	16	12.7
High school and below	13	10.3	>100	9	7.1
Junior college	15	11.9	**6. Company industry**		
Undergraduate course	83	65.9	Manufacturing industry	14	11.1
Master and above	15	11.9	Service/commerce	53	42.1
\			High - tech industry	29	23.0
			Real estate/construction	6	4.8
			Other	24	19.0

tests, and finally 12 items are formed. Specific topics and factor analysis results are shown in Table 2.

Dual entrepreneurship learning. According to the previous analysis, dual entrepreneurial learning can be divided into exploitative entrepreneurial learning and exploratory entrepreneurial learning. Learning from the research scale of Politis et al. (2004), and combining with the research of Ge Baoshan et al. (2016), the specific items are modified to form the scale that meets the needs of this article. Finally, 8 items are used to measure exploitative entrepreneurial learning and exploratory entrepreneurial learning. Specific topics and factor analysis results are shown in Table 2.

New ventures performance. Chen's (2009) research scale on new ventures performance was mainly used for reference and improved. Finally, four items were used to measure new ventures performance. Specific topics and factor analysis results are shown in Table 2.

Control variable. It mainly focuses on the characteristics of new enterprises and entrepreneurs that have important influences on variables such as exploratory

Table 2. Variable exploratory factor analysis and reliability test

Factor		Factor Measurement Index	Load Value	Interpretable Variance (%)	The Reliability Value Cronbach α
Entrepreneurial self-efficacy	Innovation and change	I like to break through existing things and do not like to stick to conventions.	0.822	63.90	0.788
		I can put forward novel ideas and creative suggestions.	0.769		
		I can easily accept new ideas and viewpoints.	0.740		
	Opportunity identification	I can find a new potential demand in the market.	0.768		
		I can explore valuable market segments.	0.735		
		I can find entrepreneurial opportunities through an analysis of the market environment.	0.777		
	Risk-taking	I can work and study efficiently under high pressure.	0.706		
		I can respond quickly and effectively to unexpected situations.	0.688		
		I can anticipate the risks in the entrepreneurial process in advance and try to minimize the risk.	0.771		
	Relationship coordination	I can communicate effectively with others.	0.723		
		I can cooperate with others happily and finish the task smoothly.	0.740		
		If you encounter obstacles in communicating with others, you also have the confidence to solve them through your own efforts.	0.725		

continues on following page

entrepreneurship learning, exploitative entrepreneurship learning and new ventures performance. These variables may be influenced by factors such as the age of entrepreneurs, the educational background of entrepreneurs, the number of years of enterprises, the scale of enterprises, and the industries in which enterprises are located (Zhu et al. 2014). Therefore, this paper takes the entrepreneur's age, educational background, enterprise years, enterprise scale and enterprise industry as control variables.

Table 2. Continued

Factor		Factor Measurement Index	Load Value	Interpretable Variance (%)	The Reliability Value Cronbach α
Dual entrepreneurial learning	Exploitative entrepreneurial learning	I think learning is to refine the existing knowledge.	0.771	61.59	0.784
		I like to be in an area where I can rely on previous knowledge.	0.722		
		When problems arise, I prefer to find common and widely accepted methods to solve them.	0.860		
		I tend to emphasize the use of knowledge related to existing product/ service experience.	0.780		
	Exploratory entrepreneurial learning	I like to explore new fields instead of repeating existing ones.	0.764	61.66	0.791
		I like to be in a new field that I have never been before.	0.753		
		I attach more importance to seeking new field information to be tested, and seek ways to enable enterprises to enter products/markets in new fields with uncertain risks.	0.818		
		I prefer that the strategic market demand is not targeted when collecting information, so as to ensure the test in the development of new products and services.	0.804		
New ventures performance		The overall operating performance of the company has grown steadily.	0.764	60.57	0.783
		The financial situation of the enterprise is good, and its profit and profit have increased rapidly.	0.822		
		Enterprise sales are growing rapidly.	0.726		
		The market share of enterprise products continues to rise.	0.798		

Common Method Deviation Test

This paper adopts two ways to control the deviation of the common method. One is to carry out prior control in the questionnaire issuing stage to encourage the interviewees to revise the questionnaire “intuitively”. The second is to use Harman single factor test method to detect the deviation of the common method, and put the items of all the research variables together to do exploratory factor analysis.

Using principal component analysis, the factor whose feature root is greater than 1 without rotation extraction is obtained in this paper. In this paper, the contribution of first principal component factor is only 23.878%, and there is no phenomenon that the contribution rate of factor variance is more than 40%. The sample can be used.

HYPOTHESIS TESTING AND RESULTS

Reliability and Validity Test

The results of empirical research need to be tested for reliability and validity. Cronbach'α coefficient is generally used to measure the reliability of each variable item. The results in Table 2 show that Cronbach'α of each variable is greater than 0.7, indicating that the reliability of all variables has good consistency. The general method to test validity is factor analysis. This study uses SPSS software to do exploratory factor analysis. The test results show that the indexes have good goodness of fit, and the discriminant validity and convergent validity of the questionnaire are good. The reliability and validity tests are shown in Table 2.

In order to further explore the relationship between variables, Pearson correlation analysis was carried out for each variable by SPSS 22.0 software in this study. The statistical results of the correlation between variables are shown in Table 3. It can be seen from the table that the absolute values of the correlation coefficients among the variables are all less than 0.7, indicating that there is no collinearity problem among the variables. In addition, entrepreneurial self-efficacy is significantly positively correlated with new ventures performance, $\beta = 0.537$, $p<0.01$; Entrepreneurial self-efficacy is significantly positively correlated with exploratory entrepreneurial learning, $\beta = 0.291$, $p<0.01$; Exploratory entrepreneurial learning is significantly positively correlated with new ventures performance, $\beta = 0.604$, $p<0.01$. This shows that there is a significant correlation between these variables and the analysis can continuc.

Hypothesis Testing

This study uses multiple linear regression analysis to verify the internal relationship among entrepreneurial self-efficacy, dual entrepreneurial learning and new venture performance. In order to further verify the proposed hypothesis, this study constructed multiple regression models, and also conducted multiple collinearity tests. The test results are shown in Table 4. The results show that all VIF values are far less than the critical value of 10, indicating that there is no obvious multiple collinearity problem (Hair et al. 1998).

Table 3. Variable correlation coefficient matrix

	1	2	3	4	5	6	7	8	9
1. AE	1								
2. LE	-0.327**	1							
3. EA	0.501**	-0.017	1						
4. SC	0.069	0.246**	0.556**	1					
5. CI	0.118	-0.076	0.021	-0.091	1				
6. ESE	0.162	0.143	0.150	0.137	-0.026	1			
7. EIVE	-0.002	-0.027	-0.064	-0.007	-0.135	0.046	1		
8. EORY	-0.320**	0.343**	-0.035	0.242**	-0.444**	0.291**	0.204*	1	
9. NVP	-0.093	0.245**	0.136	0.393**	-0.160	0.537**	0.122	0.604**	1

Note: AE age of entrepreneur, LE level of education, EA enterprise age, SC size of the company (employees), CI company industry, ESE entrepreneurial self-efficacy, EIVE exploitative entrepreneurial learning, EORY exploratory entrepreneurial learning, NVP new ventures performance

* $p < 0.05$;** $p < 0.01$; *** $p < 0.001$

Table 4. Multiple collinearity test results of regression equation

Independent Variable	Tolerance	Variance Inflation Factor (VIF)
Entrepreneurial self-efficacy	0.915	1.093
Exploitative entrepreneurial learning	0.958	1.044
Exploratory entrepreneurial learning	0.879	1.138

For the test of hypothesis H1, this study constructs model 5 and model 6. Model 5 is the research on the influence of control variables on new ventures performance, and model 6 is the research on the relationship between independent variables' entrepreneurial self-efficacy and new ventures performance. The results in table 5 show that entrepreneurial self-efficacy has a significant impact on new ventures performance (model 6: $\beta=0.517$, $p<0.001$). Therefore, the hypothesis H1 (entrepreneurial self-efficacy has a significant positive impact on new ventures performance) proposed in this study is well supported by the data.

For the test of hypothesis H2a and H2b, this study constructs model 1- model 4. Model 1 and model 3 are respectively the effects of each control variable on exploratory and exploitative entrepreneurial learning, model 2 is the relationship model between independent variable entrepreneurial self-efficacy and exploitative entrepreneurial learning, and model 4 is the relationship model between entrepreneurial self-efficacy and exploratory entrepreneurial learning. The results in table 5 show that entrepreneurial self-efficacy has no significant effect on exploitative entrepreneurial

Table 5. Regression results

Variables	DV=EIVE		DV=EORY		DV= NVP				
	Model 1	Model 2	Model 3	Model 4	Model 5	Model 6	Model 7	Model 8	Model 9
CV									
AE	0.06	0.048	-0.213*	-0.277*	-0.037	-0.152	0.095	-0.157	-0.023
LE	-0.032	-0.042	0.199*	0.142	0.129	0.027	0.006	0.031	-0.039
EA	-0.12	-0.12	-0.019	-0.020	-0.055	-0.057	-0.042	-0.047	-0.048
SC	0.051	0.048	0.183	0.163	0.384***	0.349***	0.270**	0.345	0.273**
CI	-0.137	-0.135	-0.387***	-0.378***	-0.110	-0.094	0.133	-0.082	0.083
IV									
ESE		0.052		0.286***		0.517***		0.512***	0.383***
EIVE							0.012	0.087	
EORY							0.621***		0.468***
R^2	0.026	0.029	0.353	0.429	0.196	0.443	0.449	0.45	0.568
Adj.R^2	-0.014	-0.02	0.326	0.400	0.163	0.415	0.416	0.418	0.542
F-value	0.651	0.591	13.109***	14.905***	5.862***	15.776***	13.709***	13.814***	22.155***

Note: CV control variable, IV independent variable, AE age of entrepreneur, LE level of education, EA enterprise age, SC size of the company (employees), CI company industry, ESE entrepreneurial self-efficacy, EIVE exploitative entrepreneurial learning, EORY exploratory entrepreneurial learning, NVP new ventures performance

* $p < 0.05$;**$p < 0.01$; ***$p < 0.001$

learning (model 2: β=0.052, p>0.05), while entrepreneurial self-efficacy has significant effect on exploratory entrepreneurial learning (model 4: β=0.286, p<0.001). Therefore, the hypothesis H2b (entrepreneurial self-efficacy has a significant positive impact on exploratory entrepreneurial learning) put forward in this study is well supported by the data, while the hypothesis H2a (entrepreneurial self-efficacy has a significant positive impact on exploitative entrepreneurial learning) has not been verified.

In order to verify the hypotheses H3a and H3b, this study constructs models 5 and 7, namely, the models of the influence of control variables and intermediary variables on new ventures performance. The results in table 5 show that the regression coefficient of exploitative entrepreneurial learning to new ventures performance is 0.012 but not significant (model 7: β = 0.012, p>0.05); The regression coefficient of exploratory entrepreneurial learning to new ventures performance is 0.621 and significant (model 7: β=0.621, p<0.001). Therefore, the hypothesis H3b (exploratory entrepreneurial learning has a significant positive impact on the performance of new ventures) proposed in this study is supported by the data, while the hypothesis H3a (exploitative entrepreneurial learning has a significant positive impact on the performance of new ventures) has not been verified.

In order to verify the mediating effect of exploitative entrepreneurial learning, this study builds model 8 on the basis of models 2, 6 and 7. Model 8 is the impact model of entrepreneurial self-efficacy and exploitative entrepreneurial learning on new ventures performance. The data in table 5 show that the independent variable entrepreneurial self-efficacy has no significant effect on exploitative entrepreneurial learning (model 2: $\beta=0.052, p>0.05$). entrepreneurial self-efficacy positively affects new ventures performance (model 6: $\beta=0.517$, $p<0.001$). When considering both entrepreneurial self-efficacy and exploitative entrepreneurial learning, exploitative entrepreneurial learning cannot positively affect new ventures performance (model 8: $\beta=0.087$, $p>0.05$), while entrepreneurial self-efficacy still positively affects new ventures performance (model 8: $\beta=0.621$, $p<0.001$). According to the above analysis, exploitative entrepreneurial learning does not play a mediating role in the process of the impact of entrepreneurial self-efficacy on new ventures performance. Therefore, the hypothesis H4a proposed in this study (exploitative entrepreneurial learning has a significant mediating effect between entrepreneurial self-efficacy and new ventures performance) has not been confirmed by data.

Then, in order to verify the mediating effect of exploratory entrepreneurship learning, this study builds model 9 on the basis of models 4, 6 and 7. Model 9 is a model of the impact of entrepreneurial self-efficacy and exploratory entrepreneurial learning on new ventures performance. The results in table 5 show that entrepreneurial self-efficacy positively affects exploratory entrepreneurial learning (model 4: $\beta=0.286, p<0.001$), and entrepreneurial self-efficacy positively affects new ventures performance (model 6: $\beta=0.517$, $p<0.001$). Considering both entrepreneurial self-efficacy and exploratory entrepreneurial learning, exploratory entrepreneurial learning positively affects new ventures performance (model 9: $\beta= 0.468, p<0.001$), and the regression coefficient of entrepreneurial self-efficacy decreases but still positively affects new ventures performance (model 9: $\beta=0.383$, $p<0.001$). Based on the above analysis, the regression results show that exploratory entrepreneurial learning plays a part in mediating the effect of entrepreneurial self-efficacy on new ventures performance. Therefore, the hypothesis H4b (exploratory entrepreneurial learning has a significant mediating effect between entrepreneurial self-efficacy and new ventures performance) proposed in this study is also supported by the data.

CONCLUSION

Research Results and Discussions

In the complex and changeable environment of the emerging economy, the high volatility and unpredictability of the environment have brought many operational risks and challenges to new ventures. The high failure rate has always been an important problem faced by new ventures (Ma et al. 2018). Entrepreneurial self-efficacy plays an important role in entrepreneurs' personal will, behavior and decision-making. Meanwhile, dual entrepreneurial learning also plays an important role in the construction of enterprises and the promotion of competitive advantages. Therefore, this paper explores the relationship between entrepreneurial self-efficacy and new ventures performance and introduces dual entrepreneurial learning as an intermediary variable, obtaining some enlightening research findings:

1. The results of this study found that entrepreneurial self-efficacy has a significant positive impact on the performance of new ventures. In the face of high pressure or difficulties, entrepreneurs who are full of confidence in their own abilities will still maintain a high entrepreneurial passion and put into entrepreneurial activities. In terms of decision-making and behavior choices, they are more inclined to make innovation changes that are not afraid of failure, actively seek external opportunities, stabilize and develop their interpersonal relationships than people with low self-efficacy in entrepreneurship, thus improving the ability to identify entrepreneurial opportunities, helping enterprises seize opportunities and occupy markets, and eventually leading to further improvement of enterprise performance. Some scholars have studied the relationship between entrepreneurial self-efficacy and entrepreneurial performance. Research shows that entrepreneurial self-efficacy promotes the improvement of entrepreneurial performance. The conclusion of this study confirms that entrepreneurial self-efficacy has a positive impact on new ventures performance, and also verifies the viewpoints of Zhong et al. (2012), Su et al. (2018), that entrepreneurial self-efficacy promotes entrepreneurial performance, deepening and expanding the theoretical framework of entrepreneurial self-efficacy and new ventures performance.
2. The results of this study show that entrepreneurial self-efficacy helps entrepreneurs to carry out exploratory entrepreneurial learning, while entrepreneurial self-efficacy has no significant effect on exploitative entrepreneurial learning. The internal reason for the difference may mainly lie in the willingness of high entrepreneurial self-efficacy to innovate, take risks and actively identify new market opportunities. At the same time, the essence of exploratory entrepreneurial learning is to attach importance to innovation, break existing behaviors and practices to find new fields and new development trends. These two variables are identical in some connotations. Exploitative entrepreneurial learning is a low-level learning method, emphasizing learning only on the basis of existing knowledge, avoiding innovation and reducing changes as much as possible (Levinthal and March 1993). Therefore, it is often

not the best choice for individuals with high entrepreneurial self-efficacy, so entrepreneurial self-efficacy can promote exploratory entrepreneurial learning, but has no positive impact on exploitative entrepreneurial learning.

3. The results of this study show that exploratory entrepreneurial learning has a significant positive impact on the performance of new ventures, while exploitative entrepreneurial learning has no significant impact on the performance of new ventures. The reason why the two learning methods produce different results may be that exploratory entrepreneurial learning can expand the breadth of knowledge, make up for the short-sighted and outdated problems existing in the existing knowledge, facilitate entrepreneurs to think about problems from multiple angles, make innovative decisions and valuable entrepreneurial behaviors, and further enable enterprises to obtain huge competitive advantages from "ordinary" entrepreneurial enterprises under the leadership of entrepreneurs and finally stand out. However, exploitative entrepreneurial learning to concentrate on one's own field and refine and tap existing knowledge and abilities is not conducive to its competition with other mature enterprises. New ventures have problems of small scale and shortage of resources. Only using traditional behavior to compete with mature enterprises will not be successful (Lee et al. 2001). Although it has the characteristics of low cost, this characteristic is not enough to offset the losses caused by the rapid depreciation of existing knowledge resources. Therefore, exploratory entrepreneurial learning is the most important learning method for new ventures.
4. This study attempts to introduce dual entrepreneurial learning as the mediating variable of entrepreneurial self-efficacy affecting new ventures performance. The results show that exploratory entrepreneurial learning plays a part in mediating the relationship between entrepreneurial self-efficacy and new ventures performance, while exploitative entrepreneurial learning has no significant mediating effect. The above mentioned that entrepreneurs' high self-efficacy will promote them to carry out exploratory entrepreneurial learning, and this learning method is conducive to entrepreneurs guiding enterprises to win a place in a highly volatile environment. Through innovative and experimental learning, entrepreneurs can obtain information on industry frontier knowledge, market trends, policy changes, etc. It is conducive to entrepreneurs making good judgments on the market, reducing market uncertainty, helping entrepreneurs to pay close attention to changes in the external economic environment, seize opportunities to create new products or services that meet the needs of the market and customers, and thus improving the entrepreneurial performance of enterprises. However, entrepreneurs with low entrepreneurial self-efficacy tend to adopt conservative strategies and operate cautiously, and are afraid of high-risk market opportunities. They often imitate other people's innovative

behaviors instead of creating by themselves, and often do not use exploratory entrepreneurial learning to make changes. The mediating effect of exploitative entrepreneurial learning is not significant. Entrepreneurs with high sense of efficiency tend to carry out creative learning. Entrepreneurs with low sense of efficiency cannot significantly improve entrepreneurial performance by choosing exploitative learning. The main reason is that the founding team of a new venture is usually only a few people, and the initial resources of the enterprise come from a few people. No matter how to use them, the available knowledge will depreciate rapidly with the changes of time and environment, so it cannot play a mediating role in entrepreneurial self-efficacy and new venture performance.

The theoretical contributions of this paper are mainly reflected in the following aspects: First, paying attention to the path and mechanism of the impact of entrepreneurial self-efficacy on new venture performance, making up for the existing research deficiencies, helping to further open the black box of entrepreneurial self-efficacy on new venture performance in the future, and providing practical enlightenment for entrepreneurs and enterprises to improve their performance; Secondly, this study puts forward and verifies the effect of entrepreneurial self-efficacy as a pre-variable on dual entrepreneurial learning, and at the same time expands the literature on entrepreneurial self-efficacy and dual entrepreneurial learning. Finally, this paper attempts to analyze the impact of entrepreneurial self-efficacy on new venture performance from the perspective of learning, and adds dual entrepreneurial learning as an intermediary variable to build a research model of entrepreneurial self-efficacy, dual entrepreneurial learning and new venture performance. At the same time, the research on the relationship between the three is almost blank in China. In addition, although some scholars have studied the impact of organizational learning on new venture performance from the organizational level, However, few scholars probe into the relationship between entrepreneurs' self-efficacy and learning model and performance from the individual level. Therefore, dual entrepreneurial learning has theoretical and practical research value on the mediating effect of entrepreneurial self-efficacy and new venture performance.

Theoretical Model Revision

Through relevant empirical research, the theoretical model proposed in this paper has been basically verified and adjusted according to the results of data analysis, as shown in Figure 2.

Figure 2. Modified model

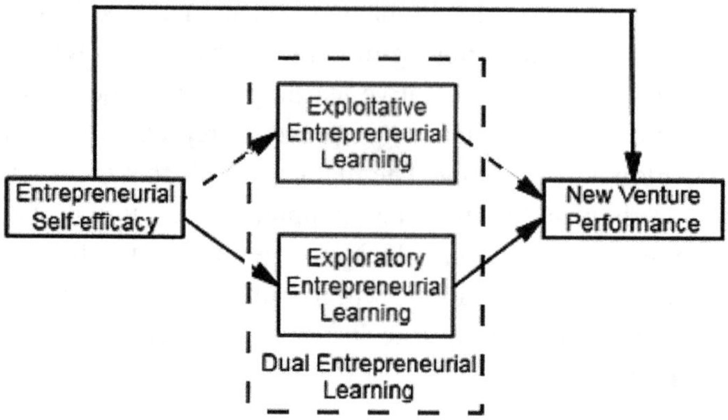

Research Inspiration

This study proposes and verifies the relationship between entrepreneurial self-efficacy and new venture performance. This relationship shows that entrepreneurs can improve the performance of new ventures by improving entrepreneurial self-efficacy, and points out the role of entrepreneurial self-efficacy in practice. Exploratory entrepreneurial learning is conducive to the formation and improvement of new venture performance, and plays an intermediary role in the impact of entrepreneurial self-efficacy on new venture performance, which illustrates the importance of exploratory entrepreneurial learning for entrepreneurs and start-ups to improve new venture performance. For entrepreneurs in real situations, effective entrepreneurial learning is crucial. In order to improve the performance of new ventures and maintain their competitive advantages, entrepreneurs should pay more attention to exploratory entrepreneurial learning, enhance their ability to acquire resources and match them with resources suitable for entrepreneurial projects.

Research Limitations and Prospects

In this study, firstly, in the process of data collection, although the universality and integrity of data have been ensured as far as possible, the samples still have limitations. In the future, the sample size and diversity should be expanded and further tested. Secondly, in future research, we will try to clarify the relationship between exploratory learning and exploitative learning, instead of taking exploratory learning and exploitative learning as independent variables. Finally, the relationship between entrepreneurial self-efficacy and new venture performance is very complex, and the research entry points are also diverse. In the future, other perspectives can be selected to further improve the theory of entrepreneurial self-efficacy and new venture performance.

REFERENCES

Baum, L. (2004). Social cognitive theory of posttraumatic recovery: The role of perceived self-efficacy. *Behaviour Research and Therapy*, *10*(42), 1129–1148. PMID:15350854

Cai, L., Tang, S. Q., Ma, Y. L., & Gao, X. (2014). Research on the relationship among entrepreneurial learning, entrepreneurial ability and new enterprise performance. *Studies in Science of Science*, *32*(8), 1189–1197.

Chen, C. C., Greene, P. G., & Crick, A. (1998). Does entrepreneurial self-efficacy distinguish entrepreneurs from managers? *Journal of Business Venturing*, *13*(4), 295–316. doi:10.1016/S0883-9026(97)00029-3

Chen, C. J. (2009). Technology commercialization, incubator and venture capital, and new venture performance. *Journal of Business Research*, *62*(1), 93–103. doi:10.1016/j.jbusres.2008.01.003

Ge, B. S., Tan, L. F., Sheng, F., & Ma, H. J. (2016). Research on the relationship among innovation culture, dual Learning and dynamic ability. *Studies in Science of Science*, *34*(4), 630–640.

Hair, J. F. Jr, Anderson, R. E., Tatham, R. L., & Black, W. C. (1998). *Multivariate data analysis* (5th ed.). Englewood Cliffs: Prentice Hall.

Han, L. Z., &Fu, H. (2009). Construction of college students' entrepreneurial self-efficacy scale. *Journal of Nanjing Normal University (Social Science Edition)*, *2009*(1), 114-118.

Jill, K. N., & Robert, S. D. (2005). Measure for measure: Modeling entrepreneurial self-efficacy onto instrumental tasks within the new venture creation process. *New England Journal of Entrepreneurship*, *8*(2), 39–47. doi:10.1108/NEJE-08-02-2005-B005

Khedhaouria, A., Gurău, C., & Torrès, O. (2015). Creativity, Self-efficacy and small-firm performance: The mediating role of entrepreneurial orientation. *Small Business Economics*, *44*(3), 485–504. doi:10.100711187-014-9608-y

Lee, C., Lee, K., & Pennings, J. M. (2001). Internal capabilities, external networks, and performance: A study on technology-based ventures. *Strategic Management Journal, 22*(6/7), 615–640. doi:10.1002mj.181

Levinthal, D. A., & March, J. G. (1993). The myopia of learning. *Strategic Management Journal, 14*(S2), 95–112. doi:10.1002mj.4250141009

Liu, J. J. (2011). Research on the relationship among entrepreneurial learning, dynamic capabilities and performance of new ventures - Adjustment of environmental dynamics. *Studies in Science of Science, 29*(5), 728–734.

Lucas, W. A., & Cooper, S. Y. (2005). *Measuring Entrepreneurial Self-efficacy.* Paper Presented to the SMU EDGE Conference, Singapore.

Ma, H. J., Wu, J., & Lang, C. T. (2018). The formation mechanism of improvisation to convention in new venture: Based on the perspective of entrepreneurial learning. *Foreign Economics & Management., 40*(11), 116–128.

Murnieks, C. Y., Mosakowski, E., & Cardon, M. S. (2014). Pathways of passion: Identity centrality, passion, and behavior among entrepreneurs. *Journal of Management, 40*(6), 1583–1606. doi:10.1177/0149206311433855

Politis, D., & Gabrielsson, J. (2004). Exploring the role of experience in the process of entrepreneurial learning. *RENT XVIIl Conferellce.*

Scherer, R. F., Adams, J. S., Carley, S. S., & Wiebe, F. A. (1989). Role model performance effects on development of entrepreneurial career preference. *Entrepreneurship Theory and Practice, 13*(1), 53–71. doi:10.1177/104225878901300306

Su, X. H., Yang, S. N., Wu, J. Z., & Zhou, Y. (2018). Research on the relationship among entrepreneurial self-efficacy, decision logic and entrepreneurial performance. *South China Journal of Economics, 2018*(10), 113-131.

Tang, J., &Jiang, Y. F. (2007). Research on career choice of newborn entrepreneurs: based on self-efficacy. *Science of Science and Management of S & T, 2007*(10), 180-185.

Tang, Q., & Gu, J. P. (2016). The effect of entrepreneur's spiritual capital and self-efficacy on entrepreneurial performance. *Enterprise Economy, 2016*(9), 111-117.

Wood, R., & Bandura, A. (1989). Social Cognitive Theory of Organizational Management. *Academy of Management Review, 14*(3), 361–384. doi:10.5465/amr.1989.4279067

Xie, Y. P., Chen, X. Y., & Ye, D. R. (2016). Does entrepreneurial passion contribute to entrepreneurial success? *Management Review*, *28*(11), 170–181.

Yang, X. P., Tang, L. B., & Yu, X. Y. (2013). Entrepreneurial network, entrepreneurial learning and new venture growth. *Management Review*, *25*(1), 24–33.

Yi, Z. H., Duan, H. X., & Ren, S. G. (2018). Entrepreneurial self-efficacy, entrepreneurial orientation and performance of small and micro technology enterprises. *Science Research Management*, *39*(8), 99–108.

Zhang, W. W., & Zhao, W. H. (2017). A study on the relationship between industry internal and external connections, entrepreneurial learning and entrepreneurial performance. *Science of Science and Management of S & T*, *38*(04), 162–170.

Zhang, Z. H., & Li, A. (2019). The influence of social network on the performance of technological new ventures. *Contemporary Economic Research, 2019*(4), 55-62.

Zhao, Y. B., Li, Y., Lee, S., & Chen, L. B. (2011). Entrepreneurial orientation, organizational learning, and performance: Evidence from China. *Entrepreneurship Theory and Practice*, *35*(2), 293–317. doi:10.1111/j.1540-6520.2009.00359.x

Zhong, W. D., & Huang, Z. X. (2012). An empirical study on the relationship among entrepreneur's relationship strength, self-efficacy and entrepreneurial performance. *Forum on Science and Technology in China, 2012*(1), 131-137.

Zhu, X. M., Kong, X. Q., & Bao, M. X. (2014). Learning orientation and competitive advantage of new enterprises: A study on the mediating effect of dual entrepreneurial learning. *R & D Management*, *26*(2), 9–16.

Chapter 13
Sustainable Entrepreneurship Guided by Policy Support in a Transitional Economy:
A Research Based on a Chinese High-Tech Enterprise

Fan Sheng
School of Economics and Management, Harbin Engineering University, China

Baoshan Ge
Jilin University, China

Shiying Zhang
Institute of Business and Economic Research, Harbin University of Commerce, China

Xinyu Liu
Dalian University of Technology, China

ABSTRACT

For countries in the process of economic transition, improvement of industrialization is no longer the sole goal of their economic development. While upgrading the level of industrial development, these countries also gradually attach importance to resource utilization efficiency and environmental protection, which is why sustainable entrepreneurship has become increasingly popular in recent years. With the intensification of policy guidance, a new "sea area" named sustainable entrepreneurship ushers in more and more "treasure hunters" exploring "the

DOI: 10.4018/978-1-7998-3495-3.ch013

treasure" therein. Based on this, this chapter constructs the model of "Green Ocean Treasure Hunting" for green entrepreneurial enterprises to analyze the role played by their government's relevant policies and puts forward the research proposition of this chapter based on the relevant literature. On this basis, this chapter chooses and analyzes a medium-sized, high-tech enterprise in China that follows a certain typical green entrepreneurial process as evidence of the propositions the authors have put forward.

INTRODUCTION

In recent years, with the continuous improvement of industrialization, people have been plagued by increasing environmental pollution and a lack of resources, in addition to more convenient living. This has caused countries to pay more attention to environmental protection and sustainable development. Developing Countries are under great economic and environmental pressure and trying to achieve growth through minimal resource consumption by promoting entrepreneurship in a sustainable way. China is no exception, after extensive catching-up economically and ensuring that it met the livelihood needs of people throughout the country, it began to gradually increase its protection of the environment and resources and turned to a sustainable economic growth model. Both the "Scientific Outlook on Development" proposed by the Third Plenary Session of the 16th CPC Central Committee and the "Ecological Civilization Building" proposed by the 18th CPC Congress directly address the practical problems of resource constraints and environmental pollution, in order to lead China's development in a green and harmonious direction. In order to achieve this goal, the Chinese government has formulated many policies to standardize and guide the development of domestic industries, such as the "Law of the People's Republic of China on Promoting Circular Economy", the "Decision on Accelerating the Cultivation and Development of Strategic Emerging Industries", the "National Environmental Protection Standard for the Thirteenth Five year Development Plan" and so on. Under the support and guidance of a series of relevant policies, some entrepreneurs and entrepreneurial enterprises have begun to choose a more environmentally friendly, economical and ecological means of development, that is, to embark on sustainable entrepreneurship. However, this road is not smooth, but full of challenges.

This article studies the innovation process of sustainable entrepreneurial enterprises, analyzes the innovative search and resource acquisition of sustainable entrepreneurial enterprises, and explores the role of policy support in promoting and supporting sustainable entrepreneurship. So as to identify the challenges faced by entrepreneurs in the process of sustainable entrepreneurship, and provide a assistance for relevant government policy development. On this basis, it is easier to understand the practice of sustainable entrepreneurship through the metaphor of a treasure hunt in the Green Ocean, and thus to clarify why and how entrepreneurs and entrepreneurial enterprises try to start green businesses and face challenges. After theoretical analysis, we then continue by analyzing a high-tech enterprise in China that undertakes sustainable entrepreneurship, in order to pursue a deeper theoretical and practical contribution.

THEORETICAL BASIS

Sustainable Entrepreneurship

When it comes to sustainable entrepreneurship, one cannot ignore green technologies, which are products, services or processes that deliver value with less resources or pollution than current standards(Marra et al., 2015,2017). Sustainable entrepreneurial enterprises pursue the goal of using green technologies to protect the environment and resource enterprises. Many scholars had conducted relevant research around the topic of sustainable entrepreneurship. Scholars have given their own definitions to it and also introduced different terms such as sustainable entrepreneurship, environmental entrepreneurship, eco-entrepreneurship and sustainable entrepreneurship in order to describe it. In this paper, we choose the term "sustainable entrepreneurship" to indicate this phenomenon. The following is a list of some definitions of these scholars, as shown in Table 1.

It can be seen that, although a recognized definition has not yet been made for sustainable entrepreneurship, there are still commonalities that exist. First of all, sustainable entrepreneurship is a way to achieve environmental goals through entrepreneurship, in the process of which the identification, exploitation and other processes of opportunities were emphasized. Secondly, sustainable entrepreneurship has emerged due to market imbalances, resource allocation imbalances and other stimulating conditions, with ensuring environment protection and sustainable development being one of its main purposes. Thirdly, sustainable entrepreneurship also needs innovation, foresight and risk-taking to develop and promote new products, technologies and services. Based on this, the sustainable entrepreneurship in this paper mainly considers the research, development, improvement and promotion of products, technologies and services by organizations or individuals exploiting entrepreneurial opportunities for environmental protection and sustainable development.

Table 1. Definitions of sustainable entrepreneurship.

Author	Definition
Dean and Mcmullen(2007)	Sustainable entrepreneurship is the result of individuals in the market who wish to stop activities that led to environmental damage and are willing to pay for it. Sustainable entrepreneurship is the process of identifying, assessing and using environmental-related opportunities emerging from market failures that are detrimental to sustainability.
Kai and Wüstenhagen (2010)	Identifying and exploiting opportunities through the emergence of market imbalances, this therefore shifts sectors towards being more socially and environmentally sustainable.
Shepherd and Patzelt(2011)	Sustainable entrepreneurship is the pursuit of opportunities for the future products, processes and services, which focuses on the protection of nature, life and society.
Kate and Eva(2012)	Sustainable entrepreneurship is bringing new products, technologies and services to the market to try and guide the industry and consumer in a way that is environmentally and socially beneficial in this process.
Silajdžić, Kurtagić and Vučijak(2015)	Sustainable entrepreneurship is the entrepreneurship and the sale of green products and services based on the principle of sustainable development of strong potential green values.
Corbett and Montgomery(2017)	Sustainable entrepreneurship is the response of individuals or organizations to address issues of uncertainty and resource allocation through novel and unique ideas and perspectives and to improve the environment by identifying, discovering, developing, innovating and exploiting opportunities.

Sustainable Entrepreneurship and Policy Support

Policy support has an impact on entrepreneurship. Fonseca et al. (2001) believe that sustainable entrepreneurship is the main power for sustainability, their study has shown that the policy combinations can effectively promote sustainable entrepreneurs to provide sustainable products/services. Higher entrepreneurial costs will inhibit entrepreneurs' willingness to start their business and thus can reduce the speed with which new businesses in a country are established. Ge et al. (2016) believe that policy support, such as the incentives, innovative protection and government programs, can play a role in promoting the development of entrepreneurial activities and lowering the threshold for market access. Furthermore, for sustainable entrepreneurship, Pinkse and Groot (2015) argue that in the face of market barriers such as imperfect information, monopolies and price mechanism imbalances, sustainable entrepreneurial enterprises tend to engage in political activities to gain government support for smooth entry into their target industry. However, research by Kai and Wüstenhagen (2010) examines government internalization of external costs through taxation and other policy measures, and shows that policy support plays an important role in promoting the commercialization of sustainable innovation outcomes. Therefore, to encourage sustainable entrepreneurship by enterprises, more should be learnt about policy. Moreover, the development of sustainable entrepreneurship is a complex process that requires the comprehensive utilization of technologies, policies, markets and more, and the government's greatest responsibility is to provide entrepreneurs with the appropriate and necessary support to address uncertainties and risks, so as to help businesses to navigate barriers more smoothly (Silajdžić et al., 2015). Therefore, in this study, the analysis of the role of policy support in sustainable entrepreneurship is emphasized, which also matches the important role of government in the transitional economy.

Innovative Research

Many scholars have conducted research on innovative research. For example, Katila and Ahuja (2002) argue that innovative research is an attempt by enterprises to solve problems in a fuzzy world and that this process may involve the creation and consolidation of technologies. Sofka and Grimpe(2010) define innovative research as the research and integration of external knowledge across boundaries by companies to help them innovate successfully and enhance the novelty of innovation. From the perspective of innovative research, this behavior can be further decomposed. For example, according to the target of research, innovative research can be divided into market knowledge research about customer preferences and technical knowledge research for the design, production and technology, etc. of products and services (Köhler et al., 2012). It can also be divided by the direction of the innovative research, such as the breadth of research for heterogeneous knowledge beyond existing knowledge and the depth of research for knowledge of the enterprise's own knowledge reserve (Katila and Ahuja, 2012).

MODEL BUILDING

In the Blue Ocean Strategy, Kim and Mauborgne (2005) divided the market into the blue oceans (unknown market spaces), which consist of non-existent industries and the red oceans (known as market spaces), which consist of existing industries. This metaphor gave us inspiration. Sustainable entrepreneurship is about novel entrepreneurship that is environmentally and socially friendly, which makes sustainable entrepreneurship supported by the government and the general public as people like to live in a beautiful environment. Such support is often reflected in environmental factors, such as policies and cultures. Therefore, we compare the market for sustainable entrepreneurial enterprises to a "Green Ocean", where external environmental factors such as policies play an important role in this green ocean. Guided by the external environment, sustainable entrepreneurial enterprises in this ocean exploit the opportunities and resources it identified and accessed to carry out the corresponding innovation activities to explore the "treasure of the sea". In other words, researching and developing, or improving the production process for, more environmentally friendly products and services. This kind of "Green Ocean", on the one hand, possesses characteristics of the blue ocean, that is, the innovation results from the country's demand for sustainable development and people's demand for a green and healthy ecological environment. Therefore, sustainable entrepreneurial enterprises offer unique competitive advantages. On the other hand, "Green Ocean" also possesses some characteristics of the red ocean. That is, the fruits of many sustainable entrepreneurial enterprises are just innovations in manufacturing processes, but not much different from other non-green products in terms of the function and performance of the product itself, both of which have strong alternatives. These companies will still face fierce competition in the market with a large number of alternative products. In this case, what troubles them is how their innovative costs can be remedied.

At present, in order to develop, enterprises not only need to seize and use opportunities to create value, but also to take into account any social benefits, combined with considering the relevant laws and regulations. This makes companies' development strategies place more emphasis on sustainability in addition to their day-to-day operations, namely in addition to meeting economic, technical and customer needs. This quest seeks to achieve sustainable product manufacturing with cheaper and more abundant ingredients (Cappa et al., 2016). For enterprises, the pursuit of more sustainable development is based on their recognition of the scarcity of natural resources and the need for businesses to take responsibility for the use of social resources. Thus, in the pursuit of green development, enterprises will use their resources and capabilities for business activities in a more sustainable manner (Rodriguez et al., 2002). Many companies choose sustainable entrepreneurship and make innovations in a sustainable way under the influence of multiple factors such as politics, society and themselves. These companies often need to keep an eye on changes in market demand and rapidly respond to them (Schaltegger and Waner, 2011). Therefore, it is necessary to explore the innovation of enterprises in order to achieve green and sustainable development in the research of sustainable entrepreneurship. Thus, in this paper, we study the sustainable entrepreneurship problem in terms of policy support in the transition economy and build a research model, mainly considering the role of policy support, the technological complexity that enterprises face in their innovative research and the innovative outcomes they have achieved.

Block (2008) found that policy support has played a significant role in the technological innovation of enterprises. The government helps enterprises to obtain resources through funding and support for the commercialization of new technologies in order to help enterprises to carry out technological innovation smoothly. Sofka and Grimpe(2010) argue that innovative research is the process by which companies cross boundaries to gain external knowledge resources and use them for business innovation. For researchers and developers, a high level of technological complexity puts them in a dilemma, making them spend more time exploring the various components and their interactions in complex technologies, as opposed to lower technological complexity which reduces the need for tedious explorations (Baldwin and Clark, 2000; Fleming and Sorenson, 2001). Therefore, we can start from a similar point of view when we study sustainable entrepreneurship. This paper mainly focuses on analysis of the impact of policy support and the enterprise's innovative research on their resource acquisition, and also the technological complexity faced by them in the innovation process, and then analyzes how the above factors affect the innovative outcomes of sustainable entrepreneurial enterprises (as shown in Figure 1). It should be noted that the resources mentioned here include not only the operating resources of enterprises, but also the knowledge resources.

Figure 1. Research framework of "Green Ocean Treasure Hunting".

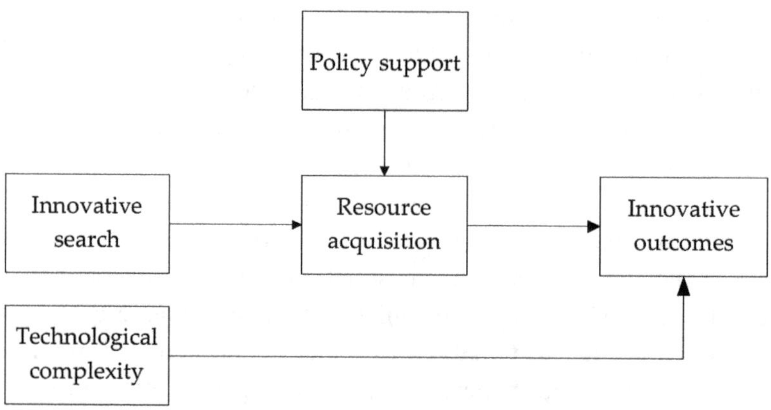

To show the process more vividly, we analogize that the process of sustainable entrepreneurship, and the individuals and organizations that start a green business, are like "treasure hunters" in this "Green Ocean", where they explore the "treasure department "under policy support (potential business opportunities). Sustainable entrepreneurship uses its own unremitting innovation as a driving force to find and tap into the "treasure" and build the "Green Ocean Treasure Hunting" model (as shown in Figure 2). Based on the metaphor of green ocean and referring the mechanics of gravity, buoyancy and other principles, we show the way in which entrepreneurial enterprises are supported and hindered during this process. This is

Figure 2. "Green Ocean Treasure Hunting" model.

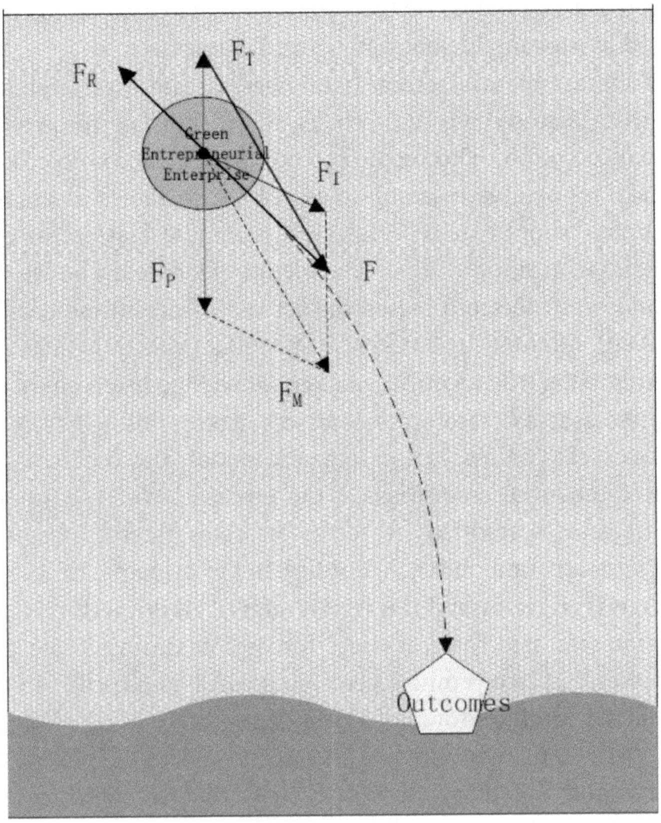

in order to show sustainable entrepreneurship more intuitively through the process by which enterprises continuously explore and pursue innovative achievements under the influence of various forces.

If an entrepreneurial enterprise is likened to a uniform, solid sphere of water and related policies as external environmental factors are viewed as a field, then the role of policy support, F_p, for entrepreneurial enterprises can be compared to the gravitational force, G, that the sphere is subjected to. Similarly, for sustainable entrepreneurial enterprises, policy support, like gravity, is a downward force. In other words, the force of policy supports in promoting enterprises' innovation and brings them closer to the green product and technology development. The supportive role of policy support for sustainable entrepreneurship is related to the intensity of policy support, that is, the intensity of the incentives, subsidies and tax relief provided by the relevant policies. From the perspective of R&D subsidies, research and development costs plus deductions, scientific research awards and so on, the intensity of impact on the entrepreneurial enterprise is related to its input and achievement in sustainable entrepreneurship. Based on this, we use F_P in Figure 2 to express the force of policy support received by sustainable entrepreneurial enterprises.

Sustainable entrepreneurial enterprises need to innovate and improve their products, services, technologies and processes, etc. for environmental protection and resource conservation. This requires entrepreneurial enterprises to take the initiative to make innovative research to get closer to their "destination". In this process, enterprises should make efforts on technical aspects to enhance their understanding and utilization of their knowledge (technical knowledge research). On the other hand, while the entrepreneurial activity of an entrepreneurial enterprise is purposeful, it still requires the enterprise to conduct research on its own initiative to help them explore the true location (market knowledge research) of their targeted R&D outcomes so as to avoid their innovative behavior falling astray and resulting in financial losses. Therefore, in this paper's model, the innovative research of sustainable entrepreneurial enterprises is the force, F_I, which is roughly oriented towards the "treasure" provided by the enterprises themselves, which have a horizontal and vertical component. According to the principle of resultant force in physics, the force is a vector and the vector sum of multiple forces acting on the same object is the resultant force of these forces. According to the parallelogram law, the motivation, F_M, that promotes entrepreneurial enterprises to be successful in innovations is the resultant force of F_P and F_I.

Most of the sustainable entrepreneurial enterprises are innovative new ventures or small and medium-sized businesses (SMEs) that are able to respond more positively to the demand for green products than large ones in almost any market segment, but they also often face higher technical uncertainty (Marra et al., 2017; Ndubisi and Nair, 2009). For sustainable entrepreneurial enterprises, they need to overcome the technological complexity in pursuing innovation achievements, such as green products and services. In this paper's model, this process is manifested in the entrepreneurial enterprises' efforts to overcome the buoyancy of "green sea" and move to the "seabed". In physics, the buoyancy that an object receives in a liquid can be expressed as F_{float}. When comparing the technological complexity faced by green enterprises to achieve buoyancy, and considering that the technological complexity of their corresponding fields is higher, the obstacles for successful innovation will therefore be larger. When a kind of technology required by various countries faces greater obstacles, these countries tend to make efforts to increase the attractiveness to provide such technologies (Lewis and Wiser, 2007). This also reflects the difficulties and technological complexity required for innovation. Taking these aspects into consideration, the technological complexity faced by sustainable entrepreneurial enterprises can be expressed by F_T in Figure 2.

On this basis, according to the parallelogram law, we can add up the impetus of the enterprise and the buoyancy caused by technological complexity, consequently then, the resultant force, F, is the force that influences the actual trajectory of sustainable entrepreneurship of enterprises. In addition, in the course of their movement in the "Green Ocean", enterprises are constantly hindered by resistance which is contrary to their direction of movement. For ordinary moving objects, this resistance can be simply expressed as f. For sustainable entrepreneurial enterprises, considering that various resources are essential to their entrepreneurial processes and the cornerstones of their innovation, the difficulty of acquiring knowledge and other kinds of resources can be a further obstacle to them. This obstacle relates to the enterprise's current level of requirement on these resources and also the influence of organizational structure, personnel composition, relevant domain knowledge and resource availability on the process of acquiring these resources needed for entrepreneurship. The result of the combination of these two aspects is the difficulty faced by enterprises in acquiring knowledge and other resources, which can be expressed by F_R in Figure 2.

MECHANISM ANALYSIS ON SUSTAINABLE ENTREPRENEURSHIP GUIDED BY POLICY SUPPORT

In a study of wind power industry enterprises in 12 countries, such as China and Brazil, Lewis and Wiser (2007) found that direct and indirect policy support, such as fiscal incentives, tax credits, government purchases and feed-in tariffs, can help promote the development of the wind energy industry. This process happens with the emergence of a large number of new entrants, products and technologies in the industry. Stigson et al. (2009) studied the energy and climate policies of Sweden, and considered that enterprises are paying increasing attention to corresponding policies when making investment decisions for related industries. Since the government cannot directly control the emissions of enterprises, but can only adopt policy measures to regulate and motivate enterprises to reduce their emissions, investment direction should be guided by policy measures.

In the light of the externality theory, the production process of enterprises in real life tends to be accompanied by certain external influences, in other words the private benefits brought by their production activities are less than the social benefits (positive externality), or the private costs are less than the social costs (negative externality). Moreover, unlike the hypothetical enterprises in neoclassical economics, which can perfectly use resources, actual enterprises can hardly achieve full utilization of resources in the production process. As Cohen and Winn (2007) have written, market failures such as externality and inefficiency can provide enterprises with opportunities for sustainable entrepreneurship, and these opportunities are abundant in reality. Therefore, for the government, in order to deal with the problem of environmental pollution and lack of resources, it is necessary to guide enterprises through policies to sustainable entrepreneurship, so that enterprises can produce positive externalities or reduce negative externalities and increase the efficiency of their resource utilization. For many entrepreneurial enterprises, market logic is the main code of conduct, that is, they decide whether to take advantage of these opportunities based on whether these business opportunities are profitable (Shane and Venkataraman, 2000), so whether or not enterprises are willing to adopt sustainable entrepreneurship and where it is going are also affected by policy. That is to say, enterprises will measure the costs and benefits that may be brought by sustainable entrepreneurship as an important reference point for decision-making, while direct or indirect policy support, such as tax incentives and subsidies, can help enterprises reduce costs or generate additional revenue. Therefore, when the government formulates or adjusts corresponding policies, the organization or individual will decide whether to take the opportunity to conduct sustainable entrepreneurship based on its measurement of the risks and benefits (Mcwilliams and Siegel. 2001). Policy support at this time is equivalent to a "Green Ocean Treasure Map" provided by the government. The "treasure hunters" who were attracted will explore where the "Treasure" is located according to the "Treasure Map". At the same time, the government also holds a role in using policy support to guide the development of sustainable entrepreneurship. Taking the new energy industry as an example, as shown in Figure 3, since the promulgation and implementation of the "National long-term science and technology development plan" and "Renewable Energy Law" in 2006, the number of new domestic energy enterprises registered in China has experienced rapid growth, with new energy enterprises established after 2006

Figure 3. The time of establishment of China's newly registered energy enterprises. (Source: Tencent Finance, Jusfoun Bigdata, 2017).

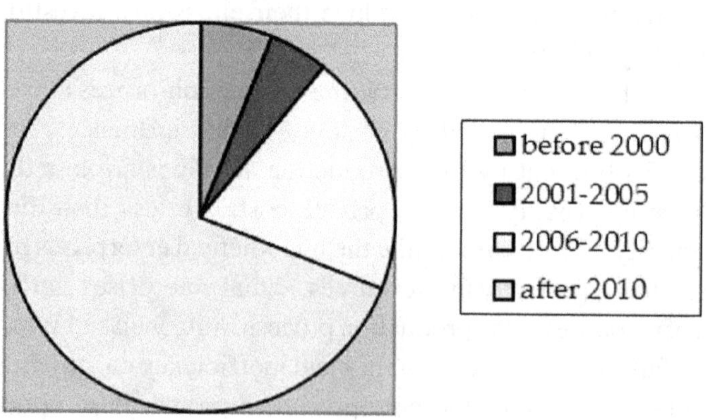

accounting for nearly 90% of the total number of new energy enterprises. Therefore, this paper puts forward Proposition 1.

Proposition 1. *Policy support can guide the direction of sustainable entrepreneurship.*

A good institutional environment can promote entrepreneurship (Busenitz et al., 2000). Based on the Porter (1995) Hypothesis, Ramanathan et al. (2017) suggest that flexible environmental regulations that encourage enterprises to innovate can drive enterprises to dynamic innovation and have a positive impact on their performance and sustainability. For sustainable entrepreneurship, policy support can also provide momentum. Specifically, due to the environmental and social demands for sustainable entrepreneurship, policy support such as tax credits, R&D subsidies and achievement rewards formulated and promulgated by the government can directly or indirectly provide enterprises with resources, enhance the competitiveness of their products (such as encouraging green consumption, enhance environmental standards, etc.) or expand the market for enterprises (such as government procurement, introduction of planning for promotion, etc.), thus reducing the enterprises' cost of design, research and development, production and transaction. Thus, for sustainable entrepreneurial enterprises, these policy supports boost their entrepreneurial activities (F_P), which can, on the one hand, make enterprises more successful at overcoming obstacles to accessing knowledge and other resources(F_R), as well as understanding technological complexity(F_T) in the process of R&D. On the other hand, policy support also makes enterprise less risky, that is, reducing the likelihood of unsellable products by expanding demand.

As shown in Figure 4, when policy support efforts (F_P) improve from F_P to $F_P^¢$, in order to analyze the function of F_p, we take the control variable methods to control F, F_T and F_R, so that then the $F_I^¢$ record is obviously smaller than F_I. That is to say, the effort to conduct innovative research of sustainable entrepreneurial enterprises under the influence of policy support is less than the effort when there is a lack of policy support or the policy support is weak. As such, policy support has brought impetus to the enterprise's sustainable entrepreneurial activities. Therefore, this paper puts forward Proposition 2.

Proposition 2. *Policy support can give impetus to an enterprise's sustainable entrepreneurship.*

For sustainable entrepreneurial enterprises, policy support alone will not be enough in completing innovative research and development of new products, services or technologies. There is also a need to ensure successful access to innovations through innovative research activities. According to the research of Sofka and Grimpe(2010)

Figure 4. The promoting role of policy support.

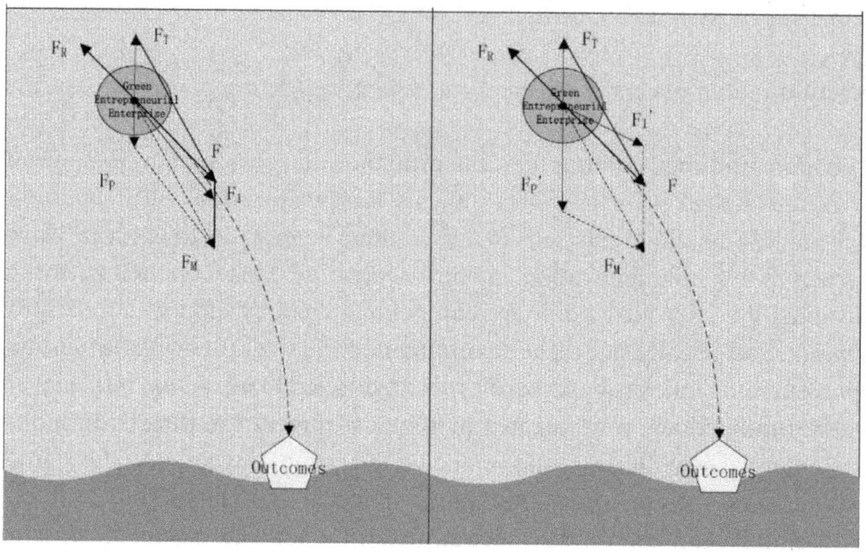

and Köhler et al.(2012), on the one hand, enterprises need to research the technical knowledge, skills, techniques, processes and other aspects required in the design, R&D and production of new products or services, thus helping them overcome technological complexity. On the other hand, enterprises also need to research market knowledge in order to understand customer preferences, market demand and other conditions, so as to improve the design, development, production and other processes and to adjust the direction of design and R&D and other activities within entrepreneurial process at any time. Therefore, enterprises are able to avoid wasting time and resources or even experiencing failure because of a deviation in their direction. In addition, sustainable entrepreneurship requires a significant amount of investment in the innovation of products and services and these inputs put pressure on enterprises. Moreover, there is the continuous deepening of the process of sustainable entrepreneurship and the continuous clear about the ultimate innovative outcomes that can be obtained, in order to reduce the burden caused by this pressure, the efforts by entrepreneurial enterprises into the market knowledge research will be appropriately shifted to technical knowledge research, allowing greater purpose and the ability to complete the "treasure hunt" process as soon as possible. As shown in Figure 5, the size of the innovative research represented by F_I is constant and the direction is deflected downward to F_I¢, that is, part of the input in market knowledge research in the horizontal direction is switched to the research of the technical knowledge in the vertical direction. Therefore, this paper puts forward Proposition 3.

Proposition 3. *Innovative research by sustainable entrepreneurial enterprise not only provides impetus for their entrepreneurial activities, but also serves to correct their trajectories.*

CASE STUDY

Methods and Sample

Case studies examine the complexities of samples and help researchers to provide solid analyses (Yin, 2013). A single case study approach helps us to capture and track new phenomena and emerging issues resulting from management practices, as well as providing a better view of issues raised within the research framework (Pettigrew, 1990; Siggelkow, 2007). A detailed study of individual cases can provide deeper insights into the complexities of the enterprise and offer a more detailed presentation of their operational state (Dyer and Wilkins, 1991). At present, the selection of typical cases is common practice based on a study of case studies. As Eisenhardt (1989) points out, for the case study approach, random samples are not only unnecessary but generally not desirable. Pettigrew even repeatedly emphasized that it is more appropriate to select a typical and extreme case to study (1990). The same holds true for Yin (2013), who argues that case studies require sample selection to be either significant or extreme. Therefore, this paper selects a typical case with which to study sustainable entrepreneurship under the policy support in a transitional economy.

This paper follows common practice in the research of sustainable entrepreneurship and selected enterprises in industries with green attributes during the sample selection (OECD, 2017). Based on the research purpose of this article, it is necessary to conduct an in-depth analysis of how green enterprises reflect on policy support and any changes to their innovative research behavior during the process of sustainable entrepreneurship. Therefore, we use a typical case study approach to analyze data obtained through a follow-up survey, in-depth interviews, and web-based collection.

In terms of sample selection, we select a Chinese company Firm A. Firm A is a high-tech enterprise established in 2013, which has set up an area of 250,000 square meters in the Songyuan Petrochemical Park in Jilin Province. Its main business is the deep processing of agricultural wastes, such as straw, to produce biomass energy and biomass materials. Its products mainly include biomass energy like bio-butanol, bio-ethanol, and biomass gas and lignin materials. On the basis of in-depth cooperation with research institutes such as Chinese Academy of Sciences and Chinese Academy of Forestry, Firm A not only made developments in biomass energy, but also gained a deeper understanding of lignin materials. In 2017, it

Figure 5. Entrepreneurial research changes with the development of sustainable entrepreneurship.

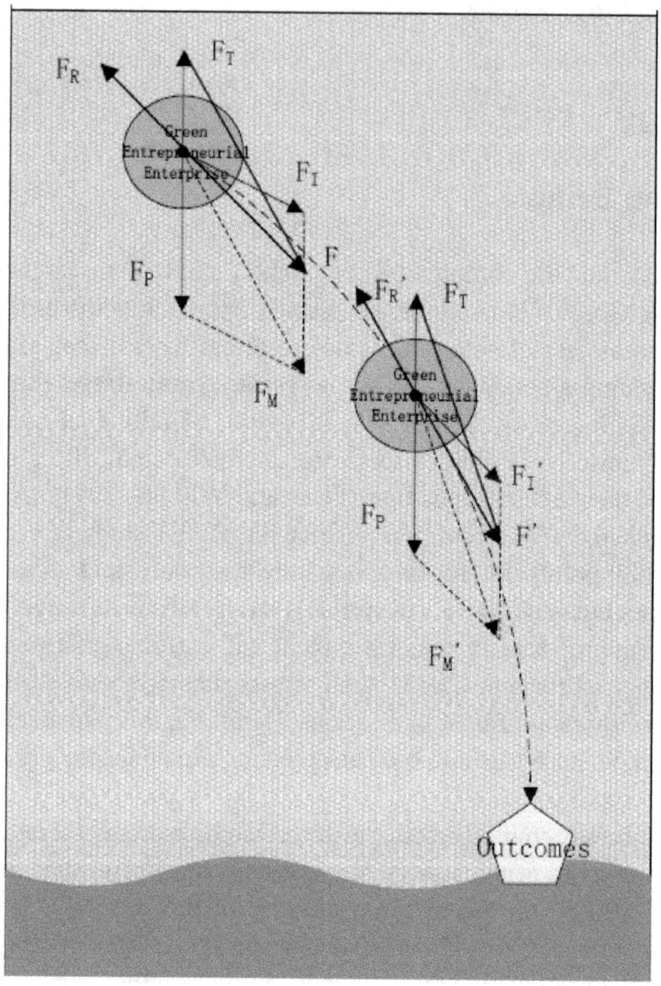

established Firm B in Beijing. At present, Firm B cooperates with large enterprises such as Craft Master to engage in building materials and decoration materials based on lignin, such as doors, windows, floors, interior and exterior wall panels, floors, furniture and biological polyurethanes. After many years of design, research and development and other innovative activities, the product series of Firm A and Firm B are basically complete, forming their own products and technology systems. Its core technology is supported by more than 20 patents, mainly involving the separation and directional conversion of three components of agricultural wastes such as straws, non-polluting gas explosions and the simultaneous fermentation of xylose and glucose to produce ethanol, butanol, acetone and bio-natural gas technologies. Some of the technologies have reached advanced levels by both international and domestic standards. At present, Firm A and Firm B have reached a stable production ability and are trying to carry out product industrialization.

The main reasons for choosing this company are as follows: firstly, the industry is typical. Firm A has engaged in the energy industry and the construction industry which are closely related to the daily needs of human beings. The green development of the energy industry and the construction industry is also a current concern in China and throughout the world. Thus, the sustainable entrepreneurship of Firm A covers the business of these two industries, showing a certain degree of typicality. Secondly, most of the sustainable entrepreneurial enterprises are innovative new ventures or small and medium-sized businesses (SMEs) that are able to respond more positively to the demand for green products than large ones in almost any market segment (Marra, 2017; Ndubisi and Nair, 2009). As a mid-sized enterprise that continuously undertakes sustainable entrepreneurship, Firm A has entered the construction industry after undertaking sustainable entrepreneurship in the energy industry. Studying it will help us to have a deeper understanding of why enterprises start sustainable entrepreneurship and the process of sustainable entrepreneurship. This is also of great significance to a large number of small and medium-sized enterprises that are interested in sustainable entrepreneurship. Thirdly, Firm A owns a number of advanced technologies and its technological innovation places it in a leading position within the industry. Its industrialized production technologies of bio-ethanol and bio-butanol and the production technology of lignin building materials and decoration materials have reached an advanced level within China or even the world. Firm A has strong motivation and innovation in the research and development of green technologies while also undertaking the risks brought by the technical and market uncertainties in the process, showing a strong entrepreneurial orientation. Fourthly, the availability and reliability of research data is relatively high. The research team for this paper continued to track the sustainable entrepreneurial process of Firm from 2014 onwards, as well as conducting several investigations and in-depth exchanges with many senior executives of the enterprise. Therefore, we are familiar with the growth path, operation mode and other aspects of the enterprise, so the reliability and consistency of the information and data we obtain can be guaranteed. Finally, Firm A is a mid-sized enterprise engaging in sustainable entrepreneurship, since its establishment, Firm A has been engaged in the research, development and production of green and clean energy and environmental protection materials. At present, its research and development achievements are in the transitional phase from a small-scale production process to incremental production. In other words, the company has just undergone the completion of the "treasure hunting" stage and reached the "treasure excavation" stage of "Green Ocean Treasure Hunting". Its development is most in line with the current entrepreneurial environment in China. Thus, compared with enterprises that have been engaged in sustainable entrepreneurship for many years or have just started sustainable entrepreneurship, Firm A is more suitable as a reference for those enterprises that are or will soon start sustainable entrepreneurship. Therefore, this paper chooses Firm A as the research object to analyze the role policy support plays, in addition to the enterprises themselves, in product improvement, research and development, etc., in the process of sustainable entrepreneurship. This paper believes Firm A to be proof of its earlier propositions.

The Guiding Role of Policy Support

China's policy support for renewable energy was relatively weak before 2005. Since the promulgation of the Renewable Energy Law in 2005, policies on support and management of renewable energy have been promulgated one after another, and the policy support on renewable energy industry has also significantly increased. However, due to limitations resulting from technology development level and cost, the focus of policy support mainly lies in the fields of wind energy and solar energy utilization, which require relatively low cost and technical difficulty in the early stages. The support for renewable energy in other fields, such as biomass energy, was relatively weak, as shown by the "Renewable Energy Industry Development Guidance Catalog" issued by the National Development and Reform Commission(NDRC) in 2005, where more than half of projects, 58 out of a total of 88 projects, supported wind energy and solar energy projects. With the gradual improvement of technical skills, China has started to increase support for renewable energy in other fields such as biomass energy. For example, the "Medium and Long-term Development Plan for Renewable Energy" formulated by the NDRC in 2007 emphasizes that the technology to use non- grain raw materials to produce fuel ethanol has met preliminary commercial development conditions. The "12th Five-Year Plan for Biomass Energy Development" compiled by the National Energy Administration of China in 2012 focuses on the field of biomass energy, and emphasizes the development of non-grain biological liquid fuels as a key task, establishing a corresponding bio-ethanol and other cellulosic bio-fuels industrialization demonstration project. As China's support for biomass energy is gets increasingly stronger, the attractiveness of this field is gradually increasing. Mr. S, the founder of Firm A, who has been engaged in the production and sales of grain alcohol and possesses an in-depth understanding of the liquid fuel industry, has a strong interest in this field after noticing that China encouraged the production of biomass energy products. Therefore, since it was established Firm A has aimed at this field and hopes to take a place in this area.

As a large agricultural country, China produces a large amount of agricultural waste every year. In order to make full use of this waste and reduce pollution, China has promulgated many policies. For example, the "Opinions on Accelerating the Comprehensive Utilization of Crop Straw", which the State Council General Office issued in 2008, emphasizes the prohibition of open burning crop straw and strengthening the comprehensive utilization of straw. In his experience in the liquid fuel industry, Mr. S learned that there are a large number of crop straws in China, and that these straws are often incinerated without utilization, resulting in huge waste and pollution. Since straw is rich in cellulose, which has the potential to be used as a raw material in biomass liquid fuel production, the only thing missing is the industrial production technology to make use of this straw in the manufacture of biomass fuels. After studying relevant policies, Mr. S believes that policy support of biomass energy is gradually increasing, and its future market is worth to looking forward to. There are sufficient low-cost sources of agricultural waste in China and since the industrialized production of bio-ethanol and bio-butanol from this agricultural waste is technically possible to achieve, Mr. S decided to create Firm A and engage in business in this area.

With the development of Firm A's R&D activities to produce biomass fuels from straw, the lignin produced during this process is found to be an excellent material with strong stability and anti-aging properties. Increasingly serious concerns about the current damage caused by indoor air pollution have led to China's regulations on the quality of building decoration materials to address the hazards of formaldehyde and other decoration pollution like "Indoor Air Quality Standards". Firm A began to consider the use of lignin due to its excellent characteristics suitable for building decoration materials, and after repeated research and testing found that lignin materials have many excellent features, such as being flame retardant, waterproof, non-deforming, anti-aging, formaldehyde-free and having high pressure resistance, which is difficult to achieve with general wood. In recent years, China has introduced a series of policies to encourage prefabricated building to deal with the problem of inefficient use of resources in the construction industry, for instance prefabricated buildings are planned to account for 50% of new buildings until 2025 in the "Construction Industry Modernization Development Program" promulgated in 2015 by the Ministry of Housing and Urban-Rural Development. In 2016, the "Guiding Opinions on Vigorously Developing Prefabricated Buildings" promulgated by the State Council opened the door to Firm A for its application of lignin materials. In order to maximize the advantages of lignin materials, Firm A invested to set up Firm B to specialize in the production and application of lignin materials and to make corresponding innovations in response to the promising prospect of the prefabricated buildings promoted by China. Their intention is to further perfect and industrialize the use of lignin materials to produce building decorating materials and encourage the use of these new eco-friendly materials in the process of prefabricated building and decoration.

From the process by which Firm A was created and chose to enter into the biomass energy industry, invest in the establishment of Firm B and enter into the construction industry, we can see that a guiding role was played by policy support. The attraction brought by the corresponding policies promulgated by the government encouraged them to enter these two industries and make unremitting efforts.

The Driving Effect of Policy Support

In its sustainable entrepreneurship, Firm A constantly carries out product innovation, research and development. In addition to its continuous input in this process, policy support also provides impetus to it. For example, the "Renewable Energy Law" stipulates that in addition to encouraging enterprises to produce biological liquid fuels, the state also requires oil sales companies to include biological liquid fuels into their sales systems (such as ethanol gasoline). Biological liquid fuels also belong to the project of developing special fund support projects and allowing financial institutions to provide preferential loans with financially discounted interest. As well as regulations like the "Opinions on Accelerating the Comprehensive Utilization of Crop Straw" issued by the General Office of the State Council, the "Circular on Further Accelerating the Comprehensive Utilization of Crop Straw and Prohibition of Burning" promulgated by NDRC and other departments stipulates to prohibit the burning of straw and implement preferential tax policies to encourage its comprehensive utilization. These policies also subsidize the R&D of straw fuel ethanol production technology and equipment and encourage financial banking institutions to provide credit support and other policies for the enterprises to carry out straw storage, processing and utilization. In its R&D, purchase of equipment, procurement of materials and trial production, Firm A has invested a lot of resources, although policy support such as subsidies, tax incentives, credit support, and lending incentives has lessened the pressure on the company. Taking the cellulosic ethanol production business of Firm, a as an example, since 2012 the government's policy support of grain-based fuel ethanol has been gradually phased out, while subsidies for non-grain ethanol produced from raw materials such as cassava and cellulose have been relatively stable. Firm A, which started its cellulosic ethanol production line in 2014, also received some policy support during the production and sales of these products. On the one hand, the government's promotion of fuel ethanol and the reduction of support for grain-based fuel ethanol has opened up more market space for cellulosic ethanol. On the other hand, the subsidy policy has also been effective in reducing the cost of its products. The production data of Firm A shows that the cost of producing cellulosic ethanol per ton is about 7600 CNY, of which, 6 tons of raw materials (agricultural waste) costs about 3600 CNY and the processing cost is about 4000 CNY. The price of cellulosic ethanol entering China's automobile fuel ethanol system is about 8300 CNY per ton. At the same time, Firm A can produce 2 tons of by-product lignin thermoplastic materials (5000 CNY per ton) and 500 cubic meters of CNG (about 1750 CNY in total). Accordingly, the benefits are very substantial.

Since 2015, prefabricated building related policies have been intensively promulgated. For example, in 2015, the "Construction Industry Modernization Development Program" promulgated by the Ministry of Housing and Urban-Rural Development planned to make prefabricated buildings account for more than 20% of new buildings by 2020, reaching 50% by 2025. The "Industrial building evaluation standards" at the end of the same year also opted to comprehensively promote prefabricated buildings nationwide starting in 2016. The "Guiding Opinions on Vigorously Developing Prefabricated Buildings" promulgated by the General Office of the State Council in 2016 also required the development of prefabricated concrete structures, steel structures and modern wood structure buildings. These policies all emphasize that increasing the development of prefabricated buildings, thus expands the market for prefabricated buildings domestically and increases the demand for prefabricated buildings and related green building materials and prefabricated decoration. This demand also became the driving force that prompted Firm A to set up Firm B and enter into the construction industry. The "Guiding Opinions on Vigorously Developing Assembled Buildings" provides subsidisation policies and tax rebate policies on eligible prefabricated building related products and encourages local governments to implement support in planning, land supply, financial and other aspects. Moreover, there is additional direct policy support that can help Firm B's sustainable entrepreneurship relating to prefabricated buildings. The construction materials and furniture provided by Firm B is made by processing the lignin obtained from the biological refining of straw. Chinese policies promoting the comprehensive utilization of crop straw also provide tax support and credit support for this process. This direct policy support directly relieves the pressure on Firm B's resources for product research and development, trial production and other processes so that it can smoothly complete the research and development, production and construction of a wide range of environmental-friendly building and decoration materials. At present, Firm B has successfully used these environmental-friendly materials to build a building-decoration integrated sample of a prefabricated house.

We analyzed the process by which Firm A entered into the biomass energy industry to R&D, produce and sell cellulosic liquid fuels and of Firm B using lignin to research and produce building materials and entering into the field of prefabricated buildings. We found that national and local policies play a supportive role and it is this policy support that has helped to boost Firm A's development and reduce pressure from resource constraints and technological complexity.

Innovative Research in Sustainable Entrepreneurship

Firm A's sustainable entrepreneurship process was carried out after identifying potential opportunities to make biomass energy products from agricultural waste. It also constantly conducted innovative research during product development. On the one hand, there were many kinds of agricultural waste that could be used by Firm A (such as straw, weeds, fruit shells etc.) and there were also many potential products (such as fuel ethanol and bio-diesel). In addition to the technical possibilities, the question of which kind of raw materials to use to eventually produce the product requires market knowledge research. After broad market knowledge research, wasted straws, which caused serious pollution, and fuel ethanol, which was promoted by the government, became Firm A's main goal. On the other hand, as the market knowledge research continued, technical knowledge research also allowed Firm A to deepen its understanding of related knowledge. Their targeted innovation achievements gradually became locked on cellulose ethanol, bio-gas and lignin and other products produced by further processing agricultural waste, such as straw. At this time, in order to relieve the pressure caused by resource consumption in the process of product innovation and R&D, Firm A paid more attention to overcoming the technological complexity that hindered the industrial production of products such as cellulosic ethanol by straw. This process required repeated exploration in order achieve the desired results. In the process, the leading team, management personnel and technicians of Firm A continued to work day and night and minimized other expenses to focus on innovation, eventually realizing the technology to convert agricultural waste to cellulose ethanol on an industrial scale in 2014. In the scientific and technological appraisal done by the Chinese Academy of Sciences and the Department of Industry and Information of Jilin Province, this technology has been identified as at an advanced level internationally.

The same applies to the R&D and utilization of lignin materials and the company's entry into the field of prefabricated buildings. While researching market knowledge, Firm A identified the opportunity brought by its lignin products in the production of environmental-friendly building materials, as well as China's efforts to promote prefabricated buildings, leading them to invest establish Firm B, which specializes in this business. During this process, Firm B understood consumer preferences and market needs through constant market knowledge research, and adjusted and improved the performance of its lignin materials and the design and construction of its prefabricated buildings through technical knowledge research. Therefore, they produced building materials and furniture with better performance and better application of lignin materials in the prefabricated buildings and prefabricated decoration, managing to realize a near perfect integration of materials, construction and decoration.

We analyzed the process of developing and producing biomass energy products from agricultural waste by Firm A and the process of developing and manufacturing building materials and innovative prefabricated building technology with the use of lignin by Firm B. Through this analysis it can be found that innovative research plays an essential role in sustainable entrepreneurship. One the one hand, technical knowledge research helps it to overcome technological complexity. On the other hand, market knowledge research helps it to determine its own development direction more accurately and move its sustainable entrepreneurial activity forward towards its targeted innovative achievements.

CONCLUSION AND OUTLOOK

This paper studies sustainable entrepreneurial activities under the guidance of policy support in the transitional economy, and gives a more in-depth understanding of sustainable entrepreneurship by making the process analogous to process of conducting a "treasure hunt in the sea". On this basis, we construct the "Green Ocean Treasure Hunting" model and regard the factors that affect the development of sustainable entrepreneurial enterprises, such as government support, innovative research and technological complexity, as the forces acting on enterprises. We use this mechanics model to analyze the influences that the enterprise will face in its pursuit of innovation achievement during the process of sustainable entrepreneurship. Based on the analysis process, several propositions are proposed, and the case of a high-tech enterprise in China is selected as a proof of these propositions. This paper constructs and analyzes the theory of the "Green Ocean Treasure Hunting" model, which draws on physics principles that can make the process of sustainable entrepreneurship more visible and easier to understand. In practice, the research in this paper may be a reference for individuals and organizations that are willing to conduct sustainable entrepreneurship. It propounds that they should give full consideration to the motivation and resistance of sustainable entrepreneurship before making decisions. As for those enterprises that are already undertaking sustainable entrepreneurship, they should make full use of policy support and innovative research so as to reduce the negative impact caused taking a wrong direction.

The research in this paper draws on the principles of physics, but for the impact of various forces that affect the sustainable entrepreneurial enterprises, we mainly did qualitative analysis. Future research could conduct quantitative research based on more primary and secondary data, so as to better reflect the role of the mechanical model. In addition, this paper mainly studies the sustainable entrepreneurship process under the guidance of policy support. In order to make the research process clearer, it ignores the influence of other factors in the process of building and analyzing models. Future research could also consider the role of culture, enterprise structure and other internal and external factors on sustainable entrepreneurial enterprises.

REFERENCES

Baldwin, C. Y., & Clark, K. B. (2000). *Design Rules: The Power of Modularity*. Cambridge, MA: MIT Press. doi:10.7551/mitpress/2366.001.0001

Block, F. (2008). Swimming against the current: the rise of a hidden developmental state in the united states. *Politics & Society*, *36*(2), 169-206.

Busenitz, L. W., Gomez, C., & Spencer, J. W. (2000). Country institutional profiles: Unlocking entrepreneurial phenomena. *Academy of Management Journal*, *43*(5), 994–1003.

Cappa, F., Sette, F. D., Hayes, D., & Rosso, F. (2016). How to deliver open sustainable innovation: An integrated approach for a sustainable marketable product. *Sustainability*, *8*(12), 1341. doi:10.3390u8121341

Chen, J., Chen, L., Chen, J., & Kefan, X. (2018). Mechanism and policy combination of technical sustainable entrepreneurship crowdfunding in china: A system dynamics analysis. *Journal of Cleaner Production*, *177*, 610–620. doi:10.1016/j.jclepro.2017.12.217

Cohen, B., & Winn, M. I. (2007). Market imperfections, opportunity and sustainable entrepreneurship. *Journal of Business Venturing*, *22*(1), 29–49. doi:10.1016/j.jbusvent.2004.12.001

Corbett, J., & Montgomery, A. W. (2017). Environmental entrepreneurship and interorganizational arrangements: A model of social-benefit market creation. *Strategic Entrepreneurship Journal*, *11*(4), 422–440. doi:10.1002ej.1250

Dean, T. J., & Mcmullen, J. S. (2007). Toward a theory of sustainable entrepreneurship: Reducing environmental degradation through entrepreneurial action. *Journal of Business Venturing*, *22*(1), 50–76. doi:10.1016/j.jbusvent.2005.09.003

Dyer, W. G. Jr, & Wilkins, A. L. (1991). Better stories, not better constructs, to generate better theory: A rejoinder to Eisenhardt. *Academy of Management Review*, *16*(3), 613–619. doi:10.5465/amr.1991.4279492

Eisenhardt, K. M. (1989). Building theories from case study research. *Academy of Management Review*, *14*(4), 532–550. doi:10.5465/amr.1989.4308385

Finance, T., & Bigdata, J. (2017). *Big Data Interpretation of the New Energy Industry: The Top 10 Occupy 70% Market*. Available online: https://finance.qq.com/original/bigdata/xinnengyuan.html

Ge, B., Jiang, D., Gao, Y., & Tsai, S.-B. (2016). The influence of legitimacy on a proactive green orientation and green performance: A study based on transitional economy scenarios in china. *Sustainability*, *8*(12), 1344. doi:10.3390u8121344

Gümüsay, & Aslan, A. (2017). Unpacking entrepreneurial opportunities: An institutional logics perspective. *Innovation*, *20*(3), 209–222.

Hockerts, K., & Wuestenhagen, R. (2010). Greening Goliaths versus emerging Davids - Theorizing about the role of incumbents and new entrants in sustainable entrepreneurship. *Journal of Business Venturing*, *25*(5), 481–492. doi:10.1016/j.jbusvent.2009.07.005

Jonatan, P. (2015). Sustainable entrepreneurship and corporate political activity: Overcoming market barriers in the clean energy sector. *Entrepreneurship Theory and Practice*, *39*(3), 633–654. doi:10.1111/etap.12055

Katila, R., & Ahuja, G. (2002). Something old, something new: A longitudinal study of search behavior and new product introduction. *Academy of Management Journal*, *45*(6), 1183–1194.

Kearins, K., & Collins, E. (2012). Making sense of ecopreneurs' decisions to sell up. *Business Strategy and the Environment*, *21*(2), 71–85. doi:10.1002/bse.710

Kim, W. C., & Mauborgne, R. A. (2005). *Blue ocean strategy*. Boston, MA: Harvard Business School Press.

Köhler, C., Sofka, W., & Grimpe, C. (2012). Selective search, sectoral patterns, and the impact on product innovation performance. *Research Policy*, *41*(8), 1344–1356. doi:10.1016/j.respol.2012.03.020

Lee, F. (2001). Technology as a complex adaptive system: Evidence from patent data. *Research Policy*, *30*(7), 1019–1039. doi:10.1016/S0048-7333(00)00135-9

Lewis, J. I., & Wiser, R. H. (2007, March). Fostering a renewable energy technology industry: An international comparison of wind industry policy support mechanisms. *Energy Policy*, *35*(3), 1844–1857. doi:10.1016/j.enpol.2006.06.005

Marra, A., Antonelli, P., Dell'Anna, L., & Pozzi, C. (2015). A network analysis using metadata to investigate innovation in clean-tech – implications for energy policy. *Energy Policy*, *86*, 17–26. doi:10.1016/j.enpol.2015.06.025

Marra, A., Antonelli, P., & Pozzi, C. (2017). Emerging green-tech specializations and clusters - a network analysis on technological innovation at the metropolitan level. *Renewable & Sustainable Energy Reviews*, *67*(1), 1037–1046. doi:10.1016/j.rser.2016.09.086

Mcwilliams, A., & Siegel, D. (2001). Corporate social responsibility: A theory of the firm perspective. *Academy of Management Review*, *26*(1), 117–127. doi:10.5465/amr.2001.4011987

Nair, S. (2009). Green entrepreneurship (ge) and green value added (gva): A conceptual framework. *International Journal of Entrepreneurship*, *13*, 21–34.

OECD. (2017). *OECD Entrepreneurship at a Glance 2011*. Available online: https://www.oecd-ilibrary.org/docserver/download/3011021e.pdf?expires=1517390284&id=id&accname=guest&checksum=E15844D9C63CC62C99688EBE360BC2DF

Pettigrew, A. M. (1990). Longitudinal field research on change: theory and practice. *Organization Science*, *1*(3), 267-292.

Porter, M. E., & Linde, C. V. D. (1995). Towards a new conception of the environment-competitiveness relationship. *The Journal of Economic Perspectives*, *4*(4), 97–118. doi:10.1257/jep.9.4.97

Ramanathan, R., He, Q., Black, A., Ghobadian, A., & Gallear, D. (2017). Environmental regulations, innovation and firm performance: A revisit of the porter hypothesis. *Journal of Cleaner Production*, *155*, 79–92. doi:10.1016/j.jclepro.2016.08.116

Ricart, J. E., Rodríguez, M. A., & Sanchez, P. (2002). Sustainable development and the sustainability of competitive advantage: A dynamic and sustainable view of the firm. *Creativity and Innovation Management*, *11*(3), 11, 135–146.

Shepherd, D. A., & Patzelt, H. (2011). The new field of sustainable entrepreneurship: Studying entrepreneurial action linking "what is to be sustained" with "what is to be developed". *Entrepreneurship Theory and Practice*, *35*(1), 137–163. doi:10.1111/j.1540-6520.2010.00426.x

Siggelkow, N. (2007). Persuasion with case studies. *Academy of Management Journal*, *50*(1), 20–24. doi:10.5465/amj.2007.24160882

Silajdzic, I., Kurtagic, S. M., & Vucijak, B. (2015). Green entrepreneurship in transition economies: a case study of bosnia and herzegovina. *Journal of Cleaner Production*, *88*, 376-384.

Sofka, W., & Grimpe, C. (2010). Specialized search and innovation performance – evidence across europe. *R & D Management*, *40*(3), 310–323. doi:10.1111/j.1467-9310.2010.00592.x

Stigson, P., Dotzauer, E., & Yan, J. (2009). Improving policy making through government–industry policy learning: The case of a novel swedish policy framework. *Applied Energy*, *86*(4), 399–406. doi:10.1016/j.apenergy.2008.05.015

Wagner, M., & Schaltegger, S. (2012). Sustainable entrepreneurship and sustainability innovation: Categories and interactions. *Business Strategy and the Environment*, *32*(2), 110–111.

Yin, R. K. (2013). *Case Study Research Design and Methods*. Thousand Oaks, CA: SAGE Publications Inc.

Compilation of References

Abor, J., & Quartey, P. (2010). Issues in SME development in Ghana and South Africa. *International Research Journal of Finance and Economics*, *39*(6), 215–228.

Acs, Z., & Armington, C. (2004). Employment Growth and Entrepreneurial Activity inCities. *Regional Studies*, *8*(8), 911–927. doi:10.1080/0034340042000280938

Acs, Z., Autio, A., & Szerb, L. (2014). National Systems of Entrepreneurship: Measurement ssues and policy implications. *Research Policy*, *43*(3), 476–494. doi:10.1016/j.respol.2013.08.016

Adomako, S., Danso, A., & Ampadu, E. (2015). Institutional outlook of the entrepreneurial climate in Ghana. *International Journal of Social Economics*, *42*(6), 566–582. doi:10.1108/IJSE-09-2013-0206

Adusei, M. (2016). Does entrepreneurship promote economic growth in Africa? *African Development Review*, *28*(2), 201–214. doi:10.1111/1467-8268.12190

Aernoudt, R. (2004). Incubators: Tool for entrepreneurship? *Small Business Economics*, *23*(2), 127–135. doi:10.1023/B:SBEJ.0000027665.54173.23

Aerts, K., Matthyssens, P., & Vandenbempt, K. (2007). Critical role and screening practices of European business incubators. *Technovation*, *27*(5), 254–267. doi:10.1016/j.technovation.2006.12.002

Ajzen, I. (1991). The theory of planned behavior. *Organizational Behavior and Human Decision Processes*, *50*(2), 179–211. doi:10.1016/0749-5978(91)90020-T

Akhter, N., Sieger, P., & Chirico, F. (2016). If we can't have it then no one should shutting down versus selling in family business portfolios. *Strategic Entrepreneurship Journal*, *10*(4), 371–394. doi:10.1002ej.1237

Akimova, I., & Schwodiauer, G. (2005). 10. The effect of trust in courts on the performance of Ukrainian SMEs. *Trust and Entrepreneurship: A West-East Perspective*, 156.

Aldrich, H. E., & Martinez, M. A. (2001). Many are called, but few are chosen: An evolutionary perspective for the study of entrepreneurship. *Entrepreneurship Theory and Practice*, *25*(4), 41–56. doi:10.1177/104225870102500404

Allen, D. N., & Rahman, S. (1985). Small business incubators: a positive environment for entrepreneurship. *Journal of Small Business Management, 23*(3), 12.

Allen, D. N., & Levine, V. (1986). *Nurturing advanced technology enterprises: Emerging issues in state and local economic development policy*. Praeger Publishers.

Allen, D. N., & McCluskey, R. (1991). Structure, policy, services, and performance in the business incubator industry. *Entrepreneurship Theory and Practice, 15*(2), 61–77. doi:10.1177/104225879101500207

Alvarez, S., & Busenitz, L. (2001). The entrepreneurship of resource-based theory. *Journal of Management, 6*(6), 755–775. doi:10.1177/014920630102700609

Amankwah-Amoah, J., & Hinson, R. E. (2019). Contextual influences on new technology ventures: A study of domestic firms in Ghana. *Technological Forecasting and Social Change, 143*, 289–296. doi:10.1016/j.techfore.2019.01.019

Amaral, A. M., Rui, B., & Lima, F. (2007). Entrepreneurial exit and firm performance. *Frontiers of Entrepreneurship Research, 27*(5), 1-15.

Amoako, I. O., & Lyon, F. (2014). 'We don't deal with courts': Cooperation and alternative institutions shaping exporting relationships of small and medium-sized enterprises in Ghana. *International Small Business Journal-Researching Entrepreneurship, 32*(2), 117–139. doi:10.1177/0266242613484778

Andersen, P., & Petersen, N. C. (1993). A procedure for ranking efficient units in data envelopment analysis. *Management Science, 39*(10), 1261–1264. doi:10.1287/mnsc.39.10.1261

Anokhin, S., Wincent, J., & Autio, E. (2011). Operationalizing opportunities in entrepreneurship research: Use of data envelopment analysis. *Small Business Economics, 37*(1), 39–57. doi:10.100711187-009-9227-1

Aoki, M., & Hayami, Y. (2001). *Communities and Markets in Economic Development*. Oxford: Oxford University Press. doi:10.1093/0199241015.001.0001

Apa, R., Grandinetti, R., & Sedita, S. R. (2017). The social and business dimensions of a networked business incubator: The case of H-Farm. *Journal of Small Business and Enterprise Development, 24*(2), 198–221. doi:10.1108/JSBED-07-2016-0103

Ardayfio-Schandorf, E. (1994). *Family and Development in Ghana: Proceedings of International Training and Research Workshop Held at the University of Ghana, Legon on 14th-18th December, 1992*. Ghana Universities Press.

Ardichvili, A., Cardozo, R., & Ray, S. (2003). A theory of entrepreneurial opportunity identification and development. *Journal of Business Venturing, 18*(1), 105–123. doi:10.1016/S0883-9026(01)00068-4

Armstrong, J. S., & Overton, T. S. (1977). Estimating nonresponse bias in mail surveys. *JMR, Journal of Marketing Research, 14*(3), 396–402. doi:10.1177/002224377701400320

Audretsch, D. B., & Belitski, M. (2017). Entrepreneurial ecosystems in cities: Estabilshing the framework conditions. *The Journal of Technology Transfer*, *42*(5), 1030–1051. doi:10.100710961-016-9473-8

Audretsch, D., Mason, C., Miles, M. P., & O'Connor, A. (2018). The dynamics of Entrepreneurial ecosystems. *Entrepreneurship and Regional Development*, *30*(3-4), 471–474. doi:10.1080/08985626.2018.1436035

Autio, E., Keeley, R. H., Klofsten, M., Parker, G. C., & Hay, M. (2001). Entrepreneurial Intent among Students in Scandinavia and in the USA. *Enterprise and Innovation Management Studies*, *2*(2), 145–160. doi:10.1080/14632440110094632

Avram, E. G., & Avasilcai, S. (2014). Symbiosis process in business ecosystem. *Advanced Materials Research*, *3483*(1036), 1066–1071. doi:10.4028/www.scientific.net/AMR.1036.1066

Babatunde, M. A. (2009). Export performance in sub-saharan Africa: An explanation. *Journal of Economic Theory*, *3*(3), 41–52.

Bailetti, T. (2012). Technology entrepreneurship: overview, definition, and distinctive aspects. *Technology Innovation Management Review, 2012*(2), 5-12.

Balcaen, S., Manigart, S., Buyze, J., & Ooghe, H. (2012). Firm exit after distress: Differentiating between bankruptcy, voluntary liquidation and M&A. *Small Business Economics*, *39*(4), 949–975. doi:10.100711187-011-9342-7

Baldwin, C. Y., & Clark, K. B. (2000). *Design Rules: The Power of Modularity*. Cambridge, MA: MIT Press. doi:10.7551/mitpress/2366.001.0001

Balogun, W., Dahalan, J., & Hassan, S. (2016). Long Run Impacts of Interest Rate Liberalization on Stock Market Development. *Procedia: Social and Behavioral Sciences*, *219*, 126–133. doi:10.1016/j.sbspro.2016.04.053

Bandura, A. (2001). Social cognitive theory: An agentic perspective. *Annual Review of Psychology*, *52*(1), 1–26. doi:10.1146/annurev.psych.52.1.1 PMID:11148297

Barajas, A., Ralph, C., & Seyed, R. Y. (2012). *The Finance and Growth Nexus Re-examined: Do All Countries Benefit Equally?* IMF Working Paper.

Baraldi, E., & Havenvid, M. I. (2016). Identifying new dimensions of business incubation: A multi-level analysis of Karolinska Institute's incubation system. *Technovation*, *50*, 53–68. doi:10.1016/j.technovation.2015.08.003

Barbero, J. L., Casillas, J. C., Ramos, A., & Guitar, S. (2012). Revisiting incubation performance: How incubator typology affects results. *Technological Forecasting and Social Change*, *79*(5), 888–902. doi:10.1016/j.techfore.2011.12.003

Barney, J. (1991). Firm resources and sustained competitive advantage. *Journal of Management*, *17*(1), 99–120. doi:10.1177/014920639101700108

Barney, J. B. (1991). Firm resources and sustained competitive advantage. *Advances in Strategic Management, 17*(1), 3–10.

Barrell, R., Karim, D., & Ventouri, A. (2017). Interest rate liberalization and capital adequacy in models of financial crises. *Journal of Financial Stability, 33*, 261–272. doi:10.1016/j.jfs.2016.09.001

Baum, J. R., & Locke, E. A. (2004). The relationship of entrepreneurial traits, skill and motivation to subsequent venture growth. *The Journal of Applied Psychology, 89*(4), 587–598. doi:10.1037/0021-9010.89.4.587 PMID:15327346

Baum, L. (2004). Social cognitive theory of posttraumatic recovery: The role of perceived self-efficacy. *Behaviour Research and Therapy, 10*(42), 1129–1148. PMID:15350854

Beck, T., Hans, D., & Christiane, K. (2014). Is more finance better? Disentangling intermediation and size effects of financial systems. *Journal of Financial Stability, 10*(10), 50–64. doi:10.1016/j.jfs.2013.03.005

Beehr, T. A., & McGrath, J. E. (1992). Social support, occupational stress and anxiety. *Anxiety, Stress, and Coping, 5*(1), 7–19. doi:10.1080/10615809208250484

Beiler, H. (2017). Do you dare? The effect of economic conditions on entrepreneurship among college graduates. *Labour Economics, 47*(S1), 64–74. doi:10.1016/j.labeco.2017.05.003

Bergek, A., & Norrman, C. (2008). Incubator best practice: A framework. *Technovation, 28*(1-2), 20–28. doi:10.1016/j.technovation.2007.07.008

Berger & Gleisner. (2009). Emergence of financial intermediaries in electronic markets: The case of online P2P lending. *BuR Business Research Journal, 2*(1).

Bhabra-Remedios, R. K., & Cornelius, B. (2003). Cracks in the egg: improving performance measures in business incubator research. *16th Annual Conference of Small Enterprise Association of Australia and New Zealand.*

Bika, Z. (2012). Entrepreneurial sons, patriarchy and the Colonels' experiment in Thessaly, rural Greece. *Entrepreneurship and Regional Development, 24*(3-4), 235–257. doi:10.1080/08985626.2012.670915

Bird, B. J. (1988). Implementing entrepreneurial ideas: The case for intention. *Academy of Management Review, 13*(3), 442–454. doi:10.5465/amr.1988.4306970

Block, F. (2008). Swimming against the current: the rise of a hidden developmental state in the united states. *Politics & Society, 36*(2), 169-206.

Boachie-Mensah, F., & Marfo-Yiadom, E. (2007). *Entrepreneurship and small business management.* Accra, Ghana: Ghana Universities Press.

Bodlaj M, Čater B. (2019). The impact of environmental turbulence on the perceived importance of innovation and innovativeness in SMEs. *Journal of Small Business Management, 57*(sup2), 417-435.

Bollinger, L., Hope, K., & Utterback, J. M. (1983). A review of literature and hypotheses on new technology-based firms. *Research Policy, 12*(1), 1–14. doi:10.1016/0048-7333(83)90023-9

Borio, C. (2008). *The financial turmoil of 2007-? A preliminary assessment and some policy considerations*. Academic Press.

Boschma, R., & Iammarino, S. (2009). Related variety, trade linkages, and regional growth inItaly. *Economic Geography, 85*(3), 289–311. doi:10.1111/j.1944-8287.2009.01034.x

Bosma, N., & Kelley, D. (2019). *Global Entrepreneurship Monitor 2018/2019 Global Report*. Global Entrepreneurship Research Association.

Boso, N., Adeleye, I., Ibeh, K., & Chizema, A. (2019). The internationalization of African firms: Opportunities, challenges, and risks. *Thunderbird International Business Review, 61*(1), 5–12. doi:10.1002/tie.21977

Boyd, N., & Vozikis, G. S. (1994). The Influence of self-efficacy on the development of entrepreneurial intentions and actions. *Entrepreneurship Theory and Practice, 18*(1), 63–77. doi:10.1177/104225879401800404

Breugst, N., Domurath, A., Patzelt, H., & Klaukien, A. (2012). Perceptions of entrepreneurial passion and employees' commitment to entrepreneurial ventures. *Entrepreneurship Theory and Practice, 36*(1), 171–192. doi:10.1111/j.1540-6520.2011.00491.x

Bruce, E. (1999). Threshold effects in non-dynamic panels: Estimation, testing, and inference. *Journal of Econometrics, 93*(4), 345–368.

Bruneel, J., Ratinho, T., Clarysse, B., & Groen, A. (2012). The evolution of business incubators: Comparing demand and supply of business incubation services across different incubator generations. *Technovation, 32*(2), 110–121. doi:10.1016/j.technovation.2011.11.003

Bruno, A. V., Mcquarrie, E. F., & Torgrimson, C. G. (1992). The evolution of new technology ventures over 20 years: Patterns of failure, merger and survival. *Journal of Business Venturing, 7*(4), 291–302. doi:10.1016/0883-9026(92)90003-A

Brunsman, K. J., & Sharfman, M. P. (1993). Strategic choices and niche movements: a probabilistic model of organizational selection and mortality. *Academy of Management Annual Meeting Proceedings, 1993*(1), 2-6. 10.5465/ambpp.1993.10315156

Brush, C. G., Manolova, T. S., & Edelman, L. F. (2008). Properties of emerging organizations: An empirical test. *Journal of Business Venturing, 23*(5), 547–566. doi:10.1016/j.jbusvent.2007.09.002

Bruton, G. D., Ahlstrom, D., & Li, H. L. (2010). Institutional theory and entrepreneurship: Where are we now and where do we need to move in the future? *Entrepreneurship Theory and Practice, 34*(3), 421–440. doi:10.1111/j.1540-6520.2010.00390.x

Bruton, G. D., & Rubanik, Y. (2002). Resources of the firm, Russian high-technology startups, and firm growth. *Journal of Business Venturing*, *17*(6), 553–576. doi:10.1016/S0883-9026(01)00079-9

Burgelman, R. A., & Grove, A. S. (1996). Strategic dissonance. *California Management Review*, *38*(2), 8–28. doi:10.2307/41165830

Burgelman, R. A., & Grove, A. S. (2007). Cross-boundary disruptors: Powerful inter-industry entrepreneurial change agents. *Research Papers*, *1*(3-4), 315–327. doi:10.1002ej.27

Burnett, H. H. M., & McMurray, A. J. (2008). Exploring business incubation from a family perspective: How start-up family firms experience the incubation process in two Australian incubators. *Small Enterprise Research*, *16*(2), 60–75. doi:10.5172er.16.2.60

Busenitz, L. W., & Barney, J. B. (1997). Differences between entrepreneurs and managers in large organizations: Biases and heuristics in strategic decision-making. *Journal of Business Venturing*, *12*(1), 9–30. doi:10.1016/S0883-9026(96)00003-1

Busenitz, L. W., Gomez, C., & Spencer, J. W. (2000). Country institutional profiles: Unlocking entrepreneurial phenomena. *Academy of Management Journal*, *43*(5), 994–1003. doi:10.5465/1556423

Busenitz, L. W., West, G. P., & Shepherd, D. (2003). Entrepreneurship research in emergence:Past trends and future directions. *Journal of Management*, *29*(3), 285–308. doi:10.1016/S0149-2063(03)00013-8

Cai, L., Chen, B., Chen, J., & Bruton, G. D. (2017). Dysfunctional competition & innovation strategy of new ventures as they mature. *Journal of Business Research*, *78*, 111–118. doi:10.1016/j.jbusres.2017.05.008

Cai, L., Hughes, M., & Yin, M. (2014). The relationship between resource acquisition methods and firm performance in Chinese new ventures: The intermediate effect of learning capability. *Journal of Small Business Management*, *52*(3), 365–389. doi:10.1111/jsbm.12039

Cai, L., Liu, Q., Zhu, X., & Deng, S. L. (2014). Market orientation and technological innovation: The moderating role of entrepreneurial support policies. *The International Entrepreneurship and Management Journal*, 1–27.

Cai, L., Peng, X., Satish, N., & Wang, L. (2016). Entrepreneurial ecosystem: Review and prospects. *Jilin University Journal Social Sciences Edition*, *56*(1), 5–16.

Cai, L., Tang, S. Q., Ma, Y. L., & Gao, X. (2014). Research on the relationship among entrepreneurial learning, entrepreneurial ability and new enterprise performance. *Studies in Science of Science*, *32*(8), 1189–1197.

Callanan, G. A., & Zimmerman, M. (2016). To be or not to be an entrepreneur: Applying a normative model to career decisions. *Journal of Career Development*, *43*(5), 447–461. doi:10.1177/0894845316633525

Cappa, F., Sette, F. D., Hayes, D., & Rosso, F. (2016). How to deliver open sustainable innovation: An integrated approach for a sustainable marketable product. *Sustainability*, *8*(12), 1341. doi:10.3390u8121341

Cardon, M. S., Gregoire, D. A., Stevens, C. E., & Patel, P. C. (2013). Measuring entrepreneurial passion: Conceptual foundations and scale validation. *Journal of Business Venturing*, *28*(3), 373–396. doi:10.1016/j.jbusvent.2012.03.003

Carlsson, B. (2002). Institutions, entrepreneurship, and growth: Biomedicine and polymers in Sweden and Ohio. *Small Business Economics*, *19*(2), 105–121. doi:10.1023/A:1016235022728

Carpenter, M., Sanders, G., & Education, P. (2015). Strategic management: pearson new international edition: concepts and cases. *Long Range Planning, 29*(6), 907-908.

Casson, M. (1982). *The entrepreneur*. Totowa, NJ: Barnes and Noble Books.

Cecchetti & Kharroubi. (2012). *Reassessing the Impact of Finance on Growth*. BIS Working Paper.

Chandra, A., & Chao, C. A. (2011). Growth and evolution of high-technology business incubation in China. *Human Systems Management*, *30*(1-2), 55–69. doi:10.3233/HSM-2011-0739

Chen, C. J. (2009). Technology commercialization, incubator and venture capital, and new venture performance. *Journal of Business Research*, *62*(1), 93–103. doi:10.1016/j.jbusres.2008.01.003

Chen, C., Greene, P., & Crick, A. (1998). Does entrepreneurial self-efficacy distinguish entrepreneurs from managers? *Business Venturing*, *13*(4), 295–316. doi:10.1016/S0883-9026(97)00029-3

Chen, J., Chen, L., Chen, J., & Kefan, X. (2018). Mechanism and policy combination of technical sustainable entrepreneurship crowdfunding in china: A system dynamics analysis. *Journal of Cleaner Production*, *177*, 610–620. doi:10.1016/j.jclepro.2017.12.217

Chen, M. J. (1996). Competitive analysis interfirm rivalry:Toward a theoretical integration. *Academy of Management Review*, *21*(1), 100–134. doi:10.5465/amr.1996.9602161567

Chen, M. J. (2007). Competitive dynamics research:An insider's odyssey. *Asia Pacific Journal of Management*, (26), 5–25.

Chen, M. J. (2009). Competitive dynamics research: An insider's odyssey. *Asia Pacific Journal of Management*, *26*(1), 5–25. doi:10.100710490-008-9110-7

Chen, M. J., & Miller, D. (2012). Competitive dynamics:Themes,trends,and a prospective research platform. *The Academy of Management Annals*, (6): 1–89.

Chen, Z., & Peng, Y. (2006). Evaluation Indicator System and Model Construction of Regional Financial Eco-environment. *Statistics & Decisions*, (6), 31–35.

Chiles, T. H., Bluedorn, A. C., & Gupta, V. K. (2007). Beyond creative destruction and entrepreneurial discovery: A radical Austrian approach to entrepreneurship. *Organization Studies*, *28*(4), 467–493. doi:10.1177/0170840606067996

Čihák & Demirgüč-Kunt. (2013). *Financial Development in 205 Economies, 1960 to 2010.* National Bureau of Economic Research.

Ciszewska-Mlinaric, M. (2018). Export Intensity, Geographic Diversification and the Role of Public Support: The Evidence from Old and New Europe SMEs. *Entrepreneurial Business and Economics Review*, *6*(2), 45–69. doi:10.15678/EBER.2018.060203

Cohen, B. (2006). Sustainable valleyentrepreneurial ecosystems. *Business Strategy and the Environment*, *15*(1), 1–14. doi:10.1002/bse.428

Cohen, B., & Winn, M. I. (2007). Market imperfections, opportunity and sustainable entrepreneurship. *Journal of Business Venturing*, *22*(1), 29–49. doi:10.1016/j.jbusvent.2004.12.001

Cope, J. (2011). Entrepreneurial learning from failure: An interpretative phenomenological analysis. *Journal of Business Venturing*, *26*(6), 604–623. doi:10.1016/j.jbusvent.2010.06.002

Corbett, J., & Montgomery, A. W. (2017). Environmental entrepreneurship and interorganizational arrangements: A model of social-benefit market creation. *Strategic Entrepreneurship Journal*, *11*(4), 422–440. doi:10.1002ej.1250

Coviello, N. E., & McAuley, A. (1999). Internationalisation and the Smaller Firm: A Review of Contemporary Empirical Research. *MIR. Management International Review*, *39*(3), 223–256.

Crocker, J., & Wolfe, C. T. (2001). Contingencies of self-worth. *Psychological Review*, *14*(4), 593–623. doi:10.1037/0033-295X.108.3.593 PMID:11488379

Cubillas, E., & González, F. (2014). Financial liberalization and bank risk-taking: International evidence. *Journal of Financial Stability*, *11*, 32–48. doi:10.1016/j.jfs.2013.11.001

Dabo, Z. (2012). The impact of financial liberalisation on the performance of banks in Nigerian. *Procedia: Social and Behavioral Sciences*, *62*, 548–554. doi:10.1016/j.sbspro.2012.09.091

Dal Colle, A. (2018). The mechanics of commercial banking liberalization and growth. *Journal of Banking & Finance*, *86*, 194–203. doi:10.1016/j.jbankfin.2016.04.014

Dalborg, C., & Wincent, J. (2015). The idea is not enough: The role of self-efficacy in mediating the relationship between pull entrepreneurship and founder passion–a research note. *International Small Business Journal*, *33*(8), 974–984. doi:10.1177/0266242614543336

Dalitso, K., & Peter, Q. (2000). *The policy environment for promoting small and medium-sized enterprises in Ghana and Malawi*. Manchester: Institute for Development Policy and Management, University of Manchester.

Dana, L.-P. (2006). *Entrepreneurship and SMEs in the Euro-Zone: towards a theory of symbiotic entrepreneurship*. London: Imperial College Press. doi:10.1142/p445

Dandapani, K., & Shahrokhi, M. (2008). E-finance: Status, innovations, resources and future challenges. *Managerial Finance*.

Dau, L. A., & Cuervo-Cazurra, A. (2014). To formalize or not to formalize: Entrepreneurship and pro-market institutions. *Journal of Business Venturing*, *29*(5), 668–686. doi:10.1016/j.jbusvent.2014.05.002

Davidsson, P., & Honig, B. (2003). The role of social and human capital among nascent entrepreneurs. *Journal of Business Venturing*, *18*(3), 301–331. doi:10.1016/S0883-9026(02)00097-6

Dawson, C., & Henley, A. (2013). Over-optimism and entry and exit from self-employment. *International Small Business Journal*, *31*(8), 938–954. doi:10.1177/0266242612445462

De Carolis, D. M., Litzky, B. E., & Eddleston, K. A. (2009). Why networks enhance the progress of new venture creation: The influence of social capital and cognition. *Entrepreneurship Theory and Practice*, *33*(2), 527–545. doi:10.1111/j.1540-6520.2009.00302.x

Deakins, D., & Freel, M. (1998). Entrepreneurial learning and the growth process in SMEs. *The Learning Organization*, *5*(3), 144–155. doi:10.1108/09696479810223428

Dean, T. J., & Mcmullen, J. S. (2007). Toward a theory of sustainable entrepreneurship: Reducing environmental degradation through entrepreneurial action. *Journal of Business Venturing*, *22*(1), 50–76. doi:10.1016/j.jbusvent.2005.09.003

DeTienne, D. R. (2010). Entrepreneurial exit as a critical component of the: Theoretical development. *Journal of Business Venturing*, *25*(2), 203–215. doi:10.1016/j.jbusvent.2008.05.004

DeTienne, D. R., & Cardon, M. S. (2012). Impact of founder experience on exit intentions. *Small Business Economics*, *38*(4), 351–374. doi:10.100711187-010-9284-5

DeTienne, D. R., Mckelvie, A., & Chandler, G. N. (2015). Making sense of entrepreneurial exit strategies: A typology and test. *Journal of Business Venturing*, *30*(2), 255–272. doi:10.1016/j.jbusvent.2014.07.007

DeTienne, D. R., & Wennberg, K. (2016). Studying exit from entrepreneurship: New directions and insights. *International Small Business Journal*, *34*(2), 151–156. doi:10.1177/0266242615601202

Dimov, D. (2007). From opportunity insight to opportunity intention: The importance of person-situation learning match. *Entrepreneurship Theory and Practice*, *31*(4), 561–583. doi:10.1111/j.1540-6520.2007.00188.x

Dimov, D. (2010). Nascent entrepreneurs and venture emergence: Opportunity confidence, human capital, and early planning. *Journal of Management Studies*, *47*(6), 1123–1153. doi:10.1111/j.1467-6486.2009.00874.x

Djankov, S., Miguel, E., Qian, Y., Roland, G., & Zhuravskaya, E. (2004). *Who Are Russia's Entrepreneurs*. Washington, DC: The World Bank.

Drnovsek, M., Cardon, M. S., & Patel, P. C. (2016). Direct and indirect effects of passion on growing technology ventures. *Strategic Entrepreneurship Journal*, *10*(2), 194–213. doi:10.1002ej.1213

Dunne, D., & Martin, R. (2006). Design thinking and how it will change management education: An interview and discussion. *Academy of Management Learning & Education, 5*(4), 512–523. doi:10.5465/amle.2006.23473212

Dunphy, D. C., & Stace, D. (1992). *Under new management: Australian organizations in transition*. McGraw-Hill.

Dyer, W. G. Jr, & Wilkins, A. L. (1991). Better stories, not better constructs, to generate better theory: A rejoinder to Eisenhardt. *Academy of Management Review, 16*(3), 613–619. doi:10.5465/amr.1991.4279492

Eckhardt, J. T., & Shane, S. A. (2003). Opportunities and entrepreneurship. *Journal of Management, 29*(3), 333–349. doi:10.1177/014920630302900304

Edelman, L. F., Manolova, T., Shirokova, G., & Tsukanova, T. (2016). The impact of family support on young entrepreneurs' start-up activities. *Journal of Business Venturing, 31*(4), 428–448. doi:10.1016/j.jbusvent.2016.04.003

Eijdenberg, E. L., Thompson, N. A., Verduijn, K., & Essers, C. (2019). Entrepreneurial activities in a developing country: An institutional theory perspective. *International Journal of Entrepreneurial Behaviour & Research, 25*(3), 414–432. doi:10.1108/IJEBR-12-2016-0418

Eisenhardt, K. M. (1989). Building theories from case study research. *Academy of Management Review, 14*(4), 532–550. doi:10.5465/amr.1989.4308385

Elfving, J. (2008). *Contextualizing entrepreneurial intentions*. Abo: Abo Akademi Press.

Enrico, B., Ugo, P., & Arcand, J. L. (2012). *Too Much Finance?* IMF Working Papers.

Fan, W., & Wang, C. M. (2004). The research on factors affecting entrepreneurial intentions. [in Chinese]. *Science of Psychology, 27*(5), 1087–1090.

Feld, B. (2012). *Startup Communities: Building an entrepreneurial ecosystem in your city.* John Wiley & Sons.

Finance, T., & Bigdata, J. (2017). *Big Data Interpretation of the New Energy Industry: The Top 10 Occupy 70% Market*. Available online: https://finance.qq.com/original/bigdata/xinnengyuan.html

Fishbein, M., & Ajzen, I. (1975). *Belief, Attitude, Intention and Behavior: An Introduction to Theory and Research*. Addison-Wesley.

Foo, M. D. (2011). Emotions and entrepreneurial opportunity evaluation. *Entrepreneurship Theory and Practice, 35*(2), 375–393. doi:10.1111/j.1540-6520.2009.00357.x

Foss, N. J., & Klein, P. G. (2009). *Entrepreneurial Alertness and Opportunity Discovery: Origins, Attributes, Critique*. Academic Press.

Foss, N. J., Knudsen, C., & Montgomery, C. A. (1995). An Exploration of Common Ground: Integrating Evolutionary and Strategic Theories of the Firm. *Resource-Based and Evolutionary Theories of the Firm: Towards a Synthesis*.

Frenken, K., Van Oort, F., & Verburg, T. (2007). Related variety, unrelated variety and regionaleconomic growth. *Regional Studies, 41*(5), 685–697. doi:10.1080/00343400601120296

Fried, H. O., Lovell, C A K., Schmidt, S. S., & Yaisawarng, S. (2002). Accounting for Environmental Effect and Statistical Noise in Data Envelopment Analysis. *Journal of Productivity Analysis, 17*(1), 157–174. doi:10.1023/A:1013548723393

Friesen, P. H., & Miller, D. (2007). A mathematical model of the adaptive behaviour of organizations. *Journal of Management Studies, 23*(1), 1–25. doi:10.1111/j.1467-6486.1986.tb00932.x

Fritsch, M., & Storey, D. J. (2014). *Entrepreneurship in a regional context: Historical roots, recent developments and future challenges*. Routledge.

Gaglio, C. M., & Katz, J. A. (2001). The psychological basis of opportunity identification: Entrepreneurial alertness. *Small Business Economics, 16*(2), 95–111. doi:10.1023/A:1011132102464

Galbraith, C. S., DeNoble, A. F., & Ehrlich, S. B. (2012). Predicting the commercialization progress of early-stage technologies: An ex-ante analysis. *IEEE Transactions on Engineering Management, 59*(2), 213–225. doi:10.1109/TEM.2010.2068050

Gartner, W. B. (1985). A framework for describing and classifying the phenomenon of new venture creation. *Academy of Management Review, 10*(4), 696–706. doi:10.5465/amr.1985.4279094

Gatewood, E. J., Shaver, K. G., Power, J. B., & Gartner, W. B. (2002). Entrepreneurial expectancy, task effort,and performance. *Entrepreneurship Theory and Practice, 27*(2), 187–206. doi:10.1111/1540-8520.00006

Gay, B., & Dousset, B. (2005). Innovation and network structural dynamics: Study of the alliance network of a major sector of the biotechnology industry. *Research Policy, 34*(10), 1457–1475. doi:10.1016/j.respol.2005.07.001

Ge, B. S., Tan, L. F., Sheng, F., & Ma, H. J. (2016). Research on the relationship among innovation culture, dual Learning and dynamic ability. *Studies in Science of Science, 34*(4), 630–640.

Ge, B., Jiang, D., Gao, Y., & Tsai, S.-B. (2016). The influence of legitimacy on a proactive green orientation and green performance: A study based on transitional economy scenarios in china. *Sustainability, 8*(12), 1344. doi:10.3390u8121344

Gelderen, M. V., Thurik, R., & Bosma, N. (2006). Success and risk factors in the pre-startup phase. *Small Business Economics, 26*(4), 319–335. doi:10.100711187-004-6837-5

GEM. (2019). *Global Entrepreneurship Monitor 2018/2019 Global Report* (0046-5070). Retrieved from https://www.gemconsortium.org/report/gem-2018-2019-global-report.pdf

GEPA. (2017). *Report on Analysis of 2017 Non-Traditional Export statistics*. Accra, Ghana: Ghana Export Promotion Authority.

Ghemawat, P. (1995). Competitive advantage and internal organization: Nucor revisited. *Journal of Economics & Management Strategy, 3*(4), 685–717. doi:10.1111/j.1430-9134.1995.00685.x

Gimeno, J., Folta, T. B., Cooper, A. C., & Woo, C. Y. (1997). Survival of the fittest? Entrepreneurial human capital and the persistence of underperforming firms. *Administrative Science Quarterly*, *42*(4), 750–783. doi:10.2307/2393656

Ginsberg, A., & Venkatraman, N. (1985). Contingency perspectives of organizational strategy: A critical review of the empirical research. *Academy of Management Review*, *10*(3), 421–434. doi:10.5465/amr.1985.4278950

Gnyawali, D. R., & Fogel, D. S. (1994). Environments for entrepreneurship development: Key dimensions and research implications. *Entrepreneurship Theory and Practice*, *18*(4), 43–62. doi:10.1177/104225879401800403

Golesorkhi, S., Mersland, R., Randøy, T., & Shenkar, O. (2019). The performance impact of culture and formal institutional differences in cross-border alliances: The case of the microfinance industry. *International Business Review*, *28*(1), 104–118. doi:10.1016/j.ibusrev.2018.08.006

Graebner, E. M. E. (2007). Theory building from cases: Opportunities and challenges. *Academy of Management Journal*, *50*(1), 25–32. doi:10.5465/amj.2007.24160888

Granstrand O. (2000). *The economics of mul-tech:A study of multi-technology corporations in Japan, Sweden and the US*. Background paper submitted to the Dynacom Project.

Greif, A. (1994). Cultural Beliefs and the Organization of Society: A Historical and Theoretical Reflection on Collectivist and Individualist Societies. *Journal of Political Economy*, *102*(5), 912–950. doi:10.1086/261959

Grichnik, D., Smeja, A., & Welpe, I. (2010). The importance of being emotional: How do emotions affect entrepreneurial opportunity evaluation and exploitation? *Journal of Economic Behavior & Organization*, *76*(1), 15–29. doi:10.1016/j.jebo.2010.02.010

Grimaldi, R., & Grandi, A. (2005). Business incubators and new venture creation: An assessment of incubating models. *Technovation*, *25*(2), 111–121. doi:10.1016/S0166-4972(03)00076-2

Gruber, M. (2007). Uncovering the value of planning in new venture creation: A process and contingency perspective. *Journal of Business Venturing*, *22*(6), 782–807. doi:10.1016/j.jbusvent.2006.07.001

Gümüsay, & Aslan, A. (2017). Unpacking entrepreneurial opportunities: An institutional logics perspective. *Innovation*, *20*(3), 209–222.

Guo & Shen. (2016). The impact of Internet finance on commercial banks' risk taking: evidence from China. *China Finance and Economic Review*, *4*(1), 16.

Guo, H., Mao, Y., & Bai, X. (2009). The study on the effects of university education on students' entrepreneurial willingness. [in Chinese]. *Soft Sciences*, *9*, 69–74.

Haeussler, C., Patzelt, H., & Zahra, S. A. (2012). Strategic alliances and product development in high technology new firms: The moderating effect of technological capabilities. *Journal of Business Venturing*, *27*(2), 217–233. doi:10.1016/j.jbusvent.2010.10.002

Hair, J. F., Anderson, R. E., & Tatham, R. L. (1998). *Black, Multivariate data analysis*. Academic Press.

Hair, J. F. Jr, Anderson, R. E., Tatham, R. L., & Black, W. C. (1998). *Multivariate data analysis* (5th ed.). Englewood Cliffs: Prentice Hall.

Hambrick, D. C., Cho, T. S., & Chen, M. J. (1996). The influence of top management team heterogeneity on firms' competitive moves. *Administrative Science Quarterly*, *41*(4), 659–684. doi:10.2307/2393871

Han, L. Z., &Fu, H. (2009). Construction of college students' entrepreneurial self-efficacy scale. *Journal of Nanjing Normal University (Social Science Edition), 2009*(1), 114-118.

Han, H. (2019). *Evaluation of financial ecological environment of regional center cities*. Anhui University of Finance and Economics.

Hannan, M., & Freeman, J. (1977). *The population ecology of organizations*. Social Science Electronic Publishing. doi:10.1086/226424

Harper, D. A. (2008). Towards a theory of entrepreneurial teams. *Journal of Business Venturing*, *23*(6), 613–626. doi:10.1016/j.jbusvent.2008.01.002

Headd, B. (2003). Redefining business success: Distinguishing between closure and failure. *Small Business Economics*, *21*(1), 51–61. doi:10.1023/A:1024433630958

Hegger, D. L. T., Vliet, J. V., & Vliet, B. J. M. V. (2007). Niche management and its contribution to regime change: The case of innovation in sanitation. *Technology Analysis and Strategic Management*, *19*(6), 729–746. doi:10.1080/09537320701711215

Hellmann, T. F., Murdock, K. C., & Stiglitz, J. E. (2000). Liberalization, moral hazard in banking, and prudential regulation: Are capital requirements enough? *The American Economic Review*, *90*(1), 147–165. doi:10.1257/aer.90.1.147

Helmke, G., & Levitsky, S. (2004). Informal institutions and comparative politics: A research agenda. *Perspectives on Politics*, *2*(4), 725–740. doi:10.1017/S1537592704040472

Herbst, A. F. (2001). E-finance: Promises kept, promises unfulfilled, and implications for policy and research. *Global Finance Journal*, *12*(2), 205–215. doi:10.1016/S1044-0283(01)00028-X

Herron, L., & Sapienza, H. J. (1992). The entrepreneur and the Initiation of new venture launch activities. *Entrepreneurship Theory and Practice*, *17*(1), 49–55. doi:10.1177/104225879201700106

Hilmersson, M. (2014). Experiential knowledge types and profiles of internationalising small and medium-sized enterprises. *International Small Business Journal*, *32*(7), 802–817. doi:10.1177/0266242612458443

Hisrich, R. D., & Smilor, R. W. (1988). The university and business incubation: Technology transfer through entrepreneurial development. *The Journal of Technology Transfer*, *13*(1), 14–19. doi:10.1007/BF02371496

Hjortsoe, I., Weale, M., & Wieladek, T. (2018). How does financial liberalisation affect the influence of monetary policy on the current account? *Journal of International Money and Finance*, *85*, 93–123. doi:10.1016/j.jimonfin.2018.03.015

Hochberg, Y. V. (2016). Accelerating entrepreneurs and ecosystems: The seed accelerator model. *Innovation Policy and the Economy*, *16*(1), 25–51. doi:10.1086/684985

Hockerts, K., & Wuestenhagen, R. (2010). Greening Goliaths versus emerging Davids - Theorizing about the role of incumbents and new entrants in sustainable entrepreneurship. *Journal of Business Venturing*, *25*(5), 481–492. doi:10.1016/j.jbusvent.2009.07.005

Hoskisson, R. E., Wright, M., Filatotchev, I., & Peng, M. W. (2013). Emerging multinationals from mid-range economies: The influence of institutions and factor markets. *Journal of Management Studies*, *50*(7), 1295–1321. doi:10.1111/j.1467-6486.2012.01085.x

Hou, X., Gao, Z., & Wang, Q. (2016). Internet finance development and banking market discipline: Evidence from China. *Journal of Financial Stability*, *22*, 88–100. doi:10.1016/j.jfs.2016.01.001

Hu. (2009). The Assessment and Empirical Study of Regional Financial Ecological Environment. *Economic Management Journal, 2009*(6), 32-37.

Huang & Liu. (2007). An Evaluation System on Chinese Financial Ecologies. *Systems Engineering Theory & Practice, 2007*(6), 52-60.

Huang, Y., & Ji, Y. (2017). How will financial liberalization change the Chinese economy? Lessons from middle-income countries. *Journal of Asian Economics*, *50*, 27–45. doi:10.1016/j.asieco.2017.04.001

Hughes, M., Ireland, R. D., & Morgan, R. E. (2007). Stimulating dynamic value: Social capital and business incubation as a pathway to competitive success. *Long Range Planning*, *40*(2), 154–177. doi:10.1016/j.lrp.2007.03.008

Iansiti, M., Levien, R., Iansiti, M., & Levien, R. (2004). The keystone advantage: What the new dynamics of business ecosystems mean for strategy, innovation, and sustainability. *Future Survey*, *20*(2), 88–90.

Isenberg, D. (2010). How to start an entrepreneurial revolution. *Harvard Business Review*, *88*(6), 40–50.

Isenberg, D. J. (2011). *The entrepreneurial ecosystem strategy as a new paradigm for economic policy: Principles for culti- vating entrepreneurship*. Presentation at the Institute of International and European Affairs.

ITC. (2016). *SME Competitiveness in Ghana: Alliance for Action*. Geneva: International Trade Centre.

Jabareen, Y. (2009). Building a Conceptual Framework: Philosophy, Definitions, and Procedure. *International Journal of Qualitative Methods*, *8*(4), 49–62. doi:10.1177/160940690900800406

Jacobides, M. G., & Winter, S. G. (2007). Entrepreneurship and firm boundaries: The theory of a firm. *Journal of Management Studies*, *44*(7), 1213–1241. doi:10.1111/j.1467-6486.2007.00726.x

Jadiyappa, N., Vanga, N. R., & Krishnankutty, R. (2016). Financial liberalisation and Capital structuring decisions of corporate firms: Evidence from India. *Economics Letters*, *149*, 33–37. doi:10.1016/j.econlet.2016.10.004

Jafari Sadeghi, V., Nkongolo-Bakenda, J.-M., Anderson, R. B., & Dana, L.-P. (2019). An institution-based view of international entrepreneurship: A comparison of context-based and universal determinants in developing and economically advanced countries. *International Business Review*, *28*(6), 101588. doi:10.1016/j.ibusrev.2019.101588

Jamil, F., Ismail, K., & Mahmood, N. (2015). University Incubators: A gateway to an entrepreneurial society. *Journal of Economics and Sustainable Development*, *6*(6), 153–160.

Jamil, F., Ismail, K., & Siddique, M. (2016). Business incubators in Asian developing countries. *International Review of Management and Marketing*, *6*(4S), 291–295.

Jenkins, A., & McKelvie, A. (2016). What is entrepreneurial failure? Implications for future research. *International Small Business Journal*, *34*(2), 176–188. doi:10.1177/0266242615574011

Ji & Wu. (2011). Assessment and Analysis of Factors Affecting the Financial Ecological Environment in Northeast Area. *Journal of Northeastern University (Social Science), 2011*(9), 410-415.

Jiang, Y., & Chen, C. C. (2018). Integrating Knowledge Activities for Team Innovation: Effects of Transformational Leadership. *Journal of Management*, *44*(5), 1819–1847. doi:10.1177/0149206316628641

Jie, J. (2009). *A Study on Relationship of Financial Ecological Environment and Economic Development of Liaoning*. Northeastern University.

Jill, K. N., & Robert, S. D. (2005). Measure for measure: Modeling entrepreneurial self-efficacy onto instrumental tasks within the new venture creation process. *New England Journal of Entrepreneurship*, *8*(2), 39–47. doi:10.1108/NEJE-08-02-2005-B005

Jin, C., Zhe, H., & Zhang, H. (2013). Analysis of Catching-up Effect and Growth Effect of Total Factor Productivity in China's Regional Financial Industry. *Statistics & Decisions*, (3), 162–167.

Jing, Z., & Wei, P. (2012). The Study of Provincial Financial Ecological Environment Assessment. *Journal of Northwest University*, *42*(1).

Jin, X., & Xie, B. (2014). Evaluation and demonstration of regional financial ecological environment. *Statistics & Decisions*, (15): 160–162.

John, C., Sek Hong, N., & Christine, W. (2002). Psychic Distance and Internationalization: Evidence from Hong Kong Firms. *International Studies of Management & Organization*, *32*(1), 36–56. doi:10.1080/00208825.2002.11043656

Johnson, J., & Tellis, G. J. (2008). Tellis G J. Drivers of success for market entry into China and India. *Journal of Marketing*, *72*(3), 1–13. doi:10.1509/JMKG.72.3.001

Johnson, S., McMillan, J., & Woodruff, C. (2002). Property Rights and Finance. *The American Economic Review*, *92*(5), 1335–1356. doi:10.1257/000282802762024539

Jonatan, P. (2015). Sustainable entrepreneurship and corporate political activity: Overcoming market barriers in the clean energy sector. *Entrepreneurship Theory and Practice*, *39*(3), 633–654. doi:10.1111/etap.12055

Jun, P., Wang, L., & Shen, X. (2015). Financial Ecological Environment and Local Government Debt Financing Costs: Empirical Test Based on Provincial Urban Investment Debt Data. *Accountability in Research*, *3*, 34–41.

Justo, R., DeTienne, D. R., & Sieger, P. (2015). Failure or voluntary exit? Reassessing the female underperformance hypothesis. *Journal of Business Venturing*, *30*(6), 775–792. doi:10.1016/j.jbusvent.2015.04.004

Kannadhasan, M., Aramvalarthan, S., & Kumar, B. P. (2014). Relationship among cognitive biases, risk perceptions and individual's decision to start a venture. *Decision (Washington, D.C.)*, *41*(1), 87–98.

Katila, R., & Ahuja, G. (2002). Something old, something new: A longitudinal study of search behavior and new product introduction. *Academy of Management Journal*, *45*(6), 1183–1194.

Katz. (1992). A psychosocial cognitive model of employment status choice. *Entrepreneurship: Theory and Practice*, *16*, 29-37.

Kearins, K., & Collins, E. (2012). Making sense of ecopreneurs' decisions to sell up. *Business Strategy and the Environment*, *21*(2), 71–85. doi:10.1002/bse.710

Keh, H. T., Foo, M. D., & Lim, B. C. (2002). Opportunity evaluation under risky conditions: The cognitive processes of entrepreneurs. *Entrepreneurship Theory and Practice*, *27*(2), 125–148. doi:10.1111/1540-8520.00003

Kemp, R., Schot, J., & Hoogma, R. (1998). Regime shifts to sustainability through processes of niche formation: The approach of strategic niche management. *Technology Analysis and Strategic Management*, *10*(2), 175–198. doi:10.1080/09537329808524310

Khavul, S., Bruton, G. D., & Wood, E. (2009). Informal family business in Africa. *Entrepreneurship Theory and Practice*, *33*(6), 1219–1238. doi:10.1111/j.1540-6520.2009.00342.x

Khedhaouria, A., Gurău, C., & Torrès, O. (2015). Creativity, Self-efficacy and small-firm performance: The mediating role of entrepreneurial orientation. *Small Business Economics*, *44*(3), 485–504. doi:10.100711187-014-9608-y

Khelil, N. (2016). The many faces of entrepreneurial failure: Insights from an empirical taxonomy. *Journal of Business Venturing*, *31*(1), 72–84. doi:10.1016/j.jbusvent.2015.08.001

Kickul, J., & Kruegue, N. F. (2004). A cognitive processing model of entrepreneurial self-efficacy and intentionally. *Frontiers of Entrepreneurship Research*, *30*(1), 607–619.

Kim, W. C., & Mauborgne, R. A. (2005). *Blue ocean strategy*. Boston, MA: Harvard Business School Press.

Kingsley, G., & Malecki, E. J. (2004). Networking for competitiveness. *Small Business Economics*, *23*(1), 71–84. doi:10.1023/B:SBEJ.0000026022.08180.b7

Kirkpatrick, S. A., Wofford, J. C., & Baum, J. R. (2002). Measuring motive imagery contained in the vision statement. *The Leadership Quarterly*, *13*(2), 139–150. doi:10.1016/S1048-9843(02)00096-6

Kirzner Israel, M. (1973). *Competition and entrepreneurship*. Academic Press.

Kirzner, I. (1997). Entrepreneurial discovery and the competitive market process: An Austrian approach. *Journal of Economic Literature*, *35*(2), 60–85.

Kirzner, I. M. (1997). Entrepreneurial discovery and the competitive market process:An Austrian approach. *Journal of Economic Literature*, 60.

Koellinger, P. (2008). Why are some entrepreneurs more innovative than others? *Small Business Economics*, *31*(1), 21–37. doi:10.100711187-008-9107-0

Köhler, C., Sofka, W., & Grimpe, C. (2012). Selective search, sectoral patterns, and the impact on product innovation performance. *Research Policy*, *41*(8), 1344–1356. doi:10.1016/j.respol.2012.03.020

Kohli, A. K., & Jaworski, B. J. (1900). Market orientation: The construct, research propositions, and managerial implications. *Journal of Marketing*, *54*(2), 1–18. doi:10.1177/002224299005400201

Konfidants. (2019). *A Survey of Made in Ghana Goods sold in Ghana's leading supermarkets*. Retrieved from http://www.konfidants.com/2019/07/01/research-reveals-only-18-of-goods-sold-in-ghanas-leading-supermarkets-are-made-in-ghana/

Ko, S., & Butler, J. E. (2007). Creativity: A key link to entrepreneurial behavior. *Business Horizons*, *50*(5), 365–372. doi:10.1016/j.bushor.2007.03.002

Krueger, N. F. (2000). The cognitive infrastructure of opportunity emergence. *Entrepreneurship*, 185-206.

Krueger, N. F. Jr, & Brazeal, D. V. (1994). Entrepreneurship potential and potential entrepreneurs. *Entrepreneurship Theory and Practice*, *18*(3), 91–104. doi:10.1177/104225879401800307

Krueger, N. F. Jr, Reilly, M. D., & Carsrud, A. L. (2000). Competing models of entrepreneurial intentions. *Journal of Business Venturing*, *15*(4), 411–532. doi:10.1016/S0883-9026(98)00033-0

Kumar, R., & Usunier, J. C. (2001). Management education in a globalizing world. *Management Learning*, *32*(3), 363–391. doi:10.1177/1350507601323005

Kuratko, D. F., & Naffziger, D. W. (1997). An Examination of Owner's Goals in Sustaining Entrepreneurship. *Small Business Management*, *35*(1), 24–33.

Langevang, T., Gough, K. V., Yankson, P. W., Owusu, G., & Osei, R. (2015). Bounded entrepreneurial vitality: The mixed embeddedness of female entrepreneurship. *Economic Geography*, *91*(4), 449–473. doi:10.1111/ecge.12092

Law, K. S., Wong, C.-S., & Mobley, W. M. (1998). Toward a taxonomy of multidimensional constructs. *Academy of Management Review*, *23*(4), 741–755. doi:10.5465/amr.1998.1255636

Lee, C., Lee, K., & Pennings, J. M. (2001). Internal capabilities, external networks, and performance: A study on technology-based ventures. *Strategic Management Journal*, *22*(6/7), 615–640. doi:10.1002mj.181

Lee, F. (2001). Technology as a complex adaptive system: Evidence from patent data. *Research Policy*, *30*(7), 1019–1039. doi:10.1016/S0048-7333(00)00135-9

Lee, K., Lee, K., & Sharif, M. (2017). Procedural justice as a moderator of the relationship between organizational change intensity and commitment to organizational change. *Journal of Organizational Change Management*, *30*(4), 501–524. doi:10.1108/JOCM-08-2015-0139

Levinthal, D. A., & March, J. G. (1993). The myopia of learning. *Strategic Management Journal*, *14*(S2), 95–112. doi:10.1002mj.4250141009

Lewis, D. A. (2001). Does technology incubation work? A critical review. *Reviews of Economic Development Literature and Practice]*, *11*, 48.

Lewis, J. I., & Wiser, R. H. (2007, March). Fostering a renewable energy technology industry: An international comparison of wind industry policy support mechanisms. *Energy Policy*, *35*(3), 1844–1857. doi:10.1016/j.enpol.2006.06.005

Li & Guo. (2019). Research on the Impact of Capital Structure on Corporate Risk Undertaking-Based on the Dual Perspective of Property Right Heterogeneity and Financial Ecological Environment. *Wuhan Finance, 2019*(12), 44-50.

Li, C. (2014). The Measure and Correspondence Analysis on the Efficiency of China's Financial Industry. *Statistical Research*, *31*(1), 91–97.

Li, H. (2001). How does new venture strategy matter in the environment–performance relationship? *The Journal of High Technology Management Research*, *12*(2), 183–204. doi:10.1016/S1047-8310(01)00036-0

Li, H., & Atuahene-Gima, K. (2001). Product innovation strategy and the performance of new technology ventures in China. *Academy of Management Journal*, *44*(6), 1123–1134.

Li, H., & Li, J. (2009). Top management team conflict and entrepreneurial strategy making in China. *Asia Pacific Journal of Management*, *26*(2), 263–283. doi:10.100710490-007-9071-2

Li, H., & Zhang, Y. (2007). The role of managers' political networking and functional experience in new venture performance: Evidence from Chinas transition economy. *Strategic Management Journal*, *28*(8), 791–804. doi:10.1002mj.605

Li, J. F., & Garnsey, E. (2014). Policy-driven ecosystems for new vaccine development. *Technovation*, *34*(12), 762–772. doi:10.1016/j.technovation.2014.07.002

Li, J., Strange, R., Ning, L., & Sutherland, D. (2016). Outward foreign direct investment and domestic innovation performance: Evidence from China. *International Business Review*, *25*(5), 1010–1019. doi:10.1016/j.ibusrev.2016.01.008

Lindelöf, H., & Science, P. (2002). Parks and the growth of new technology-based firms—Academic-industry links, innovation and markets. *Research Policy*, *31*(6), 859–876. doi:10.1016/S0048-7333(01)00153-6

Lin, F.-J., & Ho, C.-W. (2019). The knowledge of entry mode decision for small and medium enterprises. *Journal of Innovation & Knowledge*, *4*(1), 32–37. doi:10.1016/j.jik.2018.02.001

Lin, S. (2011). The concept development and operation mechanism of entrepreneurial ecosystem. *Journal of Central University of Finance & Economics*, *4*, 58–62.

Lin, Y., Wang, Y., & Kung, L. A. (2015). Influences of cross-functional collaboration and knowledge creation on technology commercialization: Evidence from high-tech industries. *Industrial Marketing Management*, *49*, 128–138. doi:10.1016/j.indmarman.2015.04.002

Li, T., & Calantone, R. J. (1998). The impact of market knowledge competence on new product advantage: Conceptualization and empirical examination. *Journal of Marketing*, *62*(4), 13–29. doi:10.1177/002224299806200402

Liu, J. J. (2011). Research on the relationship among entrepreneurial learning, dynamic capabilities and performance of new ventures - Adjustment of environmental dynamics. *Studies in Science of Science*, *29*(5), 728–734.

Liu, J., & Li, X. (2013). Imitation or innovation: An empirical study on entrepreneurial opportunity exploitation and entrepreneurial performance. *South China Journal of Economics*, *31*, 20–32.

Liu, M., & Luo, P. (2010). The comparative research on integration innovation mode of brand mobile telephone and modularity innovation mode of mountain fastness mobile telephone based on the long tail theory. *R & D Management*, *22*(4), 1–9.

Locke, E. A. (1991). The motivation sequence, the motivation hub and the motivation core. *Organizational Behavior and Human Decision Processes*, *50*(2), 288–299. doi:10.1016/0749-5978(91)90023-M

Lorenzoni, G., & Baden-Fuller, C. (1995). Creating a strategic center to manage a web of partners. *California Management Review*, *37*(3), 146–163. doi:10.2307/41165803

Love, J. H., & Roper, S. (2015). SME innovation, exporting and growth: A review of existing evidence. *International Small Business Journal*, *33*(1), 28–48. doi:10.1177/0266242614550190

Lucas, W. A., & Cooper, S. Y. (2005). *Measuring Entrepreneurial Self-efficacy*. Paper Presented to the SMU EDGE Conference, Singapore.

Luthje, C., & Franke, N. (2003). The making of an entrepreneur: Testing a model of entrepreneurial intent among engineering students at MIT. *R & D Management*, *33*(2), 135–147. doi:10.1111/1467-9310.00288

M'Chirgui, Z. (2012). Assessing the performance of business incubators: Recent France evidence. *Business and Management Research*, *1*(1), 62. doi:10.5430/bmr.v1n1p62

M'Chirgui, Z., Lamine, W., Mian, S., & Fayolle, A. (2018). University technology commercialization through new venture projects: An assessment of the French regional incubator program. *The Journal of Technology Transfer*, *43*(5), 1142–1160. doi:10.100710961-016-9535-y

Mack, E., & Mayer, H. (2016). The evolutionary dynamics of entrepreneurial ecosystems. *Urban Studies (Edinburgh, Scotland)*, *53*(10), 2118–2133. doi:10.1177/0042098015586547

Ma, H. J., Wu, J., & Lang, C. T. (2018). The formation mechanism of improvisation to convention in new venture: Based on the perspective of entrepreneurial learning. *Foreign Economics & Management.*, *40*(11), 116–128.

Mainela, T., Puhakka, V., & Servais, P. (2014). The concept of international opportunity in international entrepreneurship: A review and a research agenda. *International Journal of Management Reviews*, *16*(1), 105–129. doi:10.1111/ijmr.12011

March, J. G. (1991). Exploration and exploitation in organizational learning. *Organization Science*, *2*(1), 71–87. doi:10.1287/orsc.2.1.71

Markman, G. D., Gianiodis, P. T., Phan, P. H., & Balkin, D. B. (2005). Innovation speed: Transferring university technology to market. *Research Policy*, *34*(7), 1058–1075. doi:10.1016/j.respol.2005.05.007

Marra, A., Antonelli, P., Dell'Anna, L., & Pozzi, C. (2015). A network analysis using metadata to investigate innovation in clean-tech – implications for energy policy. *Energy Policy*, *86*, 17–26. doi:10.1016/j.enpol.2015.06.025

Marra, A., Antonelli, P., & Pozzi, C. (2017). Emerging green-tech specializations and clusters - a network analysis on technological innovation at the metropolitan level. *Renewable & Sustainable Energy Reviews*, *67*(1), 1037–1046. doi:10.1016/j.rser.2016.09.086

Martínez-Román, J. A., Gamero, J., Delgado-González, M. L., & Tamayo, J. A. (2019). Innovativeness and internationalization in SMEs: An empirical analysis in European countries. *Technological Forecasting and Social Change*, *148*, 119716. doi:10.1016/j.techfore.2019.119716

Mason, C., & Brown, R. (2014). *Entrepreneurial ecosystems and growth oriented entrepreneurship*. Final Report to OECD.

McGaughey, S., Welch, D., & Welch, L. (1997). *Managerial influences and SME internationalisation*. Academic Press.

McGrath, R. G. (1999). Falling forward: Real options reasoning and entrepreneurial failure. *Academy of Management Review*, *24*(1), 13–30. doi:10.5465/amr.1999.1580438

McMullan, W. E., Long, W. A., & Graham, J. B. (1986). Assessing economic value added by university-based new-venture outreach programs. *Journal of Business Venturing*, *1*(2), 225–240. doi:10.1016/0883-9026(86)90016-9

Mcwilliams, A., & Siegel, D. (2001). Corporate social responsibility: A theory of the firm perspective. *Academy of Management Review*, *26*(1), 117–127. doi:10.5465/amr.2001.4011987

Merigó, J. M., Gil-Lafuente, A. M., & Yager, R. R. (2015). An overview of fuzzy research with bibliometric indicators. *Applied Soft Computing*, *27*, 420–433. doi:10.1016/j.asoc.2014.10.035

Meshram, S. A., & Rawani, A. M. (2019). Understanding entrepreneurial ecosystem international. *Journal of Social Ecology and Sustainable Development*, *10*(3), 103–115. doi:10.4018/IJSESD.2019070107

Meyer, K. E., Estrin, S., Bhaumik, S., & Peng, M. W. (2009). Institutions, resources, and entry strategies in emerging economies. *Strategic Management Journal*, *30*(1), 61–80. doi:10.1002mj.720

Mian, S., Lamine, W., & Fayolle, A. (2016). Technology Business Incubation: An overview of the state of knowledge. *Technovation*, *50*, 1–12. doi:10.1016/j.technovation.2016.02.005

Michael, M. S., Saban, G., & Abdurahman, A. Z. A. (2016). Factors affecting non-exporting small and medium enterprises' intention to export: Resource based approach. *Procedia: Social and Behavioral Sciences*, *224*, 199–206. doi:10.1016/j.sbspro.2016.05.441

Milanov, H., & Fernhaber, S. A. (2009). The impact of early imprinting on the evolution of new venture networks. *Journal of Business Venturing*, *24*(1), 46–61. doi:10.1016/j.jbusvent.2007.11.001

Miller, R. E., & Cote, M. (1987). *Growing the next Silicon Valley: A guide for successful regional planning*. Free Press.

Miner, J. B., Smith, N. R., & Bracker, J. S. (1989). Role of entrepreneurial task motivation in the growth of technologically innovative firms. *Applied Psychology*, *74*(4), 554–560. doi:10.1037/0021-9010.74.4.554

Misati, E., Walumbwa, F. O., Lahiri, S., & Kundu, S. K. (2017). The Internationalization of African Small and Medium Enterprises (SMEs): A South-North Pattern. *Africa Journal of Management*, *3*(1), 53–81. doi:10.1080/23322373.2016.1275940

Monticelli, J. M., Calixto, C. V., Vasconcellos, S. L., & Garrido, I. L. (2017). The influence of formal institutions on the internationalization of companies in an emerging country. *Revista Brasileira de Gestão de Negócios*, *19*(65), 358–374. doi:10.7819/rbgn.v0i0.3040

Moore, J. F. (1993). Predators and prey: A new ecology of competition. *Harvard Business Review*, *71*(3), 75–86. PMID:10126156

Morais, F., & Ferreira, J. J. (2019). SME internationalisation process: Key issues and contributions, existing gaps and the future research agenda. *European Management Journal*. doi:10.1016/j.emj.2019.08.001

Muralidharan, E., & Pathak, S. (2017). Informal institutions and international entrepreneurship. *International Business Review*, *26*(2), 288–302. doi:10.1016/j.ibusrev.2016.07.006

Murnieks, C. Y., Mosakowski, E., & Cardon, M. S. (2014). Pathways of passion: Identity centrality, passion, and behavior among entrepreneurs. *Journal of Management*, *40*(6), 1583–1606. doi:10.1177/0149206311433855

Nacu, C. M., & Avasilcai, S. (2014). Environmental factors influencing technological entrepreneurship: Research framework and results. *Procedia: Social and Behavioral Sciences*, *109*(2), 1309–1315. doi:10.1016/j.sbspro.2013.12.630

Nadgrodkiewicz, A. (2013). Building entrepreneurial ecosystems. *Economic Reform Features Services*, *12*, 18–21.

Nair, S. (2009). Green entrepreneurship (ge) and green value added (gva): A conceptual framework. *International Journal of Entrepreneurship*, *13*, 21–34.

Naranjo-Valencia, J. C., Jiménez-Jiménez, D., & Sanz-Valle, R. (2011). Innovation or imitation? The role of organizational culture. *Management Decision*, *49*(1), 55–72. doi:10.1108/00251741111094437

Neagu, C. (2016). The importance and role of small and medium-sized businesses. *Theoretical and Applied Economics, 23*(3), 331-338.

Neck, H. M., Meyer, G. D., Cohen, B., & Corbett, A. C. (2004). An entrepreneurial system view of new venture creation. *Journal of Small Business Management*, *42*(2), 190–208. doi:10.1111/j.1540-627X.2004.00105.x

Needleman, S. E & Fletcher, O. (2012). A start-up ecosystem forms in Chicago. *Wall street Journal*, *259*(61), 3-5.

Nelson, R. R., & Winter, S. G. (1978). Forces generating and limiting concentration under Schumpeterian competition. *The Bell Journal of Economics*, *9*(2), 524–548. doi:10.2307/3003597

Ni, J. (2018). *Research on Comprehensive Evaluation of Financial Ecological Environment and Its Relationship with Economic Growth*. Zhejiang University of Commerce and Industry.

Nikolaev, B. N., Boudreaux, C. J., & Palich, L. (2018). Cross-country determinants of early-stage necessity and opportunity-motivated entrepreneurship: Accounting for model uncertainty. *Journal of Small Business Management*, *56*, 243–280. doi:10.1111/jsbm.12400

Njikam, O. (2017). Financial liberalization and growth in African economies: The role of policy complementarities. *Review of Development Finance, 7*(1), 73-83.

North, D. C. (1990). *Institutions, institutional change, and economic performance.* Cambridge Univ Press.

North, D. C. (2005). Understanding the Process of Economic Change. Princeton University Press.

Nyame-Asiamah, F., Amoako, I. O., Amankwah-Amoah, J., & Debrah, Y. A. (2020). Diaspora entrepreneurs' push and pull institutional factors for investing in Africa: Insights from African returnees from the United Kingdom. *Technological Forecasting and Social Change, 152*, 119876. doi:10.1016/j.techfore.2019.119876

Obeng, B. A., Robson, P., & Haugh, H. (2014). Strategic entrepreneurship and small firm growth in Ghana. *International Small Business Journal, 32*(5), 501–524. doi:10.1177/0266242612463946

OECD. (2017). *OECD Entrepreneurship at a Glance 2011.* Available online: https://www.oecd-ilibrary.org/docserver/download/3011021e.pdf?expires=1517390284&id=id&accname=guest&checksum=E15844D9C63CC62C99688EBE360BC2DF

Omokaro-Romanus, C., Anchor, J. R., & Konara, P. (2018). The internationalization of Nigerian firms: Motivations and location patterns. *Thunderbird International Business Review, 61*(1), 75–88. doi:10.1002/tie.21962

Osei, B., Baah-Nuakoh, A., Tutu, K., & Sowa, N. K. (1993). Impact of structural adjustment on small-scale enterprises in Ghana. In *Small Enterprises and Changing Policies: Structural adjustment, finance policy and assistance programmes in Africa* (pp. 51–70). Practical Action Publishing. doi:10.3362/9781780445908.004

Oviatt, B. M., & McDougall, P. P. (2005). The internationalization of entrepreneurship. *Journal of International Business Studies, 36*(1), 2–8. doi:10.1057/palgrave.jibs.8400119

Özdemir, Ö. Ç., & Şehitoğlu, Y. (2013). Assessing the impacts of technology business incubators: A framework for technology development centers in Turkey. *Procedia: Social and Behavioral Sciences, 75*(75), 282–291. doi:10.1016/j.sbspro.2013.04.032

Ozili, P. K. (2018). Impact of digital finance on financial inclusion and stability. *Borsa Istanbul Review, 18*(4), 329–340. doi:10.1016/j.bir.2017.12.003

Palepu, K. (1985). Diversification strategy, profit performance and the entropy measure. *Strategic Management Journal, 6*(3), 239–255. doi:10.1002mj.4250060305

Peng, M. W. (2003). Institutional transitions and strategic choices. *Academy of Management Review, 28*(2), 275–296. doi:10.5465/amr.2003.9416341

Peng, M. W., & Luo, Y. (2000). Managerial ties and firm performance in a transition economy: The nature of a micro-macro link. *Academy of Management Journal, 43*(3), 486–501.

Penrose, E. T. (1995). The theory of the growth of the firm. Oxford, UK: Oxford University Press.

Peteraf, M. A., & Barney, J. B. (2003). Integrating management and economic perspectives on corporate strategy unraveling the resource-based tangle. *Managerial and Decision Economics*, *24*(4), 309–323. doi:10.1002/mde.1126

Pettigrew, A. M. (1990). Longitudinal field research on change: theory and practice. *Organization Science*, *1*(3), 267-292.

Phan, P. H., Wong, P. K., & Wang, C. (2002). Antecedents to Entrepreneurship among university students in Singapore: Beliefs, Attitudes and Background. *Journal of Enterprising Culture*, *10*(2), 151–174. doi:10.1142/S0218495802000189

Pierce, L. (2008). *Big losses in ecosystem niches: how core firm decisions drive complementary product shakeouts*. Ssrn Electronic Journal.

Pierce, L. (2009). Big losses in ecosystem niches: How core firm decisions drive complementary product shakeouts. *Strategic Management Journal*, *30*(3), 323–347. doi:10.1002mj.736

Podsakoff, P. M., & Organ, D. W. (1986). Self-reports in organizational research: Problems and prospects. *Journal of Management*, *12*(4), 531–544. doi:10.1177/014920638601200408

Politis, D., & Gabrielsson, J. (2004). Exploring the role of experience in the process of entrepreneurial learning. *RENT XVIll Conferellce*.

Politis, D. (2005). The process of entrepreneurial learning: A conceptual framework. *Entrepreneurship Theory and Practice*, *29*(4), 399–424. doi:10.1111/j.1540-6520.2005.00091.x

Porter, M. (1990). Competitive advantage of nations. *Competitive Intelligence Review*, *1*(1), 14-14.

Porter, M. E., & Linde, C. V. D. (1995). Towards a new conception of the environment-competitiveness relationship. *The Journal of Economic Perspectives*, *4*(4), 97–118. doi:10.1257/jep.9.4.97

Ramanathan, R., He, Q., Black, A., Ghobadian, A., & Gallear, D. (2017). Environmental regulations, innovation and firm performance: A revisit of the porter hypothesis. *Journal of Cleaner Production*, *155*, 79–92. doi:10.1016/j.jclepro.2016.08.116

Ranciere, R., Tornell, A., & Westermann, F. (2006). Decomposing the effects of financial liberalization: Crises vs. growth. *Journal of Banking & Finance*, *30*(12), 3331–3348. doi:10.1016/j.jbankfin.2006.05.019

Ratinho, T., & Henriques, E. (2010). The role of science parks and business incubators in converging countries: Evidence from Portugal. *Technovation*, *30*(4), 278–290. doi:10.1016/j.technovation.2009.09.002

Repullo, R. (2004). Capital requirements, market power, and risk-taking in banking. *Journal of Financial Intermediation*, *13*(2), 156–182. doi:10.1016/j.jfi.2003.08.005

Research Group, Luoyang Central Bank of PBC. (2006). Research on the Evaluation Target System of Regional Financial Ecological Environment. *Journal of Financial Research*, (1), 167–177.

Reynolds, P. D., Carter, N. M., Gartner, W. B., & Greene, P. G. (2004). The prevalence of nascent entrepreneurs in the United States: Evidence from the panel study of entrepreneurial dynamics. *Small Business Economics*, *23*(4), 263–284. doi:10.1023/B:SBEJ.0000032046.59790.45

Rezvani, M., Lashgari, M., & Yadolahi Farsi, J. (2019). International entrepreneurial alertness in opportunity discovery for market entry. *Journal of Research in Marketing and Entrepreneurship.*, *21*(2), 76–102. doi:10.1108/JRME-01-2018-0003

Ricart, J. E., Rodríguez, M. A., & Sanchez, P. (2002). Sustainable development and the sustainability of competitive advantage: A dynamic and sustainable view of the firm. *Creativity and Innovation Management*, *11*(3), 11, 135–146.

Robichaud, Y., & Roger, A. (2001). Toward the Development of a Measuring Instrument for Entrepreneurial Motivation. *Developmental Entrepreneurship*, *6*(2), 189.

Robinson, R. B., McDougall, P., & Herron, L. (1988) Toward a new venture strategy typology. Academy of Management Proceedings, (1), 74-78.

Robson, P. J., Haugh, H. M., & Obeng, B. A. (2009). Entrepreneurship and innovation in Ghana: Enterprising Africa. *Small Business Economics*, *32*(3), 331–350. doi:10.100711187-008-9121-2

Robson, P. J., & Obeng, B. A. (2008). The barriers to growth in Ghana. *Small Business Economics*, *30*(4), 385–403. doi:10.100711187-007-9046-1

Rosenbaum, D., More, E., & Steane, P. (2018). Planned organisational change management: Forward to the past? An exploratory literature review. *Journal of Organizational Change Management*, *31*(2), 286–303. doi:10.1108/JOCM-06-2015-0089

Roundy, P. T. (2017). Small town' entrepreneurial ecosystems: Implications for developed and emerging economies. *Journal of Entrepreneurship in Emerging Economies*, *9*(3), 238–262. doi:10.1108/JEEE-09-2016-0040

Roundy, P. T., Brockman, B. K., & Bradshaw, M. (2017). The resilience of entrepreneurial ecosystems. *Journal of Business Venturing Insights*, *8*, 99–104. doi:10.1016/j.jbvi.2017.08.002

Roundy, P. T., & Fayard, D. (2019). Dynamic capabilities and entrepreneurial ecosystems: The micro-foundations of regional entrepreneurship. *The Journal of Entrepreneurship*, *28*(1), 94–120. doi:10.1177/0971355718810296

Roxas, H. B., Lindsay, V., Ashill, N., & Victorio, A. (2007). An institutional view of local entrepreneurial climate. *Journal of Asia Entrepreneurship and Sustainability*, *3*(1), 1–28.

Ruef, M., Aldrich, H. E., & Carter, N. M. (2003). The structure of founding teams: Homophily, strong ties, and isolation among US entrepreneurs. *American Sociological Review*, *68*(2), 195–222. doi:10.2307/1519766

Saaty, T. L. (1990). How to make a decision: The analytic hierarchy process. *European Journal of Operational Research*, *48*(1), 9–26. doi:10.1016/0377-2217(90)90057-I

Sarasvathy, S. D. (2003). Entrepreneurship as a science of the artificial. *Journal of Economic Psychology*, *24*(2), 203–220. doi:10.1016/S0167-4870(02)00203-9

Sarasvathy, S. D., Menon, A. R., & Kuechle, G. (2013). Failing firms and successful entrepreneurs: Serial entrepreneurship as a temporal portfolio. *Small Business Economics*, *40*(2), 417–434. doi:10.100711187-011-9412-x

Schendel, D., & Hofer, C. W. (1979). *Strategic management: A new view of business policy and planning*. Little, Brown.

Scherer, R. F., Adams, J. S., Carley, S. S., & Wiebe, F. A. (1989). Role model performance effects on development of entrepreneurial career preference. *Entrepreneurship Theory and Practice*, *13*(1), 53–71. doi:10.1177/104225878901300306

Schmidt, A., & Hansen, M. W. (2017). Internationalization Strategies of African Firms: A Survey of 210 Food Processing Firms from Tanzania, Kenya and Zambia. Academic Press.

Schumpeter, J. A. (1934). *The theory of economic development: An inquiry into profits, capital, credit, interest, and the business cycle*. Transaction Publishers.

Schwartz, M., & Göthner, M. (2009). A multidimensional evaluation of the effectiveness of business incubators: An application of the PROMETHEE outranking method. *Environment and Planning. C, Government & Policy*, *27*(6), 1072–1087. doi:10.1068/c0897b

Schwartz, M., & Hornych, C. (2008). Specialization as strategy for business incubators: An assessment of the Central German Multimedia Center. *Technovation*, *28*(7), 436–449. doi:10.1016/j.technovation.2008.02.003

Scott, W. R. (1995). Introduction: institutional theory and organizations. *The Institutional Construction of Organizations*, 11-23.

Seglah, S. K., & Armah, S. E. (2016). *Going regional: internationalisation strategies of Ghanaian service companies within the ECOWAS market*. Academic Press.

Shan, B., Cai, L., Hatfield, D. E., & Tang, S. (2014). The relationship between resources and capabilities of new ventures in emerging economies. *Information Technology Management*, *15*(2), 99–108. doi:10.100710799-014-0177-1

Shane, S. (2012). Reflections on the 2010 AMR decade award:Delivering on the promise of entrepreneurship as a field of research. *Academy of Management Review*, *37*(1), 10–20. doi:10.5465/amr.2011.0078

Shane, S. A. (2003). *A general theory of entrepreneurship: The individual-opportunity nexus*. Edward Elgar Publishing. doi:10.4337/9781781007990

Shane, S., & Venkataraman, S. (2000). The promise of Entrepreneurship as a field of research. *Academy of Management Review*, *25*(1), 217–226. doi:10.5465/amr.2000.2791611

Shannxi, P. R. (2015). Snapshot of technology business incubators in China. *International Journal of u-and e-Service. Science and Technology*, *8*(7), 235–242.

Shapero, A. (1982). Social dimensions of entrepreneurship. In The Encyclopedia of Entrepreneurship. Englewood Cliffs, NJ: Prentice Hall.

Sheng, S., Zhou, K. Z., & Lessassy, L. (2013). NPD speed vs. innovativeness: The contingent impact of institutional and market environments. *Journal of Business Research*, *66*(11), 2355–2362. doi:10.1016/j.jbusres.2012.04.018

Sheng, S., Zhou, K. Z., & Li, J. J. (2011). The effects of business and political ties on firm performance: Evidence from China. *Journal of Marketing*, *75*(1), 1–15. doi:10.1509/jm.75.1.1

Shen, Y., & Guo, P. (2015). Internet finance, technology spillover and commercial banks TFP. *Journal of Financial Research*, *417*(3), 160–175.

Shepherd, D. A. (2003). Learning from business failure: Propositions about the grief recovery process for the self-employed. *Academy of Management Review*, *28*(2), 318–329. doi:10.5465/amr.2003.9416377

Shepherd, D. A., & Patzelt, H. (2011). The new field of sustainable entrepreneurship: Studying entrepreneurial action linking "what is to be sustained" with "what is to be developed". *Entrepreneurship Theory and Practice*, *35*(1), 137–163. doi:10.1111/j.1540-6520.2010.00426.x

Shimp, T. A., & Sharma, S. (1987). Consumer ethnocentrism: Construction and validation of the CETSCALE. *JMR, Journal of Marketing Research*, *24*(3), 280–289. doi:10.1177/002224378702400304

Siggelkow, N. (2007). Persuasion with case studies. *Academy of Management Journal*, *50*(1), 20–24. doi:10.5465/amj.2007.24160882

Silajdzic, I., Kurtagic, S. M., & Vucijak, B. (2015). Green entrepreneurship in transition economies: a case study of bosnia and herzegovina. *Journal of Cleaner Production*, *88*, 376-384.

Simón-Moya, V., Revuelto-Taboada, L., & Guerrero, R. F. (2014). Institutional and economic drivers of entrepreneurship: An international perspective. *Journal of Business Research*, *67*(5), 715–721. doi:10.1016/j.jbusres.2013.11.033

Simsek, Z., Heavey, C., Veiga, J. F., & Souder, D. (2009). A typology for aligning organizational ambidexterity's conceptualizations, antecedents, and outcomes. *Journal of Management Studies*, *46*(5), 864–894. doi:10.1111/j.1467-6486.2009.00841.x

Sitaridis, I., & Kitsios, F. (2019). Competitiveness analysis and evaluation of entrepreneurial ecosystems: A multi-criteria approach. *Annals of Operations Research*, *2019*, 1–23.

Slivko, O., & Theilen, B. (2014). Innovation or imitation? The effect of spillovers and competitive pressure on firms' R&D strategy choice. *Journal of Economics*, *112*(3), 253–282. doi:10.100700712-013-0361-5

Smilor, R. W. (1987). Managing the incubator system: Critical success factors to accelerate new company development. *IEEE Transactions on Engineering Management*, *EM-34*(3), 146–155. doi:10.1109/TEM.1987.6498875

Smith, A., & Raven, R. (2012). What is protective space? reconsidering niches in transitions to sustainability. *Research Policy*, *41*(6), 1025–1036. doi:10.1016/j.respol.2011.12.012

Sofka, W., & Grimpe, C. (2010). Specialized search and innovation performance – evidence across europe. *R & D Management*, *40*(3), 310–323. doi:10.1111/j.1467-9310.2010.00592.x

Song, M., Podoynitsyna, K., Van Der Bij, H., & Halman, J. I. M. (2008). Success factors in new ventures: A Meta-analysis. *Journal of Product Innovation Management*, *25*(1), 7–27. doi:10.1111/j.1540-5885.2007.00280.x

Sørensen Jesper, B. (2007). Closure and Exposure: Mechanisms in the Intergenerational Transmission of Self-employment. In R. Martin & L. Michael (Eds.), *The Sociology of Entrepreneurship* (Vol. 25, pp. 83–124). Emerald Group Publishing Limited. doi:10.1016/S0733-558X(06)25003-1

Soto-Rodríguez, E. (2014). Entrepreneurial ecosystems as a pathway towards competitiveness: The case of Puerto Rico. *Competition Forum. American Society for Competitiveness*, *12*(1), 31–40.

Spencer, J. W., & Gómez, C. (2004). The relationship among national institutional structures, economic factors, and domestic entrepreneurial activity: A multicountry study. *Journal of Business Research*, *57*(10), 1098–1107. doi:10.1016/S0148-2963(03)00040-7

Spiegel, B. (2015). The relational organization of entrepreneurial ecosystems. *Entrepreneurship Theory and Practice*, *41*(1), 49–72. doi:10.1111/etap.12167

Spilling, R. (1996). The entrepreneurial system: On entrepreneurship in the context of a mega-event. *Journal of Business Research*, *36*(1), 91–103. doi:10.1016/0148-2963(95)00166-2

Srivastava, A. (2014). The status and impact of E-finance on developing economy. *Golden Research Thoughts*, *3*(11).

Stam, E. (2015). Entrepreneurial ecosystems and regional policy: A sympathetic critique. *European Planning Studies*, *23*(9), 1759–1769. doi:10.1080/09654313.2015.1061484

Stam, E., Thurik, R., & Van der Zwan, P. (2010). Entrepreneurial exit in real and imagined markets. *Industrial and Corporate Change*, *19*(4), 1109–1139. doi:10.1093/icc/dtp047

Steel, W., & Webster, L. (1990). *Ghana's Small Enterprise Sector: Survey of Adjustment Response and Constraints' Industry Series Paper 41*. Washington, DC: World Bank, Industry and Energy Dept.

Stephan, U., & Uhlaner, L. M. (2010). Performance-based vs socially supportive culture: A cross-national study of descriptive norms and entrepreneurship. *Journal of International Business Studies*, *41*(8), 1347–1364. doi:10.1057/jibs.2010.14

Stigson, P., Dotzauer, E., & Yan, J. (2009). Improving policy making through government–industry policy learning: The case of a novel swedish policy framework. *Applied Energy*, *86*(4), 399–406. doi:10.1016/j.apenergy.2008.05.015

Stoica, O., Mehdian, S., & Sargu, A. (2015). The impact of internet banking on the performance of Romanian banks: DEA and PCA approach. *Procedia Economics and Finance*, *20*, 610–622. doi:10.1016/S2212-5671(15)00115-X

Storey, D. (1994). *Understanding the Small Business Sector. Routledge.*

Strese, S., Keller, M., & Flatten, T. C. (2016). CEOs' Passion for inventing and radical innovations in SMEs: The moderating effect of shared vision. *Journal of Small Business Management.*

Su, X. H., Yang, S. N., Wu, J. Z., & Zhou, Y. (2018). Research on the relationship among entrepreneurial self-efficacy, decision logic and entrepreneurial performance. *South China Journal of Economics, 2018*(10), 113-131.

Suning. (2005). Optimizing the Financial Environment and Improving the Financial Ecology. *Financial Digest, 2005*(10), 4-6.

Suresh, J., & Ramraj, R. (2012). Entrepreneurial ecosystem: Case study on the influence of environmental factors on entrepreneurial success. *European Journal of Business and Management*, *4*(16), 95–101.

Su, Z., Peng, J., Shen, H., & Xiao, T. (2013). Technological capability, marketing capability, and firm performance in turbulent conditions. *Management and Organization Review*, *9*(1), 115–138. doi:10.1017/S1740877600003193

Tabak, F., & Barr, S. H. (1999). Propensity to adopt technological innovations: The impact of personal characteristics and organizational context. *Journal of Engineering and Technology Management*, *16*(3), 247–270. doi:10.1016/S0923-4748(99)00011-9

Takyi-Asiedu, S. (1993). Some socio-cultural factors retarding entrepreneurial activity in sub-Saharan Africa. *Journal of Business Venturing*, *8*(2), 91–98. doi:10.1016/0883-9026(93)90013-U

Tang, J., &Jiang, Y. F. (2007). Research on career choice of newborn entrepreneurs: based on self-efficacy. *Science of Science and Management of S & T, 2007*(10), 180-185.

Tang, M. (2009). *The research on the relationship between entrepreneurial self-efficacy and entrepreneurial intentions* (Dissertation). Zhonglan University. (in Chinese)

Tang, Q., & Gu, J. P. (2016). The effect of entrepreneur's spiritual capital and self-efficacy on entrepreneurial performance. *Enterprise Economy, 2016*(9), 111-117.

Tang, C. (2019). *Research on Mitigating Effect of Financial Ecological Environment and Corporate Governance on Financing Constraints*. Guangxi University of Science and Technology.

Tang, J., Kacmar, K. M. M., & Busenitz, L. (2012). Entrepreneurial alertness in the pursuit of new opportunities. *Journal of Business Venturing*, *27*(1), 77–94. doi:10.1016/j.jbusvent.2010.07.001

Tang, M. F., Lee, J., Liu, K., & Lu, Y. (2014). Assessing government-supported technology-based business incubators: Evidence from China. *International Journal of Technology Management*, *65*(1-4), 24–48. doi:10.1504/IJTM.2014.060956

Tanna, S., Luo, Y., & De Vita, G. (2017). What is the net effect of financial liberalization on bank productivity? A decomposition analysis of bank total factor productivity growth. *Journal of Financial Stability*, *30*, 67–78. doi:10.1016/j.jfs.2017.04.003

Tansley, A. G. (1935). The use and abuse of vegetational concepts and terms. *Ecology*, *16*(3), 284–307. doi:10.2307/1930070

Taylor, S. E. (2011). Social support: A review. In *The handbook of health psychology* (pp. 189–214). New York: Oxford University Press.

Teece, D. J. (2007). Explicating dynamic capabilities: The nature and micro-foundations of sustainable enterprise performance. *Strategic Management Journal*, *28*(13), 1319–1350. doi:10.1002mj.640

Tesar, G., & Moini, A. H. (1998). Longitudinal study of exporters and nonexporters: A focus on smaller manufacturing enterprises. *International Business Review*, *7*(3), 291–313. doi:10.1016/S0969-5931(98)00011-0

Theodoraki, C., Messeghem, K., & Rice, M. P. (2017). A social capital approach to the development of sustainable entrepreneurial ecosystems: An explorative study. *Small Business Economics*, *51*(1), 1–18.

Theodorakopoulos, N. K., Kakabadse, N., & McGowan, C. (2014). What matters in business incubation? A literature review and a suggestion for situated theorising. *Journal of Small Business and Enterprise Development*, *21*(4), 602–622. doi:10.1108/JSBED-09-2014-0152

Thorburn, K. S. (2000). Bankruptcy auctions, costs, debt recovery, and firm survival. *Journal of Financial Economics*, *58*(3), 337–368. doi:10.1016/S0304-405X(00)00075-1

Thornton, P. H., Ribeiro-Soriano, D., & Urbano, D. (2011). Socio-cultural factors and entrepreneurial activity: An overview. *International Small Business Journal*, *29*(2), 105–118. doi:10.1177/0266242610391930

Tsai, M. T., & Li, Y. H. (2007). Knowledge creation process in new venture strategy and performance. *Journal of Business Research*, *60*(4), 371–381. doi:10.1016/j.jbusres.2006.10.003

Ucbasaran, D., Westhead, P., Wright, M., & Flores, M. (2010). The nature of entrepreneurial experience, business failure and comparative optimism. *Journal of Business Venturing*, *25*(6).

Ucbasaran, D., Shepherd, D. A., Lockett, A., & Lyon, J. (2013). Life after business failure: The process and consequences of business failure for entrepreneurs. *Journal of Management*, *39*(1), 163–202. doi:10.1177/0149206312457823

Ullah, B. (2019). Firm innovation in transition economies: The role of formal versus informal finance. *Journal of Multinational Financial Management*, *50*, 58–75. doi:10.1016/j.mulfin.2019.04.004

Urbano, D., & Alvarez, C. (2014). Institutional dimensions and entrepreneurial activity: An international study. *Small Business Economics, 42*(4), 703–716. doi:10.100711187-013-9523-7

Van Holm, E. J. (2015). Makerspaces and contributions to entrepreneurship. *Procedia: Social and Behavioral Sciences, 195*, 24–31. doi:10.1016/j.sbspro.2015.06.167

Vecchiato, R. (2019). Scenario planning, cognition, and strategic investment decisions in a turbulent environment. *Long Range Planning, 52*(5), 843–865. doi:10.1016/j.lrp.2019.01.002

Venkataraman, S. (1997). The distinctive domain of entrepreneurship research. *Advances in Entrepreneurship, Firm, Emergence, and Growth, 3*(1), 119.

Vogel, P. (2013). The employment outlook for youth: Building entrepreneurial ecosystems as a way forward. *G20 Youth Forum.*

Volchek, D., Henttonen, K., & Edelmann, J. (2013). Exploring the role of a country's institutional environment in internationalization: Strategic responses of SMEs in Russia. *Journal of East-West Business, 19*(4), 317–350. doi:10.1080/10669868.2013.851140

Von Krogh, G., & Haefliger, S. (2007). Nurturing respect for IP in China. *Harvard Business Review, 85*(4), 23–24.

Von Zedtwitz, M., & Grimaldi, R. (2006). Are service profiles incubator-specific? Results from an empirical investigation in Italy. *The Journal of Technology Transfer, 31*(4), 459–468. doi:10.100710961-006-0007-7

Voss, G. B., & Voss, Z. G. (2000). Strategic orientation and firm performance in an artistic environment. *Journal of Marketing, 64*(1), 67–83. doi:10.1509/jmkg.64.1.67.17993

Wagner, M., & Schaltegger, S. (2012). Sustainable entrepreneurship and sustainability innovation: Categories and interactions. *Business Strategy and the Environment, 32*(2), 110–111.

Walter, A., Auer, M., & Ritter, T. (2006). The impact of network capabilities and entrepreneurial orientation on university spin-off performance. *Journal of Business Venturing, 21*(4), 541–567. doi:10.1016/j.jbusvent.2005.02.005

Wang & Cheng. (2017). The boundary effect of financial development on firms' R&D investment-Based on the HECKIT model of the scale & efficiency threshold. *Studies in Science of Science, 35*(1), 110–124.

Wang, Q. (2019). Necessity Analysis and Core Principles of Internet Financial Supervision. *Academic Journal of Business & Management, 1*(2).

Wang. (2012). Analysis of the Effect of Financial Eco-environment on Financial Industry and Regional Economic Development--Taking the Effectiveness and Problems of Financial Eco-environment in Central Plains Economic Zone as an Example. *Enterprise Economy, 2012*(2), 147-151.

Wang, Z., & Zhang, R. (2006). On the Evaluation Indicator System of Regional Financial Ecological Environment. *Journal of Financial Research*, (5), 167–177.

Weifeng, J., & Xinghua, D. (2010). Research on core enterprise's knowledge flow-coupling control in technological innovation network. *Science Research Management*.

Wei, Z. (2014). Financial Ecological Environment and Corporate Financial Constraints-Evidence from Chinese Listed Firms. *Accountability in Research*, (5), 73–82.

Wellalage, N. H., & Fernandez, V. (2019). Innovation and SME finance: Evidence from developing countries. *International Review of Financial Analysis*, *101370*, 101370. doi:10.1016/j.irfa.2019.06.009

Wennberg, K., & Detienne, D. R. (2014). What do we really mean when we talk about 'exit'? - a critical review of research on entrepreneurial exit. *International Small Business Journal*, *32*(1), 4–16. doi:10.1177/0266242613517126

Wennberg, K., Wiklund, J., Detienne, D. R., & Cardon, M. S. (2010). Reconceptualizing entrepreneurial exit: Divergent exit routes and their drivers. *Journal of Business Venturing*, *25*(4), 361–375. doi:10.1016/j.jbusvent.2009.01.001

Wernerfelt, B. (1984). A resource-based view of the firm. *Strategic Management Journal*, *5*(2), 171–180. doi:10.1002mj.4250050207

Werthamer, N. R., & Raymond, S. U. (1997). Technology and finance: The electronic markets. *Technological Forecasting and Social Change*, *55*(1), 39–53. doi:10.1016/S0040-1625(96)00144-8

Wilson, F., Kickul, J., & Marlino, D. (2007). Gender, entrepreneurial self-efficacy, and entrepreneurial career intentions: Implications for entrepreneurship education. *Entrepreneurship Theory and Practice*, *31*(3), 387–406. doi:10.1111/j.1540-6520.2007.00179.x

Wood, R., & Bandura, A. (1989). Social Cognitive Theory of Organizational Management. *Academy of Management Review*, *14*(3), 361–384. doi:10.5465/amr.1989.4279067

Wplniak, R., & Grebski, M. E. (2017). Functioning of the business incubator centre in Gliwice. *Zeszyty Naukowe Politechnika Śląska. Seria Organizacja i Zarzadzanie*, *105*, 569–580.

Wu & Chen. (2015). Evaluation and Analysis of Financial Ecological Environment in Fujian. *Journal of Minjiang University, 2015*(1), 26-34.

Xiang, L. L. J. Z. C. (2010). An Empirical Analysis of Factors Influencing Financial Ecological Environment's Optimizing. *Ecological Economics*, (7), 38–42.

Xie & Zhu. (2010). An Empirical Study on Financial Competitiveness of Major Cities in China. *Wuhan Finance Monthly, 2010*(2), 19-22.

Xie, P. (2012). Research on Internet financial model. *Journal of Financial Research*, *12*, 11–22.

Xie, Y. P., Chen, X. Y., & Ye, D. R. (2016). Does entrepreneurial passion contribute to entrepreneurial success? *Management Review*, *28*(11), 170–181.

Xue, J.-H., & Klein, P. G. (2008). *A Latent-Variables Approach to Entrepreneurship*. Working Paper. Contracting and Organizations Research Institute, University of Missouri.

Xu, N. (2005). On China's Financial Ecological Environment. *Journal of Financial Research*, (2): 35–43.

Xu, X. (2005). The Assessment of Regional Financial Ecology Environment. *Journal of Financial Research*, (11), 53–62.

Yang, D., Chen, P., Shi, F., & Wen, C. (2018). Internet finance: Its uncertain legal foundations and the role of big data in its development. *Emerging Markets Finance & Trade*, *54*(4), 721–732. doi:10.1080/1540496X.2016.1278528

Yang, X. P., Tang, L. B., & Yu, X. Y. (2013). Entrepreneurial network, entrepreneurial learning and new venture growth. *Management Review*, *25*(1), 24–33.

Yeboah-Assiamah, E., Muller, K., & Domfeh, K. A. (2017). Institutional assessment in natural resource governance: A conceptual overview. *Forest Policy and Economics*, *74*, 1–12. doi:10.1016/j.forpol.2016.10.006

Ye, C. (2005). Seeking for the Micro-foundation of Development Theory: Also on the Formation of a Theoretical Paradigm of Development Economics. *Social Sciences in China*, (4), 29–40.

Ye, Y. H. (2009). The study on factors affecting undergraduates' entrepreneurial intentions. [in Chinese]. *Educational Studies*, *4*, 73–77.

Yin, R. K. (2013). *Case Study Research Design and Methods*. Thousand Oaks, CA: SAGE Publications Inc.

Yi, Z. H., Duan, H. X., & Ren, S. G. (2018). Entrepreneurial self-efficacy, entrepreneurial orientation and performance of small and micro technology enterprises. *Science Research Management*, *39*(8), 99–108.

Zacharakis, A. L., Meyer, G. D., & Decastro, J. (1999). Differing perceptions of new venture failure: A matched exploratory study of venture capitalists and entrepreneurs. *Journal of Small Business Management*, *37*(3), 1–14.

Zahra, S. A. (1996). Goverance, ownership, and corporate entrepreneurship: The moderating impact of industry technological opportunities. *Academy of Management Journal*, *39*(6), 1713–1735. doi:10.5465/257076

Zahra, S. A., & Nielsen, A. P. (2002). Sources of capabilities, integration and technology commercialization. *Strategic Management Journal*, *23*(5), 377–398. doi:10.1002mj.229

Zahra, S., & Nambisan, S. (2011). Nambisan S. Entrepreneurship in global innovation ecosystems. *AMS Review*, *1*(1), 4–17. doi:10.100713162-011-0004-3

Zapletalová, Š. (2015). Models of Czech companies' internationalization. *Journal of International Entrepreneurship*, *13*(2), 153–168. doi:10.100710843-015-0145-9

Zhang, Z. H., & Li, A. (2019). The influence of social network on the performance of technological new ventures. *Contemporary Economic Research, 2019*(4), 55-62.

Zhang. (2007). Research on Rural Financial Ecology: An Analytical Framework of New Institutional Economics. *Financial Theory & Practice, 2007*(2), 41-48.

Zhang. (2012). *Research on the Evaluation Target System of Regional Financial Ecological Environment*. Academic Press.

Zhang. (2014). Evaluation and Optimizing Suggestions of Financial Ecological Environment in Yangtze River Delta Region. *Contemporary Economics, 2014*(22), 64-65.

Zhang, W. W., & Zhao, W. H. (2017). A study on the relationship between industry internal and external connections, entrepreneurial learning and entrepreneurial performance. *Science of Science and Management of S & T, 38*(04), 162–170.

Zhang, X., Ma, X., Wang, Y., Li, X., & Huo, D. (2016). What drives the internationalization of Chinese SMEs? The joint effects of international entrepreneurship characteristics, network ties, and firm ownership. *International Business Review, 25*(2), 522–534. doi:10.1016/j.ibusrev.2015.09.001

Zhao, C. (2019). *Research on the Evaluation of Regional Sci-tech Finance Ecological Environment.* Anhui University.

Zhao, Y. B., Li, Y., Lee, S., & Chen, L. B. (2011). Entrepreneurial orientation, organizational learning, and performance: Evidence from China. *Entrepreneurship Theory and Practice, 35*(2), 293–317. doi:10.1111/j.1540-6520.2009.00359.x

Zheng, B., & Li, S. (2011). The relationship of competitive strategy, innovation selection, and firm performance. *Science Research Management, 32*(4), 59–68.

Zheng, Z., Tang, X., & Liu, Y. (2014). Will the Deposit Interest Rate Marketization Increase Bank'Risk Level? Based on an Angle of Narrowed Gap between Deposit and Loan Interest Rate. *Finance & Economics, 2*, 4.

Zhilai, Z. (2015). The influence of Internet finance of commercial banks—Based on the perspective of the influence of "Internet+" on the retail industry. *Financ Econ, 5*, 34–43.

Zhong, W. D., & Huang, Z. X. (2012). An empirical study on the relationship among entrepreneur's relationship strength, self-efficacy and entrepreneurial performance. *Forum on Science and Technology in China, 2012*(1), 131-137.

Zhou. (2004, Dec. 7). Perfecting the legal system and improving the financial ecology. *Financial Times.*

Zhou, K. Z. (2006). Innovation, imitation, and new product performance: The case of China. *Industrial Marketing Management, 35*(3), 394–402. doi:10.1016/j.indmarman.2005.10.006

Zhu, C. (2019). Big data as a governance mechanism. *Review of Financial Studies, 32*(5), 2021–2061. doi:10.1093/rfs/hhy081

Zhu, X. M., Kong, X. Q., & Bao, M. X. (2014). Learning orientation and competitive advantage of new enterprises: A study on the mediating effect of dual entrepreneurial learning. *R & D Management*, *26*(2), 9–16.

Zott, C., & Amit, R. (2008). The fit between product market strategy and business model: Implications for firm performance. *Strategic Management Journal*, *29*(1), 1–26. doi:10.1002mj.642

Zou, H., Chen, X., & Ghauri, P. (2010). Antecedents and consequences of new venture growth strategy: An empirical study in China. *Asia Pacific Journal of Management*, *27*(3), 393–421. doi:10.100710490-009-9157-0

About the Contributors

Yang Gao is the Doctor in School of Business at the Dalian University of Technology in China. He has researched in the field of strategy management and entrepreneurship for 8 years. He has presided over multiple projects at the national level of China. As a research author, he has published many academic papers. He is also the reviewers of several international journals.

Sang-Bing Tsai is currently a Professor at University of Electronic Science and Technology of China Zhongshan Institute, Capital University of Economics and Business and Wuyi University. He is both Technology Management and Business Management PhD. He has published many research articles in SCI / SSCI journals, including International Journal of Production Research, International Journal of Web Services Research, Advances in Mechanical Engineering, IEEE Transactions on Systems Man Cybernetics-Systems, Plos One, Environment and Planning B-Planning & Design, Sustainability, Renewable & Sustainable Energy Reviews,...etc. His recent research interests in Computer Science, Information Management, Big Data, Sustainability, Green Operation and Applied Mathematics. He has well over 100 published peer-reviewed journal articles. Dr. Tsai is will be the Co-Editor-in-Chief for the Journal of Organizational and End User Computing. He is currently the Associate Editor for Journal of Global Information Management, and Associate Editor for International Journal of Digital Crime and Forensics, as well as serving on the editorial boards of 10 other journals.

* * *

Datian Bi is an associate professor at school of management in Jilin University. His research focuses on information management and information system, e-commerce, big data analysis.

Linlin Chang is an undergraduate of Business School, Dalian University of Technology, majoring in human resource management.

Yuehui Cui is a lecturer of School of Economics and Management at Changchun University of Technology, China. She received her Ph.D. in Management from Jilin University. Her research interests are in the area of Entrepreneurship, Social Network and corporate innovation management.

Yuchao Ding is an undergraduate of Dalian University of Technology.

Weiwei Dong is an associate researcher, Institute of urban economics, Tianjin Academy of Social Sciences.

Haomin Du is studying in Dalian University of Technology, major in Economics. The research direction during the college is economic analytics and market prediction.

Haoyang Gao is at Dalian University of Technology, engaging in econometric finance, business analytics and economics.

Baoshan Ge is a Professor, PhD supervisor in Jilin University.

Mingwei Jin is a student in Dalian University of Technology, major in Human Resource Management.

Na Li is a lecturer at School of Management, Changchun University(www.ccu.edu.cn), China. She received her PhD in management science and engineering at Jilin University in 2018. Her research is logistics and supply chain management. she has published more than 10 articles. Also, she is the leading researcher of 3 projects and participate in more than 20 projects.

Xinyu Liu is an assistant researcher of professor at the university of DUT, China. Her research focuses on electronic markets and business model. She is interested in the research on the upgrade and challenge of new technology to the electronic market. As an assistant researcher, she assisted her supervisor in the publication of many academic papers.

Yang Liu, born in 1999, is a student of Dalian University of Technology.

Peixuan Lu is an undergraduate of Dalian University of Technology, majoring in human resource management.

Xifeng Lu is a Lecturer at College of Accounting and the Enterprise Finance and Accounting Research Center of Jilin Province, Jilin University of Finance and Economics, China. Her research interests are entrepreneurial financing, innovation management, and resource management.

Liyao Pan is currently a lecturer in the Department of Management at the University of Texas at San Antonio.

Saewoon Park is a Professor at Changwon National University.

Yu Su is an Associate Professor in School of Management, Beijing Normal University.

Lydia Nyankom Takyi is a full-time lecturer in the University of Education, Winneba, Ghana, in the College of Technology Education, Department of Management Studies Education. She is currently pursuing her PhD Entrepreneurship degree in University of KwaZulu-Natal, Durban, South Africa. She holds an MPhil in Public Administration (University of Ghana), a Bachelor of Education in Social Sciences, Management and Economics option (University of Cape Coast) and a Certificate in Entrepreneurship and Small-Scale Management from Ghana Institute of Management and Public Administration (GIMPA). Her research interests include institutions and firm internationalisation, governance and financial administration, corporate governance, female entrepreneurs and economic growth and development, competitive strategy and performance. Lydia's has taught courses at the undergraduate level for over seven years now and supervised courses taught include Strategic Management, Public Administration, Entrepreneurship and Innovation Management, Organisational Behaviour and Administration and Local Government system in Ghana, Economy of Ghana and Principles of Management. Lydia's current PhD research focuses on examining the influence of entrepreneurial institutional environments on SMEs internationalisation among Ghanaian indigenous exporters. Prior to joining the Department of Management Studies Education, she worked as lecturer at Data Link University College and Central University College. In her leisure time, Lydia enjoys listening to music, watching adventurous movies and play local Ghanaian game, Ludo.

Yu Wang, PhD in Economics, Master's supervisor in School of Business in DUT, releasing CSSCI/SSCI indexed paper in the field of Regional Financial Development or International Finance for more than 30, presiding National Social Science Fund (19CJL032), Ministry of Education Social Science Fund (16YJC790105), etc.

Kaifeng Wu is at Dalian University of Technology, engaged in finance, business analytics and economics.

Xinya Xu is major in human resource management at the school of economics and management, is an undergraduate from Dalian University of Technology. Mainly engaged in sustainable development research.

Xingqun Xue, Lecture of Business School of Dalian University of technology. Graduated from the international management and marketing major of national Changyuan University of Korea, with a doctorate in management. Research fields: institutional economics, urban economics, cross-border E-commerce. Hosting research project such as "Humanities and ocial Sciences Foundation of the Ministry of Education of China", "Liaoning social science planning fund of China" and "Liaoning Provincial doctoral research initiation fund of China".

Yuanyu Zeng is studying at Dalian University of Technology. As a Junior student, she is interested in scientific research. She always follows her teacher to explore new fields.

Ao Zhang is a lecturer of School of accounting at Jilin University of Finance and Economics, China. She received her Ph.D. from Jilin University in China. Her research interests are in the area of Entrepreneurship, Strategy Management and Internet of things.

Meng Zhang obtained her Ph.D. degree from Jilin University, now is an assistant professor of Business School at Shandong Normal University in China, as well as a visiting scholar at Department of Computer Science at University of Texas at San Antonio. She has interests in doing researches on information sharing, innovation management and entrepreneurship management. She has presided over multiple projects at the national level of China. As a research author, she has published many academic papers. She is also the reviewers of Journal of Consumer Behavior and Environment, Development and Sustainability.

Shiying Zhang is working in Institute of Business & Economic Research, Harbin University of Commerce. And she is a master tutor.

Ting Zhang is a graduate student of School of Accounting and Auditing, Guangxi University of Finance and Economics.

Index

GAIN ACCESS TO **THOUSANDS** OF REFERENCE BOOKS AT **A FRACTION** OF THEIR INDIVIDUAL LIST **PRICE**.